BEA

JOYCE BEA STERLING, DREI

Guide to Passing the AMP Real Estate Exam

FIFTH EDITION

Dearborn™
A Kaplan Real Estate Education Company

This publication is designed to provide accurate and authoritative information in regard to the subject matter covered. It is sold with the understanding that the publisher is not engaged in rendering legal, accounting, or other professional advice. If legal advice or other expert assistance is required, the services of a competent professional should be sought.

President: Dr. Andrew Temte
Chief Learning Officer: Dr. Tim Smaby
Vice President, Real Estate Education: Asha Alsobrooks
Development Editor: Jody Manderfeld

GUIDE TO PASSING THE AMP REAL ESTATE EXAM FIFTH EDITION
© 2012 Kaplan, Inc.
Published by DF Institute, Inc., d/b/a Dearborn Real Estate Education
332 Front St. S., Suite 501
La Crosse, WI 54601
www.dearborn.com

Printed in the United States of America
Fifth revision, January 2014
ISBN: 978-1-4277-2492-2 / 1-4277-2492-X
PPN: 1970-1105

CONTENTS

PREFACE

It is with pride that we present the fifth edition of *Guide to Passing the AMP Real Estate Exam*. This was the first exam guide on the market that was designed specifically for the licensing exam administered by Applied Measurement Professionals, Inc. The AMP exam questions are complex, and we believe this book will provide you with the testing edge to help you pass the exam.

Other than attending class, one of the most effective ways to prepare for your state exam is by studying exam topics and answering practice questions. *Guide to Passing the AMP Real Estate Exam* contains a streamlined review of the areas covered on the exam and 960 practice questions to help you prepare for your exam.

In writing the exam guide, the author has assumed that the reader is attending a real estate prelicense class and that this book is being used as a review of the material covered in class. Specific state information regarding fair housing, transfer of deeds, and so on, should be obtained from your classroom instructor.

ABOUT THE AUTHOR

Joyce Bea Sterling, DREI, CDEI, SFR, e-Pro, GHS, SHS, has been teaching real estate principles, practices, and law since 1986, and has helped thousands of students pass their exams. Her instructional career includes being an adjunct professor at Northern Kentucky University (previously an AMP state) and teaching continuing education classes for the Kentucky Association of REALTORS®, the Career Development Center Inc., and numerous real estate boards and brokers in Kentucky and Ohio. She was an instructor at the National Association of REALTORS® in 2003, 2004, and 2006. With a Bachelor of Arts in Education from Northern Kentucky University, and a Suggestive Accelerated Learning and Teaching Certificate from Iowa State University, Joyce is a Distinguished Real Estate Educator. She also teaches the Short Sales and Foreclosures Resources (SFR) and e-Pro classes.

As an instructor, Joyce has taught every grade from kindergarten through college. Her credentials also include loan origination, Reverse Mortgage Specialist, Senior Housing Specialist, General Housing Specialist, e-Pro, public speaking, and stress management consultation. Joyce is coauthor of *Modern Real Estate Practice in Illinois*, 3rd Edition, and audio reviews for various state exams.

ACKNOWLEDGMENTS

We wish to thank Grace Ronkaitis, Attorney, Asset Law Group, PLLC, Honor, Michigan, for her participation in the preparation of the 5th Edition of *Guide to Passing the AMP Real Estate Exam* by serving as a reviewer. Her insights and suggestions are appreciated.

This book is dedicated to my daughter, Carrie Sterling Trapp; my nieces, Kenzie Singleton and Keith Singleton; and my nephew, Branham Singleton. I am proud of your values and your accomplishments.

INTRODUCTION

ABOUT YOUR EXAM!

Knowledge is power . . . and knowledge of real estate can make or save you thousands of dollars in the future. Congratulations on your decision to secure a real estate license! To get started, you must pass the AMP exam; then you can begin your career as a real estate licensee.

Applied Measurement Professionals, Inc. (AMP), of Lenexa, Kansas, began in 1990 with the goal of supplying professional testing for future real estate agents. This introduction will help you review basic reading and study skills, understand the format of the questions, and develop an exam strategy. The remaining chapters will guide you through a review of the seven areas covered on your real estate exam.

AMP provides a candidate's handbook that contains your exam application. It is available through your school or the real estate commission and provides you with specific information regarding your own state exam. It is also available at *www .goamp.com*. Please read it carefully. This guide was written to be a streamlined review of the material presented in the classroom. More in-depth information about each subject is contained in the textbook.

USING THIS GUIDE TO PREPARE FOR YOUR EXAM

This comprehensive exam prep guide contains a variety of study tools to help prepare you for your examination. The chapters follow the subject areas presented on the national AMP outline found in the candidate's handbook (available at *www.goamp.com*).

National AMP Outline	Number of Items
Agency Relationships and Contracts	28
Real Property Ownership/Interest	14
Finance	15
Real Property	14
Marketing Regulations	8
Property Management	8
Real Estate Calculations	13

There are two sections on your exam: (1) the national section, which is reviewed in detail in this Guide; and (2) the state section, which covers individual state laws. The exam will include pretest questions that do not count toward your score. This chart shows the number of national and state test questions on your exam. It also shows if the questions are intermixed between sections or if the two sections are separate.

viii   Guide to Passing the AMP Real Estate Exam Fifth Edition

State	National Exam*	State Exam*	Presentation
Alabama	105	45	Intermixed
Georgia	105	48	Intermixed
Illinois	105	45	Separate
Missouri	105	45	Separate
Montana	105	38	Separate
Nebraska	105	55	Intermixed
New Hampshire	105	45	Intermixed
North Dakota	105	45	Intermixed
South Dakota	105	57	Separate
Washington	105	**Broker** – 35 **Managing Broker** – 45	Intermixed
Wyoming	105	37	Intermixed

*Includes the five pretest questions. This information is accurate as of the date of publication. Each state has a Candidate Handbook, which may contain more current information. The handbook can be found at *www.goamp.com*.

 In the chapters, a **light bulb icon** is placed next to the material that is vital for you to know.

At the end of each chapter is a **70-question Chapter Review**, as well as a **Matching Quiz** covering important concepts from the chapter. Both are designed to assess your knowledge of key concepts and to show you exactly where you need to return for further review and study.

There are **four 110-question exams**, which include rationales. **Two exams** are found after the chapter reviews and two are included on the **CD-ROM,** which allows computer practice for taking the exam.

There is a complete **Glossary** covering the topics found on the AMP exam.

A removable **Key Point Review-To-Go** is contained at the end of the book. The pages are perforated, so tear them out and take them with you wherever you go. Even if you have only 10 to 15 minutes to study, the repetition of reading the Key Points will help you commit them to memory. Also, review that section in the final days or hours before your exam. These pages are very effective for last-minute studying!

TIPS FOR EFFECTIVE STUDYING

Listening Effectively

Most real estate students have work, family, and many other responsibilities. That's why it is so important to concentrate intently on the information the instructor presents in class. Here are three basic rules for listening effectively.

Rule 1. Listen to what the instructor is saying, as well as to the inflections in the instructor's voice. An instructor's voice will change as important material is presented.

Rule 2.   Instructors do not know what will be on any given test. However, some material is more important than other material. Listen carefully for the material that the instructor indicates you must know for the state and national exams.

Rule 3.   Your time is valuable; make the most of it while you are in class. A student who doodles, reads other material, or goes on a mental vacation during class time is missing valuable information.

Reading Effectively

Comprehensive reading is a skill that takes practice. Here are some steps to help you develop this essential skill for studying and passing the test.

Step 1.   Begin preparation for your exam with your textbook or other instructional materials. Most text authors provide a preview of the material, as well as a summary at the end of each chapter. Read the preview, skim the headings, and read the summary to grasp the author's plan of presentation of the material. Then, with an understanding of what is to be learned, read the chapter.

Step 2.   Highlight important words and terms while you are reading. Be sure to learn the words that you do not understand, or ask your instructor their meanings. Be sure you learn the vocabulary words. This is essential for passing your exam.

Step 3.   If possible, relate the material to your own life experiences. Recall listing your property with an agent, as well as what occurred during the real estate transaction. Read the important material at least three times, and then take the test at the end of the chapter. Read the material until you understand why you missed any of the questions.

Step 4.   Next, use this guide to help you review the important material until you sit for your exam. Even if you have only a few minutes to review, it will help keep the material fresh in your mind. Remember . . . *repetition is the key to learning*.

Step 5.   When you have completed your classes, read the most important material in this guide at least three times, and then answer as many test questions as you can. You will find test questions at the end of every review area and sample salesperson tests at the end of this guide. The more questions you can answer, the easier the state exam will be.

Other Study Tips

Read the class assignment before attending class to help you identify the areas in which you want to ask questions.

Find a quiet place to study. When studying at home, resist answering the phone or engaging in any other activities that can be distracting, such as having the television or radio on in the background. Most schools have a library or classroom available for study. If you make the effort to go to the library, you will probably be able to better focus on learning the material.

Consider forming a study group or finding another individual with whom you can study. Each individual should commit to reviewing the material independently before attending the study session. Determine your goals for each group meeting, and appoint a group leader to keep you on target.

Sometimes, one person may try to dominate the study group. Be aware of any people who want to control the entire group or who think they have all the right answers. Studying in groups should be a joint effort.

UNDERSTANDING QUESTION FORMATS

The following question formats can be found on your AMP exam. Many students miss questions because they do not take the time to read them carefully.

When approaching a question on your state exam, read and answer each question three times. Read the first time to identify the format of the question being asked and its content. Read the second time to create in your mind a scenario of what the question is asking and to identify key words and phrases. Then, read each question a third time to make sure that you understand exactly what is being asked.

Answer the question in your mind, and then read the answers to find that answer. Read each answer three times. There may be a key word or phrase in one of the answers or in the question that indicates the right answer. There should be ample time to read each question and each answer three times, but pace yourself. Keep track of the time and complete the test. Let's explore some of the types of questions that you may encounter on your exam.

Questions will be classified according to one of the following three levels of learning.

1. **Recall – Tests the knowledge of vocabulary words and the ability to recognize isolated information.**

  Example:
  The document that transfers rights and interests from the grantor to the grantee is the
  A. title.
  B. deed.
  C. mortgage.
  D. note.

Answer
(B) A deed is a document that transfers rights and interest from the grantor to the grantee.

2.   **Application – Requires the use of concepts or data in a new situation.**

Example:
The primary purpose of a deed is to
A. confirm the legal description.
B. provide evidence of title.
C. reveal any deed conditions.
D. verify the signature of the grantee.

Answer
(B) The primary purpose of the deed is to provide evidence of title or proof of ownership.

3.   **Analysis – Requires the integration of various concepts to make a final decision.**

Example:
When listing a property, the agent will ask the seller to see a copy of the deed to
A. verify the amount of the liens on the property.
B. compute the annual property taxes.
C. determine the owners of the property.
D. confirm that the legal description is correct.

Answer
(C) The agent would review the deed to determine the owners. Only a surveyor can confirm that the legal description is accurate.

All three types of questions can be presented in a variety of formats. Let's look at the different ways questions may be presented.

The EXCEPT Format

When the word *EXCEPT* appears at the end of the question, it means you are looking for the *opposite* of what your logic tells you is correct.

"All of the following are true EXCEPT" means you are looking for the one answer that is false.

"All of the following are false EXCEPT" means you are looking for the one answer that is true.

The NOT Format

When *NOT* is found in a question, it means you are looking for the one answer that should not be included. This format is used to see if you really understand what is involved in a certain law or principle.

xii Guide to Passing the AMP Real Estate Exam Fifth Edition

The SITUATIONAL Format

With a *SITUATIONAL* format, a scenario is created and the possible answers may include two Yes answers and two No answers. Questions in this format test your comprehension of the material, as well as your ability to analyze each answer. There may be only one word or phrase in the answer that will make it correct.

A situational format question can be very long. Read it carefully and create the situation in your mind before answering the question.

The DEFINITION or RECALL Format

These test questions are easy . . . as long as you know the definitions of the vocabulary words. A definition is given in the question, and you must match it with the answer.

The MOST IMPORTANT Format

In questions of this type, a key word or concept makes one answer more important than another.

The LEAST Format

The *LEAST* format could include the terms *LEAST INFLUENCE* or *LEAST LIKELY*. Look for the answer that is least probable.

Example: Which of the following would LEAST LIKELY be found in an abstract of title?

The BEST Format

The word *BEST* means the most advantageous or, as it relates to the test question, the better choice. This format also can be used for recall questions.

Example: A tenancy in common interest that grants the right to interval ownership of the property would BEST describe a(n). . .

The key words in this question are *interval ownership*, which would be best described as a time-share.

The TRUE Format

"Which of the following is *TRUE*?" means there are three wrong answers and one true answer.

This format may be combined with the situational format to test your understanding of the meaning of a concept.

The FALSE Format

"Which of the following is *FALSE*?" means there are three true answers and one false answer.

The DIFFERENCE Format

With the *DIFFERENCE* format, you will make comparisons or look for the distinction between two words or concepts.

Example: The major difference between actual eviction and constructive eviction is. . .

Knowing the definitions of actual and constructive eviction, as well as the proper process for each eviction, is essential to correctly answer this question.

The HAVE IN COMMON Format

Questions using this format ask what a group of words have in common.

Example: What do the terms *possibility of reverter*, *right of reentry*, and *remainder* have in common?

To correctly answer this question, you must know the definitions of *possibility of reverter*, *right of reentry*, and *remainder*.

The MOST LIKELY Format

The *MOST LIKELY* format is asking for what would normally happen in a given situation.

Example: In a real estate transaction, the agent would MOST LIKELY represent whom?

The APPLICATION Format

The *APPLICATION* format tests to see if you can apply the information you have learned.

Example: If the net income on a property remains constant and the cap rate increases 1 percent, the value of the property will. . .

This question tests your knowledge of an appraising formula.

The ACCOUNTABLE Format

This question will set up a scenario or a situation and then ask who can be held accountable or if a certain party is accountable.

Example: A broker was asked to list a property by the executor of an estate. When the broker asked if the property was zoned commercial, the executor replied, "I think so."

Without additional verification, the broker listed and sold the property as having commercial zoning. The purchaser hired an architect to design a building and attempted to secure a building permit. The buyer was informed that the property was zoned residential. Who can be held ACCOUNTABLE for the damages?

To correctly answer this question, you must understand the law of agency.

This concludes the review of the question formats, and now you're ready to study. Remember, if you find yourself struggling with a concept, ask your instructor for additional clarification.

CHAPTER 1

Agency Relationships and Contracts

AMP Outline

I. **Agency Relationships and Contracts (28 questions)**
   A. Agency Relationships
      1. Creating Agency
      2. Types of Agency (including implied agency)
      3. Rights, Duties, and Obligations of the Parties
      4. Termination and Remedies for Non-Performance
      5. Disclosure (related to representation)

1. CREATING AGENCY

The listing, buyer agency, and property management agreements will create an agency relationship. The payment of money does not create agency. A written contract or actions of the parties create agency. To earn a commission, an agent must be licensed at the time of the transaction, have a written compensation agreement, and be the procuring cause of the sale.

2. TYPES OF AGENCY (INCLUDING APPLIED AGENCY)

The agency relationship can be **express** or **implied.**

When the parties state the contract's terms and express their intention, either orally or in writing, an **express agency** is created. Example: a listing agreement.

When the actions or conduct of the parties communicate that there is an agreement, an **implied agency** is created. Example: an implied agency established by the agent when talking with a buyer. "Take this deal. It's the best one for you."

Types of Agents

General agent—When the principal delegates a broad range of powers, and the relationship is expected to be on-going.

> Example: a property manager or a real estate agent with the agent's broker.

Special agent—When the principal delegates a specific act or business transaction.

> Example: a listing agent or a party with a durable power of attorney; an agent who entered into a buyer's agency agreement.

Universal agent—A party is given full power of attorney to represent another person.

> Example: a guardian of a minor or incompetent person.

Types of Agencies

Single agency—When a broker is representing the seller or the buyer in the transaction, but not both.

Dual agency—When an agent represents two principals in the same transaction.

Facilitator or transaction broker—One who does not represent either party in a transaction. Both parties are treated as customers in the transaction.

Designated agency—Created when an agent is appointed by a broker to act for a specific principal or client. This is used when one agent with the company listed the property and another agent within the company secured the buyer for the property. The listing agent would be the designated agent of the seller, and the buyer's agent would be the designated agent of the buyer. In many states, the broker is the dual agent of the seller and buyer, but this is determined by state law. This can occur only with the written permission of both parties. Both parties are clients.

3. RIGHTS, DUTIES, AND OBLIGATIONS OF THE PARTIES

When the property owner hires a broker to find a buyer, an agency relationship is created. The owner (**principal**) has delegated to the brokerage (**agent**) the right to act on the owner's behalf. This creates a **fiduciary relationship or a position of trust and confidence,** wherein the agent owes the seller certain duties. Sales associates represent their brokers, and their primary fiduciary relationship is with their broker. In some states, sales associates are classified as a subagent to the seller/client. A subagent is an agent of an agent. However, in states where brokers may designate salespeople to be the agents of buyers or sellers, the agency responsibility passes to the designated agents.

State laws will vary regarding the duties the brokerage firm and listing agent are required to perform when a listing is secured. In some states, the seller may waive agency duties wherein the brokerage will provide minimum services, such as only placing the property in the Multiple Listing Service. Other states require, if a property is listed, the agent to schedule appointments to show the property; advertise the property; communicate, negotiate, and deliver all written offers and counter-offers; accept earnest money; help the seller fulfill contract contingencies; attend the closing, etc. Unless the state allows a "waiver of duties," the brokerage and listing agent are required to follow the law of agency as discussed in the following paragraphs.

The payment of compensation or its source does not create the agency relationship. A contract, or the actions of the parties, creates the agency relationship.

A **listing agreement** is a personal service contract securing the employment of a brokerage firm to find a ready, willing, and able buyer. The types of listing agreements are exclusive-right-to-sell, exclusive-agency, open, net, and option. The differences are discussed in detail later in this chapter.

Responsibilities of an Agent

The acronym COALD represents the duties of the agent to the principal. The broker must act with care, obedience, accountability, loyalty, and disclosure.

- **Care**—A broker is to exercise reasonable care and skill as a professional while transacting the business of the principal. For a client who is a seller, this includes establishing the correct list price, properly representing the property, delivering appropriate forms and documents needed in the transaction, and properly marketing the property. Tax or legal advice, however, should come from experts in those fields. For a client who is a buyer, this means helping the buyer find suitable property, negotiating the offer, and directing the buyer to a lender and other experts for inspections and advice.

- **Obedience**—The agent is to act in good faith and obey the principal's instructions given in the contract; however, the agent must not obey illegal instructions.

- **Accountability**—The agent is accountable for all funds or property of others that come into the agent's possession.

- **Loyalty**—The agent must be loyal, putting the principal's interests above those of all others. This includes obtaining the best offer from a buyer when representing a seller, explaining offers to a client, and representing only the interests of the client.

- **Disclosure**—The agent must keep the principal informed, disclosing all facts and information that could affect the transaction. If representing a seller, the agent must disclose if the buyer is willing to offer more for the property. If representing the buyer, an agent needs to disclose all defects and if the seller would take less for the property.

Agents must use reasonable care and skill in performance, be honest, and disclose facts that materially affect the value of the property, regardless of whom they are representing.

Where an agent breaches a fiduciary duty to the principal, the agent will not be entitled to a commission and may be additionally liable for actual damages.

Ministerial acts are those acts that a licensee may perform for a consumer that are informative in nature and do not rise to the level of active representation.

Puffing is the exaggeration of a fact.

4. TERMINATION AND REMEDIES FOR NON-PERFORMANCE

Whether the agency is established by a listing, buyer, or property management agreement, it should state the grounds for termination and remedies for non-performance. The principal may pursue damages through civil action or file a complaint with the real estate commission. Other factors regarding termination of the agency are discussed with the various types of agreements available to the parties.

5. DISCLOSURE (RELATED TO REPRESENTATION)

Each state now has mandatory agency disclosure laws that stipulate when, how, and to whom disclosures must be made. Generally, the agency disclosure statement must be in writing. The purpose is to make sure buyers and sellers understand whether they are customers or clients in a transaction. Agency disclosure usually occurs before confidential information is given. A licensee must always disclose that he has a real estate license when purchasing or leasing property.

AMP Outline

I.   **Agency Relationships and Contracts**
   B. General Legal Principles, Theory, and Concepts about Contracts
      1. Unilateral/Bilateral
      2. Validity
   3. Void and Voidable
   4. Notice of Delivery/ Acceptance
   5. Executory/Executed
   6. Enforceability
   7. Addenda to Contracts

1. UNILATERAL/BILATERAL

Unilateral contract—Only one party is obligated to perform in a unilateral contract.

Bilateral contract—Both parties are obligated to perform in a bilateral contract.

Express contract—The parties have specifically agreed, either orally or in writing, to enter into a contract.

Implied contract—The parties by their actions or conduct enter into a contract. Examples of implied contracts include ordering food in a restaurant, securing the services of a taxi, or buying gasoline at a self-service gas station.

2. VALIDITY

A contract is **valid** if it meets all the essential elements and is an enforceable contract. To be valid and enforceable, a contract must contain the following essential elements:

The parties must be legally and mentally competent and authorized to perform. In most states, a person is legally competent at the age of 18. Other parties authorized to perform include executors, administrators, anyone operating under court order, a party with the proper power of attorney, or the party authorized by a corporation to enter into real estate contracts.

There must be an **offer and acceptance**, also known as *mutual assent* or *meeting of the minds*. An offer must be made by one party (offeror), and accepted without any qualifications or changes by the second party (offeree).

The contract must be in proper legal form. Each state's statute of frauds determines the contracts that must be in writing. Generally, most real estate contracts must be in writing to be enforceable. In many states, leases and listings for less than one year are not required to be in writing.

The contract must be entered into for a legal purpose. A contract entered into for an illegal purpose is void.

There must be legal **consideration**, which is a promise, or something of value, made by one party to induce another party to enter into a contract. In a sales contract, the consideration is the selling price of the property; therefore, earnest money, or a good-faith deposit, is not necessary to create a binding sales contract.

There must be **reality of consent**, which means the contract was entered into without duress, menace, misrepresentation, or fraud. The law protects a person who has been tricked or forced into entering a contract. That is, the contract is voidable by the innocent party, but valid as to the wrongdoer.

For contracts that are required to be in writing, there must be the signatures of the parties authorized to perform. Thus, both the buyer and seller must sign the sales contract for it to be enforceable.

3. VOID AND VOIDABLE

Void—It is missing an essential element and has no legal force and effect (i.e., the contract was not signed by the person with the authority to perform).

Voidable—It may be rescinded by one or both parties. Contracts are voidable by the innocent party if entered into under duress, under undue influence, through misrepresentation, through fraud, with a minor, or with an incompetent person. A contract with a contingency that cannot be met may be voidable.

Unenforceable—When neither party can sue the other to force performance, the contract is said to be unenforceable. Because a real estate sales contract must be in writing, an oral agreement to purchase a property is unenforceable.

4. NOTICE OF DELIVERY/ACCEPTANCE

An offer is not a contract; an offer must be accepted to create a contract. Acceptance must be unconditional, unambiguous, and in strict conformance with the offer. There cannot be any changes in any of the terms of the offer. An important part of the acceptance involves its communication to the offeror.

The acceptance is not effective until the offeror receives notice of the acceptance; this is often referred to as delivery. Delivery occurs simultaneously with the acceptance only when the acceptance occurs in the presence of the offeror, or his agent. A conditional acceptance, known as a counter-offer, is actually a rejection coupled with a new offer.

5. EXECUTORY/EXECUTED

Executory contract—One or both parties have duties to perform in an executory contract. A sales contract is executory because the buyer must financially qualify, and the seller must produce a marketable title. The terms will vary depending on the type of listing agreement. Generally, the listing agreement is an executory contract because the broker and seller have duties to perform. Most listing contracts require the broker to market the property and to help the seller find a ready, willing, and able buyer. The seller is required to cooperate with the broker in every way to bring about the sale of the property and to pay a commission when the property is sold. Most contracts are executory contracts.

Executed contract—All parties have fulfilled their duties and responsibilities in an executed contract. The sales contract becomes fully executed at closing when the deed has been conveyed and the buyer has paid the purchase price. Note that the word *execute* means to *sign a document*. This is different from an executed contract.

6. ENFORCEABILITY

For a contract to be enforceable, it must meet the state laws for the creation of that particular type of contract (for example, deed, will, note, mortgage, etc.).

After a sales contract is created and contingencies are met, the sales contract is enforceable, meaning that if the buyer or seller defaults, the other party can file a **suit for specific performance** to enforce the terms of the contract.

Many oral contracts are enforceable in a court of law. However, the **statute of frauds** requires that certain instruments, such as deeds, real estate sales contracts, and certain leases, be in writing in order to be legally enforceable.

7. ADDENDA TO CONTRACTS

To change any of the provisions in the contract, or to insert additional terms, the parties should create an *addendum* or supplement to the contract. An addendum is a part of the original contract. After a contract has been created, if additional changes are made to the contact, the parties may *amend* the contract. Appropriate parties should sign or initial and date the amendment.

AMP Outline

I.   Agency Relationships and Contracts

   C.   Purchase Contracts (Contracts Between Seller and Buyer)

   1. General Principles and Legal Concepts
   2. Purchase Contract (contract of sale, purchase and sale agreement, etc.)
   3. Options (contractual right to buy)
   4. Basic Provisions/ Purpose/Elements
   5. Conditions for Termination/Breach of Contract
   6. Offer and Acceptance (counteroffers, multiple offers, negotiation, earnest money)
   7. Contingencies
   8. Duties and Obligations of the Parties

1. GENERAL PRINCIPLES AND LEGAL CONCEPTS

A contract is an agreement between two or more parties to do, or refrain from doing, a particular action. The contract contains the terms of an obligation. It consists of an offer, an acceptance, and consideration. All of these parts must be present to have a binding contract. Additionally, a contract between the seller and the buyer must meet all of the criteria described in the previous section. In other words, the agreement between the seller and buyer must be bilateral, express, and in writing (to meet the statute of frauds). The parties must be competent and there must be valuable consideration, reality of consent, acceptance, and delivery.

Elements of a Contract

- Offer and acceptance

- Consideration

- Legally competent parties

- Consent

- Legal purpose

2. PURCHASE CONTRACT (CONTRACT OF SALE, PURCHASE AND SALE AGREEMENT, ETC.)

Contract of sale, *purchase and sale agreement*, and *offer to purchase* are three different names that can be applied to the document that contains the seller's agreement to sell and the buyer's agreement to buy. An offer to purchase must meet state law guidelines, as well as the essential elements of contract. Note that an offer is not a contract. Only where there has been a meeting of the minds and a written acceptance by the parties is a contract created.

3. OPTIONS (CONTRACTUAL RIGHT TO BUY)

In an **option** contract, an **optionor** (seller) agrees *to keep open an offer to sell or lease* real property in return for option money. While the **optionee** (buyer) does not have to buy, the optionor must sell, should the buyer exercise the option. The option money given by the buyer may or may not apply toward the purchase price; typically, it does not. Whether or not the option money is applied toward the purchase price, it is mandatory and must be non-refundable to create a binding option.

Option contracts typically contain the following information: names and addresses of the parties, an identification of the property, the terms of the sale, the sales price, the date the option expires, the method of notice by which the option is to be exercised, and provisions for disbursement of the option money should the option not be exercised.

Unless the contract states otherwise, an option contract is assignable. On its creation, it is considered a **unilateral contract** because only the seller is obligated to perform. Option contracts that have been exercised are **bilateral contracts** because the buyer is then obligated to buy and the seller is obligated to sell. These contracts are still enforceable on the death of either party.

Lease Option

In a **lease option**, the lessee (tenant) has the right to purchase the property under specified conditions or to renew or extend the lease at its end. The rent or a portion of the rent may be applied to the purchase price. Note that lending guidelines may limit the amount of rent that can be applied toward a down payment.

Land Contract

In a typical **land contract**, the **vendor** (seller) finances the property and retains title to it until the final payment is made or some other condition is met by the **vendee** (buyer). The buyer possesses the property and receives equitable title.

The vendee agrees to pay the vendor a down payment and regular installment payments. These payments may be interest only or may include payment of principal and interest, for a specified timeframe. Typically, the buyer also pays for property taxes, insurance, repairs, and upkeep on the property.

A land contract is also known as a *contract for deed,* an *installment contract, articles of agreement for warranty deed, bond for title,* or *agreement of sale.*

4. BASIC PROVISIONS/PURPOSE/ELEMENTS

The purpose of a sales contract is to expressly state *in writing* the terms of the transfer of real property from the seller to the buyer.

Usual Provisions in a Sales Contract

- Identification of the seller, buyer, and property
- Type of deed being conveyed, with any restrictions
- The price of the property and how the purchaser will pay
- Amount of earnest money and remedies for breach of contract
- Provision for real estate taxes, hazard insurance, rents, etc.
- Dates for securing loan, inspection, closing, and possession
- Personal property to be left with the real estate
- Personal property the seller intends to remove
- Transfer or payment of any special assessments
- Provision stating time period for acceptance
- Dated signatures of all parties

Following are other important terms associated with contracts:

- **Assignment**—An assignment is a transfer of rights and/or duties from one contract to another contract or from one person to another person. Contracts may include a clause that either forbids or permits assignment.

- **Novation**—When novation is granted, one contract is substituted for another contract with the intent to discharge the obligation of the original contract. It is a release of liability from the original contract.

- **Ambiguities**—Any ambiguities in a contract are construed against the writer of the contract. Contract terms must be clear and definite.

- **Contingency**—A contingency in a contract requires the completion of a certain act or promise before the contract is binding, or it may cancel contract obligations. Depending on how it is written, a contingency can make a contract voidable or unenforceable.

- **Equitable title**—In an executory contract—such as a sales contract, land contract, or trust deed— the buyer's interest in the property is called an *equitable title interest*. Although the legal title is held by another party, the buyer does have the right of possession and an insurable interest in the property.

- **Forfeiture clause**—Many contracts contain a forfeiture clause, which means that under certain circumstances, one party must forfeit or give something to the other party. If found in the sales contract, the earnest money may be given to the seller if the buyer breaches the contract.

- **Right of first refusal**—This term can have two meanings. It can mean the right of a person to have the first right to purchase or lease a property, when the owner is ready to sell or lease. For example, one neighbor says to another neighbor, "When you get ready to sell your house, I'd like to be the first to make an offer." The other neighbor agrees. It can also be a contingency clause in a sales contract. In this scenario, the seller has accepted an offer contingent on the buyer selling his house. If a seller's acceptance contained a right of first refusal, it means the seller can still continue to market the home. If another qualified buyer writes an offer, the seller must give the first buyer the right to fulfill the terms of the sales contract. If the first buyer has not sold his house and cannot fulfill the contract, then he would release the seller from the contract and he could accept the offer from the ready, willing, and able buyer.

- **Suit for specific performance**—A legal action to enforce or compel the performance of the terms of a contract.

- **Caveat emptor**—Means *let the buyer beware*.

- **Caveat venditor**—Means *let the seller beware*.

- **Exculpatory clause**—A hold harmless clause that may be found in contracts relieving a party from liability for injuries to another.

- **Indemnification clause**—A clause in which one party agrees to compensate another for a loss or damage that is sustained.

State laws determine the exact terms of a sales contract. Parties should immediately receive a copy of any signed contract.

5. CONDITIONS FOR TERMINATION/BREACH OF CONTRACT

Most contracts will contain a **cancellation** or **termination clause**, which will allow one or both parties to annul their obligations under certain conditions. For example, depending on the wording of the contingency clause, a buyer or seller may be able to void the sales contract and walk away without penalty. Typical contingency clauses include the requirement that the appraised value be equal to or greater than the contract price, that the property pass inspections, that the contract be reviewed by an attorney, and that the buyer be able to obtain insurance on the property.

A **breach of contract** occurs when one party fails to perform as promised, deviates from the specified terms of the contract, or when a person interferes with another party's performance making it impossible for the duties to be fulfilled. If an important term of the contract is breached, it is deemed material, and the non-breaching party can compel performance (specific performance) or may be entitled to collect damages.

Liquidated damages—Upfront damages, or compensation, are agreed to be paid by the breaching party in the contract. The earnest money deposit may serve as a liquidated damage in a sales contract. Generally, if the buyer defaults and the seller retains the earnest money deposit as liquidated damages, the seller may not sue for any further damages.

Actual damages are those that compensate for the cost of that which has been lost.

Punitive damages are unrelated to the cost of the loss and are merely awarded to punish the wrongdoer.

As mentioned previously, when a buyer breaches the contract, the seller often retains the earnest money deposit as liquidated damages. Where the seller breaches the contract, the buyer may force the sale by suing for specific performance.

6. OFFER AND ACCEPTANCE (COUNTEROFFERS, MULTIPLE OFFERS, NEGOTIATION, EARNEST MONEY)

To *offer* means to put forward for acceptance, rejection, or deliberation. The party making the offer is the offeror, and the party receiving the offer is the *offeree*. An offer does not become a contract unless it is accepted without changes, and the terms of the offer must be clear and definite. An offer can be revoked at any time before acceptance. Notice of revocation by the offeree, death of either party, insanity of either party, and a counteroffer all terminate an offer.

Many state laws require an offer to be presented as soon as possible. It is acceptable for offers to be presented by the buyers' agent or the listing agent. Most buyers want their agent to present their offer because the agent has knowledge of the contract terms and the buyer's qualifications. A buyer who has a sizable down payment, an earnest money check, and a preapproval letter from the lender will provide some assurances to the seller that the buyer is qualified and serious about purchasing the property.

A time for performance of the following activities is typically found in the offer:

- Time for acceptance of the offer
- Date for property, termite, lead-based paint, and other inspections
- Date for loan application to be completed
- Date for loan approval
- Closing date
- Date of possession

If *time is of the essence* is found in the contract, it means the contract must be performed within the time limit specified. The party who does not perform on time may be liable for breach of contract. If a contract does not specify *time is of the essence* or a date of performance, then it is required to be performed within a reasonable time.

One of the essential elements of a contract is **offer and acceptance** or the *meeting of the minds*. Buyers and sellers need to be in agreement on the fixtures and personal property that is to be transferred at closing; if the seller will pay for any repairs that need to be made to the property; and the return of the earnest money, if the offer is not accepted, or if an inspection reveals a repair or issue the buyer finds unacceptable.

If there are any changes made to the terms of an offer, that offer is considered **void** and a **counteroffer** is created if the other party chooses to counter. The legal positions of the parties are reversed; that is, the offeror becomes the offeree, and the offeree becomes the offeror.

Parties to the offer should know that an offer or counteroffer may be accepted, rejected, countered, or ignored. Once there has been a "meeting of the minds" and the offer or counteroffer is accepted without changes, a sales contract is created.

Because most sales contracts are written with contingencies, which may or may not be fulfilled, agents are obligated to present all offers to the seller. Even when the seller and buyer have a signed agreement, if another party wants to make an offer, the offer would need to be presented to the seller. Under these circumstances, the buyers should be informed that their offer is a back-up offer. The exception to this would be if an offer has been accepted by the seller, and the seller instructs the agent in writing not to accept additional offers.

7. CONTINGENCIES

It is essential that the buyer and seller understand the contract terms and the contingencies that must be fulfilled. Typical contingency clauses found in an offer include the requirement that the appraised value must be equal to or greater than the contract price, that the property must pass inspections, that the contract be reviewed by an attorney, and that the buyer be able to obtain financing and insurance on the property.

The timelines for fulfillment of the contingencies should be reviewed by the agent to ensure that the contingencies are met. Until the contingencies have been fulfilled, the contract is voidable or unenforceable.

State law will determine whether agents are allowed to fill in the blanks of contracts without such an action being considered a practice of law. The creation or drafting of documents is considered a practice of law and can only be performed by an attorney.

8. DUTIES AND OBLIGATIONS OF THE PARTIES

A sales contract is a results-driven agreement. Generally, the seller is required to provide a marketable or insurable title, and the buyer is required to pay market value for the property. If there are no contingencies, but these actions do not take place, a breach has occurred. Most state laws require the seller to provide a warranty deed to the buyer unless the sales contract specifies otherwise.

The sales contract should have provisions for canceling the contract. If the buyer defaults, the seller may be able to retain the earnest money as liquidated damages.

If the seller defaults, the earnest money is returned to the buyer. The contract may contain other steps to be followed when canceling the contract.

AMP Outline

I. **Agency Relationships and Contracts**
    D. Service/Listing Buyer Contracts (Contracts Between Licensee and Seller or Buyer)
        1. General Principles and Legal Concepts
        2. Basic Provisions/ Purpose/Elements
        3. Duties and Obligations of the Parties
        4. Conditions for Termination/Breach of Contract
        5. Remuneration/ Consideration/Fees
        6. Types of Service/Listing Contracts

1. GENERAL PRINCIPLES AND LEGAL CONCEPTS

A **listing agreement** is a personal service contract securing the employment of a brokerage firm to find a ready, willing, and able buyer. Most states require that this agreement be in writing to be enforceable. In some states, oral listings are legal, but not enforceable in a court of law.

When a real estate broker enters into a contract with a buyer, a **buyer agency relationship** is established and duties under the law of agency are applicable to the buyer client. If the sellers are represented by an agent, the sellers would be a client to their agent, but a customer to the buyer's agent.

2. BASIC PROVISIONS/PURPOSE/ELEMENTS

Listing agreements usually include the following:

- Type of listing
- Broker's authority and responsibilities
- Names of all parties to the contract
- Brokerage firm
- Listing price
- Real and personal property descriptions
- Term or length of time of the agreement
- Commission
- Termination and default provisions
- Broker protection or extender clause
- Warranties by the owner
- Nondiscrimination wording

- Antitrust wording

- Authorizations for subagency or designated agency, use of lockbox, For Sale signs, and so forth

- Other provisions as provided by state law

- Signatures of the parties

- Unusual deed conditions or restrictions; and written instructions from the seller should be in the listing (i.e., owner does not want a lock box on the door)

When entering into a buyer agency agreement, the agent explains the parties' rights and responsibilities. At a minimum, a buyer agency agreement should contain the following:

- Purpose of agency

- Identification of the parties

- Property type description

- Compensation and method of payment

- Disclosure of any potential conflict of interest

- Term of agreement

3. DUTIES AND OBLIGATIONS OF THE PARTIES

An agent needs to be aware of the current market condition affecting the value and sale of real estate—including interest rates, employment levels, vacancy rates, demographics, and the absorption rate.

Demographics is the statistical study of the population in reference to size, density, and distribution in a given area. A company moving into or out of the area will have an impact on the employment levels, vacancy rates, supply and demand, and absorption rate.

The **absorption rate** is an estimate of how quickly homes have sold in the neighborhood within the past year. Because an agent cannot be certain exactly how and when demographic factors will affect current market conditions, the agent can never guarantee future profits from, or appreciation of, real estate.

Duties of the Listing Agent

When scheduling the listing appointment, the agent should ask the sellers for a copy of the deed, which should show who owns the property and has the right to sign the listing agreement. Only a person(s) with the proper legal authority can authorize the sale of the property. Normally, this would be the owner, but it could also include a person with power of attorney, a guardian, a trustee, or a person authorized by the incorporation to sell a corporation's property.

Note that upon a divorce, one spouse may use a quitclaim deed to transfer that spouse's ownership to the other party. The quitclaim deed should be recorded, and the divorce decree will contain provisions for the transfer of the property. Should the couple decide to continue to own property after the divorce, both parties would be required to sign the deed. If the deed is in the name of one spouse only, both parties should sign the listing agreement to release any marital rights they have to the property. If there is a question as to the owners, a title search should be conducted and an attorney should be consulted.

When a buyer is interested in seeing a listed property, the appointment is made through the listing brokerage firm. Many brokerage firms have videos or checklists for sellers that include advice about how to make their property more marketable, thus selling faster. The information could include marketing tips on areas, such as landscaping, lawn manicuring, painting, repairing the roof, cleaning or replacing carpet, cleaning closets, and renting furniture (if the property is vacant).

Safety guidelines should be followed when showing a property. This includes indicating any potentially dangerous physical conditions of the property to the buyer as well as being prudent regarding their own personal safety.

The listing agent has duties to safeguard the property. This includes proper management of keys; recommending that the sellers remove all valuables prior to showing; and if agreed upon between the agent and seller, caring for the property if the owner is out of town for extended periods of time. The property should be locked and left in the condition as it was found.

 After you pass your test, go to *www.realtor.org* and enter the words *Safety Videos* in the search area. These videos are public, and everyone can watch them.

The brokerage firm and agent have a variety of media in which to market a listed property. Many states require that all listed property include the broker or brokerage name. The listing agent should present the sellers with a marketing plan and inform the sellers that if they decide to advertise on their own, the advertisements must be approved by the broker.

Duties of Buyer's Agent

A brokerage and buyer agent's fiduciary duties must include visually inspecting the property and recommending the buyer seek the necessary inspections of the property. Buyer agent duties also include a duty to inspect public records or permits concerning title or use of the property. Additionally, the agent must negotiate the best possible price and terms for the buyer.

Note that if the listing agent also becomes a buyer's agent, then a dual agency is created; however, some states do not allow dual agency. If dual agency is allowed in your state, be sure to read the laws regarding the fiduciary duties that are owed both parties. Some states also consider a designated agency to be a type of dual agency. Although the general aspects of agency law are fairly uniform across states, there is a great deal of variation in the specific manner in which the concepts are applied from state to state.

Capital Gains

A capital gain is the taxable profit realized from the sale or exchange of an asset.

Almost everything we own and use for personal purposes, pleasure, or investment, is a **capital asset**. When a capital asset is sold or exchanged for a profit, the profit is called a capital gain. Real estate and stocks are two examples of capital assets.

The Taxpayer Relief Act of 1997 established the exclusion of capital gains on the sale of the principal residence. **Single filers** may exclude up to $250,000, and **married** homeowners who file **jointly** may exclude up to **$500,000** from capital gains tax for profits on the sale of a principal residence.

Homeowners whose gain exceeds the maximum for exclusion must pay tax on the amount over the exclusion. The exclusion can be taken more than once; however, to claim the exclusion, the home must have been used as a principal residence for two of the preceding five years. Homeowners may not have sold or exchanged a home during the two years preceding the sale, and the rule does not apply to second homes or vacation property. Capital gains computations are covered in Chapter 7: Real Estate Calculations, and a sample capital gain calculation is shown in Figure 1.1.

FIGURE 1.1 **Sample Capital Gain Calculation— Investment Property**			
Selling Price:			$125,000
Less:	7% Commission	$8,750	
	Closing costs	+ 800	
		$9,550	
			− 9,550
Net Sales Price:			$115,450
Basis:	Original cost	$60,000	
	Improvements	+ 5,000	
		$65,000	
Less:	Depreciation	− 12,000	
		$53,000	
Adjusted Basis:			− 53,000
Total Capital Gain:			$62,450

Tax Implications for Real Estate Investments

In the past, real estate investments were advantageous because tax laws allowed investors to use losses generated by these investments to shelter income from other sources. Present-day tax benefits include tax deductions for depreciation, the deferment of capital gains when property is exchanged, and deductions of losses from real estate investments.

Depreciation, or *cost recovery*, is an income tax deduction that allows a taxpayer to recover the cost or other basis of property over the assets' useful life. It is an annual allowance for the wear and tear, deterioration, or obsolescence of the property. *Land cannot be depreciated; only the improvements on it can be depreciated.*

For investment properties purchased after 1987, the straight-line method of depreciation is used. This means the depreciation is taken periodically in equal amounts. Currently, residential investment property is depreciated for 27.5 years and commercial investment property is depreciated for 39 years. To compute the depreciation, the cost basis must be determined; refer to Figure 1.2 for a straight-line depreciation example. When the investment property is sold, the depreciation that has been taken will be recaptured.

FIGURE 1.2		
Straight-line Depreciation Example	Purchase Price	$110,000
	Closing Costs	+ 3,000
	Total Acquisition Costs	$113,000
	Percentage of cost that is a building	× 85%
	Cost Basis	$ 96,050

$96,050 Cost Basis ÷ 27.5 years = $3,493—
For Residential Investment Depreciation

$96,050 Cost Basis ÷ 39.0 years = $2,463—
For Commercial Investment Depreciation

Tax Deferred Exchange

Under **Internal Revenue Code Section 1031**, if an investor exchanges property instead of selling it, payment of the capital gain may be deferred. Usually, the property exchanged is **like kind**; that is, real estate for real estate of equal or greater value. Other rules apply if real estate is exchanged for personal property. Note that personal use property, such as a principal residence or vacation home, does not qualify for a like-kind exchange.

Sometimes, additional money or personal property is given to make up the difference between the values of the exchanged properties. This money or personal property is known as boot, and capital gains must be paid immediately on the boot.

Following government guidelines, the seller may defer the gain on the sale of an investment property. The seller has 45 days from the close of escrow on the first property to identify a replacement property or properties. The close of escrow on the second property must occur within 180 days of the close of escrow on the first property. The 180 days must be within the time the taxpayer will file a tax return for the year of the sale. If this 180 days will extend beyond the standard April 15 filing deadline, the seller should obtain an extension of time to file the return.

Reverse exchanges allow the replacement property to be acquired before the disposition of the relinquished property. The agent should advise the seller to seek advice from a CPA or other qualified tax professional for current guidelines.

Capital Improvement

Any improvement that is made to extend the useful life of a property or add to its value is called a *capital improvement*. Major repairs, such as replacement of a parking lot, roof, or building equipment, would be a capital improvement. The costs of capital improvements to business property must be capitalized and must be depreciated over the life of the property. Maintenance of the property, such as painting, is not considered a capital improvement and can be deducted from annual income taxes of the investor.

Tax Benefits of Homeownership

The federal government encourages home ownership by providing income tax advantages, such as tax deductions, deferments, and exclusions to buyers of homes. These tax benefits are different for a property used as a principal place of residence from those for property purchased for investment purposes.

In general, homeowners may deduct mortgage interest payments on first and second homes that meet the definition of **qualified residence interest** from their gross income to reduce their taxable income (see Figure 1.3):

- Real estate property taxes, but not interest paid on overdue taxes

- Certain loan discount points

- Certain loan origination fees

- Loan prepayment penalties

- Casualty losses to the real estate not covered by insurance

FIGURE 1.3		
Computing Mortgage Interest and Property Tax Deductions	Loan	$150,000
	Interest	× _0.06_
		$ 9,000 annual interest the first year
	Property taxes	+ $ 3,000
	Total deduction	**$12,000**
		$12,000 × 28% = **$3,360** tax savings if the borrower is in the 28 percent tax bracket.

Note that mortgage interest may not be deductible on loans over $1.1 million.

Also note that while property taxes are tax deductible, special assessments are not.

Special assessments are for improvements that are made to the property, such as sidewalks, water lines, and so forth.

4. CONDITIONS FOR TERMINATION/BREACH OF CONTRACT

Listings may be **terminated** by

- expiration,

- fulfillment of the contract,

- mutual consent or a rescission,

- abandonment by either party,

- death of the broker or seller,

- destruction of the premises, and

- eminent domain.

Sellers should be given a copy of the listing agreement upon the execution of the document. If the seller terminates the agency agreement without cause, the seller may be liable for the expenses incurred by the broker. The seller may refuse to sell the property even if the full list price is offered. However, the broker would be due a commission under this circumstance.

Buyer agency agreements may be terminated by

- expiration,

- fulfillment of the contract,

- mutual consent or a rescission,

- abandonment by either party, and

- death of the broker or buyer.

Buyers should be given a copy of the buyer agency agreement upon the execution of the document.

If the buyer does not purchase a property, a commission is not usually owed. However, depending on the type of buyer agency agreement (e.g., Exclusive Buyer Agency) the buyer may be liable for payment of an agent's commission whether or not the agent showed the buyer the property. Nonpayment in such a case would be a breach of contract. Remember, the payment of the commission is not the determining factor in whether an agency relationship is created. In some states, it is common for a seller to pay a buyer agent's commission; however, if the seller does not pay, then it may be the buyer who has breached the agency agreement by nonpayment.

5. REMUNERATION/CONSIDERATION/FEES

The listing agreement will contain how the brokerage will be paid. Brokers may be paid a flat fee, a percentage of the sale price, or anything else of value that is agreed upon between the parties.

It is important that the buyer understand the four options for compensating a buyer agent.

- The seller pays the fee to the listing brokerage, and a co-op fee is paid to the buyer brokerage.

- Buyer agents may be paid a **consultant fee**, which is an hourly rate or a flat fee for specific services.

- The buyers may agree to pay a **contingent fee**, whereby the buyer's agent is paid by the buyer only if the clients find and buy a home, and the seller does not agree to pay the compensation. This would be used if the buyer purchases a For Sale by Owner property, or where a buyer wants to ensure that the agent's loyalty is not swayed by the seller's payment of the commission.

- A noncontingency fee is paid to the agent whether or not the buyers purchase a home.

6. TYPES OF SERVICE/LISTING CONTRACTS

Many buyers and sellers have the misconception that real estate agents are experts in everything from environmental issues to titles and deeds. For example, first-time buyers may ask how they should hold title to the property, but that is really a question for their attorney to answer. Agents must have a basic knowledge of many different aspects of real estate so they know when to recommend that a buyer seek legal counsel or other expert opinions that are needed. It is the agent's duty to inform a buyer that the offer should be reviewed by the buyer's attorney before it is presented to a seller. A buyer who refuses should sign a waiver indicating that the agent recommended that the buyer seek legal counsel.

Types of Listing Agreements

- **Exclusive-right-to-sell listing**—One broker lists the property and other brokers have the right to sell the property, if there is a cobrokerage arrangement. The listing broker is paid, no matter who sells the property.

- **Exclusive-agency listing**—One broker lists the property and the seller retains the right to sell the property. Other brokers may sell the property through a cobrokerage arrangement. If the seller sells the property without the services of a broker, a commission is not due.

- **Open listing**—In this agreement, the seller enters into listing agreements with any number of brokerage firms and retains the right to sell the property. The broker that sells the property is paid the commission; but if the seller sells the property, no commission is due any broker.

- **Net listing**—This listing does not contain a specified sales price or commission. Net listings are illegal in most states.

It is the buyer's responsibility to conduct an inspection of the property to make sure the housing systems are functioning properly. **Home protection (warranty) plans**, in which insurance covers the repair or replacement of appliances and of electrical, plumbing, heating, air-conditioning, and other systems within the home, are available. The policy may be purchased by the agent, seller, or buyer. Typical coverage is for one year, but it can be renewed if desired. As with all insurance coverage, the policy should be reviewed for exclusions, deductibles, etc.

Lenders require that the borrower purchase a **homeowners' insurance policy** prior to closing; however, the sales contract should be reviewed to determine who is responsible for property insurance between the acceptance of the contract and the closing. Most homeowners' insurance policies require that the owner maintain insurance equal to at least 80 percent of the replacement cost of the dwelling.

Due to recent changes in the industry, homeowners' insurance policies may be difficult and expensive to obtain. Payments for claims involving mold, lead-based paint, hurricane damage, and terrorism are key factors in this change. Once an offer has been accepted, the agent should recommend that the buyers immediately contact their insurance agent to determine if there will be any insurance issues.

The **Comprehensive Loss Underwriting Exchange (CLUE)** is a database of consumer claims that insurance companies can access when they are underwriting or rating an insurance policy. The database contains property insurance claims for up to five years, and loss history from the prior owner of a home may affect the eligibility of the buyer to purchase insurance. Insurance companies use loss history because actuarial studies show a correlation between a consumer's prior loss history and the consumer's future insurance loss potential.

The determination to issue a policy is determined by not only the property's past history but the buyer's credit history, as well. Typically, an insurance company will request credit information to determine whether to issue or renew an insurance policy and to rate the borrower to determine how much premium should be charged for the insurance coverage. Insurance companies believe that credit information is a good measure of financial responsibility and that consumers who show less financial responsibility will file more claims, so they should pay more for their insurance.

The **three general categories of risk** that a homeowners' policy should include protection against are (1) destruction of the premises, (2) injury to others on the premises, and (3) theft of personal property of the homeowner or family members. **Homeowners' insurance policies** should be examined carefully to determine the terms if coverage includes repair or rebuilding the home in case of natural disaster; coverage of other structures, such as a garage, that are not attached to the house; coverage for personal property losses; additional living expenses; and liability against bodily injury or property damage lawsuits brought because of incidents that occurred on the property.

Insurance policies always include exclusions. Damages typically not covered include mold, terrorism, damages from wind or hurricanes, flood damage or sewer backups, earthquakes or mudslides, falling objects, and damage caused by the weight of snow or ice.

To protect the lender's interest, the **National Flood Insurance Reform Act of 1994** allows lenders to purchase flood insurance on behalf of borrowers/owners of properties in special flood-hazard areas and charge the cost back to the borrowers.

Types of Buyer Agency Agreements

- **Exclusive Buyer Agency**—In this completely exclusive agency relationship, the buyer is legally bound to pay the agent when the buyer purchases the property described in the contract. This is true even if the buyer finds the property.

- **Exclusive-Agency Buyer Agency**—This also creates an exclusive contract between the buyer and agent. However, the broker is entitled to payment only if the broker locates the property purchased by the buyer. The buyer can find suitable property without the obligation to pay the agent.

■ **Open Buyer Agency Agreement**—In this nonexclusive contract with the agent, the buyer can enter into similar agreements with any number of agents. The agent who finds the suitable property will be compensated.

Unless an agent is also an attorney, appraiser, accountant, property inspector, termite inspector, environmental inspector, or any other professional who might be involved in a transaction, the agent should not give an opinion. (To give an opinion, the licensee would need to be the attorney, accountant, etc., of the buyer, seller, or party being represented.) However, the agent must have enough basic knowledge in these fields to know when to advise a client or customer to seek an expert's opinion.

In this section, we will analyze the different stages of the transaction when expert advice should be sought. This list is not complete. Any unusual circumstance should be discussed with the agent's broker or manager.

Listing

■ When listing an unusual property and there are no comparable sales, an agent should refer the seller to an appraiser.

■ The seller should be referred to a CPA to discuss the tax consequences of a profit made on the sale.

■ If the seller is interested in a 1031 tax-deferred exchange, the agent should refer the seller to a CPA.

■ An agent may recommend that the seller purchase a CLUE report, which can be given to a buyer as a means of assuring the buyer that property insurance can be obtained.

Showing

■ The buyer should be referred to a loan officer to determine qualifications for purchasing a property and to secure homeowners' insurance.

■ If the buyer has questions regarding the boundary lines of the property, the agent should recommend that the buyer have the property surveyed.

■ Questions regarding zoning should be referred to the zoning board.

■ Questions regarding the school district should be referred to the school board.

■ The agent should recommend that the buyers carefully review the sellers' property disclosure statement. If the buyers decide to write an offer, the agent should recommend that they have their own property inspection and that a contingency clause be a part of the offer. If there are environmental issues, the agent should refer the buyer to the expert in that subject, such as a radon inspector, lead based paint inspector, etc.

Offers and Counteroffers

- Questions such as "How should I take title to the property?" should be referred to an attorney.

- The agent should refer buyers and sellers to their own attorneys to review contracts, contingencies, and addendums before signing the documents.

From Acceptance to Closing

- Agents should recommend property inspections and other professional inspections in a timely manner to fulfill any contingency clauses in the contract. (Examples are radon, lead-based paint, water, well inspections, etc.)

- Agents should recommend that buyers contact their own insurance agents to ensure that the buyers have a policy on property they are buying at closing.

Closing

- The agent should recommend that the buyer and seller have their own attorneys to represent them at closing.

AMP Outline

I.   **Agency Relationships and Contracts**   E.   Employment Agreements between Broker and other Licensees (Including Supervision)

For a salesperson to be **operative**, a broker must hold the salesperson's license. The salesperson is authorized to perform real estate activities on behalf of the broker, and all activities must be carried out in the name of the broker. The broker is responsible for all of the salesperson's activities.

Independent Contractors

Most agents work as **independent contractors**. According to the Internal Revenue Code, the three requirements to meet the independent contractor status are

- the individual must have a current real estate license;

- the individual must have a written contract with the broker that contains the following clause:

  "The salesperson will not be treated as an employee with respect to the services performed by such salesperson as a real estate agent for federal tax purposes"; and

- ninety percent or more of the individual's income as a licensee must be based on sales production, not on the number of hours worked.

An independent contractor assumes responsibility for paying the contractor's own income tax and Social Security. The agent cannot receive any employee benefits from the broker.

The broker can regulate the working hours, office routine, and attendance at meetings of employees. The broker withholds income tax and Social Security for the employee, and the employee may receive benefits from the broker.

Supervision: Sales Force

It is the broker's responsibility to supervise the licensees under the broker's control. The broker must ensure that the sales staff is well acquainted with the laws of agency and with federal, state, and local fair housing laws, as well as with state laws covering the general conduct of the licensee. Many brokers hire professionals to review listing and sales contracts, agency disclosure forms, property disclosure forms, and any other documents needed in transactions. The broker's license may be suspended or revoked because of an agent's illegal or inappropriate actions.

In some states, if the broker's license is suspended or revoked, all of the licenses held by the broker are immediately suspended or become inactive until those licensees associate with another broker. Check with your state to determine the status of an agent's license should a broker's license be suspended or revoked.

A salesperson or broker who fails to adequately comply with required laws and regulations may be subject to disciplinary action by the real estate commission or by state and local courts. Actions against licensees may be brought by a buyer, a seller, another broker, or the real estate commission itself.

Supervision: Trust Accounts

A trust account also is known as an *escrow account* or *impound account*. The account is set up by a broker to hold the money of others until a transaction is closed. This includes earnest money checks in sales transactions and security deposits in property management. State laws regulate the establishment, maintenance, and auditing of the account or accounts that a broker is required to have.

Should the broker deposit the client's money into a personal, operating, or general account, **commingling** has occurred. Commingling is not allowed in most states. Should the broker spend the client's money, **embezzlement** has occurred. Commingling and embezzlement are illegal.

Supervision: Records

State laws determine the length of time that brokers must retain complete and accurate records of all business transactions. The documents that must be kept include, but are not limited to, copies of sales contracts, deeds, title searches, title insurance policies, homeowners' insurance policies, surveys, inspection certificates, appraisals, and warranties or guarantees of heating, electrical, or plumbing systems.

Supervision: Notifications

The following notifications and reports are usually required by state regulatory agencies. Check your state laws to determine the details of these and other requirements.

- **Transaction files**: State law determines how long brokers must keep transaction files. Generally, brokers are required to keep any documents associated with the transaction. These files include but are not limited to the listing contract, sales contract, escrow deposits and withdrawals, agency and property disclosures, HUD-1, and addenda.

- **Licenses**: Issuance, renewal, transference from one broker to another broker, escrow of, change of surname, change of resident address.

- **Brokerage business**: Opening, relocating, or closing an office; permission to use company name or name change; notification on death of the principal broker; and appointment of ancillary trustee or working with another broker to close an existing business.

- **Escrow or trust accounts**: Providing name and location of the escrow account; permission to audit the escrow account.

Supervision: Company Policies

Company policies, procedures, and standards are set to establish a clear understanding of the relationship between the broker and the salesperson and thus to communicate the rules of the game to the sales associate to resolve as many controversies as possible before they arise, and to provide a framework and atmosphere in which people can work together and succeed. A manual of procedures, policies, and standards should include, but not be limited to, advertising and promotion, compensation, cooperative sales with outside brokers, escrow, floor duty, interoffice exchange of clients, listing, open houses, sales meetings, screening prospects, signs, and termination. Some states mandate that the broker provide written policies; others consider it a lack of supervision if the broker cannot produce a written policy manual.

Supervision: Resolving Misunderstandings

From time to time, disputes occur in any real estate office. A dispute may be between two agents, between the agent and the company, or between real estate firms. Issues vary, but often revolve around commission splits. Whenever possible, the agent and management should resolve such disputes as quickly as possible. Usually, a dispute can be quickly resolved by a review of the agent's employment agreement.

In other cases, a review of the company policy and the procedures manual may resolve the issue. When neither of these items exists, advice or even binding arbitration by an impartial, disinterested party from outside the firm may be sought. Local boards of REALTORS® require arbitration and offer mediation between members. If the dispute is between brokerage firms that are not REALTORS®, the dispute can be settled through the court system.

If the dispute involves a real estate transaction, the buyers, sellers, tenants, and owners will be looking to the agents for professional advice. The agents' knowledge and expertise should be used every step of the way to avoid ambiguities and misunderstandings.

Supervision: Sales Force Training

The training of a new agent is often done by formal classroom instruction, on-the-job training, and attendance at sales meetings. The success of a real estate office or company depends on the skill and knowledge of the sales force. At a minimum, the training should cover the following topics:

- Law of agency, state laws, and ethical standards practiced by the company
- Completing documents needed in the transaction, listing, sales, and disclosures
- Making a listing presentation
- Creating a competitive market analysis
- Prospecting for sellers and buyers
- Handling objections
- Managing paper flow within the office
- Key and yard sign procedures
- Advertising and open houses
- Developing a contact database
- Communicating with clients, customers, and follow-through and follow-up procedures
- Working effectively with buyers, qualifying, showing properties, and writing an offer
- Negotiating contracts
- Telephone communication
- Internet marketing

Supervision: Accounting

A broker must maintain accurate accounting records of income and expenses, commission records of agents, and payroll records for employees, as well as bank and escrow account statements.

If the brokerage is engaged in property management, **operating funds** are used to maintain and to repair a property or to run credit checks and to screen prospective tenants. The broker must provide an owner with a statement showing the receipt and disbursement of any funds. Escrow accounts are subject to the state real estate commission's regulation and examination. Mismanagement of escrow accounts can be cause for disciplinary action by the real estate commission.

Supervision: IRS Form 8300—Cash Payment Reporting Requirements

Each person engaged in a trade or business who, in the course of that trade or business, receives more than $10,000 in cash in one transaction, or in two or more related transactions, must file Form 8300 with the Internal Revenue Service. Any transactions conducted between a payer (or the payer's agent) and the recipient in a 24-hour period are related transactions. Transactions are considered related even if they occur over a period of more than 24 hours if the recipient knows, or has reason to know, that each transaction is one of a series of connected transactions. A copy of Form 8300 must be kept for five years from the date it is filed.

Form 8300 requires the identity of the individual(s) from whom the cash was received, the person(s) on whose behalf the transaction was conducted, a description of the transaction and method of payment, and the business that received the cash. The form must be filed by the 15th day after the date the cash was received. If that date falls on a Saturday, Sunday, or legal holiday, the form must be filed by the next business day.

Penalties may be imposed for

- failure to file a correct and complete form on time, unless a reasonable cause can be shown;

- failure to furnish a correct and complete statement to each person named in a required form;

- causing, or attempting to cause, a trade or business to fail to file a required report;

- causing, or attempting to cause, a trade or business to file a required report containing a material omission or misstatement of fact; or

- structuring or attempting to structure transactions to avoid the reporting requirements.

A minimum penalty of $25,000 may be imposed if the failure is due to an intentional disregard of the cash reporting requirements. These violations may result in imprisonment of up to five years, or a fine of up to $250,000 for individuals and $500,000 for corporations, or both.

See Appendix B for a copy of Form 8300.

The broker must maintain records showing the receipt and the disbursement of commission funds to and from other brokers, as well as to salesperson licensees.

CHAPTER 1 TEST

1. The term *fiduciary* means there is a(n)
   A. legal relationship between parties that creates a position of trust and confidence.
   B. legal relationship in which only the duties of honesty and good faith are owed to the parties.
   C. oral agreement between the parties that does not create an agency relationship.
   D. written agreement between the parties to pay a real estate commission.

2. A listing agent lost the seller's house keys. The agent has breached his fiduciary duty of
   A. accountability.
   B. care.
   C. disclosure.
   D. loyalty.

3. The BEST description of the type of agency that is created by the actions or conduct of the parties is a(n)
   A. express agency.
   B. implied agency.
   C. single agency.
   D. dual agency.

4. When a brokerage represents both parties in the real estate transaction as customers, the brokerage is acting as a(n)
   A. express agency.
   B. implied agency.
   C. transaction broker.
   D. business broker.

5. When showing property, an agent exaggerates a property's benefit. This action is
   A. common business practice and is legal.
   B. a ministerial act, which is illegal.
   C. misrepresentation of the property and is illegal.
   D. puffing, which is legal as long as there is no misrepresentation.

6. The type of listing agreement that allows the seller to have contracts with more than one brokerage, as well as the right to sell the property herself, is a(n)
   A. exclusive-right-to-sell listing.
   B. exclusive-agency listing.
   C. open listing.
   D. net listing.

7. An amendment to a contract is created
   A. before the original contract is written.
   B. by adding provisions to an accepted contract.
   C. only by attorneys before the closing.
   D. only if using fill-in-the-blank agreements.

8. A buyer signed an agreement to pay the agent when she purchased a property described in the contract. The buyer signed a(n)
   A. buyer agency disclosure agreement.
   B. exclusive buyer agency agreement.
   C. exclusive-agency buyer agency agreement.
   D. open buyer agency agreement.

9. After the buyer's offer was accepted, he applied for a loan. He could not secure a loan to purchase the property. Which contract clause would allow the seller to receive the earnest money deposit?
   A. Exculpatory clause
   B. Indemnification clause
   C. Forfeiture clause
   D. Punitive damages clause

10. A promise, or something of value, made by one party to induce another party to enter into a contract is
    A. the authorization to perform.
    B. legal consideration.
    C. reality of consent.
    D. the meeting of the minds.

11. The status of a contract that meets all the essential elements and is enforceable is called a(n)
    A. valid contract.
    B. void contract.
    C. voidable contract.
    D. unenforceable contract.

12. A contract entered into without duress, menace, misrepresentation, or fraud means that it meets the legal requirement of the
    A. meeting of the minds.
    B. proper legal form.
    C. reality of consent.
    D. valuable consideration.

13. A contract that has no legal force or effect is
    A. valid.
    B. void.
    C. voidable.
    D. unenforceable.

14. When neither party can sue the other to force performance, the contract is said to be
    A. unenforceable.
    B. valid.
    C. void.
    D. voidable.

15. The transfer of rights and/or duties from one contract to another contract, or from one person to another person, is
    A. accession.
    B. acknowledgment.
    C. assignment.
    D. attestation.

16. One contract was substituted for another contract, and there was a release of liability from the original contract. The term that defines the release is
    A. alienation.
    B. exchange.
    C. indemnification.
    D. novation.

17. A sales contract, land contract, or trust deed would give the buyer a(n)
    A. cloud on the title.
    B. equitable title.
    C. quiet title.
    D. legal title.

18. Upfront damages or compensation that are agreed upon to be paid by the breaching party in the contract are called
    A. compensatory damages.
    B. liquidated damages.
    C. punitive damages.
    D. statutory damages.

19. Legal action that may be taken to enforce the terms of the contract is
    A. suit to quiet the title.
    B. suit for possession.
    C. suit for specific performance.
    D. suit for exoneration.

20. The term that means *let the seller beware* is
    A. caveat actor.
    B. caveat emptor.
    C. caveat venditor.
    D. caveat viator.

21. The clause in a contract that is meant to relieve a party from liability for injuries to another party is the
    A. exculpatory clause.
    B. execution clause.
    C. indemnification clause.
    D. indefeasible clause.

22. The seller has accepted monetary consideration and has agreed to sell his property for an agreed upon amount within a specified timeframe, if the buyer chooses to purchase. This contract is called a(n)
    A. option contract.
    B. land contract.
    C. listing contract.
    D. sales contract.

23. A land contract, contract for deed, or install-ment contract has been reached between the seller and buyer. It MOST LIKELY means that the
    A. mortgagor finances the property and retains title until the final payment is made by the mortgagee.
    B. mortgagee finances the property and retains title until the final payment is made by the mortgagor.
    C. vendee finances the property and retains title until the final payment is made by the vendor.
    D. vendor finances the property and retains title until the final payment is made by the vendee.

24. The clause in a contract that makes timely performance a condition of the contract is called the
    A. drop dead time clause.
    B. time is of the essence clause.
    C. unity of time clause.
    D. within a reasonable time clause.

25. Every enforceable contract for the sale of real estate must be in writing and signed by all parties, in accordance with the
    A. Real Estate License Act.
    B. Uniform Commercial Code.
    C. statute of frauds.
    D. Truth-in-Lending Act.

26. Which of the following is an essential ele-ment of a contract?
    A. Notary seal
    B. Mutual assent
    C. Three-day cancellation clause
    D. Equal bargaining power

27. In a bilateral contract
    A. only one of the parties is bound to the contract.
    B. both parties to the contract have duties to be performed.
    C. a restriction is placed in the contract.
    D. consideration is not an essential element.

28. An executed contract means
    A. only one party to the contract must perform.
    B. a party has the right to sue for specific performance.
    C. all of the parties have fully performed their duties.
    D. contingencies do not have to be met.

29. To create a contract, the offeree must accept the offer
    A. within twenty-four hours of receiving the offer.
    B. without any changes to the offer.
    C. before the end of the business day of receiving it.
    D. only after it has been approved by an attorney.

30. An optionee has communicated to the optionor that the optionee will purchase the property. This option contract is now exer-cised and is BEST described as a(n)
    A. executive unilateral contract.
    B. executive bilateral contract.
    C. executory bilateral contract.
    D. executory unilateral contract.

31. An oral sales contract involving the sale of real estate is
    A. valid.
    B. void.
    C. voidable.
    D. unenforceable.

32. An agent forgot to get the buyer to sign the offer. What is the status of the offer?
    A. Valid
    B. Void
    C. Voidable
    D. Voluntary

33. An offer was accepted with contingencies. The status of this contract is
    A. valid.
    B. void.
    C. voidable.
    D. unenforceable.

34. An attorney was discussing an investment with a buyer who will be attending a foreclosure sale. The attorney said "caveat emptor." This means
    A. let the bank beware.
    B. let the neighbors beware.
    C. let the seller beware.
    D. let the buyer beware.

35. A buyer's agent would NOT recommend the buyer seek expert advice if the buyer asked
    A. "How should I take title to the property?"
    B. "Does this crack in the foundation mean there is structural damage?"
    C. "How long has the property been on the market?"
    D. "Would you recommend a radon test?"

36. The buyer's offer stipulates that the closing must take place by April 15 or the contract is null and void. The buyer may refuse to purchase on April 16 if the contract contained a
    A. time is of the essence clause.
    B. settlement clause.
    C. transfer clause.
    D. contingency clause.

37. A buyer entered into a buyer agency agreement that gave him the right to enter into agency contracts with other agents. This BEST describes a(n)
    A. exclusive buyer agency.
    B. exclusive-agency buyer agency.
    C. open buyer agency.
    D. designated buyer agency.

38. Which of the following statements is FALSE regarding offer and acceptance?
    A. To offer means to put forward for acceptance or rejection.
    B. An offer can be revoked at any time before acceptance.
    C. A counter offer reverses the legal positions of the offeror and offeree.
    D. In real estate, an oral acceptance creates a binding contract.

39. Which of the following is NOT required to create a valid sales contract?
    A. Earnest money
    B. Consideration
    C. Offer and acceptance
    D. Signatures

40. Which of the following would NOT be a required notification that a broker must file with a regulatory agency?
    A. Change of location for a branch office
    B. Opening of a new branch office
    C. Notification of death of the principal broker
    D. Notification of a new listing agreement

41. Which of the following BEST describes an independent contractor in the real estate business?
    A. An independent contractor has a current real estate license, and the contractor can receive employee benefits from the broker.
    B. An independent contractor has a current real estate license, and the broker assumes the responsibility for paying the contractor's income tax and Social Security tax.
    C. An independent contractor has a current real estate license, a written contract with the broker, and 90 percent or more of the individual's income as a licensee is based on sales production and not on the number of hours worked.
    D. An independent contractor has a current real estate license, a written contract with the broker, and the broker can regulate the working hours of the agent.

42. A broker deposited an earnest money check in his business account. The broker is guilty of
    A. embezzlement.
    B. commingling.
    C. fraud.
    D. misrepresentation.

43. The broker is accountable for which of the following?
    A. The payment of agents' income taxes.
    B. The training and supervision of licensees under the broker's control.
    C. The office hours that agents work.
    D. The number of cold calls each agent makes each day.

44. Buyers entered into an exclusive buyer agency agreement. The agency relationship that has been created can be BEST described as a
    A. general agency.
    B. universal agency.
    C. dual agency.
    D. special agency.

45. An agent received a $500 bonus check from a seller. What should she do with the check?
    A. The check is considered commission, and it should be written to and given to her principal broker.
    B. Tell the seller she can accept only cash and the broker cannot know about the bonus.
    C. Tell the seller that her broker does not allow any of the agents to accept bonus checks.
    D. Cash the check and say nothing to her broker.

46. An agent who works for ABC Realty was the buyer's agent for a property that was listed by XYZ Realty. The seller agreed to pay the commission. From whom will the agent receive her commission check?
    A. The principal broker of XYZ Realty.
    B. The principal broker of ABC Realty.
    C. Either principal broker may pay her.
    D. Directly from the buyer.

47. To earn a commission, an agent must be which of the following?
    A. The agent must be the procuring cause of the sale and also be a member of the multiple-listing service.
    B. The agent must be licensed at the time of the transaction and also must have a written compensation agreement.
    C. The agent must be licensed at the time of the transaction and also must have met all continuing education requirements.
    D. The agent must be the procuring cause of the sale and also must have met all continuing education requirements.

48. A broker has several salespeople employed at her office. Early one day, one member of the sales staff brings in a written offer with an earnest money deposit on a house listed with the broker. Later the same day, another salesperson brings in a higher written offer on the same property, also including an earnest money deposit. In accordance with the office policy, the broker does not submit the second offer to the seller until the first has been presented and rejected. The seller is not informed of the second offer. In this situation, the broker's actions are
    A. permissible, providing the commission is split between the two salespeople.
    B. permissible, if such an arrangement is written into the salespeople's employment contracts.
    C. not permissible, because the broker must submit all offers to the seller.
    D. not permissible, because the broker must notify the second buyer of the existence of the first offer.

49. A broker represents a buyer interested in a house listed by another broker who is known to be very difficult during negotiations. To BEST represent her buyer, the broker should inform her buyer to
    A. carry on negotiations with the seller directly.
    B. inform the buyer that the cooperating broker is difficult to deal with and to find another house.
    C. write an offer if she is really interested in purchasing the property.
    D. say nothing about the cooperating broker being difficult to deal with, and tell the buyer that the house just sold.

50. All of the following statements are false regarding a real estate broker's acting as the agent of the seller EXCEPT the broker
    A. can lower the sale price of the property without the seller's approval.
    B. must follow the legal instructions of the seller.
    C. can disclose the seller's personal information to a buyer if it helps secure an offer on the property.
    D. can accept a commission from the buyer without the seller's approval.

51. An exclusive-right-to-sell listing is BEST described as a
    A. personal service contract.
    B. property management contact.
    C. broker-principal contract.
    D. buy-sell contract.

52. Which of the following is TRUE regarding a trust account?
    A. A trust account must be opened by a new agent within seven days of the receipt of the agent's license.
    B. A trust account is set up by a broker to hold the money of others until a transaction is closed or released by proper procedure.
    C. Money from the trust account can be used by the broker at any time.
    D. If the buyer defaults on a sales contract, the agent may withdraw money from the trust account and pay the seller.

53. The broker entered into an exclusive-right-to-sell listing with a seller. A qualified buyer agreed to buy the property for the listed price, but the seller refused to sell. Which of the following is TRUE?
    A. The seller can refuse the offer and has no legal liability to anyone.
    B. The seller can refuse to sell, but a commission is owed the broker.
    C. The seller cannot refuse to sell because the listed price was offered.
    D. The seller cannot refuse to sell because he signed an exclusive-right-to-sell listing agreement.

54. Which of the following is NOT a responsibility of the agent when the agent is representing the buyer in a real estate transaction?
    A. To show properties that maximize the broker's commissions and select the best times to show those properties.
    B. To be fair and honest with the seller, but safeguard the buyer's interest under all circumstances.
    C. To suggest the minimum amount of earnest money deposit to be offered.
    D. To require that a seller sign a property condition statement and confirm representations of the condition of the property.

55. Which of the following is the responsibility of a seller's agent to the buyer?
    A. Disclosure of any material fact pertinent to the property
    B. Disclosure of the lowest offer the seller will accept on the property
    C. Disclosure that the seller is near bankruptcy or foreclosure
    D. Disclosure that the seller has AIDS

56. A buyer made an offer and gave the seller three days to accept. On the following day, she found an FSBO property she liked better. The buyer called her the listing agent, who was acting as the dual agent, to revoke her previous offer. The agent had no communication of acceptance from the seller. Regarding this situation, the buyer must
    A. make an immediate offer on the FSBO property before it is purchased by someone else.
    B. make sure the seller is notified of the revocation before making an offer on the FSBO property.
    C. do nothing more because she has notified the agent of her decision to rescind the offer.
    D. give the seller three days to accept or reject, as stated in the offer.

57. Which of the following is NOT TRUE regarding an exclusive-agency agreement?
    A. It may contain a broker protection clause.
    B. It excludes the seller from selling the property.
    C. It excludes other brokers from listing the property.
    D. It may contain a clause prohibiting a "For Sale" sign from being placed in the yard.

58. A seller agreed to list his house for $190,000, but he was not informed that the actual value of the property was $200,000. The agent purchased the property the next day. This is an example of a violation of which of the agent's responsibilities?
    A. Obedience
    B. Accountability
    C. Loyalty
    D. Discovery

59. The principal to whom an agent gives professional opinions and counsel is a
    A. subagent.
    B. customer.
    C. client.
    D. fiduciary.

60. An agent worked for a company that required a company jacket to be worn in all business transactions, provided health insurance, and withheld taxes. The employment relationship between the brokerage and the agent was MOST LIKELY that of a(n)
    A. independent contractor.
    B. employer/employee.
    C. joint venture.
    D. general partnership.

61. Which of the following BEST defines the law of agency?
    A. The selling of another's property by an authorized agency.
    B. The rules of law that apply to the responsibilities and obligations of a person who acts for another.
    C. The principles that govern one's conduct in business.
    D. The rules and regulations of the state licensing agency.

62. One day prior to closing, the seller learns that the listing broker is related to the buyer. If the seller refuses to pay the commission, will the broker prevail in a lawsuit for the commission?
    A. Yes. Disclosure of a relationship between the buyer and listing agent is not relevant.
    B. No. A seller can rescind a listing agreement any time prior to closing.
    C. Yes. A seller must pay because there is a ready, willing, and able buyer.
    D. No. An undisclosed dual agency was created, and a fiduciary duty to the seller was breached.

63. On a listing appointment, the seller told the agent that he was learning disabled and illiterate. He asked the agent to read the listing agreement to him. After a lengthy discussion answering all of the seller's questions, the seller said he understood the terms and placed an X where the agent indicated. Is this a valid listing contract?
    A. Yes, because the seller is illiterate, not incompetent.
    B. Yes, but only if the seller has an attorney verify what the agent said.
    C. No, because an illiterate person can never enter into a valid contract.
    D. No, an illiterate person must have a guardian explain all documents to him.

64. When the agent scheduled an open house with the sellers, she advised them to remove all jewelry, valuables, and medications that could be stolen. Several people came through the open house, one of whom asked permission to use the bathroom. The next morning the sellers called to inform the agent that three bottles of medication were missing from the medicine cabinet. Can the agent be held accountable for the missing medication?
    A. Yes, because the agent should have checked every visitor before they left the open house to see if they had stolen any property.
    B. Yes, because an agent is accountable for the money or property of others that comes into his or her possession.
    C. No, because the agent advised the sellers to remove all valuables before the open house, she is not liable.
    D. No, because the agent cannot watch everyone at an open house.

65. After an unsatisfactory home inspection, a buyer refused to purchase the property. After learning of the required repairs, the listing agent advised the seller to conceal the damage and to sell the property "as is." Later, another buyer made an offer on the property and her inspection did not reveal the damage. So, the buyer purchased the property "as is." In a lawsuit against the broker for the cost of the required repairs, will the buyer prevail?
    A. Yes, because the agent must indemnify the second inspector because he was incompetent.
    B. Yes, because the agent must disclose known material defects that are not disclosed by the seller.
    C. No, because the listing agent was fulfilling his duty of loyalty and gave him good advice that helped him sell his house.
    D. No, because the buyer purchased the property "as is."

66. An agent for ABC Realty has 15 listings. Another agent for ABC Realty has a buyer under contract that is interested in one of the company's listings. The broker appointed Agent A as the exclusive agent of the seller, and Agent B as the exclusive agent for the buyer. This arrangement is an example of
    A. express agency.
    B. implied agency.
    C. designated agency.
    D. undisclosed agency.

67. When the buyer made an offer on a property, he gave the agent $500 in cash for the earnest money. After the offer was accepted, the agent deposited the cash into his personal account, and a week later, wrote the broker a check for the $500 deposit. Is this action legal?
    A. Yes, if the broker told him to follow that procedure.
    B. Yes, if the buyer gave permission for the agent to follow that procedure.
    C. No, because it is a commingling of funds.
    D. No, because it is embezzlement.

68. Which of the following documents would NOT create an agency relationship?
    A. Property management agreement
    B. Sales contract
    C. Listing contract
    D. Buyer agency contract

69. For their down payment, the buyers brought $20,000 cash to the closing table. Which form must be filed with the Internal Revenue Service to report this transaction?
    A. 1099
    B. 1003
    C. 8300
    D. 8303

70. To insert additional terms into the contract, the agent would use a(n)
    A. addendum.
    B. adaptation clause.
    C. contingency clause.
    D. new contract.

MATCHING QUIZ

The column on the right contains a brief definition of important terms in this section.
Write the letter of the matching term on the appropriate line.

A. Novation

B. Caveat emptor

C. Executory contract

D. Equitable title

E. Assignment

F. Exculpatory clause

G. Time is of the essence

H. Meeting of the minds

I. Option contract

J. Indemnification clause

K. Voidable contract

L. Independent contractor

M. Commingling

N. Embezzlement

O. Escrow account

P. IRS Form 8300

Q. Law of agency

R. Land contract

S. Indemnification clause

T. Special agent

1. _____ Contract in which the seller finances the purchase of the property; also known as a contract for deed

2. _____ Worker who assumes responsibility for paying his/her own income tax and Social Security

3. _____ Also known as impound account; an account for other peoples' money

4. _____ The act of depositing the client's money into a personal or business account

5. _____ Outlines the duties and responsibilities of the principal and the agent

6. _____ Document used to report receiving more than $10,000 in cash as a business transaction

7. _____ Another term for an offer and acceptance; an essential element of a contract

8. _____ A hold harmless clause found in some contracts

9. _____ Substituting a new contract for an old one, which releases liability

10. _____ Term meaning "let the buyer beware"

11. _____ Transfer in writing of rights or interest in a bond, mortgage, lease, or other instrument

12. _____ The right to purchase property within a definite time at a specified price

13. _____ An agreement to compensate someone for a loss

14. _____ This clause in a contract means the contract must be performed within the time limit specified

15. _____ The right to obtain absolute ownership to property when legal title is held in another party's name

16. _____ Contract may be rescinded by one or both parties

17. _____ In this contract, one or both parties have duties to perform

18. _____ The act of spending the client's money

19. _____ The party to whom the principal has delegated the duty of a specific act or business transaction

20. _____ A clause in which one party agrees to compensate another for a loss or damage that is sustained

CHAPTER 1 TEST ANSWERS

1. **(A)** A fiduciary relationship is a legal relationship that creates a position of trust and confidence.

2. **(A)** The fiduciary duty of accountability requires a licensee to be accountable for money and property of others that comes into his/her possession.

3. **(B)** The type of agency that is created by the actions or conduct of the parties is an implied agency.

4. **(C)** If both parties are customers, then the broker would be acting as a transaction broker.

5. **(D)** Puffing is the exaggeration of a property's benefits.

6. **(C)** An open listing would allow the owner to have contracts with more than one brokerage and still give the owner the right to sell the property himself without paying a commission.

7. **(B)** An addendum is a change to an original contract. An amendment is created to make changes or to add provisions after the original contract is created.

8. **(B)** The buyer signed an exclusive buyer agency agreement, which states that whenever the buyer purchases the property described in the contract, the agent will be paid.

9. **(C)** The forfeiture clause in a contract would allow the earnest money to be given to the seller if the buyer defaults.

10. **(B)** Legal consideration is a promise, or something of value, made by one party to induce another party to enter into a contract.

11. **(A)** When a contract meets all of the essential elements and is enforceable, it is a valid contract.

12. **(C)** Reality of consent means a contract was entered into without duress, menace, misrepresentation, or fraud.

13. **(B)** When a contract has no legal force or effect, it is void.

14. **(A)** When neither party can sue the other to force performance, the contract is said to be unenforceable.

15. **(C)** The transfer of rights and/or duties from one contract to another contract, or from one person to another person, is assignment.

16. **(D)** Novation is the release of liability when one contract is substituted for another contract.

17. **(B)** The sales contract, land contract, or trust deed would give the buyer an equitable title.

18. **(B)** Liquidated damages are agreed upfront damages, which are agreed to be paid to the breaching party.

19. **(C)** Legal action that may be taken to enforce the terms of the contract is a suit for specific performance.

20. **(C)** Caveat venditor means "let the seller beware."

21. **(A)** The exculpatory clause is meant to relieve or excuse a party from liability for injuries to another party. (Hold harmless clause)

22. **(A)** In an option contract, the seller accepts option money and agrees to sell his property for a specified amount within a specified timeframe, if the buyer chooses to purchase.

23. **(D)** In a land contract, the vendor (seller) will finance the property and retain title until final payment is made.

24. **(B)** Time is of the essence means that timely performance is a condition of the contract.

25. **(C)** Contracts for the sale of real estate must be in writing to be enforceable, according to the statute of frauds.

26. **(B)** One of the essential elements of a contract is mutual assent or "meeting of the minds."

27. **(B)** In a bilateral contract, both parties are obligated to perform.

28. **(C)** An executed contract means all of the parties have fully performed their duties.

29. **(B)** An offer must be accepted without any changes.

30. **(C)** When the buyer informs the seller that he/she is going to purchase the property, the option is exercised, and an executory bilateral contract exists.

31. **(D)** An oral real estate contract is unenforceable by either party.

32. **(B)** The offer is missing an essential element and is void.

33. **(C)** The contingencies would make the contract voidable.

34. **(D)** Caveat emptor means "let the buyer beware."

35. **(C)** "How long has the property been on the market?" is not a question that would require the buyer to seek expert advice.

36. **(A)** "Time is of the essence" means that if the requirement is not met, the contract has been breached.

37. **(C)** An open buyer agency agreement would permit a buyer to enter into agency agreements with more than one agent.

38. **(D)** The oral acceptance of an offer does not create a binding contract.

39. **(A)** Earnest money is not necessary to create a binding contract.

40. **(D)** A listing agreement is not a notification that must be sent to a regulatory agency.

41. **(C)** By definition of independent contractor.

42. **(B)** A client's money must be placed in a separate escrow or trust account. When it is placed in the business account, commingling has occurred.

43. **(B)** A broker is liable for the training and supervision of activities of licensees under his or her control.

44. **(D)** A special agency is created when the principal delegates a specific act or business transaction.

45. **(A)** All commission checks must be given to the principal broker.

46. **(B)** An agent is paid by the principal broker.

47. **(B)** The three requirements for collecting a commission are (1) to be licensed at the time of the transaction, (2) to have a written compensation agreement (typically that would be the listing agreement), and (3) to be the procuring cause of the sale.

48. **(C)** All offers must be presented to the seller.

49. **(C)** When representing the buyer, an agent must negotiate the best possible deal for the buyer.

50. **(B)** This is the true statement. A broker must follow the legal instructions of the seller.

51. **(A)** Listing agreements are classified as personal service contracts.

52. **(B)** By definition of trust account or escrow account, which is an account that the broker deposits money belonging to others.

53. **(B)** A listing contract is an employment contract. When the broker found the qualified buyer, the commission had been earned.

54. **(A)** When an agent is representing a buyer, the agent must search for the best properties for the buyer to inspect, including FSBOs.

55. **(A)** The seller's agent is responsible for being honest and fair with the buyer and for disclosing all pertinent and material facts about the property.

56. **(C)** An offer can be revoked at any time before acceptance. Because the agent had no communication of acceptance from the seller, the buyer has no responsibilities for the offer once the revocation was communicated to his agent.

57. **(B)** An exclusive agency permits the seller to sell the property and not pay a commission if the buyer was procured without the assistance of the broker.

58. **(C)** Loyalty means placing the principal's interest above the interest of all others, including self-interest. Because the agent did not disclose the true market value of the property, the agent did not fulfill his responsibility of loyalty.

59. **(C)** A client is a person to whom the agent gives professional opinions and counsel.

60. **(B)** Requiring a uniform, providing employee benefits, and withholding tax payments are all indications of an employee relationship.

61. **(B)** The rules of law that apply to the responsibilities and obligations of a person who acts for another is the law of agency.

62. **(D)** An undisclosed dual agency has been created, and the listing broker has violated license law in most, if not all, states. He has also breached the fiduciary duty of acting with care and skill on behalf of the seller.

63. **(A)** Illiterate persons can enter into binding contracts when they fully understand the terms.

64. **(C)** The agent advised the seller to remove valuables, and under most circumstances, has fulfilled her duty to them.

65. **(B)** The agent must honestly disclose all facts that materially affect the value of the property, regardless of whom the agent is representing.

66. **(C)** By definition, this is a designated agency.

67. **(C)** By the definition of commingling.

68. **(B)** A sales contract does not create an agency relationship.

69. **(C)** IRS Form 8300 is used to report receiving more than $10,000 cash in a trade or business transaction.

70. **(A)** The purpose of an addendum is to legally change any of the provisions of the contract or to insert new terms.

ANSWERS—MATCHING QUIZ

1. **R**	6. **P**	11. **E**	16. **K**
2. **L**	7. **H**	12. **I**	17. **C**
3. **O**	8. **F**	13. **J**	18. **N**
4. **M**	9. **A**	14. **G**	19. **T**
5. **Q**	10. **B**	15. **D**	20. **S**

2

Real Property
Ownership/Interest

AMP Outline

II. **Real Property Ownership/**
   Interest—14 Questions
   A. Freehold Estates (rights of
      ownership)

An **estate in land** defines the degree, quantity, nature, and extent of a person's interest in land or other property. To be an estate, an interest must be possessory or may become possessory in the future, and the ownership is measured in terms of duration. Estates in land can be freehold or nonfreehold. Freehold estates include fee simple estates and life estates. (See Figure 2.1.) A freehold estate is considered to exist for an uncertain duration because no one really knows how long that person is going to own the property. (For the right amount of money, would you sell today?)

Nonfreehold estates include **leasehold estates**, which are usually based on calendar time.

A lease with a definite duration is an **estate for years**. A leasehold estate also can be for an uncertain duration, such as a **tenancy at will**. Leasehold estates are discussed on page 50.

FIGURE 2.1	Fee Simple Estates	Life Estates

Freehold Estates	1. Fee Simple Absolute
	   A. The highest form of ownership that the law recognizes
	   B. Ownership is for an indefinite duration
	   C. Ownership is freely transferable
	   D. It is an inheritable estate
	2. Fee Simple Defeasible
	   A. Special Limitation with Possibility of Reverter
	      a. Title transfers so long as the property is used for a particular purpose.
	      b. There is automatic reversion to the grantor or the grantor's heirs if the land ceases to be used for that purpose.
	      c. The possibility of reverter is the possible future interest the grantor's heir(s) could have if the property ceases to be used for that purpose.
	   B. Condition Subsequent with Right of Reentry
	      a. Title is transferred on the condition that there is an activity that the grantee must not perform.
	      b. The grantors must take legal steps to get the property back.
	      c. The right of reentry is the possible future interest of the grantor.
		1. Conventional Life Estate
		   A. Ordinary with Remainder or Reversion
		      a. Set up by a grantor.
		      b. Life tenant has full use and enjoyment of property for tenant's life.
		      c. Property reverts to grantor on the death of the life tenant (reversion).
		      d. Property is transferred to the remainderman or a party other than the grantor.
		   B. Life Estate Pur Autre Vie with Remainder or Reversion
		      a. Set up by grantor but based on the life of a third party. A conveys title to B, based on the life of C.
		      b. Should B predecease C, B's heirs would have a life estate interest in the property as long as C is alive.
		      c. Property reverts to A (grantor) on the death of the person by whose life it is measured.
		      d. Property may transfer to D, a remainderman.
		2. Legal Life Estates—Set Up by Law
		   A. Dower—A widow's interests in her husband's real property
		   B. Curtesy—A husband's interests in his deceased wife's real property
		   C. Homestead—A portion of the value of the real estate that is protected from unsecured creditors

Listing contracts and sales contracts usually identify the **appurtenances** that will be transferred in the deed. The word appurtenant in real estate means rights, benefits, or attachments that transfer with real property.

Tangible (touchable) property includes physical improvements on the property; fixtures, such as lighting, heating, and plumbing equipment, are appurtenances. A listing contract should identify fixtures that go with the property and fixtures that a seller intends to take after the sale.

Intangible (cannot touch) property includes rights and privileges that belong to and pass in the deed from the grantor to the grantee. Easements and water rights are intangible appurtenances.

AMP Outline

II.   **Real Property Ownership/**
      Interest
      B. Types of Ownership
          (Estates in Land)
          1. Joint Tenancy
          2. Tenancy in Common
          3. Condominiums

An *interest in land* means there is a legal privilege in the property. For example, an **easement** is an interest in land, but it is not an estate because it does not allow for possession of the property.

The three basic types of ownership in real estate are (1) severalty, (2) co-ownership, and (3) trust. (See Figure 2.2.) Because the interpretation of these forms of ownership varies from state to state, specific questions regarding ownership should be directed to an attorney. The deed will show how the current owner holds title to the property. Generally, listing contracts and offers to purchase stipulate that the seller will convey the property fee simple absolute. If a different type of interest will be conveyed to the buyer, it should be noted in the listing and offer to purchase.

1. JOINT TENANCY

Joint tenancy is a concurrent form of ownership characterized by right of survivorship. There must be unities of time, interest, and possession for joint tenancy to be created. Each joint tenant has the right to sell, mortgage, or lease an interest without the consent of the other owners.

2. TENANCY IN COMMON

If one joint tenant sells his or her property, the new owner would be a tenant in common with the other joint tenants.

FIGURE 2.2

Types of Ownership

Characteristic	Tenancy in Severalty	Tenancy in Common	Joint Tenancy	Tenancy by the Entirety
Number of Owners	One person or legal entity	Two or more people	Two or more people with right of survivorship	Husband and wife only; law presumes they are one
Title	One title	Each co-owner has separate legal title to that co-owner's undivided interest	One title	One title
Interest	100% ownership	Shares may be unequal; law will interpret them as equal unless stipulated otherwise	Shares must be equal	Each owns 100% of the property
Conveyance	Yes, to whomever the owner stipulates	Yes, without the consent of the other owners	Yes, without the consent of the other owners	When both owners agree
Right to Partition	Not necessary; there are no co-owners	Yes	Yes	No
Status on Death	Passes to heir(s) or devisees(s)	Passes to heir(s) or devisees(s)	Passes to surviving owners	When one spouse dies, the other spouse owns it in severalty
Probate Necessary	Yes	Yes	No	No
Unities	Possession Interest Time Title	Possession	Possession Interest Time Title	Possession Interest Time Title Person
Termination	By sale or death of the owner	By sale or death of the owner	When any of the unities are broken	By consent of the parties; death of either party; or on divorce ownership

Community Property

In **community property** states, the laws are based on the idea that a wife and husband are equal partners in a marriage. Thus, any property acquired during the marriage is deemed to have been obtained by mutual effort. Listings, deeds, and mortgages require the signatures of both spouses.

When a spouse dies, the surviving spouse automatically owns one-half of the community property, and the other half of the estate is inherited by the decedent's heirs.

Separate Property

Separate property includes not only property owned by either spouse before marriage but also property inherited during marriage or received by gift. Separate property can be sold or mortgaged without the signature or permission of the non-owning spouse.

3. CONDOMINIUMS

Condominium ownership is a way of owning real estate that blends severalty and tenancy in common ownership. (See Figure 2.3.) In a condo, the air space of the unit is owned in severalty, and there is shared ownership of the common areas.

- A **master deed** conveys the land to condominium use.

- The **declaration** allows the developer to create a condo community.

- **Bylaws** govern the operation of the homeowners' association, which manages the community.

- Each condo owner must pay a **maintenance fee** for the expenses of managing the community. A lien can be placed against individual units, which may be foreclosed if this fee is not paid.

- **Special assessments** are improvements to the property that are not covered by the maintenance fee and must be paid by the owners.

- Each unit owner has a fractional undivided interest in the common areas and facilities.

- Areas outside the individual's condo are known as *common areas*, or *elements*, and are owned and used by everyone in the community.

- Limited common areas, such as a designated parking space, can be used only by the individual with the right to do so.

FIGURE 2.3

Condominium Ownership

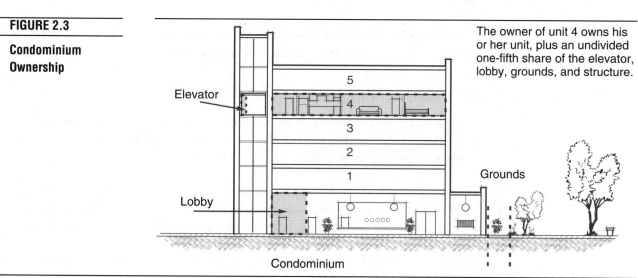

The owner of unit 4 owns his or her unit, plus an undivided one-fifth share of the elevator, lobby, grounds, and structure.

Cooperative

- In **cooperative** ownership, a corporation holds title to the property.

- The purchasers (tenants) of the cooperative receive shares of **stock** in the corporation and a **proprietary lease** that grants occupancy of a specific unit in the building.

- Cooperative tenants do not own real estate and will pay a maintenance fee to cover a prorated share of the mortgage payment, property taxes, insurance, and maintenance.

- A co-op owner has the tax benefits that arise from the owner's share of the mortgage interest and property taxes paid on the property.

- A cooperative interest can be sold, but the new lessee must meet the qualifications of the co-op before the stock and lease can be transferred.

- If one owner fails to pay a maintenance fee to the cooperative, then the other co-op owners are responsible for the payment. If the mortgage payment is not made by the cooperative, the entire building can be foreclosed on.

- A co-op tenant may be evicted for nonpayment of the monthly fee or for not following the rules and regulations.

Time-Shares

A time-share is also known as **interval ownership.** The buyer of a **time-share estate** receives a deed for the property that allows possession for an allotted time each year.

The buyer of a **time-share use** has the right to occupy the property, and use of the facilities is limited to a certain number of years. The developer retains ownership to the property, and when the specified time has expired, all interest reverts to the owner.

Conversion is the procession of changing one form of ownership to another, such as converting an apartment building to a condominium.

Town House or Row House

A town house, or row house, is an attached single-family dwelling normally with two floors. The term townhouse also describes an architectural style of condominium consisting of two floors and common walls.

Owners of a town house purchase their residential structure and the land underlying the structure. The surrounding land, including sidewalks, open spaces, and recreational facilities, is owned in common with other members of the community.

Many town house developments are **planned unit developments**. A planned unit development is designed for a high density of dwellings and a maximum use of open space.

AMP Outline

II.	**Real Property Ownership/ Interest**	3. Basic Elements and Provisions of Leases
	C. Leasehold Interest	4. Rights and Duties of the Parties
	1. Basic Concepts and Terminology	5. Remedies for Default/ Non-Performance
	2. Types of Leases	

1. BASIC CONCEPTS AND TERMINOLOGY

A **lease** is an agreement that transfers **exclusive possession** and use of real estate from the landlord/owner/lessor to the tenant/lessee. The **covenant of quiet enjoyment** requires that the lessor will not enter the property without notice, unless it is an emergency. The implied **warranty of habitability** requires the landlord to keep the property in good condition by maintaining the common areas, equipment, etc. This lease agreement can be oral or written. The owner has a **reversionary right** ... the property on the expiration of the terms of the lease. Figure 2.4 lists the ... es of leases used in property management.

... **nce clause** in a mortgage states that the mortgagee agrees not to ... ase in the event of foreclosure. However, the tenant must be in ... the lease terms.

... rest is called a **leased fee interest**, and the lessee's interest is called ... **rest**. Owners are responsible for keeping the property habitable ... ng with local building and housing codes. These responsibilities ... ep of common areas and of electrical, heating, and plumbing sys-... oval; maintenance of elevators; and any other services promised in

2. TYPES OF LEASES

FIGURE 2.4

Types of Leases—
Nonfreehold Estates

Estate for Years or Tenancy for Years
- A lease with a definite time period or specified beginning and ending dates.
- This terminology is deceptive in that a lease may last substantially less than a year.
- No notice is needed to terminate the estate.
- A tenant who remains in possession after expiration is considered a holdover.

Estate from Period to Period/Estate from Year to Year/Periodic Tenancy
- A lease with an indefinite time period. The lease automatically renews until proper notice to terminate is given.

Estate at Will or Tenancy at Will
- A lease that gives the tenant the right to possess the property with the consent of the landlord for an uncertain time period. The lease can be terminated at any time by the landlord or the tenant giving proper notice to the other party.
- Death of either party also terminates the lease.

Estate at Sufferance or Tenancy at Sufferance
- A tenancy created when a tenant remains in possession of the property without the consent of the landlord after the lease expires.
- If the landlord gives permission to a tenant to remain on the property after the expiration of a lease, the tenant may be treated as a holdover, and a tenancy at will or periodic tenancy may be created.

Assignment

Leases can be assigned or subleased unless there is a clause in the lease forbidding it. (See Figure 2.5.) A tenant who transfers *all the leasehold interests assigns the lease.* For example, the lessor executes a 20-year commercial lease with the lessee. Ten years into the lease, the business is sold. The new owner of the business (assignee) will be assigned all the leasehold interests and the landlord will receive the rent payment from the new tenant (assignee). Unless a novation is granted, the previous owner (assignor) will not be released for the liability of the rent payments.

Sublease

A sublease is created when a tenant transfers *less than all the leasehold interests* by subleasing them to a new tenant. In this arrangement, there are two landlord-tenant relationships. For example, the lessor enters into a one-year lease on an apartment with a lessee. Six months into the lease, the tenant is transferred and decides to sublease the apartment. The original lease agreement between the lessor and lessee remains, but once the apartment is sublet, another landlord-tenant relationship is created between the lessee and the sublessee. The lessor expects a rent check from the lessee, and the lessee (sublessor) expects a rent check from the sublessee. The sublessor can charge more rent and retain the profit. The sublessor's interest is called a *sandwich lease.*

FIGURE 2.5

Assignment versus Subletting

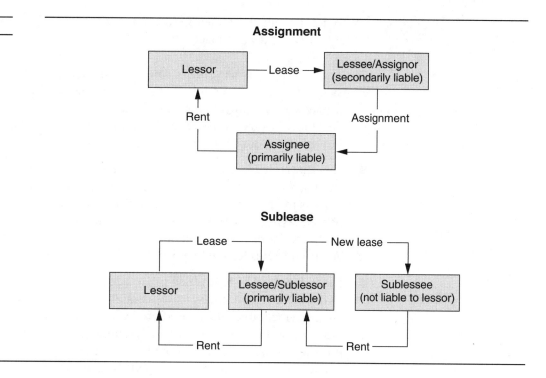

Other types of leases are as follows:

- **Lease option**—The tenant has the option to purchase the property at a specified price within a certain time. A portion of the monthly rental payment may be credited toward the purchase price.

- **Lease purchase**—The tenant agrees to purchase the property at a specified price within a certain period, which is usually the end of the lease.

- **Gross (straight) lease**—The tenant pays a fixed rental amount, and the owner pays all other ownership expenses for the property. The owner usually pays property taxes, insurance, and maintenance, while the tenant pays for the utilities.

- **Net lease**—The tenant agrees to pay ownership expenses, such as utilities, property taxes, and special assessments. In a net-net lease, the tenant pays for insurance as well. In a net-net-net lease, the tenant also pays for some agreed-on items of repair and maintenance. Thus, the terms *net, double net,* and *triple net* can be used to describe the lease, depending on the ownership expenses the tenant agrees to pay.

- **Percentage lease (used for retail space)**—The tenant agrees to pay a fixed base rental fee plus a percentage of the gross income in excess of a predetermined minimum amount of sales. The percentage lease also can be computed from the first dollar of sales. See Chapter 7 to learn how to compute the rent paid in a percentage lease.

- **Sale-leaseback**—The grantor sells the property to the grantee, and then leases it back. For example, a buyer wants to purchase a unit being used as a model in a new condominium development. The developer had intended to use the unit as a model for the next six months. The developer and buyer enter into a sale-leaseback.

The developer/owner/grantor sells the property to the buyer/grantee. When the sales transaction is complete, the grantee becomes the lessor and leases the property to the previous owner, the developer, who becomes the lessee. The developer has the property to use as a model for the next six months, and the buyer has the condo he or she wants.

- **Graduated lease**—The graduated lease is used to attract tenants to a property that is difficult to rent, to compensate for inflation, and to increase the rents as the property becomes more valuable. It allows for a periodic step-up of rent payments. For example, tenants enter into a five-year lease in which they agree to pay $400 a month for the first two years, $450 for the next two years, and $500 for the final year.

- **Index lease**—The rent is tied to an index outside the control of both the landlord and the tenant. Index leases contain an **escalation clause** that allows the lease payment to change based on the index used, for example, the consumer price index. Index leases are more common in times of inflation, when the property manager does not want to enter into long-term fixed rentals that would cause the value of the property to decrease.

Termination of Leases

Leases may be terminated by the expiration of the term of the lease, proper notice as defined in the lease, surrender and acceptance, abandonment, merger, or destruction or condemnation of the property. **Death** of the lessor or lessee does not automatically terminate a lease. Should the property be **sold,** the grantee takes the title *subject to all existing leases.* Unless the leases indicate otherwise, the new landlord cannot make any changes until each lease expires.

3. BASIC ELEMENTS AND PROVISIONS OF LEASES

A lease agreement may be prepared by an attorney or the owner, and should include the terms the manager and tenant agreed to during the negotiation process. If state law permits, a property manager may fill in the blanks of lease agreements, just a real estate agent may fill in the blanks of listings and offer-to-purchase contracts.

Before signing the lease, the lease should be reviewed by the owner, tenant, and respective attorneys. The property manager should provide a reasonable explanation to the tenant regarding the terms of the lease agreement and advise the tenant to seek legal and tax advice before signing the lease.

Lease provisions may include

- the use of the premises,
- term of the lease,
- safekeeping and return of the security deposit,
- payment for tenant improvements to the property,

- payment for maintenance of the premises,

- parking space allotment,

- condemnation clause,

- compliance clause,

- insurance clause,

- noncompliance clause,

- renewals and rent increases,

- expansion options, and

- responsibilities of the landlord and the tenant.

4. RIGHTS AND DUTIES OF THE PARTIES

The Uniform Residential Landlord and Tenant Act was designed to standardize and regulate the relationship between property owners and their tenants. Most states have enacted their own landlord and tenant laws, and the property manager should know the state and local laws. Figure 2.6 is a summary of federal law as it affects landlords and tenants.

If the lessor sells the property, any existing leases would need to be honored by the new owner, and security deposits would be transferred to the new owner at closing.

FIGURE 2.6	TENANT'S PROTECTIONS	OWNER'S RESPONSIBILITIES
Federal Tenant and Landlord Rights and Responsibilities	**No Abrogation** Tenants cannot sign away their rights in advance of signing the lease. **Security Deposits** Amount, location of, interest collected, and return of must be specified in the lease. **Estate from Period to Period** Unless the lease states otherwise, the lease is interpreted as an estate from period to period. **Fair Dealings** The court may refuse to enforce all or part of a lease that is unconscionable or grossly unfair to the tenant. **Effects of Unsigned Leases** If only one party signs and delivers a written lease and the other party pays or accepts rent, the lease is considered binding even without the other party's signature. **Tenant's Right to Vacate** The tenant may vacate the premises if the landlord breaches the lease agreement, or if the unit becomes uninhabitable due to fire or other casualty.	**Keep the Premises Safe and Habitable** Establish building rules and regulations and make sure all tenants comply **Right to Reenter** The landlord must give reasonable notice to inspect, make repairs or improvements, or show the unit. The landlord may enter the unit without notice if there is an emergency. **Tenant's Noncompliance** The covenant of quiet enjoyment assures all tenants of the use of facilities in a reasonable manner. The landlord has the right to evict a tenant if the rules and regulations are not followed. **Abandonment of the Premises** A tenant who abandons the premises before the lease expires is liable for the remaining rent. The landlord is required to make a reasonable effort to rent the abandoned property. **Use and Occupancy** This act covers only residential property and stipulates that unless there is an agreement otherwise, the tenant can only use the property for residential purposes. The tenant agrees not to conduct any illegal activities on the property.

5. REMEDIES FOR DEFAULT/ NON-PERFORMANCE

Eviction procedures will vary by state, but the proper procedure must be followed by the property manager or lessor. A tenant is usually evicted or ejected because of nonpayment of rent, unlawful use of the premises, or noncompliance with health and safety codes.

Actual eviction is when the landlord files a suit for possession because the tenant has breached the lease. **Constructive eviction** is when the landlord breaches the lease and the tenant must leave the premises because they have become uninhabitable.

AMP Outline

2. **Real Property Ownership/ Interest** D. Forms of Business Ownership 1. Sole Proprietorship	2. General or Limited Partnership 3. Limited Liability Company (LLC)

A licensee needs to be aware of basic business structures for two reasons. First, as an independent contractor, the licensee will need to decide on a business structure for working in the real estate industry. When a business structure has been decided, the licensee should check with an attorney to determine the proper local and state registration of the business. Registration with a state agency, such as the Secretary of State or Department of Commerce, is required for most business structures.

Second, when working with buyers, sellers, tenants, etc., the licensee needs to confirm that the party with whom the licensee is working has the authority to perform. Licensees should ask for the documentation, as well as check with the state to determine the owners of the business.

1. SOLE PROPRIETORSHIP

A sole proprietorship is the simplest form of business ownership by a single person. Many licensees conduct business in their own name, and most states do not require registration with the state under this type of business structure. Because there is no distinct legal difference between the person and the business, a person acting as a sole proprietor is accepting personal liability for the business.

2. GENERAL OR LIMITED PARTNERSHIP

A **partnership** is created when two or more people form a business for profit as co-owners.

When a **general partnership** is created, each person is classified as a general partner and may share in all of the decisions of running the business. This includes decisions regarding the day-to-day administration, and the sharing of profits and losses of the operation. All general partners are personally liable for debts and actions of the other general partners in the business. If one of the general partners files bankruptcy, withdraws, or dies, the partnership would need to reorganize.

When a **limited partnership** is created, one or more general partners are appointed to run the business, and the other partners are known as limited or silent partners. The general partner would be personally liable, but the limited partners are only liable for losses to the extent of their investment. If one of the limited partners files bankruptcy, withdraws, or dies, the partnership is not affected.

The significance of the Uniform Partnership Act (UPA) is that it allows real estate to be held in the partnership's name. The profits and losses of the partnership are passed through to each partner, and each individual is responsible for the payment of taxes on the income received.

3 . LIMITED LIABILITY COMPANY (LLC)

When the appropriate documents are filed, a **corporation**, or legal entity that is seen as an artificial person, is created. A **board of directors** manages the business, and a person is legally appointed to be responsible for the real estate activities. A licensee involved with a corporation should ask for a copy of the corporate documents and minutes to confirm that the person has the authority to enter into real estate contracts on behalf of the corporation.

Because the corporation is seen as an **artificial person**, the bankruptcy, withdrawal, or death of a member of the corporation will not affect the business structure. The corporation will continue to exist until it is **dissolved**, which is a legal process for closing the corporation.

If the corporation is public, individuals may purchase stock in the company. Stocks are considered personal property, and each stockholder's liability is limited to the amount of the investment.

One of the major advantages of a corporation is the corporate veil that is provided to limit the liability to the assets of the corporation, and that limited liability is passed on to the individual shareholders. One of the major disadvantages is that the profits are subject to *double taxation*. The corporation must pay taxes on its profits, and the shareholders must also pay taxes on the dividends that they receive.

A corporation may be created as a C corporation, or it may elect S corporation status. The S corporation is seen as providing members with limited liability for losses; but it is treated as a partnership for federal income tax purposes. This means S corporation will pass through income to the shareholders, who will pay taxes on the dividends they receive; however, the corporation will not pay corporate taxes at the entity level in the manner than a C corporation does.

A **limited liability company** (LLC), also provides the company the advantage of being able to pass through income to the members of the company to avoid double taxation. LLCs are classified as an **unincorporated association**, but if proper guidelines are followed, it provides limited liability to the owners as if it were a corporation.

Other Business Terminology

A **security** is defined as an act where a party joins with others in the expectation of making a profit from the efforts of others. Any pooling of money that attracts investors and meets the definition of a public offering can be federally regulated by the Securities and Exchange Commission (SEC), or by state **blue-sky laws.**

A **syndicate** is formed when two or more people unite and pool their resources to own, develop, and/or operate an investment. If the syndicate decides to pool their money for real estate investment purposes, it will need to decide how ownership will be held. Syndication may take the form of a Real Estate Investment Trust (REIT), general partnership, limited partnership, corporation, tenancy in common, or joint tenancy.

A **joint venture** is characterized by the intention of the parties to enter into a business relationship that is limited to a certain timeframe. The parties know that it will never be a permanent business relationship. Members of the joint venture share in capitol, revenues, expenses, and assets.

Real Estate Investment Trust (REIT)

The main advantage of a REIT is that investors can avoid double taxation when certain requirements are met. The trust does not have to pay corporate income tax as long as 95 percent of its income is distributed to its shareholders, 75 percent of the trust's income comes from real estate, and certain other qualifications are met. The trust sells certificates that are purchased by investors, and then the trust invests in real estate, mortgages, or both. Profits are distributed to investors.

An attorney and Certified Public Accountant (CPA) should be consulted for advice regarding the creation and taxes consequences of each business entity.

AMP Outline

II. **Real Property Ownership/Interest**
- E. Private Restrictions on Real Property / Land Use and Matters Affecting Ownership
  1. Liens
     a. Voluntary
     b. Involuntary
     c. Priority
  2. Easements/Rights-of-Way/Licenses
  3. Preexisting Leases or Other Agreements
  4. Encroachment
  5. Deed Conditions, Covenants, and Restrictions
  6. Property Owner Association Agreements

1. LIENS: VOLUNTARY AND INVOLUNTARY; PRIORITY

A **lien** is a claim against real estate to satisfy the payment of money. For a lien to be established, it must be recorded in public records at the courthouse. Recording gives constructive notice of a party's interest in a property.

- **Constructive notice**—Legal notice created by recording documents, such as deeds, mortgages, and long-term leases in the county where the property is located. Physical possession of the property also gives constructive notice of the rights of the parties that are in possession.

- **Actual notice**—Occurs when a party has actual knowledge of a fact. For example, when a grantee has actual notice of a third party's prior rights to a property and accepts the deed to the property, the party accepts the deed from a different person, and the grantee accepts the deed subject to the third party's prior rights. A person who accepts a deed with a judgment lien on the property becomes responsible for the judgment.

- **Torrens system**—A method of legal registration of land where title does not transfer and encumbrances are not effective against the property until the proper documents are registered at the Torrens office. In some states, this means that the title cannot be lost through adverse possession.

Terms Related to Liens

- **Lienor**—The party placing a claim on the property of another as security for a debt or obligation owed the party.

- **Lienee**—The party who owns the property upon which the lien has been placed.

- **Attachment**—A writ of attachment is a court order that directs the sheriff or another authorized person to retain custody of a property until a lawsuit is concluded.

- **General lien**—A claim against all property of the owner, both real and personal property.

- **Specific lien**—A claim against a particular property only.

- **Voluntary lien**—Established intentionally by the owner, such as a mortgage lien.

- **Involuntary lien**—Created by law without any action on the part of the owner (voluntary or involuntary liens may be statutory or equitable).

- **Statutory lien**—Created by law, such as a judgment.

- **Equitable lien**—Created by the court based on fairness, such as the payment of the balance on a delinquent charge account.

- **Judgment**—If a party has been found guilty in a lawsuit and does not pay, a judgment lien may be filed against the property of the guilty party.

- **Property taxes**—Specific, involuntary liens placed on the owner's property; also called **ad valorem taxes**.

- **Special assessments**—Taxes levied for improvements made to property. Special assessments are specific and statutory, but may be either voluntary or involuntary liens.

- **Mortgage lien**—A voluntary lien securing the loan for the lender until the debt is paid in full.

- **Mechanic's lien**—A lien placed on property by a party who performed labor or furnished material to improve the property (also known as materialman's lien or construction lien).

- **IRS tax lien**—A general, statutory, involuntary lien on all real and personal property owned by a debtor resulting from the non-payment of income or withholding taxes.

The **priority of liens** is generally as follows:

- Real estate taxes and special assessments are paid first.

- The debtor in the first, or senior, lien position is paid next.

The debtors in junior lien positions (second, third, and so on) are paid in the order of recording.

Mechanics' liens generally become effective on the day on which the work began, the materials were delivered, the work was completed, the contract was signed, the work was ordered, or the date that the lien was recorded.

An IRS lien becomes effective from the date of filing or recording. It does not supersede previously recorded liens.

2.   EASEMENTS/RIGHTS-OF-WAY/LICENSES

An **easement** is the right to use the land of another, but it does not include the right of possession. Easements may give the right to **ingress** (enter) and **egress** (exit) a property.

Among the various types of easements are the following:

Appurtenant Easement

- Benefits a parcel of real estate
- Involves two tracts of land owned by two different people
- The dominant estate benefits from the easement
- The servient estate is burdened by the easement (See Figure 2.7)

FIGURE 2.7

Appurtenant Easement

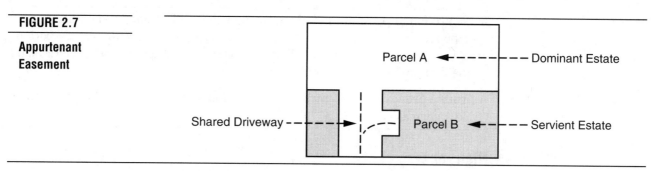

Easement in Gross

- Benefits a person or a legal entity
- Involves one tract of land
- Personal gross easements terminate on the sale of the property or death of the easement owner (e.g., the billboard)
- Commercial gross easements are usually assignable when the property is sold, or on the death of the easement owner (e.g., a utility) (See Figure 2.8.)

FIGURE 2.8

Easement in Gross

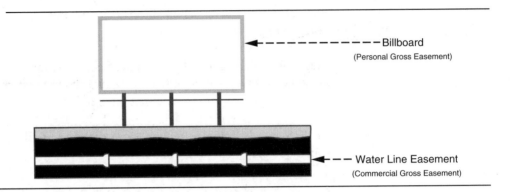

Billboard
(Personal Gross Easement)

Water Line Easement
(Commercial Gross Easement)

Easement by Necessity

■ Created when a buyer purchases a property that has been landlocked by the seller

■ Buyer must be given the access rights to ingress (enter) and egress (exit) the property

Easement by Prescription

■ Created when a claimant uses a property for a statutory period of time

■ Use must have been open, notorious, continuous, exclusive, and without the owner's approval

A **license** is the **personal privilege** to enter the land of another and use it for a specific reason, such as attending a sporting event, parking your car in a parking garage, or going to the movies. A license can be revoked at any time and terminates on the death of either party or the sale of the land.

A **profit a prendre** is the right to take crops, soil, or profit from the land of another. (Also known as profit.)

Right-of-Way

A **right-of-way** is exactly as the term implies: a right or privilege, to pass over the land of another. This right can be created by contract or the usage over a period of time. An easement is an example of a right-of-way.

3. PREEXISTING LEASES OR OTHER AGREEMENTS

When a buyer is purchasing investment property, whether single-family or multi-family, the licensee should ask for copies of the current leases. The leases should be reviewed to determine the remaining term that must be fulfilled and the rights of the current tenants.

4 . E N C R O A C H M E N T

An **encroachment** is an unauthorized intrusion of an improvement onto the real property of another. This could be an intrusion into the air, surface, or subsurface space of the property's boundary lines or building setback lines. A survey is the best way for a buyer to determine if there are any encroachments on a property.

5 . D E E D   C O N D I T I O N S ,   C O V E N A N T S ,   A N D   R E S T R I C T I O N S

Deed restrictions are provisions placed in deeds to control the future uses of the property. The restriction may be either a **deed condition** or a **deed covenant**.

A **deed condition** creates a conditional fee estate, which means that if the condition is breached, the title may revert to the grantor or the grantor's heirs. Deed restrictions normally run with the land, meaning they transfer from one owner to the next.

A **covenant** is a promise between two or more parties in which they agree to perform, or not to perform, specified acts on the property. Restrictive covenants can set the standards for all the parcels within a defined subdivision. These restrictions are available in public records, so any potential buyer has the right to review them before purchasing a property. If a deed covenant is breached, there can be a suit for money damages or injunctive relief.

Deed restrictions may be found in the deed, in the subdivision rules and regulations created by the developer, the homeowners' association of a condominium community, or in a separate document, such as a Declaration of Restrictions. Private restrictions may also be placed on the property by the owner, and these restrictions would be found in the deed. These restrictions may be enforced by any other property owner, the developer, the homeowners' association, or a lender. Any unusual deed restrictions should be included in the listing contract.

Deed restrictions are transferred from one owner to another, unless they are terminated. They may be terminated if the document contains a termination date, if there is a violation and they are not enforced, or there is a vote to change them (i.e., by following the guidelines found in the homeowners' associations bylaws).

Deed restrictions can be enforced by an interested party, such as a neighbor, the homeowners' association, or the developer.

6 . P R O P E R T Y   O W N E R   A S S O C I A T I O N   A G R E E M E N T S

Condominiums and other communities managed by a homeowners' association will have documents to govern how the association is run. Some states require that if an association is involved in the management of the community, the seller must provide certain disclosures to the potential buyer. Some states require that the buyer be given a certain timeframe to review the documents and disclosures, and provide that the sales contract is voidable where this was not done in a timely manner.

These disclosures generally include

- a copy of the declaration;

- a copy of the bylaws, rules and regulations; and

- a seller's certificate, which certifies certain information about the community.

The seller's certificate usually includes the following items:

- Does the Declaration contain a right of first refusal or other restraint that restricts the right to transfer the property? If the right of first refusal or restraint exists, where is it located in the Declaration?

- The monthly assessment for the unit.

- If there is or is not a common expense or special assessment due and unpaid by the seller to the Association. If there is an unpaid amount, what is owed?

- Are there any other fees that have not been paid by the seller that is owed to the Association? If so, what is the amount?

- What are the capital expenditures anticipated by the Association for the current, and if known, for the next two fiscal years?

- What amount is currently set aside for reserves for capital expenditures, and have the reserves been designated for a certain project?

- Current operating budget.

- Balance sheet of income and expenses.

- Are there any unsatisfied judgments against the Association?

- Does the Association provide insurance coverage for the benefit of the unit owners? If so, provide a statement describing the insurance coverage.

- Is the ownership of the community fee simple or a leasehold estate? If it is a leasehold estate, what is the remaining term of the lease and the provisions governing the renewal of the lease?

- What is the name, mailing address, and telephone number of the Association's property manager?

AMP Outline

II.	**Real Property Ownership/ Interest**	
	F. Government Powers and Control of Land Use	3. Police Powers
	1. Americans with Disabilities Act (ADA)	4. Eminent Domain
		5. Property Taxation
	2. Land Use Restrictions and Regulations (i.e., zoning)	6. Subdivision Regulations (e.g., condominiums, cooperatives, planned unit developments)

1. AMERICANS WITH DISABILITIES ACT (ADA)

The **Americans with Disabilities Act (ADA)** became effective in 1992. Its intention is to enable individuals with disabilities to become a part of the social and economic mainstream by mandating equal access to

- public accommodations,

- jobs,

- public transportation,

- telecommunications, and

- government services.

A disability is a physical or mental impairment, or history of such impairment, that substantially limits one or more of a person's major life activities. An individual with AIDS, or a person in an addiction recovery program, is protected. The law does not protect anyone using an illegal drug or a controlled substance. A disabled individual is to be given full and equal enjoyment of goods and services in places of public accommodation, including hotels, shopping centers, commercial properties, and professional offices.

Private clubs and religious organizations are exempt from the Americans with Disabilities Act.

ADA stipulates that employers with 15 or more employees must adopt nondiscriminatory employment procedures, such as making reasonable accommodations to allow a qualified person with a disability to perform essential job functions. Any changes made are to be reasonable and are not to impose an undue burden on the business. Also, changes cannot cause a direct threat to the safety or health of others.

Property owners and managers need to know the priority guidelines for making buildings accessible to disabled individuals. All existing architectural and communication barriers must be removed, if doing so can be accomplished in a readily achievable manner at a low cost. Priorities have been set for these readily achievable changes.

ADA has affected the real estate business in several areas. Real estate brokerage firms must make the necessary changes to provide full and equal opportunities to disabled individuals. Property managers must have a solid understanding of the ADA so they can advise owners of necessary changes.

Under guidelines that were implemented in March 2011, a service animal is defined as follows:

> *Service animal* means any dog that is individually trained to do work or perform tasks for the benefit of an individual with a disability, including a physical, sensory, psychiatric, intellectual, or other mental disability. Other species of animals, whether wild or domestic, trained or untrained, are not service animals for the purposes of this definition. The work or tasks performed by a service animal must be directly related to the individual's disability.

Source: ADA Title II Regulation 28 C.F.R. § 35.104

 Emotional support, therapy, and comfort animals are not service animals under the ADA.

2. LAND USE RESTRICTIONS AND REGULATIONS (I.E., ZONING)

Land in the United States is classified as the **allodial** system of ownership. This means the land is owned free and clear by individuals or other legal entities, and is not owned by the government. An owner is free to use the land for any legal purpose, but deed restrictions, homeowners' association bylaws, and zoning may restrict the land use.

There are no federal zoning laws. Zoning is a police power conferred on municipal governments by state enabling acts. Many communities have a zoning and planning board to evaluate current needs and to project and plan for future growth in a stable manner.

Municipalities and counties develop a master plan, or comprehensive plan, to guide the long-term physical development of the area. The **board classifications of land use** are agricultural, residential, commercial, industrial, and special-use properties. **Zoning ordinances** are local laws that implement the comprehensive plan and regulate the land use and structures. The **purpose of zoning** is to balance private and public land use to ensure the health, safety, and welfare of the community. A **zoning board of appeals** is established to hear complaints about the effects of zoning.

The following are terms associated with zoning:

- **Land use** is regulated by dividing the land into residential, commercial, industrial, and agricultural use districts.

- A **buffer zone** separates two different use districts. For example, a park could be planned between a residential district and a commercial district.

- **Bulk zoning** controls density or the ratio of land area to structure area. Bulk zoning is used to avoid overcrowding.

- **Aesthetic zoning** requires that owners conform to certain types of architectural styles.

- **Incentive zoning** provides a reward or incentive for a builder to meet the established objective of development. Many times, it rewards the builder with the ability to build more homes on a smaller lot size (density) if the builder will include a community improvement, such as affordable housing units. **Nonconforming property** is property in an area that was zoned for one use but for which the zoning has now changed. For example, when zoning changes the land use from residential to commercial, a residential owner usually is allowed to continue using the property as a residence until the property is sold or destroyed.

- **Performance standards** may regulate air, noise, and water pollution in industrial properties, and the term may also be used as it applies to building codes that set a standard that must be met. For example, "that walls, floor, and ceiling be so constructed as to contain an interior fire for thirty minutes."

- A **variance** may be granted in cases where the zoning creates an unnecessary hardship on the owner, but the variance must not be detrimental to zoning. Variances may be granted for setback lines, height restrictions, and the like.

- When a **special-purpose property** that benefits the public, such as a hospital, library, or museum, is approved for construction, a **conditional-use** permit is granted.

- **Spot zoning** is a change of zoning for a particular spot or lot and is generally not permitted.

If the buyers question how a property is zoned, or if their intended use will be allowed by zoning, agents should refer them to the local zoning board to find the answer. If there is no local zoning board, search the Internet for state zoning laws, or refer them to a zoning attorney.

The federal or state government may, through special legislation, regulate land use in **special study zones.** This would be used to control development in areas of a community that require additional study, such as a high-risk, flood-prone, or earthquake area. It could also include scenic easements, coastal management, and environmental laws.

3 . POLICE POWERS

The individual's right to the ownership of property is subject to certain powers by the federal, state, and/or local governments. These powers include police power, eminent domain, taxation, and escheat.

PETE is the acronym to help you remember the government powers.

P—Police Power **E**—Eminent domain **T**—Taxation **E**—Escheat

Police power—The right of the government to regulate for the purpose of promoting the health, safety, and welfare of the public (i.e., zoning and building codes).

4. EMINENT DOMAIN

Eminent domain—The inherent right of a government, a quasi-government body, or a public company to take property for public use. Just compensation must be paid to the owner. This right extends to school and sanitation districts, public utilities, and public service corporations, such as railroads and power companies, to take privately owned property for a necessary public use.

The government exercises its right to take the property by the process of **condemnation.** Just compensation is to be paid to the owner for the property.

5. PROPERTY TAXATION

Taxation—The right of the government to charge a property owner a fee to raise funds to meet the public needs. Real property taxation is ad valorem, or according to the value.

Escheat—When a property owner dies intestate; that is, leaves no will and no heirs can be found, the property reverts (escheats) to the state or the county.

6. SUBDIVISION REGULATIONS (E.G., CONDOMINIUMS, COOPERATIVES, PLANNED UNIT DEVELOPMENTS)

The individual's right to the ownership of property is also subject to certain private powers, such as deed conditions, and subdivision rules and regulations. Other rights could be acquired by adverse possession, encroachments, license, and the rights of adjoining owners.

As previously discussed, the control of land use and development is influenced by public (government), and private (nongovernment) restrictions, and public ownership of land by federal, state, and local governments. **Public controls** include state regulations aimed at protecting the public health, safety, and welfare.

A developer places **private deed restrictions** on real estate to control and maintain the desirable quality and character of a subdivision or property. This is done through the use of deed restrictions and restrictive covenants. It only takes one person to enforce a deed restriction.

Private restrictions are called covenants, conditions, and restrictions (CC&Rs). They may be placed on the land by the developer or the current owner when the property is sold.

CC&Rs cannot be imposed for an illegal purpose, such as one that would break a Fair Housing law.

Restrictions can also be found in the bylaws of condominium, cooperatives, and planned unit developments. See pages 47–48 for the review of these types of ownership.

CHAPTER 2 TEST

1. An example of the right to use the land of another, without possessing it would be a(n)
    A. lease.
    B. easement.
    C. fee simple absolute.
    D. defeasible fee.

2. An easement that involves two tracts of land, one a dominant estate and the other a servient estate, is a(n)
    A. gross easement.
    B. easement by necessity.
    C. easement by prescription.
    D. appurtenant easement.

3. The right of ingress means that the entity that has the easement has the right to
    A. enter the property.
    B. exit the property.
    C. posses the property.
    D. build on the property.

4. An easement that is created by the open, notorious, continuous, and exclusive use of a property without the owner's approval is a(n)
    A. easement by necessity.
    B. prescriptive easement.
    C. gross easement.
    D. appurtenant easement.

5. A person may enter the land of another and use it for a specific, limited time. The person knows that this privilege can be revoked at any time. The person MOST LIKELY has a(n)
    A. license.
    B. easement.
    C. personality privilege.
    D. reality privilege.

6. The right to take crops, soil, or anything of value from the land of another is called a
    A. pur autre vie rights.
    B. personal property profit.
    C. profit a prendre.
    D. profit and loss.

7. The agreement between parties to perform, or not to perform, specified acts is a
    A. concession.
    B. contingency.
    C. covenant.
    D. commitment.

8. An example of an estate that is based on calendar time is a
    A. leasehold estate.
    B. life estate.
    C. dower estate.
    D. freehold estate.

9. A person who is responsible for the management of a business and is personally liable for business losses in a partnership is the
    A. general partner.
    B. limited partner.
    C. passive partner.
    D. liability partner.

10. The type of ownership that blends severalty and tenancy-in-common ownership is a(n)
    A. cooperative.
    B. condominium.
    C. estate-in-common.
    D. estate at will.

11. A person who receives shares of stock in a corporation and has a proprietary lease to a unit within a building has purchased a
    A. cooperative.
    B. condominium.
    C. home in a subdivision.
    D. commercial building.

12. A time-share estate in which the buyer receives a deed to the property would be BEST described by the term
    A. right-to use.
    B. right-to-occupy.
    C. vacation ownership.
    D. interval ownership.

13. The process of changing an apartment building to a condominium community is called
    A. commingling.
    B. conversion.
    C. conditional use.
    D. constructive notice.

14. The developers of a special-purpose property, such as a hospital, library, or museum, would be granted a
    A. conditional-use permit.
    B. nonconforming permit.
    C. spot permit.
    D. variance permit.

15. The federal or state government may, through special legislation, regulate land use in geographical areas of a community that might be high risk. This area would be known as a
    A. county study zone.
    B. federal study zone
    C. state study zone.
    D. special study zone.

16. Which of the following is NOT one of the broad land-use classifications?
    A. Commercial
    B. Industrial
    C. Rental
    D. Residential

17. The legitimate intent of zoning is to
    A. ensure the health, safety, and welfare of the community.
    B. demonstrate the police power of the state.
    C. set limits on the number of businesses in a given area.
    D. protect neighborhoods from encroachments by industries.

18. A written lease agreement between the tenant and the owner will MOST LIKELY be interpreted as a(n)
    A. unilateral contract.
    B. bilateral contract.
    C. revocable contract.
    D. gratuitous contract.

19. A lease gives the tenant a(n)
    A. reversionary right.
    B. leased fee interest.
    C. exclusive possession.
    D. life estate.

20. A lease with a definite beginning and a definite ending date is an
    A. estate for years.
    B. estate from period to period.
    C. estate at will.
    D. estate at sufferance.

21. A lease that will automatically renew until proper notice to terminate has been given is a
    A. tenancy for years.
    B. periodic tenancy.
    C. tenancy at will.
    D. tenancy at sufferance.

22. A lease that can terminated at any time by the landlord or the tenant is an
    A. estate for years.
    B. interval estate.
    C. estate at will.
    D. estate at sufferance.

23. After the lease expires, a tenant remains in the property without the consent of the landlord. This situation is BEST described by the term
    A. tenancy for years.
    B. periodic tenancy.
    C. tenancy at will.
    D. tenancy at sufferance.

24. The landlord's interest in a leased property is called a
    A. fee simple interest.
    B. defeasible interest.
    C. leased fee interest.
    D. leasehold interest.

25. The reversionary right is the right of the
    A. tenant to possess the property until the end of the lease.
    B. lender to foreclose on the property when the tenant defaults.
    C. vendee to lease the property in a land installment sale.
    D. landlord to get possession back after the lease expires.

26. In the assignment of a lease, the assignor is the
    A. tenant.
    B. lender.
    C. owner.
    D. agent.

27. Unless a novation has been granted, who is usually secondarily liable when a lease has been assigned?
    A. The new tenant.
    B. The original tenant.
    C. Both the original tenant and the new tenant.
    D. The owner and the new tenant.

28. Less than all the leasehold interests is transferred in a(n)
    A. assignment.
    B. sublease.
    C. gross lease.
    D. net lease.

29. A tenant has agreed to pay real estate ownership expenses of property taxes, insurance, and maintenance. The tenant entered into a
    A. gross lease.
    B. percentage lease.
    C. net lease.
    D. graduated lease.

30. The lessor receives a fixed monthly rent payment, plus a percentage of the gross income based on all sales. This type of lease is called a(n)
    A. sale-leaseback.
    B. lease purchase.
    C. index lease.
    D. percentage lease.

31. The covenant that requires that the lessor give the lessee exclusive possession of the property, and that prohibits the lessor from entering the property without notice, is the
    A. covenant of quiet enjoyment.
    B. covenant of exclusive possession.
    C. covenant of seisen.
    D. covenant of further assurances.

32. Generally, the landlord is required to keep the property in good condition by maintaining the common areas. The warranty that requires this is the
    A. warranty of maintenance.
    B. warranty of habitability.
    C. warranty of transferability.
    D. warranty of good title.

33. When the lessee breaches the lease, it gives the lessor the right to proceed with
    A. actual eviction by filing a suit for possession.
    B. actual eviction by filing a suit for specific performance.
    C. constructive eviction by filing a suit for possession.
    D. constructive eviction by filing a suit for specific performance.

34. A lease would LEAST LIKELY to be terminated when the
    A. property is taken by eminent domain.
    B. life tenant who had leased the property dies.
    C. lessor sells the property.
    D. lessee buys the land from the lessor.

35. In a sale-leaseback, the grantor becomes the
    A. lessor.
    B. lessee.
    C. new owner.
    D. landlord.

36. All of the following are grounds for actual eviction EXCEPT
    A. nonpayment of rent.
    B. unlawful use of the premises.
    C. the lessor's breach of the lease.
    D. the tenant's noncompliance with health and safety codes.

37. KMK Law Firm just agreed to lease a space in downtown Cincinnati as a lessee for the next 20 years. Which of the following terms BEST describes KMK's interest in the property?
    A. Freehold interest
    B. Reversionary interest
    C. Leasehold interest
    D. Leased fee interest

38. The ABC Company (the tenant), agreed to lease a space for ten years. Five years later, ABC sold its company to XYZ. If the lease contains no provision regarding an assignment, ABC may
   A. assign the leasehold interest to XYZ.
   B. not assign the leasehold interest to XYZ under any circumstances.
   C. assign the leasehold interest to XYZ on the approval of its attorney.
   D. not assign the leasehold interest, but they may sublease the space to XYZ.

39. A landlord has defaulted on his mortgage payment. Which of the following clauses would BEST protect the tenant?
   A. Survivorship clause
   B. Nondisturbance clause
   C. Renewal clause
   D. Right of first refusal clause

40. The owner of a 20-unit apartment building sold the property to a new buyer and assigned his leased fee interest to her. At the closing, the security deposits will be
   A. returned to the tenants by the original owner.
   B. prorated between the original owner and the new owner.
   C. applied toward the current month's rent payment.
   D. transferred to the new owner.

41. Last night, an apartment building was completely destroyed by a fire. Are the tenants required to honor the remaining term of the lease?
   A. Yes, because a lease is not affected by destruction of the property.
   B. Yes, because the owner still has a mortgage payment to make next month.
   C. No, because a lease is terminated by destruction of the property.
   D. No, because the owner will file a claim with the insurance company and rebuild the property.

42. All of the following terms are associated with a net lease EXCEPT
   A. double net.
   B. triple net.
   C. property taxes and insurance.
   D. property taxes and mortgage payments.

43. When land is to be condemned or taken under the power of eminent domain, which of the following must apply?
   A. The taking must be for a public purpose.
   B. Statutory dedication must be executed.
   C. Adverse possession claim must be taken.
   D. Constructive notice must be given.

44. A person is selling limited partnerships in a real estate venture. The offering is being made within state lines, and all purchasers are residents of the state. The offering is MOST LIKELY regulated by
   A. the Securities and Exchange Commission.
   B. the real estate commission.
   C. blue-sky laws.
   D. white-sky laws.

45. Deed restrictions are a means whereby
   A. local zoning laws are enforced.
   B. the planning commission's work is made effective.
   C. villages and cities can control construction details.
   D. the seller can limit or control the buyer's use.

46. A person has a claim affecting the title to a person's property. The owner has no mortgages against the property and has been trying to sell it. The person is concerned about the possibility of a bona fide purchaser buying it before he obtains a judgment. To protect himself during the course of the court action, the person should
   A. publish a notice in a newspaper.
   B. seek an attachment.
   C. bring a quick summary proceeding.
   D. notify the owner that any attempt to sell the property will be considered fraud.

47. What is the major difference between a general lien and a specific lien?
    A. A general lien may be filed only on personal property, while a specific lien is filed on real estate.
    B. A general lien may be filed by a corporation, while a specific lien may be filed by a specific individual.
    C. A general lien may be filed by an attorney, while a specific lien can be filed by anyone.
    D. A general lien may be filed against real and personal property, while a specific lien may be filed against only a specific property.

48. When a property is abandoned, it may revert to the county or state by the process of
    A. escheat.
    B. eminent domain.
    C. testate.
    D. intestate.

49. Which of the following is NOT an example of constructive notice?
    A. Recording a deed at the courthouse
    B. A legal notice in the newspaper
    C. An unrecorded lien
    D. Possession of the property

50. The process an airport would use to take property for public use is
    A. eminent domain.
    B. escheat.
    C. adverse possession.
    D. condemnation.

51. Lis pendens is BEST described by which of the following?
    A. A notice filed when the property is foreclosed
    B. Constructive notice that a property owner is in litigation that could result in a future lien on the property
    C. Actual notice that a judgment has been secured against a property owner
    D. A notice that allows the court to maintain custody of a property until it is sold in bankruptcy

52. Three people decided to pool their resources for investment purposes. This process is called
    A. syndication.
    B. a suit for performance.
    C. a limited partnership.
    D. illegal in most states.

53. Which of the following would NOT be associated with an adverse possession claim?
    A. Title by prescription
    B. Suit to quiet the title
    C. Squatter's rights
    D. A license

54. A party's legal interests or rights to a property, which must be possessory or may become possessory in the future, and can be measured in terms of duration, refers to a(n)
    A. noninheritable estate.
    B. inheritable estate.
    C. estate in trust.
    D. estate in land.

55. The highest form of ownership that the law recognizes is a
    A. legal life estate.
    B. conventional life estate.
    C. fee simple estate.
    D. defeasible fee estate.

56. The terms remainder or reversion would be associated with which of the following types of estates?
    A. Fee simple absolute
    B. Legal life estates
    C. Defeasible fee estates
    D. Conventional life estates

57. The deed says that a property is held in severalty. This means the property is owned by
    A. one person or entity.
    B. two or more people.
    C. the grantor's two children.
    D. a spouse before a divorce.

58. When two people each have 100 percent ownership of a property, they are
    A. life estate tenants.
    B. tenants-by-the entirety.
    C. joint tenants.
    D. tenants-in-common.

59. In community property states, property owned by a spouse before marriage is called
    A. community property.
    B. personal property.
    C. separate property.
    D. dower property.

60. The word *appurtenant* is BEST defined as
    A. tangible property that is considered real property.
    B. intangible property, such as easements and water rights.
    C. any rights, benefits, or attachments that would transfer with the real property.
    D. real and personal property transferred in the deed.

61. A group of investors formed a business structure wherein one person is personally liable for the operation and the other partners can only lose the amount they have invested. This type of business arrangement BEST describes a
    A. general partnership.
    B. limited partnership.
    C. tenancy in partnership.
    D. minority partnership.

62. A pass-through entity that allows members to pay taxes on the income received and avoids taxation at the business level is a
    A. limited corporation.
    B. limited proprietorship.
    C. limited liability company.
    D. limited liability corporation.

63. When two or more parties enter into a business venture with the intention of it ending within a limited timeframe, the parties have entered into a
    A. joint administration.
    B. joint enterprise.
    C. joint interest.
    D. joint venture.

64. Which of the following is exempt from the ADA?
    A. Hotels, motels, and restaurants
    B. A church or synagogue
    C. A residential apartment building that is owner-occupied
    D. A shopping center

65. Which of the following persons can have a service animal under the ADA?
    A. A person who has a cat trained as a comfort animal.
    B. A person who has a prescription from a doctor for a therapy animal.
    C. A person who has a dog trained to assist him/her with a hearing disability.
    D. A person who has a prescription from a doctor for an emotional support animal.

66. An owner is continuing the current use of a property after the zoning board has changed the land use. The owner is said to have
    A. converted use.
    B. variance use.
    C. nonconforming use.
    D. spot use.

67. An individual seeking to be excused from the dictates of a zoning ordinance should request a(n)
    A. building of permit.
    B. alternate use permit.
    C. nonconforming use.
    D. variance.

68. A property is being sold at a foreclosure sale. Which of the following will be paid first from the proceeds of the sale?
    A. Real estate agent's commission
    B. Property taxes and special assessments
    C. Internal Revenue Service Liens
    D. Mortgage holder in the first lien position

69. A person has looked at many properties but he really likes a condo that has a great view of the city. Which of the following questions is NOT important when he makes a decision about making an offer on the property?
    A. What is the monthly assessment for the condo?
    B. How do I get a copy of the bylaws?
    C. What is the agent's commission on the sale?
    D. Are there any unsatisfied liens against the Association?

70. The unities of time, title, interest, possession, and person would be found in which type of ownership?
    A. Tenancy in common
    B. Tenancy by the entirety
    C. Joint tenancy
    D. Severalty

MATCHING QUIZ

The column on the right contains a brief definition of important terms in this section. Write the letter of the matching term on the appropriate line.

A. Syndicate

B. Suite to quiet title

C. Special assessments

D. Lis pendens

E. Government powers

F. Adverse possession

G. Judgment

H. General lien

I. Constructive notice

J. Fee simple absolute

K. Tenancy in common

L. Cooperative

M. Fee simple defeasible

N. Tenancy by the entirety

O. Condominium

P. Special study zones

Q. Leasehold interest

R. Leased fee interest

S. Constructive eviction

T. LLC

1. _____ Lien against all property of a person's property, both real and personal

2. _____ Form of ownership in which the airspace is owned in severalty, and the land and buildings are owned as tenants in common

3. _____ Legal notice or notice to the world by recorded documents

4. _____ The open, notorious, hostile, and continuous use of another's property for a statutory time, which may allow the squatter to claim the property

5. _____ Form of ownership in which a corporation holds title and the owners purchase shares of stock in the corporation and receive a proprietary lease

6. _____ A special limitation with a possibility of reverter

7. _____ Formed when two or more people unite and pool their resources to own, develop, and/or operate an investment

8. _____ Highest form of ownership recognized by law; for an indefinite duration, freely transferable, and inheritable

9. _____ Police power, eminent domain, taxation, and escheat

10. _____ Form of co-ownership by which each owner holds an undivided interest in real property as if he or she were the sole owner; characterized by unity of possession

11. _____ Legal action intended to establish or settle the title claim to a particular property

12. _____ Form of joint property ownership held by a husband and wife during marriage; characterized by unities of time, title, interest, possession, and person

13. _____ Court decision on the respective rights and claims of the parties in a lawsuit

14. _____ Regulation of land use to control development in high-risk, flood-prone, or geological areas

15. _____ Limited liability company

16. _____ This notice renders a property unmarketable because it means that litigation is pending

17. _____ Lessor's interest in a leased property

18. _____ Levees for improvements, such as sidewalks and waterlines, made to a property

19. _____ Lessee's interest in the leased premises

20. _____ Landlord breaches the lease and tenant must leave the premises

CHAPTER 2 TEST ANSWERS

1. **(B)** An easement gives the right to use the land of another, but not to possess it.

2. **(D)** An appurtenant easement involves two tracts of land, with one being the dominate estate and the other a servient estate.

3. **(A)** The right of ingress is found in an easement and it means the right to enter property.

4. **(B)** The easement that is created by the open, notorious, continuous, exclusive, and use of another's property is a prescriptive easement.

5. **(A)** When the right to enter and use the property of another for a specific time has been given, and the right can be revoked at any time, the person has a license to use the property.

6. **(C)** The right to take from the soil or anything the soil produces is a profit a prendre.

7. **(C)** An agreement or promise made between parties to perform, or not to perform, specified act/s is a covenant.

8. **(A)** The leasehold estate is based on calendar time.

9. **(A)** The general partner is personally liable in the management of a partnership.

10. **(B)** Condominium ownership blends severalty and tenancy-in-common ownership.

11. **(A)** When a person receives stock and a proprietary lease to a unit, the person is purchasing a cooperative.

12. **(D)** Interval ownership would best describe a time-share estate.

13. **(B)** Conversion is the process of changing one form of ownership to another, such as an apartment building to a condo.

14. **(A)** To build a special-purpose property, a developer would need to be granted a conditional-use permit.

15. **(D)** The federal or state governments may regulate land use in a high-risk geographical area called special study zones.

16. **(C)** The broad land-use classifications are agricultural, residential, commercial, industrial, and special-purpose properties, not rental.

17. **(A)** The major intent of legitimate zoning is to regulate for the health, safety, and welfare of the community.

18. **(B)** The lease agreement is a bilateral contract because both parties must perform.

19. **(C)** A lease gives the tenant exclusive possession of the property.

20. **(A)** When the lease has a definite beginning date and a definite ending date, it is an estate for years. (Tenancy for years)

21. **(B)** When a lease will automatically renew until proper notice has been given, it is a periodic tenancy. (Estate from period to period)

22. **(C)** When a lease can be terminated at any time by the landlord or the tenant by giving proper notice to the other party, it is called an estate at will. (Tenancy at will)

23. **(D)** When a tenant remains in the property without the consent of the landlord after the lease expires, it is called a tenancy at sufferance. (Estate at sufferance)

24. **(C)** The landlord's interest in a property is called a leased fee interest.

25. **(D)** The reversionary right is the right of the landlord to get possession of the property after the lease expires.

26. **(A)** The tenant who entered into the original lease agreement with the owner can transfer the balance of his/her rights to a new tenant under a lease assignment.

27. **(A)** The assignee is liable if he/she agreed to pay rent, but the assignor remains liable unless the landlord has granted a novation.

28. **(B)** Less than all the leasehold interest is transferred in an assignment.

29. **(C)** If the tenant is paying ownership expenses, the tenant entered into a net lease.

30. **(D)** In a percentage lease, the lessor can receive a fixed monthly rent payment plus a percentage of the gross or net of the sales.

31. **(A)** The covenant of quiet enjoyment means the landlord must give the tenant exclusive possession of the property and cannot enter the property without notice, unless it is an emergency.

32. **(B)** The warranty of habitability requires the landlord to keep the property in good condition.

33. **(A)** If the tenant breaches the lease, the lessor may file a suit for possession. (Actual eviction)

34. **(C)** Existing leases are honored when the property is sold.

35. **(B)** At the conclusion of a sale-leaseback transaction, the grantor/seller of the property becomes the lessee or new tenant.

36. **(C)** Actual eviction occurs when the tenant has breached the lease.

37. **(C)** KMK is a tenant, and the tenant's interest is best described as a leasehold interest.

38. **(A)** Unless a lease forbids assignment and subleasing, the tenant may do so.

39. **(B)** The nondisturbance clause states that if the landlord defaults on the mortgage payment and the tenant continues to pay the rent, they will not be evicted.

40. **(D)** The security deposits would be transferred to the new owner because the leases and the security deposits were assigned to the new owner.

41. **(C)** Leases normally terminate upon the destruction of the premises.

42. **(D)** The tenant pays some or all ownership expenses, but does not pay the mortgage payments in a net lease.

43. **(A)** The government has the right to take private property through eminent domain, but the taking must be for the public benefit, and just compensation must be paid.

44. **(C)** Securities sold intrastate are regulated by blue-sky laws.

45. **(D)** Deed restrictions allow the seller to limit or control the buyer's use of the land.

46. **(B)** By definition of an attachment.

47. **(D)** By the definitions of general and specific liens.

48. **(A)** When a person dies without a will and there are no heirs, the property is considered abandoned and reverts to the state by escheat.

49. **(C)** An unrecorded lien would not give constructive notice.

50. **(D)** The right of the government to take the land is eminent domain. The process is condemnation.

51. **(B)** By definition of lis pendens.

52. **(A)** By the definition of syndicate.

53. **(D)** A license is the personal privilege to be on the land of another and would not be associated with adverse possession.

54. **(D)** An estate in land is a party's legal interests or rights to a property, which must be possessory, or may become possessory, in the future.

55. **(C)** The highest form of ownership recognized by law is fee simple absolute. (Also known as fee simple or fee estate.)

56. **(D)** Remainder and reversion are terms associated with conventional life estates.

57. **(A)** Severalty ownership means that it is held by one person or entity.

58. **(B)** Only tenants-by-the-entirety can each own 100 percent ownership of the property.

59. **(C)** Separate property refers to property owned by a spouse before marriage.

60. **(C)** An appurtenant is any rights, benefits, or attachments that would transfer with real property.

61. **(B)** When a limited partnership is created, the general partner(s) have unlimited liability, but the liability of the other partners is limited to their investment.

62. **(C)** A limited liability company allows the pass-through of income to members and avoids double taxation. (It is sometimes mistakenly called a limited liability corporation, but that is incorrect.)

63. **(D)** When a joint venture is created, there is no intention for the relationship to be long term.

64. **(B)** Private clubs and religious organizations are exempt from the ADA.

65. **(C)** When a dog has been specially trained to help a disabled person perform work or tasks related to the disability, it is a service animal. (Only a dog can be a service animal.)

66. **(C)** The nonconforming use allows an owner to continue current use of the property after the land use has changed to another land use.

67. **(D)** An owner who wishes to be excused from a zoning ordinance would request a variance.

68. **(B)** Property taxes and special assessment will be paid first from the proceeds of any sale of real estate.

69. **(C)** The agent's commission on the sale would not affect a buyer's decision of whether to make an offer on the condo.

70. **(B)** The unities of time, title, interest, possession, and person would be found in tenancy by the entireties.

ANSWERS—MATCHING QUIZ

1. **H**
2. **O**
3. **I**
4. **F**
5. **L**
6. **M**
7. **A**
8. **J**
9. **E**
10. **K**
11. **B**
12. **N**
13. **G**
14. **P**
15. **T**
16. **D**
17. **R**
18. **C**
19. **Q**
20. **S**

CHAPTER 3

Finance

AMP Outline

1. EQUITY

The difference between the current market value and any liens on the property is the owner's equity.

2. LOAN-TO-VALUE RATIO

The lender will negotiate the loan on the sale price or the appraised value whichever is less. The loan-to-value ratio is the relationship between the amount of a loan and the appraised value (sale price) of a property. For example, if a borrower has a 10 percent down payment, the loan-to-value ratio is 90 percent.

3. TERM AND PAYMENT

The **term** of the loan is the length of time the borrower has to repay the lender. For home loans, the borrower generally negotiates a term of between 15 to 30 years. The longer the term, the lower the monthly payment.

The mortgage factor chart (Figure 3.1) shows how the payment is calculated based on the interest rate and the term.

FIGURE 3.1

Mortgage Factor
Chart

How To Use This Chart

To use this chart, start by finding the appropriate interest rate. Then follow that row over to the column for the appropriate loan term. This number is the *interest rate factor* required each month to amortize a $1,000 loan. To calculate the principal and interest (PI) payment, multiply the interest rate factor by the number of 1,000s in the total loan.

For example, if the interest rate is 8 percent for a term of 30 years, the interest rate factor is 7.34. If the total loan is $100,000, the loan contains 100 1,000s. Therefore, 100 × 7.34 = $734 PI only.

Rate	Term 15 Years	Term 30 Years
6	8.44	6.00
6⅛	8.51	6.08
6¼	8.57	6.16
6⅜	8.64	6.24
6½	8.71	6.32
6⅝	8.78	6.40
6¾	8.85	6.49
6⅞	8.92	6.57
7	8.98	6.65
7⅛	9.06	6.74
7¼	9.12	6.82
7⅜	9.20	6.91
7½	9.27	6.99
7⅝	9.34	7.08
7¾	9.41	7.16
7⅞	9.48	7.25
8	9.56	7.34
8⅛	9.63	7.43
8¼	9.71	7.52
8⅜	9.78	7.61
8½	9.85	7.69
8⅝	9.93	7.78
8¾	10.00	7.87
8⅞	10.07	7.96
9	10.15	8.05

4. PRINCIPAL AND INTEREST

In finance terminology, the **principal** is the loan balance, and **interest** is the charge for the use of money. In Chapter 7, we will learn how to calculate the principal and interest that is paid each month on a loan.

Interest is what a borrower **pays** when a loan is negotiated, and it is what is **earned** when his/her money is lent to other people, such as interest earned on a certificate of deposit or a savings account.

Interest on home loans is usually computed as **simple interest** and is paid in **arrears**, meaning the borrower has the benefit of the service and then pays the interest due. (As opposed to tenants who pay rent in **advance**, meaning they pay for the service before they have the benefit of living in the space.) How the interest is computed on a home loan is reviewed in the math chapter.

Some states have **usury laws** that limit the maximum interest rate that a lender can charge on certain types of loans. Note that usury laws do not set the interest rates; they establish the maximum rate that can be charged. In times of emergencies, the federal government can set aside usury laws.

5. DIRECT AND INDIRECT COSTS (POINTS, DISCOUNTS)

Primary and Secondary Mortgage Markets, Federal Reserve

The **primary mortgage market** and the **secondary mortgage market** are sources of funds for financing. Primary mortgage market lenders originate or make loans directly to borrowers, while the secondary mortgage market buys mortgages from primary market lenders.

Primary Mortgage Market

Savings and loans

- Specialize in long-term, single-family home loans

- May offer conventional, FHA, or VA mortgages

Mutual savings banks

- Located primarily in the northeastern United States

- State chartered, owned by their depositors, and originate FHA or VA loans

Commercial banks

- Have historically specialized in short-term loans (such as home improvement loans, mobile home loans, and commercial loans)

- Have become more active in the negotiation of long-term residential loans

Insurance companies

- Specialize in large-scale, long-term loans that finance commercial and industrial properties

- May require an equity kicker or participation financing in the loans they negotiate

Mortgage bankers

- Lend their own money and money of investors

- Originate loans and package mortgages, then sell the package to investors and continue to service them after they are sold

Mortgage brokers

- **Do not lend** their own money

- Bring borrowers and lenders together and are paid a percentage of the money borrowed

Credit unions

- Provide a source of funds for their members

Pension funds

- Work through mortgage bankers and mortgage brokers in real estate financing

Secondary Mortgage Markets

The secondary mortgage markets were created to provide a **rollover of funds** to the primary mortgage market. When a loan has been negotiated by a local lender, the lender may sell the loan to the secondary market and have money available to meet the demands of its new borrowers. Loans cannot be sold on the secondary market unless they conform to the secondary market guidelines. A **nonconforming loan** is one that does not meet secondary market specifications.

Loans that are purchased by the secondary market are pooled (packaged) and sold to investors in the form of **mortgage-backed securities (MBS)**. Investors purchase **pass-through participation certificates** that entitle the holders to pro-rata shares of all principal and interest payments made on the pool of loan assets.

Federal National Mortgage Association

The **Federal National Mortgage Association** (Fannie Mae) was established in 1938 for the purpose of buying FHA-insured loans from lenders; in 1945, Fannie Mae agreed to also purchase VA loans from lenders. Eventually, other types of loans were purchased from lenders, and in 1968, Fannie Mae became a government-sponsored enterprise (GSE), meaning that it was chartered by Congress as a private shareholder-owned company.

Fannie Mae's purpose today is to continue to provide liquidity and stability in the housing market by purchasing mortgages from lending institutions that negotiate loans that meet Fannie Mae guidelines. With the unstable real estate market of the last few years, Fannie Mae was taken over by the federal government in September of 2008, and the Federal Housing Finance Agency (FHFA) was appointed its conservator.

Government National Mortgage Association

The **Government National Mortgage Association** (GNMA or Ginnie Mae) is a federal agency created in 1968 when Fannie Mae was reorganized. It is owned by the government and is a division of the Department of Housing and Urban Development (HUD). Ginnie Mae specializes in high-risk and special assistance programs, such as housing for the elderly. Ginnie Mae has a mortgage-backed securities program that sells guaranteed certificates to investors. These Ginnie Mae pass-through certificates provide for a monthly pass-through of principal and interest payments directly to certificate holders.

Through a tandem plan, Ginnie Mae also works with Fannie Mae in secondary market activities when money is tight. The tandem plan provides that Fannie Mae can purchase high-risk, low-yield loans at full market rates, and Ginnie Mae will guarantee payment and absorb the difference between the low yield and current market prices. Ginnie Mae purchases FHA, VA, and certain Rural Development loans.

Federal Home Loan Mortgage Corporation

The **Federal Home Loan Mortgage Corporation** (FHLMC, or Freddie Mac) was established to assist savings and loan associations as a secondary market for conventional mortgages. Freddie Mac is a publicly owned corporation that purchases mortgages, pools them, and sells bonds in the open market as mortgage-backed securities.

Freddie Mac guarantees timely payments to investors of their mortgage-backed securities. In September 2008, Freddie Mac was also taken over by the federal government, and the Federal Housing Finance Agency (FHFA) was appointed its conservator.

Federal Reserve

The Federal Reserve (the Fed) was established to stabilize the economy by controlling the money supply and credit available in the country. It does this by creating money, regulating reserve requirements, and setting the discount rate of interest.

An oversupply of money creates inflation; an undersupply can cause a recession.

When the reserve requirements are increased, the money supply shrinks, thus increasing interest rates.

If the reserve requirements are decreased, the money supply grows, thus decreasing interest rates.

The **discount rate** of interest is the rate the Fed charges for loans to its member banks, and it can move money into, or out of, commercial banks by buying or selling government bonds.

Real estate borrowers compete with other businesses for money. When the money supply is limited, interest rates are high and qualifying buyers can be difficult. When money is plentiful, interest rates are low and qualifying buyers is much easier.

Lenders generate a yield or profit by charging upfront fees, such as loan origination and discount points, and the recurring interest fee. Information in Chapter 7 explains how to compute both of these fees.

6. RETURN ON INVESTMENT/RATE OF RETURN

The formula that investors use to calculate the return on investment, or the rate of return, is:

```
  Potential gross income
– Vacancy and rent loss
+ Additional income*
  Total anticipated revenue
– Expenses
  Net operating income before debt service
– Debt service
  Before-tax cash flow
– Taxes
  After-tax cash flow
```

* Some investors will use these steps to compute the anticipated revenue:
Potential gross income + Additional income – Vacancy and rent loss =
Total anticipated revenue

The return on investment (ROI) is one way to measure the profitability of a property. The ROI is the ratio of the property's after-tax cash flow (ATCF) to the money invested (equity [E]) in the property. The formula for computing the return on investment is

$$ROI = \frac{ATCF}{E} \times 100\%$$

The ROI also may be computed on a before-tax basis.

A property with a $10,000 ATCF in which the owner has $100,000 invested would have an ROI of 10 percent. When this formula is used to analyze the owner's investment, it is called a cash-on-cash investment, and it may be computed on either a before-tax or an after-tax basis.

The **return on investment (ROI)** is the ratio of the property's net income after taxes (ATCF) to the money invested (equity). The ROI also may be computed on a before-tax basis.

AMP Outline

III.   Finance
  B. Types of Financing
    1. Amortized
    2. Interest Only
    3. Adjustable-Rate Mortgage (ARM)
    4. Construction Loan
    5. Home Equity

1. AMORTIZED

To *amortize* means to repay the loan in monthly or other periodic payments that include principal and interest. A portion of each payment is applied to the principal balance and a portion is kept by the lender as interest on the loan.

In a **fully amortized loan** or direct reduction loan, at the end of the loan period the principal balance is zero. A 30-year fixed-rate mortgage is a fully amortized loan. If the payments are paid each month, the loan is paid in full on final payment.

In a **partially amortized loan**, or **balloon mortgage**, the principal and interest payments do not pay off the entire loan. A balance remains when the final payment is made.

In a **nonamortized loan**, periodic interest payments are made to the lender, but nothing is applied to the principal balance. These loans are called *term mortgages* or *straight mortgages*. A **construction loan** is an example of a nonamortized loan. With a construction loan, the borrower receives the money in stages, called *draws*, and makes periodic payments of interest. When the construction is complete, the borrower must have secured long-term financing and will pay off the entire principal balance.

2. INTEREST ONLY

When a borrower negotiates a **straight mortgage (term loan)**, he makes periodic payments of interest only and the principal is paid in full at the end of the term. A construction loan is an example of a straight mortgage.

3. ADJUSTABLE-RATE MORTGAGE (ARM)

An **adjustable-rate mortgage (ARM)** contains an **escalation clause** that allows the interest to adjust over the loan term. The terms associated with an adjustable rate mortgage are start rate, adjustment period, index, margin, payment cap, and rate cap. Let's review each of these.

Start rate—The interest rate at the beginning of the loan from which is fixed for a certain time frame.

Adjustment period—Based on the loan, the interest on the ARM will adjust at a certain timeframe. The interest could adjust monthly, quarterly, semi-annually, annually, every five years, and so on. Figure 3.2 shows the interest rates for different ARMs.

FIGURE 3.2	ARM	Interest Rate	Adjustment timeframe
Adjustable-Rate	3/1	Fixed for 3 years	Interest rate will adjust every year after the first 3 years
Mortgages	3/3	Fixed for 3 years	Interest rate will adjust every three years

Index—Adjustable-rate mortgages are tied to an index, such as the London Interbank Offered Rate (LIBOR), or to U.S. Treasury Securities (T-bills). This index will be reviewed at the adjustment period and used to compute the new rate.

Margin—The profit charged by the lender and added to the index to determine the interest is called the *margin*. Over the life of an adjustable-rate mortgage, the margin remains constant. Margins will range between 2 and 7 percent, so the lower margin means it is a much better loan for the borrower.

If the margin is 2 percent; that 2 percent is added to the index to determine the new interest rate.

Rate cap—The borrower should be aware of the initial, periodic, and life-of-the-loan rate caps. The initial rate cap is the maximum increase the first time the interest adjusts, while the periodic rate cap is the maximum that the interest can adjust in any subsequent adjustment periods.

The **life-of-the-loan** or aggregate rate cap is the maximum that the interest can adjust for the life of the loan.

> Example: 5/1 LIBOR ARM
>
> Interest rate is fixed for the first 5 years
> Interest rate will adjust every year thereafter
> Index: 1-year LIBOR
> Margin: 2%
> Initial rate cap: 5%
> Annual rate cap: 2%
> Lifetime rate cap: 5%

4. CONSTRUCTION LOAN

A **construction loan** is used to finance the erection of improvements on land and is also known as a *short-term* or *interim loan* because the loan is for the period of construction. The borrower pays interest only on the loan. Many lenders require the borrower to have an end loan for the permanent financing before the construction loan will be negotiated. The loan is received in a series of draws as each stage of construction is completed and inspected.

Construction loans are also classified as an **open-end mortgage,** which allows the borrower to secure additional funds, up to a maximum loan amount, without redoing the original paperwork.

5. HOME EQUITY

Equity is the difference between the market value and any existing mortgages on the property. Many homeowners will use the equity in their property to finance the purchase of a vacation home, college tuition, pay medical bills, or other business ventures. With a home equity loan, the borrowers must qualify, the property will be appraised, and a closing will take place. After the three-day right of rescission has passed, the borrower will receive a check for the loan amount. The home equity loan (HEL) is usually amortized and repaid just like the first mortgage.

Note that a home equity loan is different than a refinance. With a refinance, the equity may be withdrawn, but the borrower will have only one loan on the property. With a home equity loan, the original loan is in the first lien position, and the home equity loan is in a second lien position on the property.

If the borrower negotiates a **home equity line of credit (HELOC)**, there is a line of credit that the borrower can access whenever the borrower chooses. A checking account for the HELOC is established, and the borrower writes checks whenever money is needed.

AMP Outline

III.	**Finance**		
	C. Methods of Financing	2. Conventional	
	1. Government Programs	3. Owner-Financed	
	(e.g., FHA, VA)	4. Land Contract	

1. GOVERNMENT PROGRAMS (E.G., FHA, VA)

Unconventional mortgage—A loan that is backed by the government, such as an FHA loan that is insured by the government or a VA loan that is guaranteed by the government.

FHA-Insured Loans

The **Federal Housing Administration (FHA)** was established in 1934 to encourage improvements in housing standards, to encourage lenders to make loans, and to exert a stabilizing influence on the mortgage market after the Great Depression. FHA operates under the Department of Housing and Urban Development (HUD). FHA does not negotiate loans; FHA insures loans, which means the loan is backed by the government. Should a borrower of an FHA insured loan default, the lender would foreclose on the property. If the purchase price of the property at the foreclosure sale did not cover the amount due the lender, then FHA would pay the lender the difference.

Lenders must be qualified to negotiate FHA-insured loans. There are several FHA insured loan programs, with the most popular being the 203(b)B for owner-occupied, one-to-four-family dwellings.

Characteristics of an FHA loan are as follows:

- Every county has a maximum FHA lending limit. (This increases annually.)

- There is a one-time upfront mortgage insurance premium (MIP), which can be financed; ½ percent MIP is added to the monthly payments.

■ There is a minimum down payment, and the borrower must have cash for it. The down payment may be a gift, but it cannot be a loan.

■ Interest rates are negotiable, and as a rule, FHA does not set income limits for borrowers.

■ Discount points may be paid by the buyer or seller.

■ Prepayment penalties are not allowed, and the maximum origination fee a lender can charge is 1 percent.

■ If an FHA-insured loan is assumed by another borrower, the borrower must meet FHA qualifying guidelines. (If a borrower is assuming an FHA-insured loan negotiated prior to December 15, 1989, the borrower would not have to meet FHA qualifying guidelines.)

■ When the loan is assumed, the lender will issue a certificate of reduction to verify the existing principal balance.

VA-Guaranteed Loans

The **Serviceman's Readjustment Act of 1944** initially established the Veterans Administration, now known as the Department of Veterans Affairs (VA). One of its purposes was to make government-backed loans available to qualified veterans and un-remarried widows or widowers of veterans. A qualified veteran can negotiate a VA or GI loan with a 100 percent **loan-to-value ratio**, or with a minimum down payment, at relatively low interest rates. The VA *guarantees* loans to lenders and normally does not directly negotiate loans. If a qualified lender is not readily available, as in an isolated rural area, the VA will negotiate a loan.

Other characteristics of a VA-guaranteed loan are as follows:

■ A qualified person can secure a VA-guaranteed loan on a one-to-four-family dwelling that will be owner-occupied.

■ The amount of a loan that a veteran can obtain is determined by the lender.

■ There is a limit on how much the VA will guarantee. Should the borrower default and the lender receive less than the mortgage balance after a foreclosure sale, the VA guarantees the lender a certain amount, based on a sliding scale of the value of the property.

■ To determine the amount the VA will guarantee, a veteran must apply for a **certificate of eligibility**, which establishes the maximum guaranty entitlement of the veteran.

■ A **certificate of reasonable value (CRV)** is issued by the VA for the property being purchased. The CRV states the current market value based on a VA-approved appraisal and places a ceiling on the amount of the VA loan allowed for the property.

■ The borrower or seller also must pay a funding fee to the VA. This is a percentage of the loan amount and depends on the eligibility status and down payment of the veteran. The funding fee may be financed as a part of the loan.

- Discount points may be paid by the buyer or seller when a VA-guaranteed loan is negotiated.

- No prepayment penalties are allowed on VA mortgages.

- A VA loan is assumable. If another qualified veteran assumes the loan, that veteran's certificate of eligibility may replace the existing certificate. The original borrower is granted a novation by the lender, and his or her full eligibility is reinstated by VA.

- If a nonveteran assumes the loan, the original borrower remains liable for the loan. A novation agreement with the lender does not reinstate the eligibility of the veteran. Only the VA can reinstate the eligibility.

FHA-insured and VA-guaranteed loans are assumable loans. For FHA-insured loans originated after December 1, 1986, and VA-guaranteed loans originated after March 1, 1988, the buyer must meet approval requirements. A third party can buy the property subject to the mortgage or assume the mortgage. These concepts are explained more fully in the assumption of mortgage section on pages 95 and 96.

Rural Economic and Community Development

- Federal agency under the Department of Agriculture that negotiates loans to people in rural areas

- Negotiates loans for the purchase of property, to operate farms, or to purchase farm equipment

- Bases the interest paid on the loan on the income of the borrower

- Originates loans either through a private lender or directly by the agency

2 .   C O N V E N T I O N A L

- **Conventional mortgage**—Not insured or guaranteed by the government.

- **Conventional uninsured mortgage**—Typically, the borrower has a 20 percent or greater down payment, and the lender accepts the creditworthiness of the borrower and the property as security for the loan.

- **Conventional insured mortgage**—Typically, the borrower has less than a 20 percent down payment and the lender requires private mortgage insurance.

- **Unconventional mortgage**—A loan that is backed by the government, such as an FHA loan that is *insured* by the government, and a VA loan that is guaranteed by the government.

Private Mortgage Insurance

If a borrower has less than a 20 percent down payment, the lender may require that the borrower purchase **private mortgage insurance (PMI)**. Payment for PMI can be a one-time premium, but typically it is a percentage added to each monthly payment. When the loan balance is paid down to 80 percent of the total value, the PMI payment will be dropped, if the proper procedures are followed. If the property is sold at foreclosure for less than the mortgage balance, the PMI pays the lender up to the amount of the insurance, typically the top 20 to 25 percent of the loan.

3. OWNER-FINANCED

A **purchase-money mortgage** (PMM) is a creative financing technique that developed when interest rates were high. The seller agrees to finance a portion or the entire purchase price. The buyer will receive the deed and title at the closing and the seller will put a lien on the property. If the seller finances a portion of the purchase price, he records the note and will be in a second lien position. If the seller finances the entire amount, he records the note and will be in a first lien position. A PMM is also known as a *take-back mortgage.*

Here is an example of a purchase-money mortgage: A buyer has a 5 percent down payment, and the seller agrees to lend the borrower 15 percent of the sale price. The lender will negotiate an 80 percent loan and will not require private mortgage insurance. This is known as an 80/15/5 loan. (There is also an 80/10/10 loan.)

At the closing, the seller pays off an existing loan and takes back a mortgage on the property just sold. To secure the loan, the seller establishes a junior lien on the property and receives payments from the buyer until the loan is paid in full. This occurs with the approval of the lender negotiating the 80 percent loan.

4. LAND CONTRACT

In a **land contract**, the seller/vendor agrees to finance the sale of the property. Typically, the buyer/vendee makes a down payment, then monthly payments until the balance is paid in full. The seller normally retains title to the property until the final payment. Should the buyer default, the seller can evict the buyer and regain possession. Whether or not the buyer would lose all of the money they have paid the seller is a matter of state law and the contract itself. Many state laws give a defaulted buyer more legal protection, and the seller must foreclose on the property to reclaim it.

Be aware that there is no mortgage involved in a land contract. A mortgage is a pledge of property to a lender as security for the payment of a debt, but the land contract is itself the security instrument.

The buyer's interest in a land contract is an equitable interest or equitable title. An **equitable title** represents the buyer's interest in the property when the legal title is held by another party. It also is an insurable interest, meaning the buyer can secure insurance on the property. Most land contracts stipulate that the buyer secure insurance, pay property taxes, and maintain the property.

AMP Outline

1. BASIC ELEMENTS AND PROVISIONS OF FINANCING INSTRUMENTS

- **Equity**—The difference between the market value and any liens on the property

- **Mortgage**—A pledge of property to a lender; collateral for the debt (note)

- **Mortgagor**—The borrower

- **Mortgagee**—The lender

- **Note**—The promise to pay a debt and evidence of the debt; states the terms of repayment

- **Obligor/promissor**—The borrower in a note

- **Obligee/promisee**—The lender in the note

Types of Mortgages

An **adjustable-rate mortgage (ARM)** contains an **escalation clause** that allows the interest to adjust over the loan term. ARMs were discussed in detail on page 85.

A **blanket mortgage** may be used by a builder or developer. This mortgage covers more than one tract of land and contains a partial release clause, which allows the borrower to obtain a release of any one lot or parcel, and thus gives the buyer a marketable title.

A **buydown mortgage** allows the borrower to buy down the interest rate, thus reducing the monthly payment for a number of years. To buy down the interest rate, the borrower must pay interest in advance.

A **budget mortgage** includes principal, interest, taxes, and insurance payments (PITI). The tax and insurance portions of each monthly payment are put into an escrow account and paid when those payments are due.

A **construction loan** is used to finance the erection of improvements on land and was discussed in detail on page 86.

A **graduated-payment mortgage (GPM)** is also known as a *flexible-payment plan*. The borrower makes lower monthly payments for the first few years and larger payments for the remainder of the loan term. If the lower monthly payments do not cover all the interest charges, the lender adds the unpaid interest to the principal balance. This creates **negative amortization** because the loan balance increases instead of decreases.

A borrower who has negotiated a **growing-equity mortgage (GEM)** realizes that there will be periodic increases in the monthly payment. However, the increase is applied directly to the principal, thus reducing the term of the loan.

Package mortgages are usually used in the sale of new homes in a subdivision or in condominium sales. This type of loan covers both real and personal property.

An **open-end mortgage** allows the mortgagor to borrow additional funds, up to a maximum dollar amount, all of which are secured by the same original mortgage.

In a **shared-appreciation mortgage (SAM)**, the lender agrees to originate the loan at below-market interest rates in return for a guaranteed share of the appreciation the borrower will realize when the property is sold. This typically is used in the financing of commercial projects.

When a borrower negotiates a **straight mortgage (term loan)**, he makes periodic payment of interest only and the principal is paid in full at the end of the term. A construction loan is an example of a straight mortgage.

A **reverse annuity mortgage (RAM)** or reverse mortgage allows homeowners 62 years of age or older to borrow against the equity in their homes without income or credit ratio qualifications. The money may be taken in a lump sum, line of credit, monthly payment (to the owner), for a specified term, or a combination of the above. The loan comes due when the borrower no longer permanently resides in the property. Reverse mortgages are nonrecourse loans.

A **wraparound mortgage** is also known as an *all-inclusive* or *overriding loan*. It is a junior loan that wraps around an existing senior loan. For example, an owner has an existing mortgage and equity in his property. When he goes to the lender to negotiate a loan against the equity, the lender agrees to do so and wraps it around the existing first mortgage. The borrower makes only one monthly payment to the lender that is applied to both mortgages.

To create a wraparound mortgage, the original loan must be assumable, and all aspects of the senior loan must be disclosed to the junior lender. With the decline in the real estate market, there has been a revival of this idea as a form of seller financing. The borrower obtains a mortgage loan and the seller finances the buyer's down payment, which is wrapped around the buyer's mortgage loan. The buyer then makes one payment to the seller, who in turn makes the mortgage payment on behalf of the buyer.

Other Basic Elements of a Financing Instrument

Prime and Subprime Loans   Lenders will classify a borrower with a down payment and a good credit history as **A paper**, or the person who can secure a **prime loan**. Such a borrower can negotiate for the best interest rate because he or she is considered to be a low risk.

Borrowers who are classified as **B, C, or D paper** are classified as a high risk and will be given a **subprime loan** or one with a higher interest rate and less-favorable loan terms. A previous bankruptcy, late payments on other debts, such as a credit card or rent payments, very little savings, or too much debt, are all factors that would place a borrower in the subprime category.

Prepayment   An **open mortgage** usually allows a borrower to pay off the loan at any time over the life of the loan without a penalty. This is allowed by a **prepayment privilege clause** in the mortgage. When a borrower repays the loan ahead of schedule, the lender collects less interest. Some lenders allow the prepayment of the mortgage, and others charge a prepayment penalty. This penalty is a percentage of the remaining mortgage balance.

Interest Rates   The **interest** paid by the borrower is a charge for the use of money, and the lender normally computes simple interest on residential loans. A **fixed** interest rate is constant over the life of the loan. An **adjustable** interest rate can change over the life of the loan.

The **lock-in clause** in the note typically means that upon loan application, the lender has agreed to lock the rate for a specified time period, or it could mean that the loan cannot be prepaid unless all interest is paid.

Hypothecation means to pledge property to the lender as collateral, without giving up possession of it.

Release   When the mortgage is paid in full, the lender must release its interest in the property. In lien-theory states, a mortgage release or satisfaction piece is recorded. In title-theory states, a defeasance clause provides that the lender release its interest in the title. If the mortgage document was a **trust deed**, the reconveyance deed must be recorded to release the lender's title interest.

If a lien is not released at settlement, the lien will run with the land, or stay attached to the property. This is why a title search is conducted to protect the interest of the buyer and the lender.

Due-on-Sale   A **due-on-sale clause** in a mortgage allows the lender to collect full payment from the mortgagor when the property is sold. This clause prevents owners from selling the property to a buyer on a loan assumption, subject to the mortgage or land contract.

Alienation   Mortgages may contain an **alienation clause**, which provides that if the property is conveyed to any party without the lender's consent, the lender can collect full payment. This is different than a due-on-sale clause. For example, a borrower negotiated a loan for a principal place of residence. Several years later, the borrower coverts the principal place of residence to rental property and does not disclose the change to the lender. When the lender discovers that it is being used for rental property, the lender can call the note due and payable.

Subordination   Under certain circumstances, a lender with a first lien position will agree to switch positions (**subordination**) and take a second lien position on the property. For example, a borrower has a first mortgage with lender XYZ and a line of credit with lender ABC. The borrower decides to refinance her loan with XYZ. When she refinances, her current mortgage with XYZ is paid in full, and technically, ABC would move into a first lien position. XYZ will agree to refinance only if ABC will subordinate, or move from the first lien position to the second lien position. Usually, a subordination fee will be charged if an agreement to subordinate is reached.

Escalation   An **escalation clause** is found in an adjustable-rate mortgage and in certain leases. In a mortgage, it allows the interest rate to adjust over the life of the loan. In a lease, it allows the lease payment to adjust over the life of the lease.

Acceleration   Notes, mortgages, and security instruments contain an **acceleration clause** that allows the lender to call the note due and payable in advance of the loan term. The lender could enforce the acceleration clause in a mortgage if the borrower defaults on the payments, there is destruction of the premises, or there is a sale of the property to another party. If this clause were not in the note and/or mortgage, the lender would have to sue the borrower for each individual monthly payment.

The **acceleration clause** allows the lender to call the entire balance due, not just the months the borrower is behind.

Rescission   The process of **rescission** means that the contract has been canceled, terminated, or annulled and the parties have been returned to the legal positions they were in before they entered the contract. A contract may be rescinded due to mistake, fraud, or misrepresentation. For example, if the seller cannot provide a marketable title, the buyer is not required to purchase the property, and the contract may be rescinded.

2. LEGAL PRINCIPLES

Security instruments (documents) are used to provide collateral for the repayment of a loan. The statute of frauds requires security instruments to be in writing. These instruments consist of

- mortgages, primarily used in lien-theory states;

- trust deeds, primarily used in title-theory states; and

- land contracts, used when the seller is financing the property.

Lien-Theory State

The lender's interest in the property can be a lien interest or a title interest. In a **lien-theory state**, the borrower receives the deed at the closing, and the lender establishes a lien position by recording the note and mortgage. Should the borrower default, the mortgage gives the lender the right to foreclose on the property, the note determines how much money the lender can collect, and the lien establishes the order in which the creditors are paid.

Title-Theory State

In a **title-theory state**, the law construes the lender to have legal title to the property and the borrower to have an equitable title. Because the lender holds the title to the property, the lender has the right to possession of the property on default.

Intermediate-Theory State

Intermediate-theory states are a combination of lien theory and title theory. The law interprets the lender as having a lien on the property unless the borrower defaults. On default, the title passes to the lender.

FIGURE 3.3

Deeds of Trust

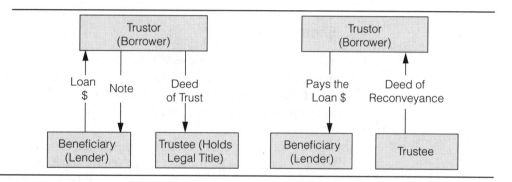

Deed of Trust

- A **deed of trust** is also known as a **trust deed**. (See Figure 3.3)

- Legal title is conveyed to the **trustee** for the benefit of the **beneficiary**.

- A **defeasance** clause stipulates that when the final payment is made, the lender's interest is defeated and a **deed of reconveyance** is given from the trustee to the **trustor**.

- If the borrower defaults, the trustee will initiate **foreclosure**.

- If the borrower defaults, a **nonjudicial foreclosure** or foreclosure by advertisement is the usual foreclosure process.

Assumption of Existing Financing

Subject to the Mortgage   When a property is sold subject to the mortgage, the original borrower remains liable for the debt, even if the third party buyer defaults. If a default occurs, the buyer loses the property and the original borrower has a foreclosure on his credit report, and possibly a deficiency judgment. Before this happens, the original borrower can attempt to salvage the situation either by buying the property or by buying the mortgage from the lender and foreclosing.

Assumption of the Mortgage   When a third party assumes the mortgage, the third party becomes liable for the debt. Should the new buyer default, that buyer is primarily liable for the debt and the original borrower is secondarily liable.

A **novation** is a substitution of one contract for another. If the lender grants novation in the assumption of an existing mortgage, the original borrower is released from liability.

3 . NON-PERFORMANCE

The **default** clause in a note and mortgage protects the lender if there is nonperformance of a duty or obligation on the part of the borrower. This clause requires the timely payment of the terms of the note, upkeep of the property, payment of property taxes and insurance, and permission from the lender for improvements to be made on the property. If the borrower defaults, the lender has the right to foreclose.

Short Sales

With the bust of the real estate bubble, many owners owe more than the current market value of their homes and are negotiating a short sale with their lender. A **short sale** means that the lender and seller are willing to take less than the outstanding loan amount; however, the bank has the final approval of the selling price.

Agents should inform buyers that this is lender process and it will not close in a short timeframe. The process will vary by state laws, and each lender has different guidelines. The short sale process will be impacted should the owner file for bankruptcy or the lender begin the foreclosure process. Agents should not attempt to answer legal questions regarding these topics but should direct buyers and sellers to the proper experts.

Foreclosure is the legal process whereby the lender forces the sale of the property to satisfy an unpaid debt. State and local laws regulate foreclosure proceedings. The three types of foreclosure are (1) judicial, (2) nonjudicial, and (3) strict.

Judicial Foreclosure

Foreclosure by **judicial sale** occurs when the property is sold though a court process, which can be expensive and time-consuming. First, the lender must bring a lawsuit against the defaulted borrower, then the judge orders an appraisal of the property and sets a foreclosure sale date. Creditors are notified, and the foreclosure is advertised. The property is sold, and when the paperwork is in order, the sale is confirmed. At that point, the owner's rights to the property have been foreclosed.

Nonjudicial Foreclosure

Nonjudicial foreclosure is also referred to as *statutory foreclosure* or *foreclosure by advertisement* and occurs when the lender uses the abbreviated foreclosure process that has been established under state law. In states that allow this process, the mortgage document must contain a *power-of-sale clause*. This clause allows the lender to sell the property at a nonjudicial public sale without being required to spend the time and money involved in a court foreclosure suit. The process is administered through the court system. The notice of default may be recorded at the county recorder's office to give public notice of the auction. The foreclosure process will take place without court intervention.

Upon default, the loan is accelerated and the defaulted borrower may redeem the property (equitable redemption) by paying off the principal and collection costs. If payment is not made during the equitable redemption period, the property is advertised and sold at auction. The defaulted borrower is then given a specified time period set by state law to redeem the property (statutory redemption) by repurchasing the property from the highest bidder. The defaulted borrower must pay the full auction sale price and all of the legal fees associated with the process. The defaulted borrower is allowed to remain in possession of the property until expiration of the statutory redemption period. (See Figure 3.4.)

Strict Foreclosure

Strict foreclosure allows the lender to foreclose on the property after appropriate notice has been given to the delinquent borrower and the proper papers have been filed in court. If full payment is not made within a prescribed time, the borrower's equitable and statutory redemption rights are waived, the property is sold, and the lender keeps all equity in the property, if there is any. A deficiency judgment is not allowed in strict foreclosure cases. Strict foreclosure of real estate is prohibited in many states because it is thought to be overly harsh and punitive.

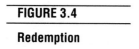

FIGURE 3.4

Redemption

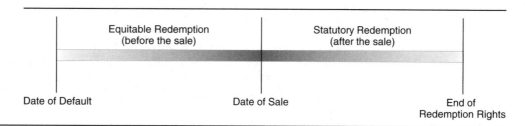

Equitable Redemption (before the sale) | Statutory Redemption (after the sale)

Date of Default | Date of Sale | End of Redemption Rights

Deficiency Judgment

If the foreclosure sale price does not pay off the loan (principal plus costs of collection and foreclosure), because the note promises to pay, the lender can bring an additional action to enforce the terms of payment. A **deficiency judgment,** which is a **personal judgment**, can be levied against the defaulted. Generally, deficiency judgments are allowed against recourse loans, but some states limit their use, especially against a defaulted borrower's principal residence.

In a **nonrecourse loan**, the borrower is not held personally liable for the note. This occurs when the lender accepts the property as adequate security for the loan. This type of loan is typically made to real estate syndicates or other real estate investors, but reverse mortgages are also nonrecourse loans.

AMP Outline

III.   Finance
    E. Government Oversight
       1. Real Estate Settlement Procedures Act (RESPA)
       2. Regulation Z

       3. Truth in Lending Act
       4. Antitrust
       5. Mortgage Fraud
       6. Equal Credit Opportunity Act

1. REAL ESTATE SETTLEMENT PROCEDURES ACT (RESPA)

The **Real Estate Settlement Procedures Act (RESPA)** is a federal act that requires that lenders disclose to the buyer and seller all settlement costs on federally related mortgage loans, and first and second liens for the purchase or refinancing of one-to-four-family dwellings.

RESPA requires that lenders and settlement agents make certain disclosures at the time of the loan application and at the closing of the loan. These include the following:

The booklet *Settlement Costs and You* must be given to a prospective borrower within three business days from the time that person receives or prepares a loan application.

Internet Search – Settlement Costs and You Booklet

The booklet is available in English and Spanish at *http://portal.hud.gov/hudportal/HUD?src=/program_offices/housing/rmra/res/settlement-cost-booklet03252010*.

Within three business days of application, the lender must provide the borrower with a Good-Faith Estimate (GFE) of the settlement costs the borrower will likely incur. The new GFE discloses the charges that cannot change, those that can increase up to 10 percent at settlement, and those that can change at settlement (See Figure 3.5).

FIGURE 3.5

Good-Faith Estimate Settlement Charges

These charges **cannot increase** at settlement:	The total of these charges **can increase up to 10%** at settlement:	These charges **can change** at settlement:
■ Our origination charge	■ Required services that we select	■ Required services that you can shop for *(if you do not use companies we identify)*
■ Your credit or charge (points) for the specific interest rate chosen *(after you lock in your interest rate)*	■ Title services and lender's title insurance *(if we select them or you use companies we identify)*	■ Title services and lender's title insurance *(if you do not use companies we identify)*
■ Your adjusted origination charges *(after you lock in your interest rate)*	■ Owner's title insurance *(if you use companies we identify)*	■ Owner's title insurance *(if you do not use companies we identify)*
■ Transfer taxes	■ Required services that you can shop for *(if you use companies we identify)*	■ Initial deposit for your escrow account
	■ Government recording charges	■ Daily interest charges
		■ Homeowner's insurance

Source: HUD, *http://portal.hud.gov/hudportal/documents/huddoc?id=gfestimate.pdf*

Internet Search – Good Faith Estimate or visit *http://portal.hud.gov/hudportal/documents/huddoc?id=gfestimate.pdf*.

The Uniform Settlement Statement (HUD-1 Form) must be used to itemize all charges related to the transaction. Borrowers have the right to review the HUD-1, to the extent to which they are available, within 24 hours of the closing.

The lender is prohibited from receiving any kickbacks or other referral fees from service providers.

Lenders **cannot** charge a fee for the preparation of the settlement statement. The buyer and seller must receive a copy of the HUD-1 at the closing.

RESPA limits the amount of money a lender may require the borrower to hold in an escrow account for payment of taxes, insurance, etc., and requires the lender to provide initial and annual escrow account statements to the borrower.

RESPA does not apply to a land contract; a purchase-money mortgage, where the seller is solely financing the property; or a transaction where the buyer is assuming the seller's existing loan and the lender charges less than $50 for the assumption.

Internet Search – Frequently Asked Questions

www.hud.gov/offices/hsg/rmra/res/respa_hm.cfm

HUD-1

http://portal.hud.gov/hudportal/documents/huddoc?id=hud1.pdf

2. REGULATION Z

The **Truth in Lending Act (Regulation Z)** requires that lenders disclose the true cost of credit expressed as an APR or annual percentage rate.

Regulation Z covers **all one-to-four-family** real estate financing for residential borrowers who are natural persons, but not loans that are used for business, commercial, or agricultural purposes; personal property credit transactions involving more than $25,000; and loans to the owner of a dwelling containing more than four housing units.

Regulation Z defines a **creditor** as an entity that extends consumer credit more than 25 times a year, or more than 5 times a year if the transaction involves a dwelling as security. The credit must be subject to a finance charge or payable in more than four installments by written agreement.

3. TRUTH IN LENDING ACT

The **Truth in Lending Act** was passed as a part of the **Consumer Credit Protection Act**. When negotiating a home improvement loan, refinancing a home loan, a home equity loan, and an FHA reverse mortgage, there is a three-business-day right of rescission mandated by Regulation Z. This right of rescission does not apply to owner-occupied residential first mortgage and trust deeds. Also under

Regulation Z, full disclosure is required by the lender if any of the following trigger items appears in an ad:

■ Amount of monthly payment

■ Number of payments

■ Amount of down payment

■ Finance charges

■ Term of the loan

If any of the above trigger items appears in an ad, full disclosure is required. The advertisement must include

■ cash price;

■ required down payment;

■ number, amounts, and due dates of all payments;

■ total of all payments to be made over the term of the mortgage (unless the advertised credit refers to a first mortgage or deed of trust to finance the acquisition of a dwelling); and

■ **annual percentage rate**.

As used in the previous list, *full disclosure* means that if any of the above items are used in an ad, the same ad must include the cash price; required down payment; number, amounts, and due dates of all payments; and the annual percentage rate. If the annual percentage rate is disclosed in an advertisement, it meets Truth-in-Lending requirements.

4 . ANTITRUST

The Sherman Antitrust laws prohibit price fixing, group boycotting, allocation of customers or markets, and tie-in agreements.

■ **Price-Fixing**—A brokerage firm can establish a brokerage policy regarding the commission rate that the brokerage will charge. Commission rates are negotiable between the parties. However, brokers, real estate governing bodies, such as a commission, association, or board, cannot conspire to fix prices. Agents should never make a reference to a *going rate*, *standard rate*, or *traditional rate for this area*.

■ **Group Boycotting**—Brokers may not in any way conspire to not work with other brokers, or withhold patronage, to reduce competition.

■ **Allocation of Customers or Markets**—Brokers may not divide the community into geographic areas and then agree not to compete with other brokers in that area; nor may they divide the market by price range or the types of property.

■ **Tie-in Agreements**—Brokers cannot tie or agree to sell one product based on the purchase of another product.

Internet Search – Sherman Antitrust Act

www.justice.gov/atr/public/real_estate/index.html

Other Brokerage Business Models

Full Service Discount Brokers—With this business policy, the broker firm may offer full service at a reduced commission, or offer rebates and inducements to buyers and sellers.

Fee-for-Service Brokers—Under this business model flat-fee or limited-service brokers allow buyers and sellers to select from a menu of real estate services. For example, the seller could pay for having the broker place the property in the multiple listing service (MLS), and the seller would handle all other aspects of the transaction from showing the property to writing the offer, etc.

Virtual Office Website Brokers—The Internet has created the business model of Virtual Office Web sites (VOWs) where brokerage services are offered online to registered clients. Through the National Association of REALTORS® Internet Data Exchange policy, brokers can offer their registered clients access to the MLS. Although these services make it possible to list property located out-of-state, it is important to remember that real estate licenses are issued at the state level. Only a licensee that is licensed in a particular state is allowed to perform real estate services in that state.

5. MORTGAGE FRAUD

Mortgage fraud means the lender was provided with false or misleading information on a loan application, or with falsified documents in the loan process. According to the FBI mortgage fraud Web site, the estimated annual losses from mortgage fraud are currently between $4 to $6 billion dollars (April 2011). There are usually several *players* involved in mortgage fraud. These may include appraisers, title companies, lenders, real estate agents, and investors.

The types of mortgage fraud include, but are not limited to: equity skimming, house stealing, property flipping, straw buyers, silent second, stolen identity, and rescue scams, to name a few.

- **Equity Skimming**—An **investor** negotiates with a straw buyer to purchase the property and then the straw buyer gives the investor a quitclaim deed to the property. The investor rents the property but does not make any mortgage payments. Eventually, the property is sold at foreclosure, but the investor has collected rent until the foreclosure.

- **House Stealing**—A con artist selects a house and assumes the identity of the owner by finding personal information on the Internet and public records. Once they have fake identifications, they sell the property and pocket the profits, even while the true owner is living in the house.

- **Property Flipping**—The basis for property flipping is an inflated appraisal. In this type of mortgage fraud, a property is purchased, then quickly resold at a much higher value. The home was purchased for $15,000, but within the month was sold to someone for $83,000, and the appraisal indicates an $83,000 value. Many times the borrower's loan is supported by falsified documents, such as forged paycheck stubs, fake tax returns, etc.

- **Straw Buyers**—One person sells his/her identity to another person for the purpose of negotiating a loan. The buyer of the identity is in collusion with other players and purchases the property. The straw buyer may also use fake or stolen identifications when he or she applies for the loan.

- **Silent Second**—In this scenario, the buyer negotiates a second mortgage with the seller and the fact is never disclosed to the lender. As a result, the lender believes the buyer has a larger down payment than he/she really does.

- **Stolen Identity**—A person's identity is stolen and used without his/her knowledge to apply for a loan.

- **Rescue Scams**—In this scenario, homeowners who are behind on their mortgage are told that their home can be saved by paying upfront fees and transferring the deed to the rescuer. Many times the owners are told they can stay in the property and pay rent. When their credit is good, they can then buy the house back. The rescuer will run off with the upfront fees, get a second loan on the property, or sell the home without the true owner's knowledge and consent.

Mortgage Fraud Prevention

There are many warning signs that a real estate agent can look for to prevent mortgage fraud. Agents can prevent fraud by ensuring the following:

- The property address or legal description is clearly identified and legible on the sales contract, and that all the blanks in the contract are filled in. Write the letters NA for not applicable, if the blank is not needed.

- The sales contract accurately states the consideration to be paid by the buyer for the property. If after the contract is negotiated, an agent is asked to change the consideration, the agent should not do it.

- If a buyer wants the offer written contingent upon the use of a certain appraiser, the agent should not do it.

- Any party that wants to place restrictions on how their participation is reported in the contract or HUD-1 should be reported.

- The consideration stated in the sales contract and on the deed the buyer receives at closing are for the same amount.

- Current comparables are used. Beware if the comparables that appraiser used are a year old, but they are not the most recent sales in the neighborhood.

- The seller's name/s should be the same on the sales contract and the deed given to the buyer at closing.

- The buyer states an unrealistic income for his/her occupation.

Internet Search – Mortgage Fraud

www.fbi.gov/about-us/investigate/white_collar/mortgage-fraud/

6. EQUAL CREDIT OPPORTUNITY ACT

The **Equal Credit Opportunity Act (ECOA)** prohibits discrimination based on race, color, religion, national origin, sex, marital status, age, or source of income in the granting of credit. This act requires that credit applications be considered only on the basis of income, net worth, job stability, and credit rating. If the applicant is rejected, lenders have 30 days to inform the applicant of the reasons why credit was denied. (This 30-day notice also applies to creditors that terminate existing credit.)

Community Reinvestment Act

The **Community Reinvestment Act** was passed to prevent redlining and disinvestment in central city areas. **Redlining** is the lender's refusal to negotiate loans in certain geographic areas, even to qualified borrowers. This act requires that lenders delineate the communities in which their lending activities take place, make available listings of the types of credit they offer in the communities, and make available appropriate notices and information regarding lending activities. It also gives lenders the option to close affirmative action programs designed to meet the credit needs of their communities.

AMP Outline

III.   Finance

    F.   Lending Process

        1.   Pre-Approval and Pre-Qualification (e.g., debt ratios, credit scoring, and history)

        2.   Parties to the Lending Process (e.g., loan originator, underwriter, mortgage broker)

1. PRE-APPROVAL AND PRE-QUALIFICATION (E.G., DEBT RATIOS, CREDIT SCORING, AND HISTORY)

Most real estate agents recommend that the buyers be preapproved for a loan. This will help determine the price range of the property for which they qualify, and it will also identify any credit issues to be resolved. If buyers have not viewed a free credit report, the agent should recommend they do so by visiting *www.AnnualCreditReport.com*, or by calling (877) 322-8228.

Assessing the buyer's price range depends on three basic factors: (1) stable income, (2) net worth, and (3) credit history. It seems like a simple process, but it involves more than just the use of mathematical formulas.

To determine the **stable income** of the borrower, the lender may require paycheck stubs, tax returns, W2s, and verification of employment for the past two years. To determine the **net worth**, the borrower's liabilities are subtracted from the borrower's assets. With the potential borrower's authorization, the loan officer will pull the credit report, which will include a **credit score** that takes into account the applicant's employment and credit history.

The three **credit bureaus**, Equifax, Experian, and TransUnion, use software created by Fair Isaac and Company (FICO), which analyzes the credit risk of a borrower. Factors that are analyzed include the borrower's employment history, outstanding debts, and repayment history. These factors are used to calculate a credit score, also known as the *FICO Score, BEACON Score or EMPIRICA®*. (Commonly called the FICO score.) A borrower's credit score will determine the approved loan amount, as well as the terms of the loan.

The **mortgage-to-income ratio** is the ratio of the monthly housing expense (principal, interest, taxes, and insurance) to the gross monthly income. In many loans, the mortgage expense can be no more than 28 percent of the gross monthly income. This can also be known as the *housing-to-income ratio*, or the *front-end ratio*.

The **debt-to-service ratio** expresses the relationship of the total monthly debt payments to the borrower's income. This is also known as the *debt-to-income ratio*, or the *back-end ratio*.

In most conventional loans, the total debt-to-service ratio can be no more than 36 percent of the borrower's stable monthly income. FHA debt-to-service ratios are generally 29 percent, and debt-to-income ratio is 41 percent.

VA has no front-end ratio, and the back-end ratio is 41 percent of the gross monthly income.

2. PARTIES TO THE LENDING PROCESS (E.G., LOAN ORIGINATOR, UNDERWRITER, MORTGAGE BROKER)

The four basic steps for securing a loan for the purchase of real estate are as follows:

1. Applying for the loan

2. Analysis of the borrower and the property

3. Underwriting the loan

4. Closing the loan

The lending institution will have a **loan originator** meet with the borrower to complete the loan application, collect the required documents, and verify the information received. The borrower should review the **lock-in clause** in the loan application, which guarantees that the interest rate quoted the buyer on loan application is locked for a specific time.

The loan origination fee is charged by the lender to cover the administrative costs of making the loan. The fee is a percentage of the loan amount.

The loan will be processed by the loan officer, or a **processer**, who orders the appraisal, title search, termite inspection, or other inspections required by the lender.

To confirm the borrower's **assets**, the lender will require statements from checking, savings, stock, bond, retirement, and money market accounts.

The borrower must also disclose **liabilities**, such as car payments, mortgage or rent payments, credit card debt, student loans, alimony or child support, and any other debts.

Once the loan has been processed, the completed loan package is submitted to the **underwriter,** who will review and evaluate the risk of the loan. Approval of every loan is conditioned on terms being met by the borrower. Typically, the loan commitment letter states the loan has been approved pending confirmation of items such as these:

- Satisfactory title report

- Mortgagee's title insurance

- Homeowners' insurance policy

- Survey

- Verification of job status

- Affidavit of marital status

- Copy of the settlement sheet of the house just sold

- Verification of bank accounts

- Payoff of a particular bill

- Inspection reports that are required by the lender

- Any repairs required by the appraiser

Once the required documentation is received by the underwriter, a closing date is set. The types of closing are called *face-to-face* (round table) and *closing in escrow*. In the face-to-face closing, the buyers, sellers, settlement agent, and attorneys meet at a designated time and location to finalize the sales contract.

In an escrow closing, an employee of the title company or an attorney, communicates with and collects information from buyers and sellers. The buyers and sellers rarely meet because they individually set personal appointments with the escrow agent to provide and sign needed documents.

CHAPTER 3 TEST

1. Who is the individual who obtains a real estate loan by signing a note and a mortgage?
   A. Mortgagor
   B. Mortgagee
   C. Optionor
   D. Optionee

2. Which of the following describes a mortgage that uses both real and personal property as security?
   A. Blanket mortgage
   B. Package mortgage
   C. Purchase-money mortgage
   D. Wraparound mortgage

3. Which of the following describes a mortgage that requires principal and interest payments at regular intervals until the debt is satisfied?
   A. Term mortgage
   B. Amortized mortgage
   C. First mortgage
   D. Balloon mortgage

4. What is the clause in a note, mortgage, or trust deed that permits a lender to declare the entire unpaid sum due should the borrower default?
   A. Judgment clause
   B. Acceleration clause
   C. Forfeiture clause
   D. Escalator clause

5. A mortgage must include a power-of-sale clause to be foreclosed by
   A. action.
   B. advertisement.
   C. judicial procedure.
   D. the FHA.

6. In many states, by paying the debt after a foreclosure sale, the mortgagor has the right to regain the property. What is the right called?
   A. Equitable right of redemption
   B. Owner's right of redemption
   C. Vendee's right of redemption
   D. Statutory right of redemption

7. In a title-theory state, the
   A. mortgagee takes title to the mortgaged property during the term of the mortgage.
   B. mortgagor has a lien against the property for the full amount of the mortgage.
   C. mortgagor may foreclose only by court action.
   D. mortgagor holds title to the property during the term of the mortgage.

8. A woman is qualified to obtain an FHA loan for the purchase of a new home. From which of the following may she obtain this loan?
   A. Federal Housing Administration
   B. Federal National Mortgage Association
   C. A qualified Federal Housing Administration mortgagee
   D. Federal Home Loan Mortgage Corporation

9. A mortgage instrument may include a clause that prevents the assumption of the mortgage by a new purchaser without the lender's consent. What is this clause called?
   A. Alienation clause
   B. Power-of-sale clause
   C. Defeasance clause
   D. Certificate of sale

10. The defeasance clause in a mortgage requires that the mortgagee execute a(n)
    A. assignment of mortgage.
    B. satisfaction of mortgage.
    C. subordination agreement.
    D. partial release agreement.

11. A seller enters into a contract with a buyer to sell his house for $400,000. The buyer cannot obtain complete financing, and at the closing, the buyer and seller enter into a contract for deed. On signing the contract for deed, the buyer's interest in the property is that of
    A. legal title.
    B. equitable title.
    C. joint title.
    D. mortgagee in possession.

12. Which of the following is a lien on real estate?
    A. Easement
    B. Recorded mortgage
    C. Encroachment
    D. Restrictive covenant

13. A mortgage loan that requires monthly payments of $1,175.75 for 20 years and a final payment of $25,095 is a(n)
    A. wraparound mortgage.
    B. accelerated mortgage.
    C. balloon mortgage.
    D. variable mortgage.

14. The ratio of the property's net income to the initial investment is the
    A. after-tax cash flow.
    B. before-tax cash flow.
    C. equity.
    D. return on investment.

15. The difference between the market value and any liens on the property is the owner's
    A. equity.
    B. return.
    C. cash outflow.
    D. capital asset.

16. The borrower has a 10 percent down payment and has applied for a conventional loan. The lender will MOST LIKELY require the borrower to purchase
    A. conventional mortgage insurance.
    B. private mortgage insurance.
    C. life insurance.
    D. title insurance.

17. Fannie Mae and Ginnie Mae
    A. work together as primary lenders.
    B. work together with state governments.
    C. are both private agencies.
    D. are both involved in the secondary market.

18. A deficiency judgment can be filed when
    A. a foreclosure sale does not produce sufficient funds to pay a mortgage debt in full.
    B. insufficient property taxes have been paid on real property.
    C. a foreclosure sale is not completed.
    D. property taxes on forfeited property remain unpaid.

19. When a buyer assumes the mortgage, which of the following is TRUE?
    A. The assumption is not affected by the mortgage's alienation clause.
    B. The seller is automatically released from liability when the mortgage is assumed.
    C. The mortgage must contain a due-on-sale clause in order for the buyer to assume it.
    D. The buyer who assumes a mortgage becomes liable for the debt.

20. An eligible veteran made an offer of $250,000 to purchase a home contingent upon obtaining a no down payment VA guaranteed loan. Four weeks after the offer was accepted, a certificate of reasonable value (CRV) for $247,000 was issued for the property. In this case, the veteran may
    A. withdraw from the sale with a three-point penalty.
    B. purchase the property with a $3,000 down payment.
    C. purchase the property or be in breach of contract to the seller.
    D. withdraw from the sale on payment of a $3,000 commission to the seller's broker.

21. In an FHA insured loan transaction, the
    A. discount points may be paid by the seller or the buyer.
    B. origination fee must be paid by the seller.
    C. mortgage insurance premium may be paid by the seller or buyer.
    D. the mortgage insurance premium must be paid by the seller.

22. A government-backed loan that guarantees the lender against a loss is a(n)
    A. FHA mortgage.
    B. VA mortgage.
    C. FNMA mortgage.
    D. PMI mortgage.

23. The loan which is MOST LIKELY to create negative amortization is the
    A. blanket mortgage.
    B. budget mortgage.
    C. construction loan.
    D. graduated-payment mortgage.

24. The mortgage that includes both real and personal property is called a
    A. growing equity mortgage.
    B. package mortgage.
    C. shared appreciation mortgage.
    D. wraparound mortgage.

25. Which of the following is TRUE regarding a purchase-money mortgage?
    A. The seller retains possession of the property and transfers equitable title.
    B. The seller executes and delivers a home equity line of credit at closing.
    C. The seller finances a portion of the purchase price and places a junior lien on the property.
    D. The seller agrees to assume the mortgage and repurchase the property if the buyer defaults.

26. Regulation Z applies to
    A. business loans.
    B. residential loans made to a person.
    C. commercial loans under $10,000.
    D. installment sales.

27. A seller lent money to a buyer, and in return, took a mortgage as security for the debt. The seller immediately recorded the mortgage. Later, the buyer negotiated a loan with another lender who recorded a lien on the property. The buyer defaulted and a court determined that the second lender had priority over the first lender. For this to occur, the
    A. first lender knew of the second loan prior to the first lender negotiating a loan.
    B. second lender's loan was larger than the first lender's loan.
    C. first lender signed a subordination agreement in favor of the second lender.
    D. second lender signed a satisfaction of the mortgage.

28. Borrowers who are classified as high risk will MOST LIKELY negotiate a
    A. prime loan.
    B. paper loan.
    C. subterranean loan.
    D. subprime loan.

29. In a declining market, the sellers consider themselves fortunate. Their house has the same market value as it did on the date they purchased it three years ago, when they used their life savings of $20,000 as a down payment. Since that time, they have paid $14,400 on mortgage payments, of which $10,000 was used to pay interest. In this scenario, the $24,400 that the sellers have paid toward their principal is considered their
    A. homestead.
    B. profit.
    C. redemption.
    D. equity.

30. A lender agreed to accept less than the current principal balance from a distressed homeowner. This lender process is a known as a
    A. judicial foreclosure.
    B. redemption sale.
    C. strict foreclosure.
    D. short sale.

31. Who is the beneficiary in the deed of trust security instrument used in a title-theory state?
    A. Buyer
    B. Seller
    C. Lender
    D. Attorney

32. What is the major difference between conventional and unconventional loans?
    A. A conventional loan is guaranteed or insured by the government, while an unconventional loan is not.
    B. An unconventional loan is guaranteed or insured by the government, while a conventional loan is not.
    C. A conventional loan is sold on the secondary market, while an unconventional loan is not.
    D. An unconventional loan is sold on the secondary market, while a conventional loan is not.

33. On an adjustable-rate mortgage, a margin is added to the index to determine the new interest rate. This margin will
    A. change every six months.
    B. decrease as the term of the loan decreases.
    C. change as the index changes.
    D. remain constant over the life of the loan.

34. A defaulted borrower's right to redeem property before a foreclosure is known as the
    A. statutory right of redemption.
    B. equitable right of redemption.
    C. borrower's right of redemption.
    D. lender's right of redemption.

35. Laws that determine the maximum interest rate a lender can charge are known as
    A. statutes of fraud.
    B. usury laws.
    C. truth-in-lending laws.
    D. borrower protection laws.

36. A developer placed a mortgage on his housing development. When he sold a lot to the buyer, a partial release was obtained for the lot purchased. The mortgage the developer obtained was a(n)
    A. blanket mortgage.
    B. purchase-money mortgage.
    C. package mortgage.
    D. open-end mortgage.

37. In the purchase of a commercial property, the investors negotiated a loan in which none of the investors were personally liable for the payment of the debt. The investors negotiated a
    A. shared appreciation mortgage.
    B. purchase-money mortgage.
    C. nonrecourse loan.
    D. wraparound loan.

38. Which of the following requires that finance charges be stated as an annual percentage rate?
    A. Truth in Lending Act
    B. Real Estate Settlement Procedures Act
    C. Equal Credit Opportunity Act
    D. Community Reinvestment Act

39. In determining whether to extend a loan to the purchaser of a house, lending institutions are MOST LIKELY to place the greatest importance on the
    A. sale price.
    B. purchaser's financial stability.
    C. appraised value.
    D. interest rate of the loan.

40. The act that requires lenders to inform buyers and sellers of all settlement fees and charges is
    A. ECOA.
    B. REIT.
    C. RESPA.
    D. TILA.

41. All of the following are ways that a borrower may default on a loan EXCEPT
    A. lack of maintenance of the property.
    B. forgetting to pay property taxes.
    C. not securing permission from the lender to improve the property.
    D. making timely payments of principal and interest.

42. According to the Truth in Lending Act, a lender must reveal all of the following EXCEPT
    A. discount points.
    B. interest rate.
    C. title fees.
    D. origination fee.

43. Several brokers at a continuing education class were in the back of the room discussing the new discount broker who just opened her business. One of the brokers said, "The best way to deal with this discount broker is to not show her listings." Is this statement legal?
    A. Yes, because the comment was just one broker's opinion.
    B. Yes, because the comment was part of a hypothetical classroom discussion.
    C. No, the brokers are price fixing, which is a violation of the Sherman Antitrust Act.
    D. No, the brokers are group boycotting, which is a violation of the Sherman Antitrust Act.

44. A buyer purchased a property through a loan assumption. The seller requested that the old note and mortgage be substituted with a new note and mortgage in the buyer's name. If the lender allows this change, it is known as the granting of a(n)
    A. attachment.
    B. release of mortgage.
    C. satisfaction piece.
    D. novation.

45. A person was paid $8,000 to let someone else use his identification and credit information to obtain a loan. The person using the identification is called a(n)
    A. promissor.
    B. impostor.
    C. mortgagor.
    D. straw buyer.

46. The seller agreed to lend the buyer $10,000 as a part of the down payment to purchase the seller's property. This loan was not disclosed to the lender, and as a result, the lender believes the borrower has a larger down payment than he actually has. The term that BEST describes this type of mortgage fraud is
    A. equity skimming.
    B. house stealing.
    C. a silent second.
    D. the seller's rescue.

47. An owner negotiated a home equity loan on his property. The owner's right to rescind this agreement within three days is provided by
    A. FHA.
    B. Regulation Z.
    C. Regulation B.
    D. VA.

48. Which of the following would restore a veteran's loan benefits after he has sold under an assumption?
    A. Substitution of novation from the lender
    B. Subject to certificate of assumption taken by the seller
    C. Subject to VA mortgage taken by a buyer
    D. Substitution of eligibility by another veteran

49. A borrower negotiated a second mortgage on her property. This mortgage is subordinate to the first mortgage, and the borrower makes one monthly payment. She MOST LIKELY secured a
    A. shared-appreciation mortgage.
    B. purchase-money mortgage.
    C. wraparound mortgage.
    D. growing-equity mortgage.

50. An offer of $120,000 was accepted by the sellers. The buyers had $12,000 for the down payment. The borrowers would negotiate a loan with a(n)
    A. 80 percent loan-to-value ratio.
    B. 85 percent loan-to-value ratio.
    C. 90 percent loan-to-value ratio.
    D. 95 percent loan-to-value ratio.

51. A retired couple negotiated a loan against the equity in their property. They now receive a monthly check from the lender for the rest of their lives, as long as they reside in the property. The seniors negotiated a(n)
    A. open mortgage.
    B. closed mortgage.
    C. reverse mortgage.
    D. open-end mortgage.

52. A borrower has secured a guarantee from the lender that the interest rate quoted on a loan application will not change prior to closing. This is known as a(n)
    A. fixed-rate mortgage.
    B. anaconda agreement.
    C. extender clause.
    D. lock-in clause.

53. Which of the following parties must sign the note and the mortgage?
    A. Mortgagor/promisee
    B. Mortgagee/promissor
    C. Mortgagor/promissor
    D. Mortgagee/promisee

54. Which of the following actions is NOT a sign of possible mortgage fraud?
    A. The buyer insists that the agent write the offer contingent upon the use of a certain appraiser.
    B. Leaving blanks in an offer to purchase for the seller to fill in at a later date.
    C. Rewriting a sale contract with an inflated purchase price.
    D. The consideration stated in the sales contract and the new deed are the same.

55. A construction loan is an example of a(n)
    A. amortized loan.
    B. partially amortized loan.
    C. nonamortized loan.
    D. balloon mortgage.

56. A qualified veteran is purchasing a duplex. Under these circumstances, the VA will
    A. set the rate of interest.
    B. determine the maximum loan amount.
    C. set the limit on the guarantee.
    D. determine the term of the loan.

57. A first-time homebuyer seeks advice from an agent regarding the difference between a mortgage broker and a mortgage banker. The agent will tell him that
    A. free checking is a typical incentive to negotiate a loan through a mortgage banker, but not a mortgage broker.
    B. mortgage bankers normally deal in conforming loans, but mortgage brokers deal in nonconforming loans.
    C. mortgage bankers normally hold their loans in portfolio, but mortgage brokers sell their loans on the secondary mortgage market.
    D. mortgage bankers originate loans, package them, and sell them to investors, while mortgage brokers bring borrowers and lenders together and are paid a percentage on the loan amount.

58. The lender is requiring that a buyer set up an escrow account for taxes and insurance. This is known as a
    A. buydown mortgage.
    B. budget mortgage.
    C. balloon mortgage.
    D. blanket mortgage.

59. A VA-guaranteed loan is an example of a(n)
    A. conventional mortgage.
    B. conventional guaranteed mortgage.
    C. unconventional insured mortgage.
    D. unconventional mortgage.

60. The federal act that prohibits a lender from discriminating based on race, color, religion, national origin, sex, marital status, age, or source of income is the
    A. federal Fair Housing Act.
    B. Equal Credit Opportunity Act.
    C. Reconciliation Act.
    D. Truth in Lending Act.

61. A couple that is 70 years old owns their home, and they have no liens on their property. They would like to negotiate a loan where they make no monthly payments and have no income or credit ratios to qualify. Is there a loan product that will meet their needs?
    A. Yes, because they own their home without liens, they can negotiate a home equity line of credit with any lender.
    B. Yes, because they are over the age of 62, they can negotiate a reverse mortgage where they will make no monthly payments and have no income or credit ratios to qualify.
    C. No, there is no loan program where the borrower does not make monthly payments or have income or credit ratios to qualify.
    D. No, there is no lender who will incur the risk of lending money to a 70-year-old person.

62. A credit bureau will analyze the borrower's employment history, outstanding debts and repayment history to compute the borrower's
    A. credit score.
    B. front-end score.
    C. back-end score.
    D. debt-to-service score.

63. A veteran is negotiating a GI loan. The appraiser will issue a
    A. certificate of reduction.
    B. certificate of reasonable value.
    C. certificate of deposit.
    D. certificate of indebtedness.

64. What is the major difference between an open mortgage and an open-end mortgage?
    A. An open mortgage is negotiated on fixed-rate mortgages, and the open-end mortgage is negotiated on adjustable-rate mortgages.
    B. An open mortgage is used to purchase new construction, and the open-end mortgage is used to purchase manufactured homes.
    C. An open mortgage allows prepayment of the loan during the loan term; an open-end mortgage is expandable by increments up to a maximum dollar amount, under the original security document.
    D. An open mortgage allows a prepayment not to exceed 5 percent of the loan balance if repaid within 5 years; an open-end mortgage does not allow a prepayment penalty.

65. The act of pledging property to the lender without giving up possession rights is known as
    A. conventional pledge.
    B. unconventional pledge.
    C. conforming pledge.
    D. hypothecation.

66. Which government body is responsible for creating money, regulating reserve requirements, and setting the discount rate of interest?
    A. Federal Housing Administration
    B. Federal National Mortgage Association
    C. Federal Reserve
    D. Federal Register

67. What party will review the loan package and make the final decision regarding the risk of the loan?
    A. Loan originator
    B. Processor
    C. Settlement agent
    D. Underwriter

68. The buyer was preapproved for a loan and his offer of $160,000 was accepted. Circumstances changed, and three weeks before the closing, the seller did not want to sell and the buyer did not want to buy. Can the parties release one another from the contract?
    A. Yes, they can release each other from the contract, and the process is known as rescission.
    B. Yes, they can release each other from the contract, and the process is known as reconciliation.
    C. No, once a sales contract has been executed by both parties, changes result in mortgage fraud.
    D. No, because the broker fulfilled the terms of the listing agreement, the buyer and seller must fulfill the terms of the sales contract.

69. Which federal law requires a loan originator to provide a potential borrower with a Good Faith Estimate within three days of application?
    A. Community Reinvestment Act
    B. Equal Credit Opportunity Act
    C. Truth in Lending Act
    D. Real Estate Settlement Procedures Act

70. While listening to the radio, a consumer heard "For qualified borrowers, we have 30-year fixed-rate mortgages with an annual percentage rate of 6.35 percent. This is a limited offer, so call today." Is this loan in compliance with Regulation Z?
    A. Yes, this ad meets RESPA requirements.
    B. Yes, this ad meets Truth-in-Lending requirements.
    C. No, lenders are not allowed to advertise interest rates on the radio.
    D. No, the APR is a trigger item that requires full disclosure.

MATCHING QUIZ

The column on the right contains a brief definition of important terms in this section. Write the letter of the matching term on the appropriate line.

A. Deficiency judgment

B. Statutory redemption

C. Regulation Z

D. RESPA

E. Alienation clause

F. Mortgage Fraud

G. Sherman Antitrust Act

H. Unconventional mortgage

I. Lien-theory state

J. Amortize

K. Rescission

L. Margin

M. HELOC

N. Mortgagor

O. Mortgagee

P. Debt-to-income ratio

Q. Short Sale

R. Redlining

S. Equal Credit Opportunity Act

T. Foreclosure

1. _____ The contract has been canceled and the parties have returned to the legal positions they were in before they entered into the contract.

2. _____ When a loan is negotiated in this type of state, the law allows the mortgagee to place a lien on the property.

3. _____ Providing the lender with false or misleading information on a loan application or with falsified documents in the loan process.

4. _____ The federal law that prohibits price fixing, group boycotting, allocation of customers or markets, or tie-in agreements.

5. _____ A loan that is backed by the government.

6. _____ To repay the loan in monthly or other periodic payments that includes principal and interest.

7. _____ The lender.

8. _____ Law that requires the disclosure of the true cost of credit expressed as an annual percent rate.

9. _____ The defaulted borrower's right to redeem the property after foreclosure.

10. _____ Clause in a mortgage that allows the lender to collect full payment if the borrower transfers the property to any party without lender's consent.

11. _____ A federal law that requires the lender to give potential borrowers a GFE within three business days of loan application.

12. _____ Personal judgment levied against a defaulted borrower when the foreclosure sale does not pay the debt in full.

13. _____ A lender's illegal act of refusing to negotiate loans in certain geographic areas, even to qualified borrowers.

14. _____ Prohibits lenders from basing credit-worthiness on the borrower's race, color, religion, national origin, sex, marital status, age, or source of income.

15. _____ The relationship of the borrower's total monthly debt payments to the borrower's income.

16. _____ The borrower.

17. _____ Credit against the equity in his/her property.

18. _____ The legal process whereby the property can be sold as security for the payment of the debt.

19. _____ The lender process wherein the lender and the owner agree to accept less than the current principal amount when the property is sold.

20. _____ The premium that a lender changes in an ARM that remains constant over the life of the loan.

CHAPTER 3 TEST ANSWERS

1. **(A)** The mortgagor is the borrower, and the mortgagee is the lender.

2. **(B)** By definition of package mortgage.

3. **(B)** By definition of amortization.

4. **(B)** By definition of acceleration clause.

5. **(B)** A power-of-sale clause is found in mortgages or trust deeds in title-theory states. This clause gives the lender the right to sell the property by advertisement when the borrower defaults and other stipulations are met.

6. **(D)** Statutory right of redemption is the right a delinquent borrower has after the foreclosure sale to redeem the property, if all costs are paid.

7. **(A)** By definition of title-theory state.

8. **(C)** A lender must qualify to negotiate FHA-insured loans. FHA, FNMA, and FHLMC do not negotiate loans.

9. **(A)** The alienation clause allows the lender to call the note due if the property is transferred to another person.

10. **(B)** When the final payment is made, the lender must release its interest in the property. A satisfaction of mortgage releases the mortgage lien and clears the title.

11. **(B)** When property is purchased under a land contract, the buyer's interest is an equitable title interest.

12. **(B)** A recorded mortgage places a lien on a property.

13. **(C)** By definition of a balloon mortgage.

14. **(D)** The ratio that compares the property's net income to the money invested is the rate of return. It may be computed on an after tax flow or before tax flow basis.

15. **(A)** Equity is defined as the difference between the market value and any existing mortgage(s) on the property.

16. **(B)** If the borrower has less than a 20 percent down payment, the lender will probably require the borrower to purchase private mortgage insurance (PMI) to reduce the lender's risk.

17. **(D)** FNMA and GNMA are both members of the secondary mortgage market.

18. **(A)** When a foreclosure sale does not produce sufficient funds to pay a debt in full, a deficiency judgment may be filed against the borrower.

19. **(D)** By definition of loan assumption.

20. **(B)** The contract was written contingent upon obtaining a no down payment VA guaranteed loan. If the sale price was $250,000 but the CRV was $247,000, the veteran does not have to purchase. He still could purchase if he choose to pay a $3,000 down payment and he qualified for the loan.

21. **(A)** Discount points may be paid by the buyer or seller in an FHA-insured loan. The origination fee and Mortgage Insurance Premium (MIP) are paid by the buyer. The MIP may be a one-time fee or a percentage added to the monthly payment.

22. **(B)** VA makes a guarantee to the lender; FHA insures the lender against a loss.

23. **(D)** In a graduated payment mortgage, the payments start out low and graduate or increase at certain timeframes. If the initial payments do not cover the interest, then the interest is added to the principal and the loan balance would increase, instead of decrease.

24. **(B)** A package mortgage includes both real and personal property.

25. **(C)** By definition of purchase-money mortgage.

26. **(B)** Regulation Z applies to residential loans made to a person, not to loans made for business, commercial, or agricultural purposes or properties sold under land contracts.

27. **(C)** By definition of subordination agreement.

28. **(D)** Borrowers who are classified as high risk will most likely negotiate a subprime loan.

29. **(D)** Equity is the difference between the market value and any liens on the property.

30. **(D)** The process in which the lender and owner agree to accept less than the current principal balance is a short sale.

31. **(C)** In the deed of trust document, the lender is the beneficiary, the trustor is the borrower, and the trustee holds the legal title for the lender.

32. **(B)** FHA and VA loans are unconventional loans, which means they are backed by the government. Conventional loans are based on the credit worthiness of the borrower and the property.

33. **(D)** The index may change on an adjustable-rate mortgage, but the margin will remain constant over the life of the loan.

34. **(B)** Equitable right of redemption is the right to redeem the property before foreclosure. Statutory right of redemption is the right to redeem the property after foreclosure.

35. **(B)** Usury laws determine the maximum interest rate that lenders can charge. They are normally state laws, but the federal government could set these rates as well.

36. **(A)** Blanket mortgages cover more than one tract of land and contain a partial release clause.

37. **(C)** In a nonrecourse loan, the borrower is not held personally liable for the note. Many commercial loans and reverse mortgages are nonrecourse loans.

38. **(A)** Regulation Z, or Truth-in-Lending, requires the disclosure of the APR.

39. **(B)** Of these choices, the buyer's financial position is the most important factor that the lender uses when evaluating whether to underwrite the loan.

40. **(C)** RESPA requires that a settlement sheet be given to the buyers and sellers, disclosing the fees paid by the parties.

41. **(D)** A borrower making timely payments of principal and interest would not constitute default.

42. **(C)** Regulation Z does not require the disclosure of title fees because they are not a finance charge. (RESPA does require the disclosure because they are a settlement cost.)

43. **(D)** Group boycotting, which is an agreement not to work with, or to withhold patronage from, other brokers is a violation of the Sherman Antitrust Act. Being present during the discussion is dangerous, even if there is no overt or express agreement.

44. **(D)** By definition of a novation.

45. **(D)** A person using another person's identify to secure a loan is called a straw buyer. The straw buyer may have either stolen a person's identity, or paid another person to use it.

46. **(C)** When the seller lends money to the borrower as a part of a down payment and the lender has no knowledge of the loan, it is called a silent second.

47. **(B)** Regulation Z provides for a three-day right of rescission on home equity loans and refinancing of property.

48. **(D)** The substitution of eligibility by another veteran on a loan assumption or the payoff of the loan would release the veteran's eligibility; then the VA could restore the veteran's loan benefits.

49. **(C)** By definition of wraparound mortgage.

50. **(C)** The borrowers had a $12,000 down payment, which is a 10 percent down payment. The loan-to-value ratio is 90 percent.

51. **(C)** By definition of reverse annuity mortgage.

52. **(D)** By definition of lock-in agreement.

53. **(C)** The borrower gives a pledge or property to a lender in the mortgage document and is the mortgagor. The borrower promises to repay the debt in the note and is the promissor.

54. **(D)** The consideration stated in the sales contract and the new deed the buyer receives at closing should be the same. If not, there could be mortgage fraud in the transaction.

55. **(C)** A construction loan is interest only, which means it is a nonamortized loan.

56. **(C)** The VA will set the limit on the guarantee to the lender.

57. **(D)** By definitions of mortgage bankers and mortgage brokers.

58. **(B)** A budget mortgage includes monthly payments of principal, interest, taxes, and insurance.

59. **(D)** Unconventional mortgages are backed by the government. FHA loans are insured; VA loans are guaranteed.

60. **(B)** The Equal Credit Opportunity Act prohibits lenders from discriminating when negotiating loans.

61. **(B)** The reverse mortgage would allow them to secure a loan against a percentage of the equity in their property without making monthly payments or having income or credit ratios to qualify.

62. **(A)** Credit bureaus base a borrower's credit score on employment history, outstanding debts, and repayment history.

63. **(B)** The appraiser would issue a certificate of reasonable value on a GI, or VA-guaranteed loan.

64. **(C)** By the definitions of open mortgage and open-end mortgage.

65. **(D)** Hypothecation means pledging property to the lender without giving up possession rights.

66. **(C)** Those are the responsibilities of the Federal Reserve.

67. **(D)** The underwriter is the party who reviews the loan package and evaluates the risk of the loan.

68. **(A)** By the definition of rescission.

69. **(D)** RESPA requires that potential borrowers be given a GFE within three business days of loan application.

70. **(B)** As long as the annual percentage rate is included in an advertisement, it meets truth-in-lending guidelines.

ANSWERS—MATCHING QUIZ

1. **K**	6. **J**	11. **D**	16. **N**
2. **I**	7. **O**	12. **A**	17. **M**
3. **F**	8. **C**	13. **R**	18. **T**
4. **G**	9. **B**	14. **S**	19. **Q**
5. **H**	10. **E**	15. **P**	20. **L**

CHAPTER 4

Real Property

AMP Outline

In some states, a street address is sufficient to identify the property in a listing and sales contract. Other states require the legal description in these contracts, as well as in deeds, mortgages, notes, and other real estate documents. Metes and bounds, lot and block, and the rectangular or government survey are the legal descriptions commonly used. The purpose of the legal description is to describe the property so it can be uniquely identified when compared to any other properties.

1. METES AND BOUNDS

The **metes-and-bounds** survey method or the **boundary survey** involves describing land by the **metes (distance)** and **bounds (direction)**. A starting point must be identified that future surveyors can use, and it is known as a **point of beginning (POB)** or a **point of commencement (POC)**. The surveyor travels around the property being described until the lot closes; that is, the surveyor returns to the point of beginning.

A metes-and-bounds legal description typically uses feet and inches as the units of measurement to describe the distance between monuments. Direction is given by the bearing of one monument in respect to another monument, described by using north, south, east, and west in relationship to degrees, minutes, and seconds.

FIGURE 4.1

Reading a Bearing

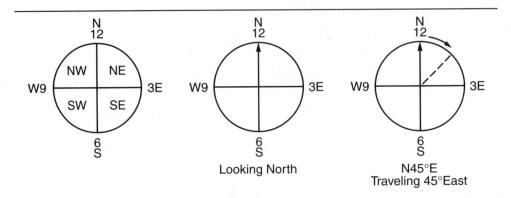

For example, imagine a circular clock with a line drawn from 12 to 6, and another line from 9 to 3. North is 12 o'clock, east is 3 o'clock, south 6 o'clock, and west 9 o'clock. The four quadrants, then, are NE, NW, SE, and SW. A legal description reading N45°E means that a surveyor is moving 45° eastward from due north. On the imaginary clock, the surveyor is facing the position of the hour hand at 1:30 pm. (See Figure 4.1)

Other survey terms include the following:

- **Monuments**—used to physically identify the POB and the intersections of the boundary lines of the area being surveyed.

- **Benchmark**—a permanent reference point used to establish elevations and altitudes above sea level.

- **Datum**—a point, line, or surface from which elevations are measured to determine such things as the heights of structures or grades of streets.

2. RECTANGULAR SURVEY

The **government** (rectangular or geodetic) **survey** is based on a system of imaginary lines called **principal meridians**, which run north and south, and **base lines**, which run east and west.

- The largest square is called a *check* and measures 24 miles by 24 miles. Each check has 16 townships.

- A **township** measures 6 miles by 6 miles. Each township has 36 sections. (See Figure 4.2.)

- A **section** measures 1 mile by 1 mile and contains 640 acres.

- **Correction lines** are used to compensate for the earth's curvature.

- **Oversized** or undersized sections are called *fractional sections*.

FIGURE 4.2

Sections of a Township

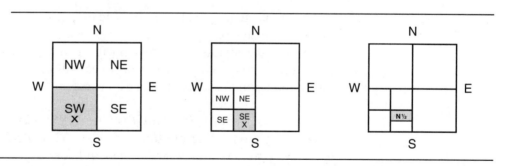

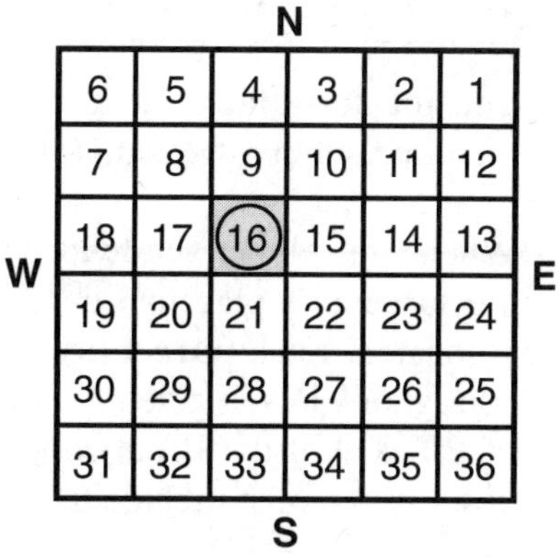

A government survey description could read "The NW¼ of the NE¼ of the SW¼ of Section 32, Township 12 North, Range 3 West of the tenth Principal Meridian." When asked to locate the legal description of a parcel of land using the government survey, read the description backward. Use Figure 4.3 as an example to locate the N½ of the SE¼ of the SW¼: begin by locating the SW¼, then locate the SE¼ of the SW¼, then the N½ of the SE¼ of the SW¼.

To compute the acreage of the N½ of the SE¼ of the SW¼, remember there are 640 acres in one section of land. Divide 640 by the denominators: 640 ÷ 4 ÷ 4 ÷ 2 = 20 acres of land.

If a question asks to compute the acres in the SW¼ of the NE¼ of the NE¼, and the N½ of the SE¼ of the SW¼, the words indicate that there are two parcels of land, as shown in Figure 4.4. Again, divide 640 acres by the denominators, but compute the acreage for the two tracts separately. Thus, 640 ÷ 4 ÷ 4 ÷ 4 = 10 acres, and 640 ÷ 4 ÷ 4 ÷ 2 = 20 acres; 10 + 20 = 30 acres of land.

FIGURE 4.3

Locating a Parcel of Land in the Government Survey

FIGURE 4.4

Locating Two Parcels of Land in the Government Survey

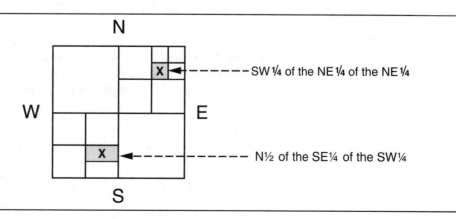

3. LOT AND BLOCK

The **lot-and-block** method of legal description is used on maps and plats of recorded subdivided land (also known as a *recorded plat* or a *recorded map*).

When a developer subdivides a tract of land for the development of a subdivision, the surveyor's plat map is recorded in the county courthouse where the property is located. Each **parcel (lot)** of land is assigned a lot number, and each group of contiguous lots is given a **block number**. A description might read "Lots 5 and 6 of Block 9 of the Brentwood Subdivision." Because all states use this method, a description must include the county and state to distinguish it from another area.

AMP Outline

IV.   **Real Property**
    B. Methods of Measurement
        1. Structures (space and volume)
        2. Livable Area
        3. Land Measurement

1. STRUCTURES (SPACE AND VOLUME)

The square footage of a property is many times used as one of the factors to determine the value of the property, or the rent that is paid in a commercial lease. However, computing the square footage of property can be challenging, so many brokers and real estate boards require agents only to provide the room dimensions of the property.

If an agent is quoting the square footage of a property, the source needs to be disclosed to the buyers. Did the agent compute the square footage, was it taken from tax records, the appraiser, seller listing agent, or another source? If the square footage is used, most multiple listing services will have a disclaimer stating that the square footage that is quoted is an estimate.

The American National Standards Institute (ANSI) has established a standard measurement for computing the square footage of single-family homes that is used by many appraisers. Many real estate regulatory agencies are adapting the ANSI standards so agents and appraisers will be quoting the same square footage of the property.

Note that the owner of a condominium has purchased the air space within the unit, and the volume or cubic footage will be used in the legal description. Square footage and volume math questions are found in the Chapter 7.

2. LIVABLE AREA

Finished area—An area that is suitable for **year-round use**. The space must be connected to the house. This is sometimes referred to as the gross living area (GLA).

Unfinished area—An area that is not suitable for year-round use.

Above grade—The area of the house that is entirely above grade or ground level.

Below grade—The area of a house that is wholly or partially below grade.

To compute the square footage of a single family home, the external dimensions of the building are measured. A garage, porch, patio, or unfinished areas are not used when computing the square footage of a property. Unfinished areas are included in another section of the appraisal report.

3.   LAND MEASUREMENT

The accuracy of the lot size is essential in both residential and commercial properties. If there is a discrepancy between the lot size quoted in the listing contract or deed and the actual lot size, the actual lot size found by the survey will prevail.

Other terms associated with lot size include the following:

- **Floor area ratio**—the ratio of the floor area to the land area on which the building sits.

- **Livability space ratio**—requires a minimum square footage of nonvehicular outdoor area in a development for each square foot of total living area.

- **Front footage**—the linear measurement of a property along the street line or water line is always given first when dimensions are stated (if a lot measures 100' × 200', then the first dimension given [100'] refers to the front footage).

- **Setback**—the amount of space required between the lot line and the building line.

AMP Outline

IV. Real Property	3. Comparative Market Analysis (performed by a real estate licensee)
C. Property Valuation	
1. Basic Concepts and Terminology	4. Broker Price Opinion
2. Influences and Characteristics Affecting Value	5. Real Property (e.g., fixtures vs. personal property [e.g., chattel])

1.   BASIC CONCEPTS AND TERMINOLOGY

An **appraisal** is the process of developing and communicating an objective opinion of an estimate of a property's **market value**. The market value is the most **probable price** a buyer will pay for the property in an arm's-length transaction—a transaction wherein the buyer doesn't have to buy, the seller doesn't have to sell, both have a knowledge of the market, and there is no other relationship between them (such as being relatives). **Market price** is the actual selling price of the property. **Cost** is the actual dollars spent to produce an asset. Value, price, and cost could be the same, but they are usually different.

In a real estate transaction, the appraiser is usually hired by the lender to develop and communicate an estimate of a property's value. The appraiser's opinion is an objective opinion, because it is supported by facts. (The buyer pays for the appraisal.) Appraisers are also hired by attorneys to determine the value property when parties are getting a divorce, by state and local governments when property is being taken by eminent domain, by insurance companies, and in many other transactions involving real estate.

The location of a property is one of the major factors in determining its value. **Location**, or **situs**, is the preference people have for a certain area. When determining the value of a property, an adjustment may be necessary to compensate for differences of location within the neighborhood.

Improvements are added to the land and will usually increase the value of the property. Improvements to land include buildings, additions such as a family room, or the replacement of a roof. Improvements of land include streets, sidewalks, and utilities.

The life cycle of a community includes growth, stability, decline, and gentrification or revitalization. An appraiser evaluates the community to determine which cycle the property is in and how that affects the value of the property. The **economic base** is reviewed for activities that will attract business and income to the community. Other economic factors that will affect a property's value include interest rates, taxes, employment levels, and population.

2. INFLUENCES AND CHARACTERISTICS AFFECTING VALUE

The principles of value that an appraiser will use in the appraisal process are the following:

- **Anticipation**—The value of the property will adjust with any anticipated change within the community, such as the change of zoning from residential to commercial, or the expansion of the airport that will increase the noise levels in nearby communities.

- **Competition**—The interaction of supply and demand wherein excess profits attract competition.

- **Conformity**—The maximum value is achieved when the property is in harmony with its surroundings.

- **Contribution**—The value of any part of the property is measured by its effect on the value of the whole.

- **Highest and best use**—The most reasonable, probable, and profitable use of the property.

- **Increasing returns**—When money spent on an improvement increases the property value.

- **Decreasing returns**—When adding improvements to the land does not produce a proportional increase in property values.

- **Plottage**—The value that is created when two or more tracts of land are merged into a single, larger one; **assemblage** is the process of merging the parcels of real estate.

- **Progression**—The value of a modest home will increase if it is surrounded by larger, more expensive properties.

- **Regression**—A larger, more expensive home will be adversely affected if it is surrounded by smaller, more modest homes.

- **Substitution**—The foundation for all approaches to appraising; the maximum value of a property tends to be set by the cost of purchasing an equal substitute property.

- **Supply and demand**—The amount of goods available in the market to be sold and the demand or need for the good.

DUST is the acronym to help you remember the four elements of value.

D—Demand is the number of properties (goods) that people are willing and able to buy at a given price.

U—Utility asks the question, "How has the land and improvement been utilized?" (A one-bedroom home versus a three-bedroom home.)

S—Scarcity means that when the supply is limited, the price will increase.

T—Transferability means that there must be a good and marketable title to the property.

Depreciation is a loss of property value due to any cause. This could include ordinary wear and tear, damage caused by fire or vandalism, or damage caused by acts of nature, such as hurricanes, floods, earthquakes, and so forth. The three types of depreciation that the appraiser determines are physical, functional, and external. Please remember that land does not ordinarily depreciate; only the improvements are depreciated.

Terms Associated with Depreciation

- **Depreciation** causes a loss of property value.

- **Curable depreciation** is reasonable and economically feasible to correct.

- **Incurable depreciation** is not economically feasible to correct.

- **Physical depreciation** may be curable or incurable and is caused by lack of maintenance and ordinary wear and tear. Depreciation of the property can occur through deterioration, which may be the effect of either normal wear and tear or natural elements.

- **Functional obsolescence** may be curable or incurable and occurs because of poor floor plan, outdated items, or changes in technology. Examples: A low ratio of bathrooms to bedrooms; an older home with limited electrical outlets in a room; or a new home built with a one-car garage.

■ **External obsolescence** is incurable and occurs because of factors located outside the property. External obsolescence is also known as *economic, locational,* or *environmental obsolescence.* Examples: nearby nuclear power plant, pig farm, or rising interest rates.

3. COMPARATIVE MARKET ANALYSIS (PERFORMED BY A REAL ESTATE LICENSEE)

When listing a property, an agent will develop a comparative market analysis (CMA) to help the seller determine the listed price or to help buyers determine what they should offer. The buyer probably isn't going to pay more than what recent buyers just paid for a similar property. If the listed property is worth more, that value needs to be justified in the CMA.

The CMA is developed by finding and analyzing every type of sale that is similar to the listed property. This would include recent sales of **like-kind properties**, properties currently on the market, properties under contract, listings that have expired or properties sold at foreclosure, estate sales, or short sales.

Need for an Appraisal at Listing

When an agent lists a property with unusual circumstances, an independent appraisal should be recommended. For example, there has been major growth in a community within the past three years. The agent is listing a 100-acre farm surrounded by this growth. There are no comparable properties, so determining the highest and best use of the farm requires an appraisal.

Also, some sellers may seek an independent appraisal before a property is listed because they want to know the estimated value before contacting an agent. This could happen if the property has historic value.

To negotiate the loan, the lender will require an appraisal to determine the fair market value of the property. The loan will be computed on the sale price or appraised value, whichever is less.

4. BROKER PRICE OPINION

Many agents are hired by lenders to perform a broker price opinion (BPO), which can also be called a broker opinion of value (BOV). Some lenders will use a BPO to determine the value of a property that is going into foreclosure, an estate sale, or a short sale. Lenders may also use a BPO for a refinance or home equity loan. The theory is that licensees are producing Comparative Market Analyses, and the same steps would be taken to create the BPO. This is less expensive than hiring an appraiser to appraise the property.

A *drive-by BPO* means the licensee is securing information about the outside of the property, while an *internal BPO* means the interior of the house is viewed.

5. REAL PROPERTY (E.G., FIXTURES VS. PERSONAL PROPERTY [E.G., CHATTEL])

The words *land, real estate,* and *real property* are often interchanged but have distinct definitions. (See Figure 4.5.) The **bundle of legal rights** associated with real estate includes the right to possess, control, enjoy, exclude, and dispose of real property. A *divided interest* means that one party can own the air and surface rights while another party owns the subsurface or mineral rights. Unless a contract stipulates otherwise, or mineral rights have been previously sold or leased, air, surface, and subsurface rights are purchased together.

FIGURE 4.5

Land, Real Estate, and Real Property

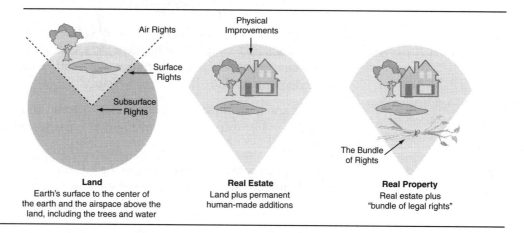

Land
Earth's surface to the center of the earth and the airspace above the land, including the trees and water

Real Estate
Land plus permanent human-made additions

Real Property
Real estate plus "bundle of legal rights"

Water Rights

Riparian rights are water rights granted to owners of land along the course of a river, stream, or lake. **Flowing water rights**: Land adjoining navigable rivers is usually owned to the water's edge, while land adjoining nonnavigable streams and lakes is owned to the center of the stream or lake.

Littoral rights are water rights of owners whose land borders on large, navigable lakes, seas, and oceans. **Nonflowing water rights**: Ownership ends at the mean high-water mark.

The action of water may affect the quality of land ownership. An owner is entitled to all land that is accumulated by **accretion**, or the increase in land resulting from the deposit of soil by the water's action. The deposits are **alluvion** or alluvium.

When water recedes, new land is acquired by **reliction**. **Avulsion** is the sudden loss of land as a result of an act of nature, such as an earthquake. The gradual wearing away of land is **erosion**.

Physical and Economic Characteristics of Real Estate

The physical characteristics of real estate can be remembered by the acronym **HID**.

■ **H—Heterogeneity** or nonhomogeneity means that every parcel of land is different.

- **I—Immobility** means the geographic location of a parcel of land can never be changed.

- **D—Durable** refers to land that is indestructible, meaning improvements can depreciate or be destroyed, but the land still remains.

The economic characteristics of land that affect its value are scarcity, improvements, permanence of investment, and area preference.

- **Scarcity** means that when the supply is limited, the price will increase. This could be the scarcity of land in a given location or the scarcity of a certain type of zoning (e.g., multifamily).

- **Improvements** will increase or decrease the property value. For example, building a four-bedroom home on a vacant lot would increase value; an announcement that a nuclear power plant will be built nearby will probably decrease the surrounding property values.

- **Permanence** of investment refers to the capital and labor used to develop a large fixed investment. Examples: water lines, sewage systems, electricity, and roads.

- **Area preference** or **situs** refers to the location of the property and is based on factors such as reputation, aesthetic beauty (e.g., a river view), geography, and convenience. People will pay more for location.

Emblements

Trees, grasses, and perennial shrubbery that do not require annual cultivation are considered real property (fructus naturales or fruits of nature).

Emblements, or crops that require annual planting, are considered personal property. When a farm is being sold, the contract should stipulate who will have the right to harvest and profit from the annual crop. Usually, former owners and tenants are entitled to harvest the crops that are a result of their labor.

Fixtures and Trade Fixtures

A **fixture** is an item that was once personal property but has become affixed to the land or improvement so that the law construes it to be a part of the real estate. Most items that are a permanent part of a building are considered fixtures.

A fixture can be excluded from the sale of the property. What goes and what stays should be discussed in detail with the seller when the property is listed. To reach a meeting of the minds, the buyer must have an understanding of the contents of the listing agreement.

A **trade fixture** (chattel fixture) is an item that is owned by the tenant and attached to a rented space to conduct business. Trade fixtures usually can be removed from the property before the lease expires. If trade fixtures remain on the property after the lease expires, they generally belong to the landlord.

Personal and Real Property Differences

Personal property, also known as **personalty** or **chattels**, is all property that does not fit the definition of real property. It includes movable items not attached to real estate, such as furniture, cars, and clothing. It also includes items that were once attached but have been severed from real estate, such as trees, crops, and chandeliers.

Should a question arise as to whether an item is real or personal property, the courts use five tests to determine the status of the property. The acronym **MARIA** will help you remember the tests to determine if an item is real or personal property.

- **M—Method of annexation**. Was the item permanently attached? Can it be removed without causing damage?

- **A—Adaptation to real estate**. Is the item custom made? For example, house keys are movable but are considered to be real property because of their adapted use to the property.

- **R—Relationship to the parties**. Emblements are considered the personal property of the tenant; but in the purchase of a farm, emblements could belong to the seller or buyer, depending on what is negotiated.

- **I—Intention**. What was the intention of the owner when the item was installed? Did the owner intend for it to remain permanently or to take it when the property was sold? (Courts have ruled that this intention is the most important factor in determining if an item is real or personal property.)

- **A—Agreement**. What was the agreement in the sales contract?

Remember, **real property** is transferred in the **deed**, while personal property is transferred with a bill of sale.

AMP Outline

IV.	**Real Property**	2. Cost Approach
	D. Methods of Valuation (Performed by an Appraiser)	3. Income Analysis Approach
	1. Sales Comparison (Market Data) Approach	4. Appraisal Process/ Procedure

1. SALES COMPARISON (MARKET DATA) APPROACH

- Used to appraise residential property and vacant land

- Also known as *market data approach* or *direct sales comparison*

- Value of subject property is determined by comparing it with at least three comparable properties that have recently sold

  - **SBA—Subject Better Add**. If the subject property has an amenity that the comparable does not, add the value of the amenity to the comparable property.

■ **CBS—Comparable Better Subtract.** If the comparable property has an amenity that the subject does not, subtract the value of the amenity from the comparable property.

FIGURE 4.6

Sales Comparison Approach

	Subject Property	Comparable Properties A	B	C
Sales price		$260,000	$252,000	$265,000
Financing concessions	none	none	none	none
Date of sale		current	current	current
Location	good	same	poorer +6,500	same
Age	6 years	same	same	same
Size of lot	60' × 135'	same	same	larger –5,000
Landscaping	good	same	same	same
Construction			same	
Style	brick	same	same	same
No. of rooms	ranch	same	same	same
No. of bedrooms	6	same	poorer +500	same
No. of baths	3	same	same	same
Sq. ft. of living space	1½	same	same	better –500
Other space	1,500	same	same	better –1,000
(basement)	full basement	same	poorer	same
Condition—exterior	average	better –1,500	+1,000	better –1,500
Condition—interior	good	same	same	better –500
Garage	2-car attached	same	same	same
Other improvements	none	none	none	none
Net adjustments		–1,500	+8,000	–8,500
Adjusted value		$258,500	$260,000	$256,500

Note: The value of a feature that is present in the subject but not in the comparable property is *added* to the sales price of the comparable. Likewise, the value of a feature that is present in the comparable but not in the subject property is *subtracted*. A good way to remember this is: CBS stands for "comp better subtract"; and CPA stands for "comp poorer add." The adjusted sales prices of the comparables represent the probable range of value of the subject property. From this range, a single market value estimate can be selected.

Note that an appraiser will never average the prices of comparable properties to determine the value of the subject property.

2. COST APPROACH

■ Used to appraise special purpose properties: houses of worship, libraries, and new properties at their highest and best use

■ Also known as *replacement* or *cost estimate*

■ The value of the improvement is computed using the reproduction or replacement cost. The **reproduction cost** is the dollar amount required to construct an exact duplicate of the subject property. **Replacement cost** is the dollar amount required to construct improvements of equal utility using current materials. Land value is determined by the sales comparison approach to appraising.

Math questions regarding the cost approach are found in Chapter 7.

3. INCOME ANALYSIS APPROACH

Used to Appraise: Investment or Income-Producing Property

Also Known As: Capitalization

Description: The appraiser capitalizes or determines the present net worth of future benefits or income the property will generate

Math questions regarding the income approach are found in Chapter 7.

4. APPRAISAL PROCESS/PROCEDURE

The steps in the appraisal process are as follows:

1. State the problem.

2. List the data needed and the sources.

3. Gather, record, and verify the necessary data.

4. Determine the highest and best use.

5. Estimate the land value.

6. Estimate the value by the three approaches.

7. Reconcile the estimate of value received from the direct sales comparison, cost, and income approaches to arrive at a final value estimate for the subject property.

8. Report the final value estimate.

The first step of the appraisal process is to state the problem or the purpose for conducting the appraisal. Is the property being appraised to determine the market value because it is being sold? Is it being appraised to determine the cost to rebuild for insurance purposes? The second step of the appraisal process is to collect market data and to classify the data by type and by source.

General data refers to information that would be appropriate for many properties. This includes outside factors, such as social, economic, environmental/physical, and government forces that would affect the value of the property. Other examples of general data include labor statistics, weather studies, transportation studies, and so forth.

Specific data refers to the information used in the analysis of the subject property and the comparable properties that will be used in the valuation process. The legal description, environmental reports, and survey would be gathered on the subject property.

Specific data on comparable properties is found under the Value Adjustments section of the appraisal report. (See Figure 4.6.) The sources of data include the primary and secondary data. **Primary data** are collected directly by the appraiser and include sketches, office files, and sales information. **Secondary data** are prepared by someone other than the appraiser, but they are used by the appraiser in determining value. Information from the multiple-listing service, conversations with other appraisers, and publications of all sold properties in the county are examples of secondary data.

AMP Outline

IV.	**Real Property**	5. Deeds
	E. Conveyance of Real	6. Will
	Property	7. Court-Ordered Sale (e.g.,
	1. Definition of Clear	foreclosure)
	(Marketable) Title	8. Adverse Possession
	2. Matters Affecting Title	9. Settlement Procedures
	3. Recordation	(closing the transaction)
	4. Title Insurance	

1. DEFINITION OF CLEAR (MARKETABLE) TITLE

When a sales contract has been negotiated between the buyer and the seller, the buyer will apply for the loan. One of the steps in processing the loan is to order a title search. Even though the law allows anyone to conduct a title search, it is usually conducted by an **abstractor,** or someone trained by a title company. An abstractor is liable for mistakes in the abstractor's search of the public records. The abstractor is not liable for forgery, missing heirs, or encroachments not found in the search.

The abstractor searches public records at the courthouse and then summarizes the information in chronological order. An **abstract (of title)** is a condensed legal history of all transactions affecting the property; it includes conveyances, wills, records of judicial proceedings, recorded liens, and encumbrances affecting the property, and their current status. Upon reviewing the abstract, an attorney will give an opinion of title.

Note that there is no guarantee of title; there is only an opinion based on the information discovered on the day the title search is conducted.

A **marketable title** or merchantable title is one that is free from reasonable objections; that is, one that will not place the buyer in a position of legal liability or threaten the buyer's right to quiet enjoyment of the property. If buyers accept a deed and then have a problem with the title, they may sue the seller based on the covenants found within the deed, if there are any, or call on their title company to defend the title if they have an owner's policy.

Easements, restrictions, violations of zoning ordinances, lis pendens notices, mortgages, liens, federal tax liens, property tax liens, and encroachments could render a title unmarketable, though slight encroachments usually do not. An unmarketable title does not prevent the property from being transferred by deed. The buyer may accept the property with certain defects that may limit or restrict ownership. However, a lender may refuse to negotiate a loan if the title is unmarketable.

2 . MATTERS AFFECTING TITLE

Title problems occur when there is a hidden mistake in a prior deed, will, mortgage, or other document that may give someone else a valid legal claim against a property. These hidden defects include

- ■ incorrect information, such as a wrong name, in a deed, mortgage, or other documents of public record that would affect the title; an incorrect legal description;

- ■ a lien or claim against the property or seller that could become the new owner's responsibility after the sale, such as unpaid mortgages, taxes, sewer and water assessments, or bills owed to workers or other creditors; it would also include attachments;

- ■ claims to ownership, including a claim to a marital interest by the spouse of a former owner, or by a child of the former owners, who was not mentioned in his or her parents' wills; and

- ■ the transfer of an invalid deed, such as transfer by a previous seller who did not actually own the property, or by a previous owner who was not mentally or legally competent.

A **cloud on title** is any claim that creates a defect of title or casts doubt on the title's validity. An example is when a mortgage has been paid in full but the mortgage release or satisfaction document has not been recorded to verify the payoff.

3 . RECORDATION

For a valid transfer of real estate, the deed must be signed by the grantor and accepted by the grantee. (The deed must meet the requirements of state laws.) There is nothing that requires the grantee to record the deed. However, to best protect the grantee's interest against the claims of other parties, it is recommended that the deed be recorded. When a deed is not recorded, it creates a gap in the title, which can create a question regarding the ownership of the property.

For a lien to be established, it must be recorded in public land records in the county where the property is located. **Recording** gives constructive notice of a party's interest in a property. If the property is located in more than one county, the proper recording document will need to be recorded in all counties.

Note that a deed that meets state laws and is signed by the grantor and accepted by the grantee is a valid conveyance of the property. However, most land record offices have additional recording requirements that must be met before they will accept a document for recording.

Examples of recording requirements that do not affect validity include minimum font and margin sizes, and the requirement that a deed be notarized before it can be recorded.

- ■ **Constructive notice**—Legal notice created by recording documents, such as deeds, mortgages, and long-term leases in the county where the property is located. Physical possession of the property also gives constructive notice of the rights of the parties that are in possession.

- **Actual notice**—A party has actual knowledge of the fact. When a party has actual notice of a third party's prior rights to a property and still accepts the deed to the property, the party accepts the deed subject to the third party's prior rights. For example, a person who accepts a deed with a judgment lien on the property becomes responsible for the judgment.

- **Torrens system**—A method of legal registration of land where title does not transfer and encumbrances are not effective against the property until the proper documents are registered at the Torrens office. In some states, this means that the title cannot be lost through adverse possession.

Licensees are checking public land records for the number and amount of liens on a property when it is listed. If the property value is less than the encumbrances, the agent may not be able to help the seller.

A buyers' agent should ask if the seller is behind on the mortgage, property taxes, or insurance payments on the property before an offer is made.

4. TITLE INSURANCE

Title insurance indemnifies (protects) the policyholder against losses that arise from certain title defects that occurred before the policy was issued and that were not found in the title search. The title insurance company will defend any covered claim made against the policyholder. Whether purchasing an owner's or a lender's policy, the premium is paid only once, generally at closing. Title insurance does not cover all title defects. Figure 4.7 provides details of standard coverage, extended coverage, or defects not covered by either policy.

FIGURE 4.7

Title Insurance

Standard Coverage	Extended Coverage	Not Covered by Either Policy
Defects found in public records	Standard coverage plus defects discoverable through the following: ■ Property inspection, including unrecorded rights of persons in possession ■ Examination of survey ■ Unrecorded liens not unknown to policyholder	Defects and liens listed in policy Defects known to buyer Changes in land use brought about by zoning ordinances
Forged documents		
Incompetent grantors		
Incorrect marital statements		
Improperly delivered deeds		

Owner's Policy

When a buyer purchases property, the buyer should seriously consider purchasing an owner's title policy to protect the buyer's interest. For a one-time premium, an owner's title insurance policy remains in effect as long as the insured or the insured's heirs retain an interest in the property. If the owner is a corporation, its successors by dissolution, merger, or consolidation are included.

Mortgagee's Policy

A mortgagee's (lender's) policy covers the loan balance and decreases as the balance is reduced. The coverage continues until the loan is repaid in full or the property is conveyed to a new owner.

Should there be a claim, the title insurance company negotiates with the claimant to settle the claim, defends the title in court (if necessary), satisfies any covered claim, and pays for the costs incurred in defending the title. When a title insurance company settles a claim, the company requires that the policyholder **subrogate (substitute)** rights to the claim to the title company. This means if compensation is paid to the policyholder, the title company now stands in the policyholder's position and has the right to sue the claimant to collect any money it paid to cover the claim. The more common legal procedures that would affect the property are as follows:

- **Suit to quiet title**—A court action intended to establish or settle the question of ownership of, or interest in, a particular property. This could include the release of abandoned easements, dower or curtesy rights, adverse possession claims, foreclosures, bankruptcy, and judgments.

- **Bankruptcy**—A statutory process in which debtors obtain financial relief by a judicially supervised reorganization, or liquidation of assets for the benefit of their creditors.

- **Foreclosure**—A legal procedure to terminate a defaulted mortgagor's interest in the property.

- **Judgment**—Court decision on the respective rights and claims of the parties in a suit; a general, involuntary, equitable lien on both real and personal property of the debtor that normally covers only the property in the county where the judgment is rendered.

- **Lis pendens notice**—Recorded to give constructive notice that an action affecting the property has been filed in court, meaning that a lawsuit has been filed, but a judgment has not been decreed; warns of a future lien on the property and renders a property unmarketable.

- **Writ of attachment**—Creditor asks the court to retain custody of the property while a court suit is being decided, thus preventing the debtor from transferring unsecured real estate before a judgment is rendered; ensures that the property will be available to satisfy the judgment.

- **Writ of execution**—A court order authorizing an officer of the court, such as a sheriff, to sell the property of a defendant to satisfy a judgment.

5. DEEDS

A **deed** is the written instrument that transfers the title from the grantor/seller to the grantee/buyer. Different types of deeds can be used to convey the title, and the distinguishing characteristics are the covenants or promises made by the grantor. State laws have their own requirements for the creation of a valid deed. Remember, it is the grantor's responsibility to bring the deed the buyer will receive to the closing.

Alienation is the act of transferring property to another. Alienation may be voluntary, such as by gift or sale; or involuntary, such as through eminent domain or adverse possession.

An alienation clause in a mortgage allows the lender to collect full payment when the property is conveyed.

Essential Elements of a Valid Deed

- The name of the **grantor**

- A **grantee** identified with reasonable certainty (a deed cannot be transferred to a deceased person or to a corporation that does not exist)

- **Consideration** will be stated and may or may not be the actual selling price

- A **granting clause** or words of conveyance

- An optional **habendum clause**, which means *to have and to hold* and defines ownership

- **Restrictions** or limitations placed on the conveyance of the property

- An accurate **legal description**

- The **signature of the grantor** or party with the legal authority to transfer the property

- **Delivery** and acceptance of the deed by the grantee

A deed must be signed by the party with the legal authority to perform. This is usually the owner, but it could be someone with power of attorney (known as the attorney-in-fact), a guardian, executor, administrator, etc.

A deed must pass or be offered by the grantor to the grantee while the grantor is alive.

Acknowledgment

In most states, a deed must be acknowledged and attested to be recorded. The primary purpose of **acknowledgment** is to verify that the person who signed the written document did so voluntarily and of his or her own free will. The secondary purpose of acknowledgment is to verify the identity of the signer. **Attestation** is the act of witnessing the person sign the document.

Types of Deeds

A **general warranty deed** is the best deed for the buyer to receive because it contains five covenants or promises made by the grantor. They are as follows:

- **Covenant of seisin**—promises the grantor owns the property and has the right to convey.

- **Covenant against encumbrances**—promises that there are no encumbrances other than those stated in the deed.

- **Covenant of quiet enjoyment**—promises that the grantor has a superior title and no one will object to the conveyance.

- **Covenant of further assurances**—promises that the grantor will correct any title defects found in the future.

- **Covenant of warranty forever**—promises that the grantor will defend the title in disputes brought by third parties.

A **special warranty deed** contains the following three warranties:

- **Grantor** received title

- Property was unencumbered by the grantor

- Grantor will defend the title for his or her period of ownership only

A **bargain and sale deed**

- This implies that the grantor holds title and possession but includes no express warranties.

A **quitclaim deed**

- This contains no express or implied covenants; it conveys whatever interest the grantor has, if any, on that given day.

- This is used to correct an error in a deed or release an interest in the property.

Special purpose deeds include the following:

- A **cession deed** is used to give property to the government, such as giving land for a park.

- A **sheriff's deed** transfers the interest in a property that was foreclosed.

- The **executor's** or **administrator's deed** is given by a court-appointed party to settle the estate of a deceased person.

- A **tax deed** is given at property tax sale.

- The **gift deed** is used to give property as a gift. The consideration would be stated as love and affection. If the grantor gave the property as a gift to avoid creditors, the creditors could seize the property.

In a **deed in trust**, the trustor conveys title to a trustee, who manages the property for the beneficiary.

- An **inter vivos** trust means to set up a trust during one's life.

- A **testamentary trust** means that the trust is established by will.

- A **deed of reconveyance** is used in a deed in trust or a deed of trust to reconvey the title to the trustor. There are federal, state, and security regulations that govern trust agreements.

6. WILL

When a person dies, that individual's estate is distributed through a legal process called *probate*. All liabilities are paid from the assets, and the remaining property is distributed to the heirs. A person can die **testate**, meaning with a will, or **intestate**, without a will. Let's review the terms associated with each.

Probate—The legal process of settling a deceased person's estate by confirming the validity of the will, identifying the heirs, determining assets, payment of the estate liabilities, and distribution of the remaining assets to the heirs.

Valid Will—A will that has been written by someone of legal age, who is also of sound mind, and that meets the state requirements for a valid will.

Executor (male)/Executrix (female)—A party named in a will to settle the estate.

Testate—The deceased person left a valid will.

Testator—The writer of the will.

Devise—To leave real property to someone in a will.

Devisee—The party receiving real property in a will.

Bequest—A gift left in a will.

Legacy—Money is left to someone in a will.

Intestate—A deceased person left no will.

Administrator (male)/Adminstratrix (female)—A person appointed by the court to settle the estate of someone who died intestate.

Laws of Descent and Distribution—State laws that determine how the assets will be distributed when someone died intestate. If a person dies intestate and owns property in another state, the laws in the state where the property is located determine who receives the property.

Descent—The method of receiving real property when someone dies intestate.

Holographic Will—A handwritten will that may be legal in many states.

Nuncupative Will—An oral will in which someone distributes personal property in contemplation of imminent death. There must be at least two witnesses, and if a written will is found, the nuncupative will cannot contradict the written will.

When a licensee is asked to list the property that is in an estate, the licensee should check at the public records office to determine the owner(s) of record.

---

7. COURT-ORDERED SALE (E.G., FORECLOSURE)

A **suit for partition** is filed to break up a joint tenancy or tenancy in common ownership. This may be done by dividing the property; but if necessary, the court will order a sale and divide the proceeds from the sale.

Foreclosure—A legal procedure to terminate a defaulted mortgagor's or debtor's interest in the property. See pages 96–97 for additional details.

8. ADVERSE POSSESSION

If a person uses someone else's property for a statutory period, and if the use is open, notorious, hostile, and continuous; the person may acquire title to the property through **adverse possession.** The rights of the party in possession are called **squatter's rights.**

To acquire a title through adverse possession, the squatter must file a **suit to quiet title** after the statutory period has been met. Periods of ownership by different squatters can be **tacked** or combined, enabling a party who has not been in possession for the entire time to establish a claim. Adverse possession is an involuntary alienation or conveyance of property. When a squatter receives a title through an adverse possession claim, it is called a **title by prescription** or a **prescriptive title.**

An **encroachment** is an unauthorized intrusion of an improvement onto the real property of another. This could be an intrusion into the air, surface, or subsurface space of the property's boundary lines or building setback lines. A survey is the best way for a buyer to determine if there are any encroachments on a property and to determine the exact boundary lines of the property.

9. SETTLEMENT PROCEDURES (CLOSING THE TRANSACTION)

A real estate settlement, or closing, takes place to consummate or finalize a real estate transaction. Before closing, the buyer makes a final inspection to ensure the property is in the same condition as promised in the sales contract. Both parties receive a copy of the settlement or closing statement, which they inspect to ensure that all monies have been accounted for properly. Each party may have an attorney present at the closing.

A **face-to-face closing** is a formal meeting of all parties involved, and a settlement agent presides over the closing. A **closing in escrow** means that a disinterested third party is authorized to act as an escrow agent for the buyer and the seller and to handle all closing activities.

The settlement agent sees that all documents are prepared for closing and conducts the closing. The settlement agent may file Form 1099-S with the IRS. A settlement agent could be a closing agent from the title company, an attorney, a lender, or a real estate agent. Proration calculations will be reviewed in Chapter 7.

A **mortgage** is a pledge of property to the lender for security for the payment of the debt.

A **note** is the evidence of the debt and states the terms of repayment.

An **affidavit of the seller** is a document in which the seller affirms that, from the time the sales contract was accepted until the date of closing, the seller has done nothing to burden the title that would not be revealed in the title search.

A **bill of sale** is used to show the transfer of personal property.

A **payoff statement** indicates the payoff of the seller's existing note(s).

An **insurance policy** is required by buyer to show payment of homeowners insurance.

Real estate transfer taxes, or RETTs, are state, county, and/or municipal sales taxes most often used as general revenue. However, RETTs can be devoted to specific uses, such as affordable housing development or open space protection. Transfer taxes are normally paid by the seller or lessor when the property is conveyed by a deed, contract for deed, lease, sublease, or assignment. The transfer tax may be paid by the purchase of tax stamps and are sometimes called documentary stamp taxes.

CHAPTER 4 TEST

1. The survey that would have a POB, and usually uses feet and inches as the units of measurements, is the
   A. lot and block.
   B. government.
   C. metes-and-bounds.
   D. township.

2. A permanent reference monument used to establish elevations and altitudes above sea level is a
   A. benchmark.
   B. datum.
   C. monument.
   D. POC.

3. The type of legal description that would MOST LIKELY be used to subdivide a tract of land for the development of a subdivision, or that would be used to describe a vacant city lot, is the
   A. lot-and-block.
   B. metes and bounds.
   C. rectangular.
   D. government.

4. The survey that uses the terms *check*, *township*, and *sections* is the
   A. lot-and-block survey.
   B. metes and bounds survey.
   C. government survey.
   D. cartographic survey.

5. An area of land that is 1 mile by 1 mile is a
   A. section and contains one acre of land.
   B. section and contains six hundred and forty acres.
   C. township and contains thirty six acres.
   D. check and contains twenty four acres.

6. Oversized or undersized sections are called
   A. correction sections.
   B. fractional sections.
   C. township sections.
   D. check sections.

7. The linear measurement of a property along the street line or water line is
   A. setback ratio.
   B. square footage.
   C. floor area ratio.
   D. front footage.

8. An appraiser has measured a building to compute the GLA. This means the appraiser measured the
   A. gross living area above grade.
   B. gross living area below grade.
   C. gross living area above and below grade.
   D. gross living area including the garage, porch, or patio.

9. Which of the following is NOT a method that could be used to transfer ownership?
   A. Sale
   B. Testate succession
   C. Intestate succession
   D. Lease

10. Location, or situs, is one of the major factors in determining the value of a property. Another factor that the appraiser will review is the ability of the community to attract income and business. This is known as the community's
    A. economic base.
    B. life cycle.
    C. market value.
    D. zoning plan.

11. Rising interest rates would be an example of
    A. curable depreciation.
    B. incurable depreciation.
    C. functional obsolescence.
    D. external obsolescence.

12. The principle of appraising, which states a property's value will adjust with any change, such as a change of zoning from residential to commercial, or a factory closing, is the principle of
    A. anticipation.
    B. change.
    C. competition.
    D. highest and best use.

13. Economic, locational, environmental, and external obsolescence refer to
    A. lack of maintenance and ordinary wear and tear.
    B. outdated items and changes in technology.
    C. factors affecting value outside of the property boundary lines.
    D. obsolescence that is reasonable and economically feasible to correct.

14. The life cycle of a community is defined by stages of development. These include
    A. growth, stability, decline, and gentrification.
    B. vacant land, development, maintenance, and decline.
    C. farms, subdivisions, commercial buildings, and special purpose properties.
    D. improvement of land and improvements to land.

15. Sales or financing concessions, location, age, and condition are examples of
    A. general data.
    B. specific data.
    C. neighborhood data.
    D. regional data.

16. The right to possess, control, enjoy, exclude and dispose of real property is only found in the definition of
    A. land.
    B. real estate.
    C. real property.
    D. improvements.

17. Littoral water rights would be found in the deed of a property whose boundary lines abut a
    A. navigable lake.
    B. small river.
    C. neighborhood creek.
    D. man-made pond.

18. An owner is entitled to all land that accumulates from the deposit of soil by the action of water. The deposits of the additional soil are called
    A. avulsion.
    B. alluvium.
    C. accretion.
    D. accession.

19. The physical characteristic of real estate that means that every parcel of land is different is known as
    A. durability.
    B. immobility.
    C. heterogeneity.
    D. scarcity.

20. All of the following terms are associated with the economic characterizes of real estate EXCEPT
    A. improvements.
    B. permanence of the investment.
    C. area preference.
    D. license.

21. Fructus naturales would be classified as
    A. nontransferable property.
    B. personal property.
    C. intangible property.
    D. real property.

22. An annual crop that is considered personal property is called a(n)
    A. fixture.
    B. emblement.
    C. sessonus fructus.
    D. share-crop.

23. Personal property attached to a rented space in order to conduct a business is known as a
    A. fixture.
    B. trade fixture.
    C. rental fixture.
    D. real property.

24. Personalty or chattels would be referring to
    A. real property.
    B. personal property.
    C. real and personal property.
    D. intangible property.

25. An appraiser is hired to develop and communicate
    A. an estimate of a property's market value.
    B. the selling price of the property.
    C. the subjective value of the property.
    D. value the buyer needs to negotiate a loan.

26. The principle of appraising, which states that the maximum value is achieved when the property is in harmony with its surroundings, is the principle of
    A. competition.
    B. conformity.
    C. contribution.
    D. highest and best use.

27. Assemblage is the process of merging two or more parcels of real estate into one parcel. The value that is created by assemblage is called
    A. market value.
    B. market cost.
    C. plottage.
    D. price.

28. A smaller home is surrounded by larger, more expensive homes. The value of the smaller home will
    A. decrease because of the larger, surrounding properties.
    B. increase because of the larger, more expensive properties.
    C. not be affected by surrounding properties.
    D. be anticipated to increase for the first five years.

29. The four elements of value are
    A. regression, progression, supply, and demand.
    B. assemblage, plottage, supply, and demand.
    C. demand, utility, scarcity, and transferability.
    D. heterogeneity, nonhomogeneity, immobility, and durability.

30. An appraiser does NOT
    A. gather, record, and verify the necessary data.
    B. determine the highest and best use.
    C. report the final value estimate.
    D. average the prices of properties that have recently sold.

31. A buyer could learn the exact boundary lines of a property by
    A. reviewing the legal description with the seller.
    B. reviewing the mortgage location survey with the lender.
    C. paying for a cadastral survey.
    D. paying for a stake survey.

32. A buyer's offer was accepted. To determine the value, the appraiser will MOST LIKELY be hired by the
    A. agent.
    B. buyer.
    C. lender.
    D. seller.

33. When an owner sold a parcel of real estate, he gave the buyer a quitclaim deed. On receipt of the deed, the buyer may be certain that
    A. there is only one owner of the property.
    B. there are no encumbrances against the property.
    C. he now owns the property subject to certain claims of the seller.
    D. all of the owner's interests in the property, as of the date of the deed, belong to the buyer.

34. Which of the following is TRUE regarding a deed and title?
    A. A deed can be prepared only by an attorney, while a title can be prepared by an attorney or an owner.
    B. A deed is valid only if it is recorded, and a title does not have to be recorded to show ownership.
    C. The purpose of a title is to transfer the bundle of rights from the grantee to the grantor.
    D. The purpose of a deed is to convey title from the grantor to the grantee.

35. An owner transfers property to a buyer with a special warranty deed. Which of the following is TRUE?
    A. The owner is making additional warranties beyond those given in a warranty deed.
    B. The property is Torrens property.
    C. The owner is warranting that no encumbrances have ever been placed against the property that have not been satisfied or released.
    D. The owner warranties are limited to the time he owned the property.

36. The state, county, and/or municipal sales tax is many times used as general revenue and is normally a debit to the seller on the HUD-1 statement. It is sometimes called a documentary stamp tax and may also be called a(n)
    A. recording fee.
    B. environmental tax.
    C. transfer tax.
    D. real estate tax.

37. A buyer purchased property but did not record the deed. Under these circumstances, the
    A. transfer of property between buyer and seller is ineffective.
    B. buyer's interest is not fully protected against third parties.
    C. deed is invalid after 90 days.
    D. deed is invalid after six months.

38. For a deed to be valid, the
    A. grantor must be legally competent.
    B. signature of the grantor must be witnessed.
    C. documents must pass through the hands of an escrow agent.
    D. grantee must sign the deed.

39. A defect or cloud on the title to property may be perfected by
    A. obtaining quitclaim deeds from all other interested parties.
    B. bringing an action to register title.
    C. paying cash for the property at the closing.
    D. bringing an action to repudiate title.

40. When a buyer is required to purchase mortgagee's title policy, the title insurance policy will
    A. indemnify the buyer against some, but not all, of the possible defect in the title.
    B. indemnify the lender against some, but not all, of the possible defects in title.
    C. protect the buyer from all defects in the title.
    D. protect the seller from a lawsuit if defects are found in the title.

41. Normally, a deed is considered valid even if
    A. signed by an authorized attorney-in-fact rather than the seller.
    B. the grantor's name was forged.
    C. the deed was signed by a minor and not the guardian of the minor.
    D. the grantor did not deliver the deed.

42. The owner gave the buyer a deed, which guaranteed that the property was not encumbered during the time the owner held title, except as noted in the deed. The type of deed the owner gave the buyer is a
    A. general warranty deed.
    B. quitclaim deed.
    C. special warranty deed.
    D. limited quitclaim deed.

43. Which of the following is NOT usually prorated between buyer and seller at the closing?
    A. Recording charges
    B. Property taxes
    C. Rents
    D. Utility bills

44. Which of the following transfers is an involuntary alienation of property?
    A. Quitclaim
    B. Devise
    C. Eminent domain
    D. Gift

45. All of the following are intended to convey legal title to real estate EXCEPT
    A. a warranty deed.
    B. a deed of trust.
    C. a trustee's deed.
    D. an equitable title.

46. The words *to have and to hold* in a deed
    define the ownership that is being transferred.
    This phrase is known as the
    A. granting clause.
    B. habendum clause.
    C. alienation clause.
    D. distributor clause.

47. For a deed to be recorded, it must be
    acknowledged. The primary purpose of
    acknowledgment is to
    A. convey title to the grantee.
    B. ensure the identity of the grantee.
    C. verify that the deed was signed without
       duress.
    D. guarantee a marketable title.

48. Which of the following statements is TRUE
    regarding title insurance?
    A. Title insurance is paid monthly and is
       included in the mortgage payment.
    B. Title insurance covers losses due to a
       defect in the title, but it does not pay for
       the cost of defending the title.
    C. There are two types of title polices that
       may be purchased. The owner's policy
       covers the owner, while the mortgagee's
       policy covers the lender.
    D. Title insurance normally does not cover
       defects caused by forgery.

49. Which of the following is FALSE regarding
    taxes?
    A. Ad valorem is another term for real prop-
       erty taxes.
    B. Unpaid ad valorem taxes could create a
       general lien on the property.
    C. Ad valorem taxes are paid on the value of
       the real property.
    D. Unpaid ad valorem taxes could create a
       specific lien on the property.

50. A closing is scheduled to take place April
    15. In January, the owner paid the taxes for
    the entire year, and the buyers are assuming
    responsibility for taxes attributable to the
    period following the closing. At the closing,
    on the settlement statement, the adjustment
    made for property taxes appears as
    A. a debit to the buyer and a credit to the
       seller.
    B. credit to the buyer and a debit to the
       seller.
    C. credit to the buyer.
    D. debit to the seller.

51. Some time ago, a special assessment was lev-
    ied against a property for sidewalk and street
    improvements in front of a house. Under the
    agreement with the purchaser, the buyers
    will not assume the special assessment. If
    the assessment has not been paid off prior to
    the closing, the amount remaining due will
    appear as a
    A. credit to the buyer.
    B. debit to the seller.
    C. credit to the seller and a debit to the
       buyer.
    D. debit to the seller and a credit to the
       buyer.

52. Expenses involved in the closing of a real
    estate transaction are shown on the settlement
    as a
    A. debit to either the buyer or the seller.
    B. credit to either the buyer or the seller.
    C. debit to both the buyer and the seller.
    D. credit to both the buyer and the seller.

53. A testamentary trust means the trust was
    established by a
    A. deceased person's will.
    B. lender in a lien theory state.
    C. lender in a title theory state.
    D. person while he/she was alive.

54. Which of the following is TRUE regarding an abstract of title?
    A. It can be developed only by an attorney.
    B. It contains the names of missing heirs.
    C. It contains information taken from public records.
    D. It is necessary before a property can be listed.

55. An owner's title insurance policy normally covers all of the following EXCEPT
    A. missing heirs.
    B. incorrect marital status.
    C. zoning changes.
    D. forgery.

56. At a closing, the buyer received a deed in which the grantor implied possession and ownership of the property. The buyer MOST LIKELY received a
    A. general warranty deed.
    B. bargain and sale deed.
    C. special warranty deed.
    D. grantee's deed.

57. A buyer wishes to take title to a property with a deed that BEST protects his interest. The buyer should ask for a(n)
    A. fee simple interest conveyed by a quit-claim deed.
    B. estate for years interest conveyed by a bargain and sale deed.
    C. fee simple interest conveyed by a warranty deed.
    D. periodic estate interest conveyed by a grant deed.

58. An owner signed a deed conveying her property to her best friend. She told no one and placed the deed in her safe-deposit box. Several months later, she died intestate and the deed was found. Who receives the property?
    A. Her best friend because the deed has been signed by the owner.
    B. The owner's heirs, as determined by the laws of descent and distribution.
    C. Another friend who gave her property on her death bed.
    D. The state, because she died intestate.

59. All of the following documents would MOST LIKELY be recorded EXCEPT
    A. a general warranty deed.
    B. a mortgage.
    C. a mortgage release.
    D. a sales contract.

60. Which of the following would NOT be associated with testate succession?
    A. Will
    B. Devisee
    C. Probate
    D. Descent

61. Mr. and Mrs. Buyer declined to purchase an owner's title policy, but the lender required them to purchase a lender's title policy. Six months after the closing, a man knocked on their door. He explained that he had an ownership interest in the property because his wife sold the property while he was in another country. The man at the closing table, who said he was the husband, was not. If the man's claim is true, are the buyers covered under the lender's policy?
    A. Yes, because the closing took place only six months ago, they would be covered.
    B. Yes, because the lender's policy protects the buyer against forgery.
    C. No, because the buyers are not covered by the lender's policy.
    D. No, because the owner's policy does not protect against forgery.

62. All of the following actions would create a cloud on the title EXCEPT
    A. undisclosed dower rights.
    B. lis pendens notice.
    C. writ of execution.
    D. mortgage release.

63. Which of the following covenants would NOT be found in a general warranty deed?
    A. Covenant of seisin
    B. Covenant to renew
    C. Covenant of warranty forever
    D. Covenant of quiet enjoyment

64. At the closing table, the grantor executed a notarized deed. The grantee accepted the deed and took possession. Six months later, the grantor performed a title check and noticed that the grantee had not recorded the deed. Is there a valid transfer between the parties?
    A. Yes, the grantor signed and the buyer accepted a notarized deed, so the transfer is valid between the parties.
    B. Yes, because the grantee took possession of the property the day of closing, there is a valid transfer between the parties.
    C. No, because the grantee did not record the deed, there is not a valid transfer between the parties.
    D. No, because the grantee did not record the deed and the seller has a voidable title, so the transfer is not valid between the parties.

65. A person's principal place of residence is in Chicago. He purchased a 200-acre farm in Kentucky. The title search showed that the farm was located in Boone County, Kentucky, and Kenton County, Kentucky. The deed should be recorded in
    A. Chicago, Illinois, where he lives.
    B. Boone County, Kentucky.
    C. Kenton County, Kentucky.
    D. Boone and Kenton counties in Kentucky.

66. While searching the Internet, a buyer found property that she was interested in buying. State laws require the seller to disclose in the deed the actual selling price of the property. Can the buyer go to the county land records, conduct her own title search on the property, and determine what the seller paid for it?
    A. Yes, if her attorney goes with her.
    B. Yes, because recorded records are public documents.
    C. No, because she has not made an offer on the property.
    D. No, because only attorneys and abstractors can search public documents.

67. A couple contracted with a builder to construct their retirement home and paid cash for the property. At closing, they had their attorney represent them and they purchased an owner's title policy. Three months later, it was determined that the builder had not paid the subcontractors. Before the title company will make a payment to settle the claim, the owners will need to
    A. pay an additional title insurance premium.
    B. subordinate their rights to their attorney.
    C. have their attorney negotiate with the subcontractors.
    D. subrogate their rights to the title company.

68. Which of the following legal descriptions must include airspace above a datum?
    A. Survey of a cemetery plot
    B. Survey of a condominium
    C. Survey of a single-family home
    D. Survey of mineral rights

69. Which of the following BEST describes a lis pendens notice?
    A. A recorded notice that allows all lien holders to collect before a judgment
    B. A recorded notice that is filed only when a property is in foreclosure
    C. A recorded notice that is filed on final determination of a suit to quiet title
    D. A recorded notice that a property is in litigation that could result in a future lien being placed on the property

70. A house built in the 1940s has never had any of the electrical panels updated. This appraiser would classify this aspect of the house as
    A. physical depreciation.
    B. functional obsolescence.
    C. locational obsolescence.
    D. environmental obsolescence.

MATCHING QUIZ

The column on the right contains a brief definition of important terms in this section. Write the letter of the matching term on the appropriate line.

A. Setback

B. Objective Value

C. Curable Depreciation

D. Broker Price Opinion

E. Riparian Rights

F. Marketable Title

G. Metes and Bounds

H. Indemnify

I. Suit to Quiet the Title

J. General Warranty Deed

K. Quitclaim Deed

L. Probate

M. Devise

N. Descent and Distribution

O. Highest and Best Use

P. Transfer Tax

Q. Bill of Sale

R. Principal of Substitution

S. Adverse Possession

T. Benchmark

1. _____ This legal description is characterized by degrees, minutes, and seconds.

2. _____ The most reasonable, probable, and profitable use of the property.

3. _____ To protect someone from loss.

4. _____ Paid by the seller upon conveyance of the title.

5. _____ The amount of space required between the lot line and the building line.

6. _____ Court action intended to resolve the question of ownership of, or interest in, a particular property.

7. _____ The best deed for the buyer to receive.

8. _____ The best deed for the seller to give.

9. _____ The process of settling a deceased person's estate.

10. _____ A permanent reference point used to establish elevations and altitudes above sea level.

11. _____ The transfer of real property by a will.

12. _____ The method of determining heirs and settling an estate when someone died intestate.

13. _____ An estimated value of a property provided by a real estate licensee to a lender.

14. _____ A title that is free from reasonable objections that will not place the lender or owner in a position of legal liability.

15. _____ A person's claim to property by squatter's rights.

16. _____ An appraiser's opinion of value based on facts.

17. _____ Water rights granted to owners of land along the course of a river, stream, or lake.

18. _____ Document used to show the transfer of personal property.

19. _____ The foundation for all the approaches to appraising.

20. _____ Depreciation that is reasonable and economically feasible to correct.

CHAPTER 4 TEST ANSWERS

1. **(C)** The metes-and-bounds survey would have a point of beginning or a point of commencement and use feet and inches as the units of measurements.

2. **(A)** The benchmark is a permanent reference point used to establish elevations and altitudes above sea level.

3. **(A)** The lot and block survey would be used to subdivide vacant land for the development of a subdivision.

4. **(C)** The government or rectangular survey uses the terms check, township, and sections.

5. **(B)** A section is one mile by one mile and contains six hundred and forty acres.

6. **(B)** Oversized and undersized sections are called fractional sections.

7. **(D)** The linear measurement of a property along the street line or water line is front footage.

8. **(A)** The GLA is the gross living area above grade.

9. **(D)** A lease is not used to transfer ownership of property.

10. **(A)** The economic base measures the ability of a community to attract business and income.

11. **(D)** External obsolescence are factors that affect the value of the property, which are outside the property boundary lines. Rising interest rates is an example of external obsolescence.

12. **(A)** The principle of anticipation states that a property's value will adjust with any change.

13. **(C)** Economic, location, environmental, and external obsolescence refer to factors affecting the value of a property, which are outside of the property's boundary lines.

14. **(A)** The life cycle of a community is defined by the stages of growth, stability, decline, and gentrification.

15. **(B)** Specific data is information that is used in the analysis of the subject property and the comparable properties, such as sales or financing concessions, location, age, and condition.

16. **(C)** Real property includes the bundle of legal rights, which includes the right to possess, control, enjoy, exclude, and dispose of real property by the owner.

17. **(A)** Littoral rights are water rights of owners whose land borders on large navigable lakes, seas, and oceans.

18. **(B)** The deposits of soil by the action of water are called alluvium.

19. **(C)** Heterogeneity or nonhomogeneity means that every parcel of real estate is different.

20. **(D)** The economic characteristics of real estate are scarcity, improvements, permanence of investment, and area preference, not a license.

21. **(D)** Fructus naturales are fruits of nature, such as trees that do not require annual planting. Fructus naturales are classified as real property.

22. **(B)** Emblements require annual planting and are considered personal property of the owner.

23. **(B)** When a tenant attaches personal property to a rented space to conduct business, it is a trade fixture. If, however, they are attached, they maintain their character as personal property.

24. **(B)** Personalty or chattels are other names for personal property.

25. **(A)** An appraiser is hired to develop and communicate an estimate of the property's value.

26. **(B)** The principle of appraising that states that the maximum value is achieved when the property is in harmony with its surroundings is the principle of conformity.

27. **(C)** Plottage value is the value created by assemblage.

28. **(B)** The principle of progression states that the smaller home will increase in value when surrounded by larger, more expensive homes.

29. **(C)** The four elements of value are demand, utility, scarcity, and transferability (DUST).

30. **(D)** An appraiser does not average the prices of properties that have recently sold.

31. **(D)** The stake survey would determine the exact boundaries of a property.

32. **(C)** The appraiser is generally hired by the lender.

33. **(D)** A quitclaim deed makes no warranties. It transfers whatever interest the giver has, if any.

34. **(D)** A deed conveys the title from the grantor to the grantee.

35. **(D)** By definition of special warranty deed.

36. **(C)** By the definition of a transfer tax.

37. **(B)** When the grantee does not record the deed, his interests are not protected against third parties.

38. **(A)** The grantor must be legally competent when the grantor signs the deed. The signature must be acknowledged and attested if it is to be recorded, but not for validity.

39. **(A)** Quitclaim deeds signed by the parties that have an interest in the property are the best way to perfect a title.

40. **(B)** Indemnification is an agreement to reimburse someone for a loss. The holder of title insurance is indemnified against some, but not all, possible defects. A mortgagee's policy indemnifies the lender.

41. **(A)** A deed must be transferred by a competent party. The attorney-in-fact is considered a competent party.

42. **(C)** By definition of special warranty deed.

43. **(A)** The recording fee is an expense of the buyer and is not prorated.

44. **(C)** Alienation in real estate means conveyance. Eminent domain is involuntary alienation of real estate.

45. **(D)** An equitable title is an insurable title, but it does not transfer legal title.

46. **(B)** By definition of habendum clause, which means to have and to hold.

47. **(C)** The primary purpose of acknowledgment is to verify that the document was executed without duress. The secondary purpose is to ensure the identity of the party signing the document.

48. **(C)** The owner's policy covers the owner, while the lender's policy covers the lender and decreases as the mortgage balance is reduced.

49. **(B)** Unpaid property taxes create a specific lien on the property, not a general lien.

50. **(A)** The taxes were paid in advance for the entire year; therefore, they are a debit to the buyer and a credit to the seller.

51. **(B)** The buyers will not assume the assessment; therefore, the entry will be a debit to the seller.

52. **(A)** Expenses could be a debit to either the buyer or the seller on a settlement sheet.

53. **(A)** A testamentary trust means the trust was established by a deceased person's will.

54. **(C)** An abstract of title is a history or digest of information taken from public records.

55. **(C)** Zoning changes or zoning regulations are not covered under title insurance.

56. **(B)** By definition of bargain and sale deed, in which the grantor implies ownership and possession.

57. **(C)** A fee simple absolute ownership conveyed by a general warranty deed would best protect the grantee's interest.

58. **(B)** The deed was not delivered during the lifetime of the grantor; therefore, the property transfers to the owner's heirs by the laws of descent and distribution in the state where the property is located.

59. **(D)** The sales contract is not usually recorded.

60. **(D)** When a person dies intestate, the state laws of descent and distribution determine who receives the property of the deceased person. Descent would not be associated with testate, which is the status of a party who has died with a will.

61. **(C)** No, they would not be covered. The lenders policy does not cover the owners.

62. **(D)** A mortgage release would not create a cloud on the title.

63. **(B)** The covenant to renew is not found in the general warranty deed. It may be found in a lease.

64. **(A)** There is a valid transference between the parties. Usually, buyers or their lenders will record the deed, but a buyer is not required by law to record the deed. It is the best way for the buyers to protect their interests in the property.

65. **(D)** The deed should be recorded in all counties where the property is located.

66. **(B)** Public records can be searched by anyone.

67. **(D)** The owners will subrogate their rights to the title company so that the insurance company can take action against the builder.

68. **(B)** A survey of a condominium must contain the legal description of the elevations of floor and ceiling surfaces and the vertical boundaries in reference to an official datum. Thus, it must include the airspace above the datum.

69. **(D)** By definition of lis pendens.

70. **(B)** Outdated electrical panels would be classified as functional obsolescence.

ANSWERS—MATCHING QUIZ

1. **G**	6. **I**	11. **M**	16. **B**
2. **O**	7. **J**	12. **N**	17. **E**
3. **H**	8. **K**	13. **D**	18. **Q**
4. **P**	9. **L**	14. **F**	19. **R**
5. **A**	10. **T**	15. **S**	20. **C**

CHAPTER 5

Marketing Regulations

AMP Outline

1. ENVIRONMENTAL CONCERN (E.G., LEAD-BASED PAINT; RADON)

Landlords Disclosure: Lead Warning Statement

Housing built before 1978 may contain lead-based paint. Lead from paint, paint chips, and dust can pose health hazards if not managed properly. Lead exposure is especially harmful to young children and pregnant women. Before renting pre-1978 housing, lessors must disclose the presence of known lead-based paint and/or lead-based paint hazards in the dwelling. Lessees also must receive a federally approved pamphlet on lead poisoning prevention.

Note that tenants do not have ten days to inspect the property for lead-based paint hazards. The landlord is required to give tenants any known lead-based paint and lead hazards reports before the lease takes effect.

Seller's Disclosure: Lead Warning Statement

Every purchaser of any interest in residential real property on which a residential dwelling was built prior to 1978 is notified that such property may present exposure to lead from lead-based paint that may place young children at risk of developing lead poisoning. Lead poisoning in young children may produce permanent neurological damage, including learning disabilities, reduced intelligence quotient, behavioral problems, and impaired memory. Lead poisoning also poses a particular risk to pregnant women.

The seller of any interest in residential real property is required to provide the buyer with any information on lead-based paint hazards from risk assessments or inspections in the seller's possession and notify the buyer of any known lead-based paint hazards. A risk assessment or inspection for possible lead-based paint hazards is recommended prior to purchase.

Remember...

- Buyers have ten days to inspect for lead-based paint hazards

- Buyers must pay for the inspection

- Buyers may waive their right to the inspection

- Buyers and tenants have the right to any prior inspection records and reports

- Federal law requires that the disclosures be kept for three years

The Landlord and Sellers Lead Based Paint Disclosures and the *Protect Your Family from Lead in Your Home* can be found at the EPA Web site: *www.epa.gov/lead /pubs/leadprot.htm* (see Figure 5.1).

FIGURE 5.1

EPA Lead-Based Paint

Lead poisoning is a danger to everyone, including adults. Intact lead-based paint is usually not a hazard; but chipping, peeling lead paint, or lead dust from friction sources, such as windows and doors is the major source of lead poisoning.

The law does not require any testing or removal of lead-based paint by sellers or landlords, and it does not invalidate leasing and sales contracts. The law does not apply to the following:

- Housing built after 1977

- Zero-bedroom units, such as efficiencies, lofts, and dormitories

- Leases for less than 100 days, such as vacation houses or short-term rentals

- Housing for the elderly (unless children live there)

- Housing for the handicapped (unless children live there)

- Rental housing that has been inspected by a certified inspector and found to be free of lead-based paint

- Foreclosure sales

Agents must ensure the following:

- Sellers and landlords are made aware of their obligations under this rule

- Sellers and landlords disclose the proper information to lessors, buyers, and tenants

- Sellers give purchasers the opportunity to conduct an inspection

- Lease and sales contracts contain the appropriate notification and disclosure language and proper signatures

Sellers, lessors, and real estate agents share responsibility for ensuring compliance with the law. A party who fails to give the proper information can be sued for triple the amount of damages.

Lead-Based Paint Ruling for Contractors

Beginning April 22, 2010, contractors performing renovation, repair, and painting projects that disturb lead-based paint in homes, child care facilities, and schools built before 1978 must be certified by the EPA and must follow specific lead-safe work practices to prevent lead contamination. Individuals can become certified renovators by taking an eight-hour training course from an EPA-approved training provider.

Radon

Radon is a cancer-causing radioactive gas that is produced by the natural decay of radium, which is produced by the natural decay of uranium.

According to EPA's 2003 *Assessment of Risks from Radon in Homes,* radon is estimated to cause about 21,000 lung cancer deaths per year.

Nearly 1 out of every 15 homes in the U.S. is estimated to have elevated radon levels. The two main sources of radon are air and water. When the source of water is a well, or the public water supply source is groundwater, the water should be tested for radon.

The EPA Action Level is 4 picocuries per liter of air. (4 pCi/L)

Testing is inexpensive, and every home and building should be tested. The average cost to mitigate a home is between $800 and $2,500.

 You can find more information about radon at the EPA Web site: *http://www.epa .gov/radon*. (See Figure 5.2.)

Surgeon General Health Advisory

"Indoor radon is the second-leading cause of lung cancer in the United States and breathing it over prolonged periods can present a significant health risk to families all over the country. It's important to know that this threat is completely preventable. Radon can be detected with a simple test and fixed through well-established venting techniques." January 2005

FIGURE 5.2

A Citizen's Guide to Radon

United States
Environmental Protection
Agency

EPA 402/K-09/001 | January 2009 | www.epa.gov/radon

A Citizen's Guide To Radon

The Guide To Protecting Yourself And Your Family From Radon

Indoor Air Quality (IAQ)

Other Environmental Issues

Consumers are aware of other environmental issues that can affect their health, as well as the value of the property. (See Figure 5.3) Depending on the type of property being purchased, the buyer should ask the seller about disclosure of the following environmental hazards:

■ **Urea formaldehyde**—used in building materials, especially insulation; emits gases that can cause respiratory problems and eye and skin irritations.

■ **Asbestos**—because asbestos provides heat insulation and is fire resistant, it was used in more than 3,000 types of building materials. **Asbestos Containing Materials (ACMs)** include insulation, floor tiles, roof shingles, and siding, to name a few. Intact asbestos is generally not a hazard. Disturbed or exposed asbestos can release microscopic fibers, which is breathed into the lungs and can result in respiratory diseases. **Friable ACM**, is defined as any material containing more than 1 percent asbestos and that, when dry, can be crumbled, pulverized, or reduced to powder by hand pressure.

■ **Non-friable ACM** is any material containing more than 1 percent asbestos that when dry, **cannot be crumbled**, pulverized, or reduced to powder by hand pressure.

■ **Carbon monoxide**—an odorless and colorless gas that occurs as a byproduct of incomplete combustion when burning fuels, such as wood, oil, and natural gas. Proper ventilation is needed when burning these fuels. Carbon monoxide inhibits the blood's ability to transport oxygen, which can cause nausea and even death.

■ **Underground storage tanks (USTs)**—commonly found where gas stations, auto repair shops, printing and chemical plants, and dry cleaners used tanks for storage of chemicals. If USTs are used to store toxic wastes and the tanks are neglected, they may leak hazardous substances into the environment and thus contaminate the soil and groundwater. More than 90 percent of the world's total supply of drinking water is groundwater. Approximately one half of the people in the United States use ground water for drinking water.

■ **Mold**—found almost everywhere, but excess moisture allows mold to grow rapidly, and mold can destroy property. Some people are sensitive to mold, which can cause allergic reactions or more serious health problems.

■ **PCBs or Polychlorinated biphenyls**—formerly used in electrical transformers; equipment leaking PCBs should be replaced. PCBs are considered a health hazard. Toxic Substances Control Act (TSCA) placed prohibitions on the manufacture, processing and distribution of PCBs in commerce. The law requires Cradle **to Grave** management of PCBs from manufacturing to disposal.

FIGURE 5.3

Environmental Hazards

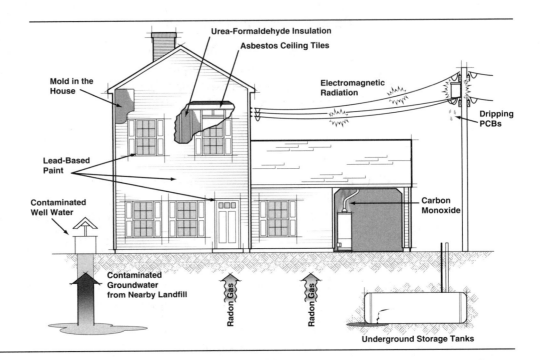

Comprehensive Environmental Response, Compensation, and Liability Act (CERCLA) is a 1980 law that taxed the petroleum industry, created a national inventory of hazardous waste sites, and identified **potentially responsible parties (PRPs)** for cleanup of the sites. The four classes of potentially liable parties are as follows:

- **Current owners and operators** of a facility

- **Past owners and operators** of a facility at the time hazardous wastes were disposed

- **Generators** and parties that arranged for the disposal or transport of the hazardous substances

- **Transporters** of hazardous waste that selected the site where the hazardous substances were brought

The law became known as the **Superfund** when Congress collected over $12 billion to cleanup sites when a PRP could not be identified. Federal authority was given to respond directly to releases, or threatened releases, of hazardous substances. A **hazardous substance** is any material that poses a threat to public health or the environment.

Potentially Responsible Parties' Liability

- **Retroactive liability**—Parties may be held liable for acts that happened before Superfund's enactment in 1980.

- **Joint and several liability**—Any one potentially responsible party (PRP) may be held liable for the entire cleanup of the site, when the harm caused by multiple parties cannot be separated.

- **Strict liability**—A PRP cannot simply say that it was not negligent or that it was operating according to industry standards. If a PRP sent some amount of the hazardous waste found at the site, that party is liable.

Any real estate can involve an **Environmental Site Assessment (ESA)**, and many commercial transactions involve a Phase I, Phase II, and/or Phase III assessment. The purpose of an ESA is to **identify potential or existing** environmental liabilities.

- **Phase I ESA**—A Phase I ESA will show that **environmental due diligence** was taken to confirm the presence or absence of environmental issues; and to access liability of ownership prior to its acquisition. This action will hopefully qualify a buyer for the innocent landowner defense under the CERCLA should environment issues be discovered in the future.

- **Phase II ESA**—If potential environmental issues are identified in Phase I, there will be a Phase II ESA, which involves the collection and analysis of samples to document the presence or absence of regulated substances.

- **Phase III ESA**—Phase I and Phase II results are studied to determine an appropriate and reasonable solution for any environmental issues that are found. This includes the design and implementation of the remediation of the site and all necessary reports and permits to achieve cleanup of the site to the agreed upon site specific standards.

Real estate licensees are not expected to be experts in environmental issues; however, they need to know how to identify possible issues and direct buyers, sellers, tenants and owners to the experts.

2. PROPERTY CONDITION

Buyers are generally concerned about the physical condition of the structure, nearby stigmatized properties, and environmental issues of the property and surrounding properties. To help identify the defects of the physical structure, many buyers write their offers contingent upon an inspection by an independent third party or property inspector. Many buyers and lenders may require a pest control report showing that the property is free and clear of any live, visible infestation by wood-destroying organisms. Depending on the type of property, lenders may also require a flood certification and environmental assessment before negotiating a loan on the property.

Developers want to ensure that there is an adequate and safe water supply and that the disposal of sewage meets health and safety standards. To ensure the health, safety, and welfare of homeowners, there are local, state, or municipal building and construction standards that must be met. These standards include the regulation and control of design, construction, quality, use, occupancy, location, and maintenance of all buildings and structures.

A **building permit** must be issued for the construction of a new building or other improvement, and for any substantial repair of an existing structure or the demolition of a building. The purpose of the permit is to ensure compliance with the **building code**, or minimum standards of construction. A violation of code and failure to disclose violations may constitute misrepresentation and make the contract voidable. When the building meets code, a **certificate of occupancy** is issued. Building codes are established by local governments, but it should be noted that not all areas have building codes. If there is a question if a building meets code, the agent should direct the buyer to the local zoning board to determine the answer.

Property owners who use septic tanks are required to have a **percolation test** (perk test), which tests the soil's absorption or drainage capacity. Only if the soil has the ability to absorb and drain water can the land be developed.

There are two types of potential defects in a property:

■ **Latent defects** are hidden structural defects not easily discovered by inspection.

■ **Patent defects** are easily visible when inspecting a property.

Most states require that the seller complete a **seller's disclosure of property condition statement**, which provides information regarding the house systems (plumbing, electrical, heating and cooling, etc.), foundation, structural damage, leaking basement, the roof, drainage problems, boundary issues, source of water supply, source of sanitation, improvements to the property, and environmental issues, such as mold, lead-based paint, and radon. Sellers are also required to disclose major repairs resulting from fires, hurricanes, or other natural disasters.

■ The property disclosure statement should be completed by the seller or a person with the legal authority, such as the executor of an estate.

■ Licensees should review the document to ensure that the seller has totally completed the form. (Did the seller sign the form? Have all the boxes been checked?)

■ The property disclosure form is not intended to be a warranty or a substitute for the buyer's securing an independent property inspection.

■ If a licensee questions the accuracy of the property disclosure form, it should be discussed with the seller. Remember, the law of agency requires the disclosure of any material facts that would affect the transaction.

■ Generally, the form is given to the buyer before the offer is made. If the buyer is purchasing a for-sale-by-owner property, the law may allow the disclosure to be given after the offer is accepted. The timeframes for presenting the seller's disclosure form is a matter of state law, and the consequences of the failure to make a timely disclosure vary. Remember, all written offers need to be presented to the seller even if the property disclosure form has not been completed by the seller.

An agent is liable for not disclosing known defects and may be liable for defects about which the agent should have known. **Misrepresentation** means a party is making a decision based on information that is not true, and may be intentional or negligent. The property is being misrepresented when defects are not disclosed to the buyer. The buyer may be able to rescind the sales contract or receive **compensatory damages**, which are actual damages for the repair of the defect. **Punitive damages** are damages assessed as punishment.

Buyers should be informed that the seller's property disclosure form is **not a substitute** for hiring their own property inspector, and that the buyers should rely on the opinions of their inspector. Depending on the property, the agent may recommend the buyer also have a radon, mold, lead-based paint, and water and well inspection, and to ask the seller for a CLUE report. (See page 21.)

A **material fact** is defined as a fact that is significant or essential to the issue or matter at hand. It is information that, if known, could change the decision of the party.

In a real estate transaction, a **material fact** can be anything from disclosure that a property is stigmatized, to zoning verification, property taxes, building codes, building permits, certificates of occupancy, and other land-use restrictions that may apply. The local zoning administrator or county attorney will assist the public in answering these questions.

Any other encumbrances, such as deed restrictions and conditions, regulations of the homeowners' association, special assessments, or any other condition that would burden the use, enjoyment, or disposition of the property, also need to be disclosed. For example, is the property in foreclosure, short sale, or an estate sale? Are there any other circumstances that might prevent the property from being readily transferable? If so, this information should be disclosed to the buyer.

Survey

The purpose of the survey is to determine the exact area of the land being purchased, to identify any existing encroachments and easements, and to determine compliance with setback and other zoning requirements. Most lenders require a **mortgage location survey** that assures the lender that the lot is as represented in the legal description, and that the improvements are within the lot lines. A mortgage survey is not a stake survey created by a civil engineer where monuments are identified and land areas are measured. A lender may also require buyers to purchase a title policy endorsement to protect the lender against survey problems.

Agents should not indicate that the fence line, row of trees, or any other monuments represent the boundary lines. If the buyers want to confirm the exact boundary lines, they will need to pay for a stake survey.

Stigmatized Property

A property may be **stigmatized** if the history of the property makes it undesirable, or if a sex offender lives in the neighborhood. A stigma may be created by a homicide, suicide, shooting, illegal drug sales, methamphetamine lab, or if the house is said to be haunted. Some states have laws requiring the disclosure, or nondisclosure, of stigmatized properties. If there are no state laws, a broker should seek competent legal counsel when dealing with a stigmatized property.

Meth Labs

According to the U.S. Drug Enforcement Administration (DEA), there were 10,064 seizures of methamphetamine labs (meth labs) in 2009. The illegal use of methamphetamine is a major drug threat in the United States. Meth labs can be set up almost anywhere and are often found in private residences, apartments, trailers, automobiles, campgrounds, and hotel and motel rooms.

According to the U.S. Department of Justice, the average meth lab produces five to seven pounds of toxic waste for every pound of meth produced. When a meth lab is found in a home, the site is deemed a toxic waste site. When these chemicals are dumped, contamination of soil and nearby water supplies is possible.

Most property disclosure documents do not specifically ask about the production of methamphetamine or other illegal drugs. A prudent buyer's agent would recommend that the buyer ask the seller to sign a statement that methamphetamine has never been made or used on the property.

Brownfields

A **brownfield site** is real property, for which the expansion, redevelopment, or reuse is complicated by the presence, or potential presence, of a hazardous substance, pollutant, or contaminant. Brownfields include abandoned factories, former dry cleaners, vacant gas stations, illegal drug labs, old dumps, and mine-scarred lands. Unaddressed brownfields will increase the risk of potential environmental hazards, which affect human health, urban sprawl, urban blight, and decreased property values in neighborhoods.

AMP Outline

V.	**Marketing Regulations (purchase and rental)**	2. Do-Not-Call List
		3. CAN-SPAM Act
	B. Licensee Advertising	4. Fair Housing (e.g., blockbusting, steering)
	1. Antitrust	

Real estate brokerage firms advertise their company, their agents, properties for sale and properties for rent. Licensees may also maintain their own websites for self promotion, listed properties and rental properties. State and federal advertising laws must be followed and advertising should not be false, misleading or deceptive in any way.

Agents also need to be aware of the liability of postings on their websites and social media sites. **Defamation** is the act of harming the **reputation of another** by making **false statements** to a third person. When the defamation assertion is expressed in a transitory form, especially **speech,** it is called **slander.** When a defamatory statement expressed in a **fixed medium**, especially writing but also a picture, sign, or electronic broadcast, it is called **libel.**

The following list provides examples of the many types of advertising that are available to agents, but it not intended to be all-inclusive.

Types of Advertising

- Announcements

- Brochures

- Business cards

- e-blasts, e-mail

- Fliers

- Multiple listing service flyers

- Newsletters

- Refrigerator magnets

- Stationary

- Web sites (broker and agent owned)

- Social media sites

- Yard signs

1. ANTITRUST

The Sherman Antitrust Act or state antitrust laws do not allow brokers to price fix, boycott, allocate customers or markets, or have tying agreements; however, brokers or agents can advertise the commission rate that they charge. The following statements should be avoided in conversations and advertisements.

- "The standard commission rate in this area is _____ percent."

- "It's true that XYZ Company charges a flat fee to list properties, but nobody shows their listings."

- "I'd like to lower my commission rate, but the state association has a rule, and I can't."

Commissions are negotiated between the parties and listing agreements should not be preprinted with a commission rate or a certain timeframe.

2. DO-NOT-CALL LIST

The two databases that a licensee should check before making a phone call to solicit business are the database maintained by the Federal Trade Commission (FTC) and brokerage firm database.

- Complaints may be filed with the FTC, the U.S. Justice Department, the state Attorney General's office, or private parties.

- Consumers may bring a private suit where actual damages can be $50,000 or more.

- Civil fine—Up to $11,000 per violation. (Each call is a separate violation.)

- Telemarketers are required to check the do-not-call list every 31 days.

A **telephone solicitation** is defined as a live or recorded communication sent by a telephone; or a message sent by a facsimile machine to a residential, mobile, or telephone paging device or telephone number, including a call made by an automatic dialing or a recorded message device. The telephone solicitation includes calling someone for the purpose of any of the following:

■ Soliciting a sale of consumer goods or services, offering an investment, business, or employment opportunity, or offering a consumer loan to the person called.

■ Obtaining information that will or may be used for the solicitation of a sale of consumer goods or services, the offering of an investment, business, or employment opportunity, or the offering of a consumer loan to the person called.

■ Offering the person called a prize, gift, or anything else of value, if payment of money or other consideration is required in order to receive the prize or gift, including the purchase of other merchandise or services, or the payment of any processing fees, delivery charges, shipping and handling fees, or other fees or charges. It also includes offering the person called a prize, gift, or other incentive to attend a sales presentation for consumer goods or services, an investment or business opportunity, or a consumer loan.

Telemarketers can call for any of the following reasons:

■ There has been a prior or there is an existing business relationship with someone. This exception applies to existing clients and customers and extends for up to 18 months after the end of a transaction. If a consumer makes an inquiry, the telemarketer can call the person for up to three months after the inquiry.

■ There has been an express request from someone to call.

■ There is an existing debt or contract with the company.

■ They are soliciting only donations for charities.

■ They are promoting a political candidate.

■ They are calling a business.

Note that other than the items previously listed, do not call anyone until the Do-Not-Call List has been checked.

■ A licensee may call a For Sale By Owner whose number is on the Do-Not-Call list if a buyer is interested in seeing the property.

■ A licensee may not call a For Sale By Owner whose number is on the Do-Not-Call list to solicit the listing.

■ If a listing has expired, the listing agent and other agents within the brokerage firm may contact the seller for up to 18 months after the expiration date. Agents from other brokerage firms would need to check the Do-Not-Call list, and if the number is on the list, they cannot call.

Do-Not-Fax

The federal Junk Fax Prevention Act of 2005 allows someone to send a fax based on a prior business relationship. The basic requirements are as follows:

- The sender must have an established business relationship with the recipient, or **written consent** from the recipient prior to sending unsolicited advertising faxes.

- The sender must have voluntarily received the recipient's fax number.

- The fax must include an opt-out process to prevent receiving future unsolicited advertising faxes.

- If an opt-out is received, it must be honored within 30 days of receipt.

3. CAN-SPAM ACT

The **Controlling the Assault of Non-Solicited Pornography and Marketing Act** (CAN-SPAM Act) established the guidelines for sending unsolicited e-mails. If an e-mail is commercial in nature, then it must follow these guidelines:

- The header information cannot be false or misleading.

- The subject line cannot be deceptive.

- The message must be identified as an advertisement.

- Your message must include a valid physical postal address.

- A method to opt-out from receiving future emails must be prominent.

- Opt-out requests must be honored within 10 business days. (Opt-out mechanisms must be able to process the opt-out request for at least 30 days after the message is sent.)

- If using a third party to send emails, you must monitor what others are doing on your behalf.

If the email contains transactional or relationship content; that is, it facilitates an already agreed-upon transaction or updates a customer in an existing business relationship, it may not contain false or misleading routing information, but it is otherwise exempt from most of the provisions of the law.

Penalties

- There can be a fine of up to $16,000 for each separate unsolicited e-mail.

- Damages are up to $250 per violation.

- There are treble damages for willful violations.

- A maximum fine of $2 million.

- Punishable by up to five years in prison.

4. FAIR HOUSING (E.G. BLOCKBUSTING, STEERING)

The **Civil Rights Act of 1866** was the first law written to prohibit discrimination based on race. The law reads as follows: "All citizens of the United States shall have the same right in every state and territory as is enjoyed by white citizens thereof to inherit, purchase, lease, sell, hold, and convey real and personal property."

Many state and local laws are more strict than the federal regulation, and a licensee should be aware that failure to comply with these laws is a criminal act and grounds for disciplinary action.

Currently, the federal Fair Housing Act of 1968, as amended, prohibits discrimination based on race, color, religion, sex, national origin, familial status, and disability. Let's define each of these.

Race—An anthropological system of classifying groups of people according to physical characteristics, such as skin color, hair texture, eye shape, or color. The U.S Supreme Court has been generous in its interpretation of race and has allowed the definition to include people who share a common history, language, culture, or ancestry.

Color—This classification occurs because of skin color. The 1896 Supreme Court decision *Plessy v. Ferguson* established the **separate but equal** doctrine that was followed in many parts of the country. Anyone who wasn't white was colored, and the Jim Crow laws allowed separate accommodations for restaurants, water fountains, hotels, waiting rooms, etc.

Jim Crow laws were legal in this country until 1965. Do an Internet search on Jim Crow images and visit *www.JimCrowHistory.org*.

Religion—A system of beliefs and practices relating to the sacred and divine. People of the same religion many times will congregate to the same community or neighborhoods. People always have the right to choose where they want to live based on their financial ability to pay. Real estate licensees cannot steer people into, or out of, communities based on religion or any other protected class.

Sex—The physical characteristics that make a person male or female. Note that the federal Fair Housing laws do not protect someone because of sexual orientation. Some state and local laws offer this protection. Under the Code of Ethics of the National Association of REALTORS®, sexual orientation is a protected class.

National Origin—The country of birth or ancestry. Owners and property managers may ask for an applicant for citizenship or immigration status documentation during the screening process, but only for the purpose of determining lawful entry or work status in the United States. Discrimination against a non-US citizen that is lawfully in this country is illegal.

Familial status—The head of a household (adult) who is responsible for a minor child or children. A minor is a person under the age of 18. This includes protection for a pregnant woman or someone in the process of obtaining custody or adoption.

Landlords cannot refuse to rent to someone with children unless the property is exempt.

Disability—A person is considered disabled if he/she has had a major life activity that has been impaired. This includes a physical or mental impairment, the history of impairment, or being regarded as having an impairment. A person with AIDS is given a protected status, and this information cannot be disclosed in a real estate transaction. People who use illegal drugs or have been convicted of the illegal manufacture or distribution of a controlled substance are not protected under this law.

Landlords must allow a disabled person to make reasonable changes in the property to accommodate the disabled person's needs. For example, a blind person with a service animal would be allowed to keep the animal in the rented space, even if the landlord had a no-pet policy.

A disabled person's has the right to reasonably modify the space at their expense. The landlord has the right to approve the modifications and may insist that the changes be made by qualified contractors. The landlord may also require the tenant to place money in an escrow account to restore the space to its original condition when the tenant moves out.

The **federal Fair Housing Act** regulates the sale or rental of residential dwellings and any vacant land offered for sale for residential construction or use.

The following actions have been found to be discriminatory when they are based on a protected class:

- Refusing to sell, rent, negotiate, or deal with a person, or telling a person that a dwelling is not available for inspection, sale, or rent when it is available

- Changing or misrepresenting the terms or services for buying or leasing housing

- Discriminating through any statement or advertisement that indicates a preference for a certain race, color, sex, familial status, religion, national origin, or disability (See Figure 5.4)

- Blockbusting, or panic peddling, which means inducing owners to sell or rent now because persons of a protected class are moving into the neighborhood

- Steering or channeling, which is directing buyers into or out of certain neighborhoods

- Denying or altering any terms or conditions for a loan to purchase, construct, repair, or improve a dwelling

- Limiting or denying membership in any real estate organization, such as the MLS or any other facilities related to the selling or renting of housing

- Any act considered intimidation or influence by using fear, such as threatening or evicting a tenant who filed a complaint against the management for possible discriminatory acts

- Charging higher rents and higher deposits to families with children

- Deliberately slowing down the processing of a contract to hinder the sale or lease of a property

- Recording racially restrictive covenants in order to prevent a member of a protected class from purchasing or leasing

- Selectively checking the credit of a member of a protected class

- Eviction of tenants because of interracial marriage or religion

- Appraisal reports that state that population transitions are illegal

- Failure to display the equal housing opportunity poster

- Failure to use the Fair Housing logo or slogan in advertising

- Redlining, the practice of lenders refusing to negotiate loans in certain geographic areas, even when the borrower qualifies

There are no exemptions to the Civil Rights Act of 1866, and there are no limits to punitive damages against those found guilty of discrimination because of race. *Jones v. Mayer* is a 1968 Supreme Court case that upheld the Civil Rights Act of 1866.

Exemptions to the Federal Fair Housing Act

The sale or rental of a single-family home is exempt if

- an owner who is not occupying the home has only one sale in 24 months;

- no more than three homes are owned at any one time;

- the services of a broker, or any other person who is engaged in the business of selling or leasing real estate, are not used; and

- no discriminatory advertising is used.

Other exemptions include the following:

- A one-to-four-family dwelling is exempt if the owner occupies one of the units, no discriminatory advertising is used, and no agent is used.

- A nonprofit religious organization can discriminate on a religious basis only. Membership in that religious organization cannot be discriminatory.

- A nonprofit private club may restrict rentals or occupancy of lodgings to members only. Membership in the nonprofit private club, such as the YMCA, cannot be discriminatory.

- Housing is exempt from the familial status rule if one of the two senior housing guidelines are followed: (1) if a building is occupied, or intended to be occupied, solely by persons aged 62 or older, it is exempt; and (2) if 80 percent of the units are occupied by someone 55 years of age or older, the building is exempt.

- The prospective tenant may be rejected if the number of people occupying the rental unit exceeds occupancy codes.

There are many groups of people that the Federal Fair Housing Act does not protect. Examples: Marital status, sexual orientation, age, or illegal alien status.

Review your state and local laws, which may include other protected classes. The term to remember for Fair Housing is **Equal Professional Services** for everyone.

Complaints and Penalties

Complaints of violations of the federal Fair Housing Act may be filed with the Department of Housing and Urban Development (HUD) and taken directly to a federal district court. Complaints of a violation of state or local Fair Housing laws may be filed on a state and/or local level. Action also may be taken by the attorney general of the United States. An aggrieved party or the secretary of HUD must file a complaint within one year of the discriminatory act.

Federal penalties include

- a fine of up to $100,000 and imprisonment for up to one year for failure to attend or provide testimony at a hearing or failure to answer lawful inquiries;

- a fine of up to $16,000 for the first offense, up to $37,500 for the second offense within five years of the filing date of the complaint, and up to $65,000 for the third offense within seven years;

- a fine of up to $1,000 and/or up to one year in jail for intimidation; and

- a fine of up to $10,000 and/or up to 10 years in jail for bodily injury; for death, the penalty can be any jail term up to life.

Affirmative Marketing

An affirmative marketing program is designed to inform all buyers in a minority community of the availability of homes for sale without discrimination. The purpose of affirmative marketing is to encourage the integration of minority groups into housing.

Community Reinvestment Act

The **Community Reinvestment Act** was passed to prevent redlining and disinvestment in central city areas. This act requires that lenders delineate the communities in which their lending activities take place, make available listings of the types of credit they offer in the communities, and make available appropriate notices and information regarding lending activities. It also gives lenders the option to disclose affirmative action programs designed to meet the credit needs of their communities.

	Characteristic	Rule	Permitted	Not Permitted
FIGURE 5.4 **HUD's Advertising Guidelines**	Race Color National Origin	No discriminatory limi- tation/preference may be expressed	"master bedroom" "good neighborhood"	"White neighborhood" "no French"
	Religion	No religious preference/ limitation	"chapel on premises" "kosher meals available" "Merry Christmas"	"no Muslims" "nice Christian family" "near great Catholic school"
	Sex	No explicit preference based on sex	"mother-in-law suite" "master bedroom" "female roommate sought"	"great house for a man" "wife's dream kitchen"
	Disability	No exclusions or limita- tions based on handicap	"wheelchair ramp" "walk to shopping"	"no wheelchairs" "able-bodied tenants only"
	Familial Status	No preference or limita- tion based on family size or nature	"two-bedroom" "family room" "quiet neighborhood"	"married couple only" "no more than two children" "retiree's dream house" "adults only" "Empty Nesters"
	Photographs or Illustrations of People	People should be clearly representative and nonexclusive	Illustrations showing ethnic races, family groups, singles, etc.	Illustrations showing only singles, African American families, elderly white adults, etc.

CHAPTER 5 TEST

1. Before a buyer makes an offer on the property, the buyer should have received and read the
   A. broker policy manual.
   B. property disclosure form.
   C. independent contract agreement.
   D. general warranty deed.

2. Information that is important to buyers that could change their decision to buy a property is
   A. always found in the property disclosure form.
   B. always found during the property inspection.
   C. known as a material fact.
   D. known as a physical defect to the property.

3. A property that has an undesirable reputation because of an event that occurred on or near it is
   A. considered dangerous.
   B. considered polluted.
   C. a stigmatized property.
   D. a physical hazard.

4. The gas that is a produced by the natural decay of radium is
   A. carbon monoxide.
   B. formaldehyde.
   C. mold.
   D. radon.

5. One of the major environmental hazards that can contaminate the underground water supply is
   A. eliminating the use of asbestos in plumbing applications.
   B. encasement of lead-based paint.
   C. legal restriction of the use of PCBs.
   D. leaking underground storage tanks.

6. The environmental issue that would render a property a toxic waste site would be when
   A. mildew was found on a shower curtain.
   B. intact lead-based paint was discovered.
   C. the radon level was 3 pCi/l of air.
   D. the property was used as a meth lab.

7. Hidden defects not easily discovered by inspection are called
   A. patent defects.
   B. fraudulent defects.
   C. latent defects.
   D. observable defects.

8. A residential home that was built in 1951 is currently on the market. By federal law, the buyer should be given the
   A. agency disclosure form.
   B. consumer's guide to agency relationships.
   C. zoning disclosure form.
   D. lead-based paint disclosure form.

9. Directing buyers into or out of certain neighborhoods based on a protected class is the illegal practice of
   A. intimidation.
   B. blockbusting.
   C. steering.
   D. redlining.

10. If a community is occupied solely by persons aged sixty-two or older; or if 80 percent of the units are occupied by someone fifty-five or older, the building is exempt from discrimination based on
    A. race.
    B. sex.
    C. national origin.
    D. familial status.

11. The transaction that would be exempt from the federal Fair Housing laws if the owner did not place a discriminatory ad and the services of a broker were not used is the
    A. sale of a single-family home where the seller does not own more than three homes.
    B. sale or rental of a twenty unit apartment building owned by a real estate agent.
    C. rental of a four bedroom condominium owned by an off-site, sole investor.
    D. sale of a four bedroom condominium owned by four or fewer investors.

12. According to the Civil Rights Act of 1866, discrimination because of race would have a maximum fine of
    A. up to $11,000 for the first offense.
    B. up to $27,500 for the second offense committed within five years.
    C. up to $55,000 for the third offense committed within seven years.
    D. no limit.

13. Which of the following is an environmental hazard associated with leakage near electrical equipment?
    A. Urea formaldehyde
    B. Radon
    C. Polychlorinated biphenyls (PCBs)
    D. Asbestos

14. Which of the following BEST defines blockbusting?
    A. Limiting the number of multi-family units that can be built in a minority neighborhood
    B. Informing owners that minorities are moving into the area and they better sell now
    C. Discriminating against minorities by limiting the neighborhoods in which homes are shown
    D. A lender who refuses to negotiate loans to qualified buyers in minority neighborhoods

15. The federal Fair Housing Act applies to all of the following types of property EXCEPT
    A. one-to-four family property.
    B. residential vacant land sales.
    C. two hundred unit condo community.
    D. commercial and industrial properties.

16. A landlord, who is also an attorney, owns a duplex. One of his tenants moved out, and his ad in the local paper reads: For Rent: 2-bedroom apartment in a duplex. Steep stairs. No children or pets. Is the ad legal?
    A. Yes, because he is an attorney, and he does not have to follow fair housing guidelines.
    B. Yes, because the property has steep stairs, he is protecting children, and that is legal.
    C. No, because a duplex is exempted from the fair housing laws.
    D. No, because children can only be excluded if the property meets the guidelines for the elderly.

17. To install a septic tank, a person would have to conduct a
    A. hydroponics test.
    B. percolation test.
    C. septic soil test.
    D. topography test.

18. The lead-based paint disclosure form must be given to potential buyers and tenants when the property was built before
    A. 1956.
    B. 1968.
    C. 1976.
    D. 1978.

19. Potential buyers have written an offer on a property that falls under the guidelines for lead-based paint disclosures. If the buyers want to have the property inspected, how many days do they have to conduct a lead-based paint inspection?
    A. 5
    B. 10
    C. 12
    D. 15

20. Which of the following statements is FALSE regarding the federal lead-based paint disclosure law?
    A. Tenants have ten days to inspect for lead-based paint before the lease agreement is binding.
    B. Buyers may waive their rights to have the property inspected for lead-based paint.
    C. Buyers and tenants have the right to any prior inspection records and reports.
    D. Federal law requires that disclosures be kept for three years.

21. All of the following would be except from the federal lead-based paint disclosure laws EXCEPT
    A. the rental of units in an apartment building constructed in 1951.
    B. a two-week vacation lease in a building constructed in 1977.
    C. the sale of units in a senior citizens community constructed in 1960.
    D. a property sold at a foreclosure sale that was constructed in 1975.

22. Which of the following parties is NOT responsible for giving the *Protect Your Family From Lead in Your Home* document to potential buyers and tenants?
    A. Seller
    B. Landlord
    C. Real Estate Agent
    D. Settlement Agent

23. According to the EPA, approximately how many homes in the United States have elevated radon levels?
    A. 1 out of 4
    B. 1 out of 10
    C. 1 out of 15
    D. 1 out of 20

24. The two major sources of radon entry into a building are
    A. basement and roof.
    B. air and water.
    C. pets and people.
    D. computers and cell phones.

25. The EPA recommends that every building home be tested for radon. The EPA Action Level for mitigation is
    A. 1 pCi/L.
    B. 2 pCi/L.
    C. 4 pCi/L.
    D. 10 pCi/L.

26. Any materials that contain more than 1 percent asbestos and that will crumble by hand pressure when dry are known as
    A. friable ACMs.
    B. non-friable ACMs.
    C. water resistance ACMS.
    D. high electrical conductivity ACMS.

27. A homeowner had a problem with water leaking into the basement. Estimates to repair the leak ranged between $15,000 to $20,000. The owner couldn't afford the repairs, so he constructed a false floor over the entire basement. Next, he installed carpet over the false floor. When he listed the house, he did not disclose the leak nor the false floor on the property disclosure form. This is an example of a
    A. patent defect, and the agent may be liable for not discovering the false floor.
    B. patent defect, and the agent is not liable for not discovering the false floor.
    C. latent defect, and the agent may be liable for not discovering the false floor.
    D. latent defect, and the agent is not liable for not discovering the false floor.

28. The level of airplane noise in the neighborhood or possible environmental issues in surrounding properties would be BEST classified as
    A. material defects.
    B. material facts.
    C. material information.
    D. material breach.

29. Abandoned factories, former dry cleaners, and vacant gas stations that may contain environmental hazards are classified as
    A. brownfields.
    B. green fields.
    C. wetlands.
    D. priority list sites.

30. Telemarketers are required to check the do-not-call list every
    A. 7 days.
    B. 14 days.
    C. 31 days.
    D. 60 days.

31. A licensee should check which of the following databases before making phone calls to solicit a listing?
    A. Google and Microsoft databases
    B. Antitrust and fair housing databases
    C. Real estate commission and REALTOR® databases
    D. Federal Trade Commission and brokerage firm databases

32. A listing has expired. How many months may the agents in the listing office call a seller who is on the do-not-call list?
    A. 12 months
    B. 18 months
    C. 24 months
    D. 36 months

33. Which of the following statements is FALSE in regards to the do-not-call laws?
    A. A licensee may call a FSBO whose number is on the do-not-call list if he/she has a buyer interested in seeing the property.
    B. A licensee may not call a FSBO whose number is on the do-not-call list to solicit the listing.
    C. When a listing has expired, only agents from the brokerage firm who listed the property may call the owner for the timeline allowed by law.
    D. When a consumer calls an agent to request information about a listed property, the agent may call the potential buyer at any time in the future.

34. The Can-Spam Act established guidelines for sending
    A. solicited facsimiles.
    B. unsolicited facsimiles.
    C. solicited e-mail.
    D. unsolicited e-mail.

35. A commercial email must include an opt-out method. Which of the following statements is FALSE regarding the opt-out requirements?
    A. The words opt-out must be easily seen by the sender of the email.
    B. Requests to opt-out must be honored within 10 business days.
    C. The receiver must be able to opt-out for at least 30 days after the message is sent.
    D. The email must contain the words opt-out prominently in the email.

36. In regards to property defects, compensatory damages are defined as
    A. actual damages for the repair of the defect.
    B. damages to punish the person who did not disclose.
    C. incidental damages that occur in every real estate transaction.
    D. special damages because of the inconvenience to the party.

37. Which of the following is NOT a member of the protected classes under the federal fair housing laws?
    A. Familial status
    B. National origin
    C. Sex
    D. Marital status

38. A lender refuses to negotiate a loan with a qualified borrower because the property is located in a geographic area that the lender considers high-risk. The lender is guilty of
    A. disintermediation.
    B. disobeying usury laws.
    C. redlining.
    D. steering.

39. All of the following actions are legal EXCEPT
    A. a broker who displays the Equal Housing Poster in the main office.
    B. an appraisal report stating the racial composition of the neighborhood.
    C. refusing to add a racially restrictive deed covenant to a deed.
    D. discussing with homeowners the importance of the Fair Housing laws.

40. Which of the following is FALSE in regards to fair housing penalties?
    A. There can be a fine for the first offense of up to $16,000.
    B. There can be a fine of up to $1,000 for intimidation.
    C. The maximum fine for racial discrimination is $65,000.
    D. There can be a fine of up to $100,000 for failure to attend a hearing.

41. All of the following types of properties are EXEMPT from the federal Fair Housing laws EXCEPT
    A. a one-to-four family dwelling that is owner-occupied, no discriminatory advertising is used, and the services of a brokerage or agent are not used.
    B. a non-profit religious organization can restrict residential facilities to persons of that religion as long as membership in the religion is not discriminatory.
    C. an owner-occupied single family home that uses the services of a broker and that asks an agent not to sell the property to a buyer of a certain religion.
    D. a non-profit private club that may discriminate and refuse to allow someone who is not a member to reside in a residence.

42. All of the following terms would be allowed in the advertisement of a property EXCEPT
    A. master bedroom.
    B. kosher meals available.
    C. retiree's dream home.
    D. mother-in-law suite.

43. Which of the following advertisements would be legal under the antitrust laws?
    A. "We charge the same as everyone else—6 percent commission—but our service is priceless!"
    B. "List with us! We're a traditional real estate firm and other traditional brokers show our listings!"
    C. "We're having a sale! List with us between now and April 30th and the commission rate is only 4.5 percent!"
    D. "You get what you pay for! Flat fee companies don't work as hard as we do! We're worth our standard 7 percent fee!"

44. Lead poisoning is a danger to
    A. children.
    B. pregnant women.
    C. seniors.
    D. everyone.

45. The environmental hazard that people need to be aware of when burning fuels, such as wood, oil, and natural gas without proper ventilation is
    A. mold.
    B. carbon monoxide.
    C. radon.
    D. urca formaldehyde.

46. The federal law that taxed the petroleum industry and created a national inventory of hazardous waste sites is
    A. CERCLA.
    B. SARA
    C. TSCA.
    D. CWA.

47. A person owned a dry cleaning business from 1960 to 1979. He, like other dry cleaners in the area, dumped perchloroethylene (PERC) on to the ground in the backyard of the building. If the previous owner is named as a potentially responsible party, his liability will MOST LIKELY be classified as
    A. joint and several liability.
    B. retroactive liability.
    C. strict liability.
    D. individual liability.

48. The purpose of an Environmental Site Assessment is to
    A. identify potentially responsible parties for past environmental issues.
    B. determine appropriate and reasonable solutions for environmental issues.
    C. collect and analyze samples of soil and water to test for environmental issues.
    D. identify potential or existing environmental issues.

49. While inspecting a property, the inspector pointed to a twelve-inch crack that started at the corner of a window and moved in a somewhat vertical direction down the wall. The crack is an example of a(n)
    A. latent defect.
    B. patent defect.
    C. structural defect.
    D. environmental defect.

50. According to the Department of Justice, the average meth lab will produce how many pounds of toxic waste for every pound of meth that is produced?
    A. One to two
    B. Three to four
    C. Five to seven
    D. Seven to nine

51. Under the federal do-not-call law, the civil fine for each violation can be up to
    A. $1,000.
    B. $5,000.
    C. $11,000.
    D. $25,000.

52. A licensee sent out a broadcast fax to announce a reduced price on a listed property. A person who received the fax chose to opt-out from receiving additional faxes from the licensee. The opt-out request must be honored within
    A. seven days.
    B. ten days.
    C. fourteen days.
    D. thirty days.

53. Under the Can-Spam Act, the fine for sending an unsolicited email can be up to
    A. $1,000.
    B. $5,000.
    C. $10,500.
    D. $16,000

54. The 1896 Supreme Court case that established the separate but equal doctrine that was practiced in many parts of this country was
    A. *Plessy v. Ferguson.*
    B. *Jones v. Mayer.*
    C. *Dred Scott v. Sandford.*
    D. *Shelley v. Kraemer*

55. A landlord has a no-kids policy. This is legal if
    A. the building is an owner-occupied, one-to-four family unit.
    B. it applies to all pregnant women.
    C. everyone living in the apartments is at least sixty-two years of age.
    D. the landlord also has a no pet policy.

56. All of the following terms would be illegal in an advertisement EXCEPT
    A. Adults Only.
    B. Empty Nesters.
    C. Married Couple.
    D. Wheelchair Ramp.

57. A foreign student is in the United States to study at a university. When filling out an application to rent an apartment, the landlord asks for documentation to determine his citizenship and/or immigration status. Is this action legal?
    A. Yes, because landlords may ask for citizenship and/or immigration status documentation during the screening process if HUD guidelines are met.
    B. Yes, because the Uniform Landlord Tenant Act requires prospective tenants to provide citizenship and/or immigration documentation.
    C. No, because foreign students would fall into a protected class based on national origin.
    D. No, because it is illegal for a foreign student to be asked to show citizenship and/or immigration status documentation.

58. A person with a physical disability has found an apartment that must be remodeled to accommodate her needs. Which of the following actions would be illegal for the landlord to require?
    A. Because she is disabled, she will be required to pay a larger security deposit than other tenants.
    B. The landlord can review the renovation plans and require qualified contractors to perform the work.
    C. Money must be placed in an escrow account to return the apartment to its original condition when she moves out.
    D. The landlord can require the tenant to pay for all the renovations.

59. The landlord would have the right to evict all of the following tenants EXCEPT
    A. a tenant who is late with the rent payment.
    B. a tenant who has revealed that he/she has AIDS.
    C. a tenant who disturbs other tenants.
    D. a tenant who uses the property for an illegal purpose.

60. A lender has the right to deny lending money to a minority applicant when the applicant
    A. applies in geographic locations that are not acceptable to the lender.
    B. does not financially qualify to purchase the property.
    C. agrees to let the lender alters the terms of the loan.
    D. agrees to pay a higher interest rate.

61. As of April 2010, contractors performing renovation, repair, and painting projects that disturb lead-based paint in homes, child care facilities, and schools built before 1978 must be certified by the
    A. Federal Lead-Based Paint Commission.
    B. state Lead-Based Paint Commission.
    C. Environmental Protection Agency.
    D. Brownfield Prevention Agency.

62. A family going on a two-week vacation turned off their air conditioning unit even though it was predicted to be a very hot July. While they were gone, the washing machine water hose burst and spewed water in the basement for several days. The environmental issue that the owners will MOST LIKELY discover when they return home is
    A. radon.
    B. formaldehyde.
    C. polychlorinated biphenyls.
    D. mold.

63. When an agent has the owner complete a seller's property disclosure form and provides it to the buyer in a timely manner, the agent is BEST protecting the liability of the
    A. buyer.
    B. broker.
    C. ender.
    D. seller.

64. A buyer is purchasing a new home in a subdivision. Which document should the buyer confirm has been issued before he moves in?
    A. Certificate of no defense
    B. Certificate of occupancy
    C. Building certificate
    D. Code certificate

65. Before constructing an addition to an existing building, a person should secure a
    A. building permit.
    B. business license.
    C. building loan.
    D. building contractor.

66. While looking at a property, the potential buyers asked, "Is that fence the boundary line?" The agent should recommend that the buyers
    A. read the legal description.
    B. ask the owners.
    C. have a stake survey.
    D. ask the neighbors.

67. The act of harming the reputation of another by making false statements to a third person is known as
    A. misrepresentation.
    B. fraud.
    C. deception.
    D. defamation.

68. When the defamatory statement is expressed orally, it is called
    A. lying.
    B. fraud.
    C. libel.
    D. slander.

69. When a defamatory statement is expressed in a fixed medium, such as on online post, it is called
    A. intentional misrepresentation.
    B. negligent misrepresentation.
    C. libel.
    D. slander.

70. Potential tenants have how many days to have the property inspected for lead-based paint before the lease becomes effective?
    A. 0
    B. 5
    C. 10
    D. 12

MATCHING QUIZ

The column on the right contains a brief definition of important terms in this section. Write the letter of the matching term on the appropriate line.

A. 1978

B. Radon

C. Friable ACMs

D. ESA

E. Certificate of Occupancy

F. Material Fact

G. Stigmatized Property

H. Brownfields

I. Blockbusting

J. 4 pCi/L

K. Redlining

L. Steering

M. CERCLA

N. Civil Rights Act of 1866

O. $16,000

P. 18 months

Q. 10 days

R. 3 years

S. Building Code

T. PCBs

1. _____ This is the EPA action level for the mitigation of radon.

2. _____ This federal law taxed the petroleum industry and created a national inventory of hazardous waste sites.

3. _____ Inducing owners to sell or rent now because a minority is moving into the neighborhood.

4. _____ Housing built prior to this year may contain lead-based paint.

5. _____ An illegal act of a lender refusing to negotiate a loan of the geographic location of the property.

6. _____ Environmental Site Assessment to identify potential or existing environmental problems.

7. _____ Directing buyers into or out of neighborhoods based on a protected class.

8. _____ The federal law that makes it illegal to discriminate because of race in a real estate transaction.

9. _____ A radioactive gas that is produced by the natural decay of radium.

10. _____ The Can-Spam Act allows a fine of up to this amount for sending unsolicited e-mail.

11. _____ The timeframe that the Do-Not-Call laws allow a licensee of the listing brokerage firm to call a previous client.

12. _____ The law requires Cradle to Grave management of this substance.

13. _____ This code sets a minimum standard for construction.

14. _____ Issued when construction meets code.

15. _____ A property that is undesirable because of an event that has occurred there or in a surrounding property.

16. _____ The timeframe that the Can-Spam laws requires that an opt-out request to be honored.

17. _____ Any material that contains more than 1 percent asbestos and will crumble when dry.

18. _____ Abandoned factories, former dry cleaners, and vacant gas stations are examples of these types of properties.

19. _____ The timeframe that the lead-based paint disclosure form must be kept.

20. _____ Information that if known, could change the decision of the party.

CHAPTER 5 TEST ANSWERS

1. **(B)** The buyer should receive and read a property disclosure statement before making an offer on the property.

2. **(C)** Information that could change a party's decision is a material fact.

3. **(C)** A property has an undesirable reputation because of an event that has occurred on or near it is considered stigmatized.

4. **(D)** The gas that is produced by the natural decay of radium is radon.

5. **(D)** Leaking underground storage tanks are one of the major environmental hazards that could contaminate the underground water supply.

6. **(D)** When a property is used for a meth lab, it is considered a toxic waste site.

7. **(C)** Latent defects are hidden defects.

8. **(D)** If a buyer is purchasing a property built prior to 1978, the buyer should receive the lead-based paint disclosure form. Agency disclosures are a matter of state law.

9. **(C)** Steering is the illegal practice of directing buyers into or out of neighborhoods.

10. **(D)** A community designed for occupancy where 100 percent of the people living there are sixty two years of age or older, or 80 percent of the units are occupied by someone fifty-five or older would be exempt of the familial status class.

11. **(A)** The sale or rental of a single-family home when fewer than three homes are owned, no discrimination is used in advertising, and the services of a broker are not used, is exempt.

12. **(D)** There is no limit to the maximum fine for discrimination because of race.

13. **(C)** PCBs can be found in electrical equipment.

14. **(B)** Blockbusting occurs when a licensee informs owners that minorities are moving into the neighborhood and they better sell now.

15. **(D)** Fair housing laws apply to any residential property and vacant land that will be used for residential purposes. It does not apply to commercial or industrial properties.

16. **(D)** Only housing that meets the requirements of the designation of housing for the elderly can exclude children. (The ad would probably read Adult Community.)

17. **(B)** The purpose of the percolation test is to determine how quickly the ground will absorb water, and the perk test would be conducted to determine if a septic tank could be installed.

18. **(D)** The lead-based paint disclosure form must be given to potential buyers and tenants if the property was built before 1978.

19. **(B)** The potential buyers have ten days to have the lead-based paint inspection.

20. **(A)** Under the law, tenants are not given ten days to inspect for lead-based paint. Only the buyer is given that right.

21. **(A)** The typical apartment lease is not exempt from the lead-based laws. Leases for less than 100 days, housing for seniors, dormitories, and properties sold at foreclosure are exempt.

22. **(D)** The settlement agent is not responsible for giving the document *Protect Your Family From Lead in Your Home*. Sellers, landlords, and real estate agents involved in the transaction are responsible for providing the document.

23. **(C)** Approximately 1 out of 15 homes in the United States has elevated radon levels.

24. **(B)** The two major sources of radon entry into a home are air and water.

25. **(C)** The EPA Action Level for mitigation is 4 pCi/L. (4 picocuries per liter of air)

26. **(A)** When asbestos-containing materials that contain more than 1 percent asbestos, and that when dry will crumble, is called friable.

27. **(D)** It is a latent defect, and agents are not liable for the discovery and disclosure of latent defects.

28. **(B)** A material fact is information that if known that would change the decision of the party. Materials facts may or may not involve the structure of the property. Stigmatized property, airplane noise, and environmental issues in surrounding properties may be material facts to some buyers.

29. **(A)** Brownfield sites include any properties that are abandoned, which may be environmental hazards.

30. **(C)** Telemarketers are required to check the do-not-call list every 31 days.

31. **(D)** A licensee should check the FTC and brokerage firm databases for numbers on the do-not-call list.

32. **(B)** If there has been a prior, or there is an existing business relationship with someone whose number is on the do-not-call list, agents working for the listing brokerage firm may call for up to 18 months after the transaction.

33. **(D)** Agents may call consumers who make an inquiry for up to 3 months after the inquiry.

34. **(D)** The Can-Spam laws establish guidelines for sending unsolicited e-mail.

35. **(A)** The opt-out must be seen by the receiver, not the sender of the e-mail.

36. **(A)** Compensatory damages would be monetary payment for the repair of the defect.

37. **(D)** Federal fair housing law prohibits discrimination based on race, color, religion, sex, national origin, familial status, and disability. It does not include marital status, age, or sexual orientation. State or local laws may include those and others as members of a protected class.

38. **(C)** Redlining is the practice of lenders who refuse to make loans in certain geographic areas, even when the borrower qualifies for the loan.

39. **(B)** Appraisal reports cannot contain the racial composition of the neighborhood.

40. **(C)** There is no limit to the fine for discrimination because of race.

41. **(C)** The owner of a single family home cannot discriminate on the basis of religion.

42. **(C)** The term *retiree's dream home* is advertising for a particular person and not the property.

43. **(C)** It is acceptable to advertise your commission rate.

44. **(D)** Lead poisoning is a danger to every person, but it is especially dangerous to children and pregnant women.

45. **(B)** When burning fuels such as wood, oil, and natural gas, there needs to be proper ventilation because of carbon monoxide.

46. **(A)** CERCLA or the Comprehensive Environmental Response, Compensation and Liability Act taxed the petroleum industry. It is known as the Superfund. An amendment to the act was the Superfund Amendments and Reauthorization Act (SARA). TSCA stands for the Toxic Substances Control Act, which regulates PCBs. CWA represents the Clean Water Act.

47. **(C)** The previous owner's liability would MOST LIKELY be classified as strict liability. He would still be liable for acts committed before CERCLA was enacted.

48. **(D)** The purpose of an Environment Site Assessment (ESA) is to identify potential or existing environmental liabilities.

49. **(B)** Patent defects are easily visible when inspecting the property.

50. **(C)** The average meth lab will create five to seven pounds of toxic waste for every pound of meth produced.

51. **(C)** Under the federal do-not-call laws, the fine can be up to $11,000 for each violation.

52. **(D)** When someone chooses to opt-out of receiving additional faxes, the request must be honored within 30 days.

53. **(D)** Under the Can-Spam Act the fine can be up to $16,000 for sending an unsolicited email.

54. **(A)** *Plessy v. Ferguson* is the Supreme Court case that established the *separate but equal doctrine* that was followed in many parts of the country until the mid 1960s.

55. **(C)** If a community is designed for seniors and everyone living there is sixty-two years of age or older, or 80 percent of the people living there are fifty-five or older, the community is exempt and children are not allowed to live there.

56. **(D)** An advertisement may describe the property and wheelchair ramp is a property description. The other terms describe people, not property.

57. **(A)** Landlords may ask for citizenship and/or immigration status documentation during the screening process if HUD guidelines are met.

58. **(A)** Landlords cannot require a disabled tenant to pay a larger security deposit than other tenants.

59. **(B)** The landlord would not be able to evict a tenant because the tenant has AIDS, nor can a landlord refuse to rent to a qualified tenant who has AIDS.

60. **(B)** Any lender has the right to deny negotiating a loan with someone who does not financially qualify.

61. **(C)** Contractors performing renovation, repair, and painting projects that disturb lead-based paint in homes, child care facilities, and schools built before 1978 must be certified by the EPA.

62. **(D)** Excess moisture that is not cleaned up immediately can create a mold issue.

63. **(B)** When the licensee has the seller complete the property disclosure form and it is given to the buyer in a timely manner, the licensee is reducing the liability of the broker because the laws have been followed.

64. **(B)** A certificate of occupancy should be issued when a buyer is purchasing a new home.

65. **(A)** When constructing an addition or adding onto an existing building, or when demolishing a building, a person should secure a building permit.

66. **(C)** To determine the exact boundaries of a property, the licensee should recommend the buyers have a stake survey.

67. **(D)** The act of harming the reputation of another by making a false statement to a third person is known as defamation.

68. **(D)** When the defamation assertion is expressed in a transitory form, especially speech, it is called slander.

69. **(C)** When the defamation assertion is expressed in a fixed form, it is called libel.

70. **(A)** Tenants do not have any days to conduct a lead-based paint inspection, but they must be given the lead-based paint pamphlet and full disclosure.

ANSWERS—MATCHING QUIZ

1. **J**	6. **D**	11. **P**	16. **Q**
2. **M**	7. **L**	12. **T**	17. **C**
3. **I**	8. **N**	13. **S**	18. **H**
4. **A**	9. **B**	14. **E**	19. **R**
5. **K**	10. **0**	15. **G**	20. **F**

CHAPTER 6

Property Management

AMP Outline

A. GENERAL PRINCIPLES OF PROPERTY MANAGEMENT AGREEMENTS

An owner can manager his own property without a license. In most states, an owner can hire an employee who does not have a real estate license to manage the property of the owner. Review your state laws to determine under what circumstances a person would need a license to manage property for others. A property management agreement is a **personal service contract**, which means it is terminated upon the death of either party.

The owner may also enter into a contract with a brokerage firm to manage property. If the brokerage firm is hired to manage the property, an agent for the brokerage may be the property manager. A written management agreement between the owner and the brokerage stipulates whether payment is to be on a flat-fee basis or a percentage of the gross income.

Whichever relationship or method of payment is negotiated, the brokerage firm and property manager have a fiduciary relationship with the owner. The property manager would be the general agent of the owner, meaning the manager is involved in an on-going business relationship and can enter into contracts on behalf of the owner.

The property manager has a fiduciary relationship with the owner, which includes the duties of care, obedience, accounting, loyalty, and disclosure.

- The *duty of care* means to use care and skill while managing the property, binding the owner to contracts, and being responsible in every way to the owner.

- The *duty of obedience* means to carry out, in good faith, the owner's instructions. The property manager should immediately terminate the relationship if asked to do something illegal or unethical.

- The *duty of accounting* means to maintain and accurately report to the owner the status of all funds received on behalf of, or from, the property owner.

- The *duty of loyalty* means to put the property owner's interests first and act without self-interest in every transaction.

- The *duty of disclosure* means to keep the owner informed of all material facts regarding the management of the property.

Property managers may specialize in a particular type of property, such as condominium communities, apartment buildings, warehouses, factories, industrial parks, hotels, office buildings, and so on.

B. BASIC PROVISIONS/PURPOSE/ ELEMENTS OF PROPERTY MANAGEMENT AGREEMENTS

There is a difference between a management plan and a management agreement. The property manager will be responsible for creating a **management plan** that meets the owner's objectives, a budget of projected revenues and expenses, and occupancy and absorption rates.

The **management agreement** is negotiated between the owner and the brokerage/ property manager, and it creates an agency relationship with fiduciary duties to the owner.

If a brokerage firm is hired to manage property, the broker may hire an agent to manage the property. The agreement is between the brokerage firm and the owner, not the agent and the owner.

States may have specific laws regarding such agreements; but generally, the following must be included to establish the scope of the agent's authority:

- Identification of the parties

- Identification of the property, which may include a legal description

- Statement of owner's purpose

- Duties and responsibilities of the manager

- Responsibilities of the owner

- Rate and schedule of compensation

- Accounting and report requirements

- Starting date, termination date, and provisions for renewal options

- Amount and method of determining the minimum security deposit to be collected from the tenants for each unit managed

- Procedure for returning or retaining the security deposit

- Provision setting forth the conditions under which the manager is authorized to pay expenses of the property being managed and any other authority given to the manager

- Copy of the lease that will be used

- Antitrust provisions

- Fair housing provisions

- Signatures of the parties

The property manager will develop an operating budget, cash flow report, profit and loss statement, and budget comparison statement.

Operating Budget

An operating budget is based on the anticipated revenues and expenses. When the property manager develops the budget, it must reflect the owner's long-term goals. The budget will allocate money for continuous, fixed expenses, such as employees' salaries, property taxes, and insurance. It will also establish a cash reserve fund for variable expenses, such as repairs and supplies.

Cash Flow Formula

Most owners require that the property manager create a monthly report of income and expenses.

	Potential gross rental income*
+	Additional income (vending equipment, parking garage fees, etc.)
−	Vacancy rates and credit losses
	Effective gross income

* The gross income of an apartment complex may be based on the room count of the space, whereas commercial properties may be computed by the square footage of the space.

The following also may be used to compute the effective gross income. They are different from the above steps.

	Potential gross income
−	Vacancy rates and credit losses
+	Additional income
	Effective gross income

Effective gross income
– Operating expenses
Net operating income before debt service (Debt service is the mortgage payment.)

Net operating income before debt service
– Debt service
Cash flow (also known as before-tax cash flow)

Cash flow
– Taxes
After-tax cash flow

The return on investment (ROI) is one way to measure the profitability of a property. The ROI is the ratio of the property's after-tax cash flow (ATCF) to the money invested (equity [E]) in the property.

The formula for computing the return on investment is

$$ROI = \frac{AFCF}{E} \times 100\%$$

The ROI also may be computed on a before-tax basis.

A property with a $10,000 ATCF in which the owner has $100,000 invested would have an ROI of 10 percent. When this formula is used to analyze the owner's investment, it is called a cash-on-cash investment, and it may be computed on either a before-tax or an after-tax basis.

Profit and Loss Statement

Quarterly, semiannual, or annual profit and loss statements are compiled from the monthly cash flow reports. From this, the owner can analyze how the property was managed, decide what changes should be made, and make projections for the next year.

Only the interest portion of each mortgage payment should be deducted as an expense on the profit and loss statement; whereas on the monthly reports, the entire debt service is used.

The following is an example of a profit and loss statement:

Profit and Loss Statement

Period: January 1, XXXX, to December 31, XXXX

Receipts	$198,948.43
Operating Expenses	– 74,343.89
Operating Income	$124,604.54
Total Mortgage Payment	– 54,567.89
Mortgage Loan Principal Add-Back	+ 6,493.20
Net Profit	$ 76,529.85

The profit and loss statement may be compared with the operating budget that was prepared for the year. Such a comparison can measure the performance of the property manager and determine the changes that will need to be made in the future.

Budget Comparison Statement

The purpose of the budget comparison is to compare the actual income and expenses with the projected budget.

C. TYPES OF CONTRACTS

The tenant may be represented by an attorney when negotiating the lease agreement, or the property manager may act as the owner's agent, the lessee's agent, or a dual agent.

Unless the property manager is also an attorney, the property manager may only fill in the blanks of lease agreements; they may not write them. When the lease is negotiated between the owner and the tenant, a bilateral contract is created, and exclusive possession is given to the tenant. It is the owner's responsibility to provide the lease agreement that is to be used by the property manager.

Whether leasing residential, commercial, or industrial property, qualifying the tenant is one of the major responsibilities of the property manager. Filling out a lease application that may ask for verification of identity, authorization to secure a credit report, financial statement, special needs of the tenant, and securing rental history is a part of the process.

The lease negotiations could include concessions, such as free rent to influence a prospect to become a tenant, rent reductions and rebates, length of the lease period, tenant alterations, expansion options, noncompeting tenant restrictions, and lease buy-out, assumption, and subletting.

The provisions of a valid lease are essentially the same as for any valid contract. There must be an offer and acceptance by parties with the legal capacity to contract. The terms of a lease include

- names and addresses of the parties,
- description of the property,
- term of the lease,
- security deposit (amount and location of the deposit),
- possession and use of the premises,
- rights and obligation of the parties,
- consideration (when and to whom rent payments are made),
- late payments,
- payment of utilities and appliances,
- provisions for assignment and sublease,
- provisions for maintenance and condition,
- pets and alterations,
- loss of damage,
- default,
- lead-based paint disclosure,
- default and termination provisions,
- warranty of quiet enjoyment,
- warranty of habitability,
- surrender, and
- signatures of the parties.

Types of Leases

Estate for Years or Tenancy for Years

- A lease with a definite time period or specified beginning and ending dates.
- No notice is needed to terminate the estate.
- A tenant who remains in possession after expiration is considered a holdover.

Estate from Period to Period/Estate from Year to Year/Periodic Tenancy

- A lease with an indefinite time period that automatically renews until proper notice to terminate is given.

Estate at Will or Tenancy at Will

- A lease that gives the tenant the right to possess the property with the consent of the landlord for an uncertain time period. The lease can be terminated at any time by the landlord, or by the tenant giving proper notice to the other party.

- Death of either party also terminates the lease.

Estate at Sufferance or Tenancy at Sufferance

- A tenancy created when a tenant remains in possession of the property without the consent of the landlord after the lease expires.

- If the landlord gives permission to a tenant to remain on the property after the expiration of a lease, the tenant may be treated as a holdover, and a tenancy at will or periodic tenancy may be created.

Termination of Leases

Abandonment by the tenant—When the tenant abandons the lease, the tenant is still liable for the terms of the lease. In a residential lease, the landlord is responsible for mitigating damages by attempting to find another tenant in a timely manner.

Death of one of the parties—Unless the lease agreement specifies that the lease is terminated when the landlord or tenant passes, the lease agreement is still binding and effective. (Mortgages, credit cards, and other contracts the deceased person entered into are also binding. They become a part of the estate settlement.) Exceptions to this rule include the following:

- When the owner of a life estate passes, all lease agreements the life tenant may have entered into are terminated.

- The death of either party will terminate a tenancy at will.

Destruction of the premises—The lease agreement should specify the status of the lease when the premises are destroyed. In a residential lease, most state laws will terminate the lease upon the destruction of the premises. Many commercial leases are binding upon the destruction of the premises.

Fulfillment of the terms—A lease is terminated when the parties have fulfilled the obligations of the lease.

Merger—If the tenant purchases the property, the lease agreement is terminated.

Mutual agreement—The landlord and tenant may mutually agree to terminate the lease.

Operation of law—Bankruptcy of either party or the process condemnation will terminate a lease agreement. Condemnation can mean the property is found uninhabitable, or the government is taking it through eminent domain.

Sale of the property—The sale of the property does not terminate a residential lease agreement, and the new owner would need to honor the existing leases. Many commercial leases do terminate upon the sale of the property, and the commercial lease should address that issue. If the new owner has the right to terminate the lease, a sale clause will be found in the lease, which gives the tenant some time-frame before the lease is terminated.

See pages 50–52 for a review of additional types of lease agreements.

D. DUTIES AND OBLIGATIONS OF THE PARTIES

The property management and lease agreements will stipulate the specific duties and responsibilities of each party. The following is a summary of the primary duties of each party.

Owner's Duties

- Provide specific goals and objectives to the property manager.

- Provide the lease agreement to the property manager.

- Keep the property safe and habitable. This includes snow and ice removal, adequate lighting in parking lots and hallways, working sprinkler systems, smoke detectors, etc. Comply with health and building codes. Follow federal, state and local laws.

- Give reasonable notice to inspect, make repairs for improvements, and to enter the property.

- If a residential tenant abandons the property before the lease expires, the owner must make reasonable efforts to rent the abandoned space.

- Set up a trust or escrow account for security deposits. Note that some states prohibit security deposits from being commingled with earnest money deposits.

- Set up a business account for other monies.

- Maintain proper insurance on the property.

- Provide lead-based paint disclosures and reports to tenants.

- Follow eviction laws.

- Unless paid by the tenant, the owner must pay property taxes, special assessments, and utilities.

- Provide the tenant with building rules and other laws that must to be followed. (This will be a part of the lease agreement.)

- Notify the tenant of the location of the security deposit and the terms for its return. (This will be a part of the lease agreement.)

Property Manager's Duties

- Meet the goals and objectives of the owner by generating the highest net operating income while maintaining the property.

- Develop a management plan, operating budget, profit and loss statement, cash flow reports, and budget comparison reports.

- Analyze rental rates, screen and select qualified tenants, collect the rent, and evict tenants.

- Market and advertise the property. Comply with all advertising and fair housing laws.

- Maintain good relations with the tenant.

- Maintain the property by hiring qualified contractors to make repairs.

- Evaluate risk management and make recommendations to the owner.

- Comply with federal, state, and local laws; such as providing the lead-based paint disclosures and being in compliance with the Americans with Disabilities Act.

- Be aware of environmental issues and comply with laws.

- Be accountable for money, employees, and service contracts.

- Hire, supervise, and discharge employees and contractors.

- Enter into contracts with service providers on behalf of the owner (phone, electricity, water, trash removal, etc.).

Tenant Duties

- Read the lease agreement to ensure compliance and understanding of the terms.

- Use the property for legal purposes and keep the property in a habitable condition.

- Pay the full rent due in a timely manner.

- The tenant may not use the property in any way that interferes with the rights of neighbors or other tenants.

- The tenant may not alter the property unless it is allowed within the terms of the lease agreement.

- The tenant agrees to obey federal, state, and local laws in regards to the use of the property.

- Notify the owner or property manager of needed repairs.

- Give proper notice when moving. Proper notice is determined by state law or the terms of the lease. Generally, in a residential lease, proper notice is the timeframe when the rent is paid. If rent is paid every 30 days, then 30 days' notice would be required. If rent is paid every two weeks, then two weeks' notice would be required.

E. MARKET ANALYSIS AND TENANT ACQUISITION

A property manager can choose from a range of advertising media to reach a target audience. This could include placing a sign on the property identifying the management firm and the person to call for further information; as well as flyers, newspaper advertising, regional magazines and trade journals, radio, television, direct mail and brochures, and Internet sites.

The first step in the development of a marketing plan is to determine if there is a low or high vacancy rate in the area for the type of property being leased. If there is a high vacancy rate, attracting tenants for immediate occupancy is the primary goal. Concessions, such as free rent or reduced rent through a graduated lease or rebates, may be offered to a tenant. If there is a low vacancy rate, an ad campaign would promote the many amenities of the property and the owner would analyze if potential tenants are willing to pay a higher rent.

A market is created when two or more people meet for the purpose of selling or leasing a commodity. These transactions occur at a national, regional, or local level. A property manager must be able to evaluate market trends to determine the rent that may be charged. This would include supply and demand and local economic conditions, as well as a neighborhood market analysis.

Regional Market Analysis

A regional market analysis should include demographic and economic information in the area where the property is located. This information includes population statistics, income and employment data, a description of transportation facilities, and supply and demand trends.

Neighborhood Market Analysis

Property managers rely on a neighborhood market analysis because much of their business is generated at a local level. The neighborhood market analysis would include boundaries and land usage, transportation and utilities, economy, supply and demand, and neighborhood amenities and facilities. Once the regional and neighborhood market surveys are complete, the property manager analyzes the data to determine the special features of the property and how it fits the needs of potential tenants.

Tenant Acquisition

The best method of renting property is to secure referrals from satisfied tenants. Many times, an owner will pay cash or rental incentives (concessions) to current tenants for such referrals. Press releases sent to local newspapers and brokers may gain free publicity for the property when leasing new or large developments. The interest also provides a new media for advertising and obtaining tenants.

The property manager also may decide to work with a **leasing agent**, who is an independent contractor and whose primary function is to show the property, follow up with prospective tenants, and lease the space. Leasing agents may be paid a flat referral fee or a split-commission basis.

Once the prospective tenant's needs have been determined, the next step is to qualify the tenant. The property manager should provide disclosures that are required by state and federal laws, such as agency disclosures, lead-based paint disclosures, and other documents required by state law. Of course, a copy of the lease agreement should be available to the tenant.

While showing the property, the manager describes the benefits of the space, building, and neighborhood as they meet the tenant's needs. If the property is occupied, the current tenant must be notified of the showing.

The occupancy terms to be negotiated include concessions, rent schedules, rebates, length of the leasing period, tenant alterations, expansion options, noncompeting tenant restrictions, and the defraying of moving expenses. The property manager must negotiate these terms to meet the needs of both the owner and the tenant.

Once the lease agreement has been negotiated, the landlord must give exclusive possession of the property to the tenant. The **covenant of quiet enjoyment** means the landlord must honor the tenant's right of possession. This means the landlord may not enter the property without the tenant's permission to provide services or make repairs, or other unusual circumstances. Landlords may always enter property if there is an emergency.

The implied **warranty of habitability** requires that the landlord keep the property in good condition. This would include maintenance of the common areas and equipment, providing utilities, and being in compliance with state and local codes.

The property manager should develop (and the owner should approve) a screening process that provides equal professional services to all potential tenants. One of the first areas of qualification of potential tenants must be in meeting a tenant's needs as far as space requirements are concerned. The needs would be totally different for a residential tenant than for a commercial tenant.

Other tenant considerations include

- motives for moving,
- the expiration of the current lease,
- projected budget for the new space,
- parking and transportation needs, and
- any special needs of the tenant.

Each prospective tenant should be required to fill out a lease application. For residential tenants, credit references, personal references, and rental history must be secured and checked by the property manager. For commercial property, a profit and loss statement of the company should be reviewed to demonstrate that the company is financially sound. All federal laws, such as fair housing and the Americans with Disabilities Act, must be obeyed when screening applicants.

In negotiating a commercial lease, the property manager must be sure that the person being interviewed has the authority to negotiate contracts for the company. This can be accomplished by asking for a copy of the articles of incorporation or partnership agreement.

A property manager establishes communication with a prospective tenant during the initial interviewing process. This communication continues and is strengthened during the screening and the negotiation of the lease. Complaints that constitute an emergency would be handled immediately, while other complaints should be resolved in compliance with the lease. The property manager and owner should develop a complaint process that is either outlined in the lease or available to the tenant as a separate document.

Tenants must know that they cannot use their space in such a way as to infringe on the rights of others and that noncompliance with building rules, violations of the law, or any activities that disrupt other tenants are grounds for eviction.

F. ACCOUNTS AND DISBURSEMENT

The property management agreement should provide the manager with the bank and account number of the business account in which the collected rents are deposited, and the trust account for the security deposits. Laws vary by state, but normally there cannot be a commingling of security deposits into business or personal accounts because the security deposit belongs to the tenant.

State laws may stipulate that the tenants be informed of the bank and the account number where their security deposits are located. State laws and the lease agreement also regulate the disbursement of security deposits and may specify who receives the interest earned from the security deposits. Some states do not allow security deposits to be placed in an interest-bearing account.

The owner may require the property manager to be bonded. The purpose of the surety bond, which is sometimes called a *fidelity bond*, is to protect the owner if the property manager is dishonest in the reporting or management of monies received on the owner's behalf. The property management agreement usually limits the dollar amount for a check the manager may write without requiring the owner's signature.

G. PROPERTY MAINTENANCE AND IMPROVEMENTS

A property manager is responsible for building security and handling emergencies. *Life safety* is the industry term for those responsibilities. The four goals of life safety programs are

- preventing emergencies and security breaches by installing smoke detectors, sprinkler systems, paging systems, closed-circuit television, video camera, and security alarms;

- detecting a breach as early as possible;

- containing or confining the damage or intrusion; and

- counteracting the damage by prompt and proper action.

This also would include the responsibility of hiring and training a life safety officer to assist in the evacuation of tenants and to enforce safety guidelines. Tenants should be educated so they know what to do in case of a disaster, such as a hurricane, tornado, earthquake, fire, bomb threat, or other accident.

Property managers and agents must have a working knowledge of hazardous substances and wastes and the laws regulating owners. A **hazardous waste** is a byproduct of a manufactured item, while a **hazardous substance** may include everyday items, such as household cleaning products and paint. The Environmental Protection Agency (EPA) was established to centralize the federal government's environmental responsibilities.

Environmental hazards that property managers will most likely encounter are asbestos, radon, contents of underground storage tanks, urea formaldehyde, polychlorinated biphenyls (PCBs), and lead paint. A review of these topics is found in Chapter 5.

Property managers must be in compliance with the antitrust laws, federal fair housing laws, the Equal Credit Opportunity Act, the Fair Credit Reporting Act, and the Lead-Based Paint Hazard Reduction Act, all of which are discussed in various chapters in this book. In addition to these laws, the property manager must be in compliance with the Americans with Disabilities Act, Megan's Law, and the Uniform Residential Landlord and Tenant Act. Many states have enacted their own Landlord Tenant laws, which must be followed.

Known lead-based paint and lead hazards must be disclosed to the tenant before the lease takes effect. Any prior lead hazard reports the owner has must be given to the potential tenant, as well as the booklet *Protect Your Family From Lead in Your Home*. Federal laws require that the disclosure form be kept for three years.

The primary goals of a property manager are to generate the highest net operating income while maintaining the property. To preserve the physical condition of the property, the manager must be able to accurately assess the various levels of maintenance operations presented in the following list.

- **Preventive maintenance**—preserves the physical building and eliminates costly problems before major repairs become necessary. (Seasonal servicing of equipment)

- **Corrective maintenance**—fulfills the owner's responsibilities to the tenant by keeping the building's equipment, utilities, and amenities functioning properly. (Making necessary repairs on equipment)

- **Routine maintenance**—includes routine housekeeping, such as maintenance of the common areas and grounds, and maintaining the physical cleanliness of the building itself.

- **New construction maintenance**—occurs to meet the needs of a tenant and could be something as simple as installing new carpeting or as complex as upgrading or remodeling the property to meet the tenant's needs. Tenants many times require a **build-out**, which involves alterations to the space to meet their needs.

Risk Management

One of the primary duties of the property manager involves risk management, which is usually done through the purchase of insurance. Risk management involves identifying the risk and deciding to avoid, control, retain, or transfer it. A property manager will monitor risks to determine the action that must take place in the future.

Types of insurance that may be purchased to protect the owner include

- fire and hazard insurance to cover losses by fire, tornados, high winds, hail, smoke, etc.;

- flood insurance to cover losses caused by heavy rains or other damages caused by water—managers should check the flood plain map at the Federal Emergency Management Agency (FEMA);

- property insurance to cover natural disasters, fires, and vandalism;

- general liability insurance to cover contractors and real and personal property;

- loss of income insurance to cover loss of rents, profits, and commissions;

- replacement cost insurance to cover the cost of a replacing a part of or the entire building;

- workers' compensation to cover liability for injury to employees;

- commercial automobile liability to cover injury and damage by vehicles; and

- machinery and equipment insurance to cover machinery and equipment.

H. EVICTIONS

Rent is paid in advance, usually on the first of the month, and the property manager must know state and local laws regarding eviction procedures as they relate to rent. The lease agreement should specify the day the rent is due, the grace period and the late fee, and when eviction procedures will begin. If a lease agreement does not specify the due date, then rent is due at the end of the leasing period.

A tenant is usually evicted or ejected because of nonpayment of rent, unlawful use of the premises, or noncompliance with health and safety codes.

Rent control is a regulation by the state or local government agencies restricting the amount of rent landlords can charge their tenants. The primary purpose of rent control is to remedy high rents caused by the imbalance between supply and demand in housing.

Actual eviction is when the landlord files a suit for possession because the tenant has breached the lease.

Constructive eviction is when the landlord breaches the lease and the tenant must leave the premises because they have become uninhabitable.

CHAPTER 6 TEST

1. The property manager has a fiduciary duty with the owner and is considered a(n)
   A. general agent.
   B. limited agent.
   C. special agent.
   D. universal agent.

2. When a property manager binds a principal/owner to a contract, the manager is directly operating under the fiduciary duty of
   A. accounting.
   B. care and skill.
   C. loyalty.
   D. obedience.

3. A leasing agent's primary responsible is to
   A. find a qualified tenant.
   B. make property repairs.
   C. hire the owner's employees.
   D. evict complying tenants.

4. A property management agreement is classified as a
   A. unilateral work-for-hire agreement.
   B. bilateral work-for-hire agreement.
   C. unilateral personal service contract.
   D. bilateral personal service contract.

5. In a mortgage, the nondisturbance clause benefits the
   A. property manager.
   B. owner.
   C. lender.
   D. tenant.

6. A property manager is responsible for the development of many documents for the owner. The creation of which of the following document is NOT a responsibility of the property manager?
   A. Operating budget
   B. Cash flow
   C. Lease agreement
   D. Profit and loss statement

7. A lease must give the tenant
   A. the personal address of the owner.
   B. exclusive possession of the property.
   C. the location of the owner's business account.
   D. 30 days to make the first rent payment.

8. A tenant who remains in possession of the property after the lease has expired is called
   A. a holder.
   B. a hold out.
   C. a holdover.
   D. homeless.

9. An owner sold his 20-unit apartment building. Which of the following statements would be TRUE in regards to the sale?
   A. The seller would keep all of the security deposits.
   B. The new owner can immediately raise the rent.
   C. The tenants will get a month of free rent.
   D. The existing lease agreements would be honored by the new owner.

10. Which of the following actions is NOT a responsibility of the landlord?
    A. Keep the property in a safe and habitable condition.
    B. Timely payment of the monthly rent.
    C. Maintaining a trust account for security deposits.
    D. Payment of property taxes and insurance.

11. If there is a low vacancy rate, the property manager should probably
    A. raise the rent.
    B. lower the rent.
    C. offer free rent.
    D. offer rebates.

12. Unless the lease agreement stipulates otherwise, the upkeep of the electrical, heating, and plumbing systems would be the responsibility of the
    A. owner/lessee.
    B. owner/lessor.
    C. tenant/lessee.
    D. tenant/lessor.

13. When a lease is assigned, the assignee is the
    A. new tenant.
    B. original tenant.
    C. owner.
    D. agent.

14. A school leased a small, commercial shopping strip. When classes started, the other tenants started complaining to the landlord that the students of the school were taking up the majority of the parking spaces and their customers had no place to park. The lease required that the students park in spaces away from the other businesses. The school asked the students to park in the assigned spaces, but most continued to park where it was convenient. The landlord evicted the school. Is this action legal?
    A. No, the landlord cannot evict the school because parking is available to the public.
    B. No, because the school asked the students to park in the assigned spaces, they cannot be evicted.
    C. Yes, the landlord can evict the school, and it is called actual eviction.
    D. Yes, the landlord can evict the school, and it is called constructive eviction.

15. In which of the following arrangements would there be two landlord tenant relationships?
    A. Assignment
    B. Lease purchase
    C. Lease option
    D. Sublease

16. A property manager collected a security deposit from a tenant and placed it in the owner's business account. Is this action legal?
    A. Yes, it is called conversion, and it is legal.
    B. Yes, it is called commingling, and it is legal.
    C. No, it is called conversion, and it is illegal.
    D. No, it is called commingling, and it is illegal.

17. Upon purchasing a small apartment complex, the owner had the in-ground swimming pool filled in with concrete. This action is an example of
    A. avoiding the risk.
    B. managing the risk.
    C. controlling the risk.
    D. transferring the risk.

18. Rent is usually
    A. paid in advance.
    B. paid in arrears.
    C. prorated between the lessor and lessee.
    D. prorated between the agent and the owner.

19. An escalation clause would be found in a(n)
    A. index lease.
    B. escalation lease.
    C. graduated lease.
    D. net lease.

20. The purpose for calculating the of the rate of return is to
    A. analyze the vacancy rate for the month.
    B. measure the profitability of the property.
    C. determine the absorption rate within the building.
    D. project future income.

21. A potential tenant is inspecting a property built in 1970. The potential tenant must be given
    A. ten days to inspect for lead-based paint.
    B. copies of prior inspections and reports regarding lead-based paint.
    C. the previous tenant's lease agreement.
    D. the owner's home address.

22. The property manager may not commingle funds. This means the property manager should
    A. place a security deposit check into an owner's escrow account.
    B. pay a vendor from the owner's business checking account.
    C. pay himself/herself from the owner's business account.
    D. place a security deposit check into the owner's business account.

23. When the lessee breaches the lease, it gives the lessor the right to proceed with
    A. actual eviction by filing a suit for possession.
    B. actual eviction by filing a suit for specific performance.
    C. constructive eviction by filing a suit for possession.
    D. constructive eviction by filing a suit for specific performance.

24. One of the property manager's responsibilities is to keep the building's equipment in working order. This action would fall under
    A. preventive maintenance.
    B. corrective maintenance.
    C. routine maintenance.
    D. new construction maintenance.

25. When the state or local government restricts the amount of rent a lessor can charge, it is called
    A. rent service.
    B. subsidy rent.
    C. economic rent.
    D. rent control.

26. A management agreement usually covers which of the following items?
    A. Authorization of payment of expenses
    B. Estoppel certificates
    C. Joint and several liability
    D. Waiver of subrogation

27. A property manager normally is charged with all of the following duties EXCEPT
    A. renting space to tenants.
    B. preparing a budget.
    C. developing a management plan.
    D. repairing a tenant's fixture.

28. Which of the following is the MOST IMPOR-TANT record kept by the property manager?
    A. Accounting report of income and expenses
    B. Tenants' complaints
    C. Property manager's personal expense account
    D. Utilities paid by the property manager

29. The tenant has agreed to pay a fixed monthly rent, a portion of the property taxes, and maintenance on a 1,200-square-foot retail space in a mall. This lease is BEST described as a
    A. percentage lease.
    B. gross lease.
    C. net lease.
    D. retail lease

30. Which of the following would a property manager LEAST LIKELY do?
    A. Screen and qualify tenants
    B. Place security deposits in the proper escrow account
    C. Accept a rebate from a service provider
    D. Negotiate a lease and present it to the owner for approval

31. Which of the following is the BEST method for attracting tenants to a property?
    A. Cooperating with brokers in the area
    B. Developing an advertising campaign
    C. Having press releases published in the local newspapers to create publicity
    D. Securing referrals from satisfied tenants

32. A person entered into a property management agreement with Barron Properties, Inc. The property management agreement MOST LIKELY stipulates that he will be paid a percentage of
    A. last year's net income.
    B. this year's potential income.
    C. this year's gross income.
    D. last year's gross income.

33. Which of the following criteria is the MOST IMPORTANT for a property manager to use to qualify and screen a potential tenant?
    A. The space requirements and financial history
    B. The projected moving dates and number of children
    C. The special needs of the potential tenant and commission earned
    D. The parking needs of the potential tenant and the number of disabled customers

34. All of the following events would probably terminate a residential lease agreement EXCEPT
   A. the property being taken by eminent domain.
   B. when the life tenant, who had leased the property, dies.
   C. when the owner sells the property.
   D. when the lessee buys the land from the lessor.

35. What is the BEST way for a property manager to minimize problems with a tenant?
   A. To talk with the tenant about the tenant's conduct.
   B. To tell the tenant to ask the other tenants to behave.
   C. To discuss and give a copy of the rules and regulations to the tenant.
   D. To say nothing until there is a problem.

36. The primary goals of a property manager are to
   A. generate the highest net operating income for the owner while maintaining the investment.
   B. generate the highest gross income for the owner while maintaining the investment.
   C. negotiate the lowest rent possible for the lessee while providing as many amenities as possible.
   D. negotiate the highest rent possible for the lessor while providing as many amenities as possible.

37. Which of the following types of insurance would protect the owner from liability when an employee has been injured?
   A. General liability insurance
   B. Workers' compensation
   C. Automobile insurance
   D. Loss of income insurance

38. A property manager must take which of the following into consideration to determine the net operating income that a property produces?
   A. Debt service
   B. IRS taxes
   C. After-tax cash flow
   D. Vacancy/rent loss

39. To compute the return on investment, a property manager must
   A. divide the before-tax cash flow by the after-cash tax flow.
   B. multiply the before-tax cash flow by the after-cash tax flow.
   C. divide the after-tax cash flow by the equity and multiply by 100 percent.
   D. multiply the after-tax cash flow by the equity and divide by 100 percent.

40. An agent has become a manager of a property that is difficult to lease. Which of the following leases would the agent MOST LIKELY use to secure a contract with a prospective tenant?
   A. Percentage lease
   B. Graduated lease
   C. Sublease
   D. Gross lease

41. The primary purpose of a profit and loss statement is to analyze
   A. how the property was managed, what changes should be made, and projections for the new year.
   B. how the operating budget was calculated and budget projections for the new year.
   C. the ratio of the operating expenses to the operating income.
   D. the ratio of the rate of return to the debt service.

42. On a profit and loss statement, all of the following are entered EXCEPT
   A. mortgage loan principal add-back.
   B. receipts.
   C. operating expenses.
   D. property manager's compensation.

43. What do asbestos, radon, and urea formaldehyde all have in common?
    A. They are classified as environmental hazards, and a property manager must be aware of them.
    B. They are all classified as hazardous substances, and a property manager must be aware of them.
    C. They are produced as a result of the natural decay of radioactive substances, so they cannot be avoided.
    D. They are produced as a result of the natural decay of organic substances, so they cannot be avoided.

44. All of the following are grounds for constructive eviction EXCEPT
    A. the nonpayment of rent by the tenant.
    B. the furnace that has not worked for five days in the middle of winter.
    C. the water is turned off because the owner did not pay the water bill.
    D. the property is declared uninhabitable by the local government.

45. An operating budget allowed $2,500 for the property manager to buy new carpet. The property manager can negotiate a contract with a carpet company to purchase carpet for the property, as well as the manager's personal residence, if
    A. directly billed to the owner.
    B. purchased without the owner's knowledge.
    C. given that authorization in an employment contract.
    D. bids have been secured from at least three companies.

46. A blind person with a seeing eye dog wants to rent an apartment from the landlord who has a no-pet policy. The landlord may
    A. charge the blind person a service animal security deposit.
    B. charge more rent because of the seeing-eye dog.
    C. refuse to rent to the blind person.
    D. charge the blind person for any damages when the tenant leaves.

47. A buyer offered to purchase an occupied fourplex. Should his offer be accepted, which of the following is TRUE regarding the current leases?
    A. The leases will be void.
    B. The leases will be unaffected.
    C. The lessee can cancel the leases.
    D. The lessor can raise the rent.

48. Which of the following would NOT be a factor in the development of a marketing plan by the property manager?
    A. Supply and demand
    B. Local economic conditions
    C. Location of the property
    D. Availability of good maintenance employees

49. Which of the following provisions is LEAST LIKELY to be found in a property management agreement?
    A. Start date, termination date, and renewal options
    B. Business bank account information and banking authorizations
    C. Policy for the return of security deposits
    D. Authorization for the manager to receive kickbacks from service providers

50. Which of the following is an environmental hazard associated with leakage near electrical equipment?
    A. Urea formaldehyde
    B. Radon
    C. Polychlorinated biphenyls (PCBs)
    D. Asbestos

51. All of the following occupancy terms are negotiated between a property manager and a prospective tenant EXCEPT
    A. expansion options.
    B. length of the leasing period.
    C. tenant alterations.
    D. the owner's profit.

52. The duties and responsibilities of a property manager would be LEAST LIKELY to include which of the following?
    A. Investing profits generated by the property for the owner
    B. Supervising the remodeling of the property
    C. Showing the property to prospective tenants
    D. Collecting the rent from current tenants

53. A property manager showed a prospective tenant an available apartment. Which of the following would NOT be a consideration in qualifying the potential tenant?
    A. Credit history
    B. Race
    C. Space requirements
    D. Personal references

54. Which of the following does NOT normally terminate a lease?
    A. Death of the lessor
    B. Nonpayment of rent
    C. Constructive eviction
    D. Condemnation of the property

55. A property manager is developing an operating budget. Which of the following is LEAST LIKELY to be considered an operating expense?
    A. Utility bills
    B. Debt service
    C. Maintenance expenses
    D. Management fees

56. The owner of a fourplex lives in one unit and has an apartment available for rent. She would like for the new tenant to be a nonsmoker. Can she advertise the unit as a nonsmoking apartment?
    A. Yes, because smoking is a behavior that is not protected by federal fair housing laws.
    B. Yes, because the fourplex is owner-occupied.
    C. No, because it would be discriminatory advertising.
    D. No, because only the owner of a duplex can discriminate because of smoking.

57. A licensee negotiated a property management agreement with an owner. The property management agreement
    A. is a personal service contract that terminates upon the death of either party.
    B. creates a special agency relationship that terminates when it expires.
    C. need not be in writing in most states and can be terminated at any time.
    D. creates a universal agency relationship that can be terminated at any time.

58. To protect the owner against the mismanagement of monies that the property manager receives, the owner may require the manager to purchase a(n)
    A. errors and omissions bond.
    B. fidelity bond.
    C. theft bond.
    D. embezzlement bond.

59. An automatic renewal clause would MOST LIKELY be found in which of the following leases?
    A. Tenancy for years
    B. Periodic tenancy
    C. Estate at will
    D. Estate at sufferance

60. A tenant pays a fixed rental amount and the owner pays all other ownership expenses for the property. The lease agreement they have negotiated is MOST LIKELY a(n)
    A. index lease.
    B. percentage lease.
    C. net lease.
    D. gross lease.

61. The owner of an investment property died at 10 pm last night. Can the property manager collect the rent checks that are due today?
    A. Yes, it is property manager's duty to collect the rent checks for the estate.
    B. Yes, the property manager should collect the rent checks because it is his job.
    C. No, the property manager should not collect the rent checks because his contract terminated upon the owner's death.
    D. No, the property manager should not collect the rent checks until the executor of her estate gives him permission to do so.

62. A hurricane destroyed several apartment buildings in a community, creating an imbalance between the supply and demand of rental units. If the local government imposes a law that restricts the amount of rent a landlord may charge, it is known as
    A. rent control.
    B. rent restriction.
    C. fixed rent.
    D. gross rent.

63. A property manager hired a contractor to build a wheelchair ramp, install Braille markings on the elevators, and make the restrooms in the lobby accessible to people with wheelchairs. The property manager is ensuring that the owner is in compliance with which law?
    A. FFH
    B. ADA
    C. ECOA
    D. CRA

64. What is the major difference between an assignment and a sublease?
    A. When a lease has been assigned, the landlord expects payment from the assignor, but when the property has been sublet, the landlord expects payment from the sublessee.
    B. Only tenants of residential properties can assign leases, and only tenants of commercial properties can sublease properties.
    C. A tenant who transfers all the leasehold interest assigns the lease, while a tenant who subleases transfers less than the leasehold interests in the property.
    D. An assignment is used for long-term leases, but a sublease is used for short-term leases.

65. The implied warranty of habitability is BEST defined as the
    A. landlord's responsibility to keep the property in good condition.
    B. landlord's reversionary right to occupy the property upon the expiration of the lease.
    C. tenant's duty to safeguard the property.
    D. tenant's duty to maintain insurance on the property.

66. Property management agreements must be
    A. notarized.
    B. in writing.
    C. for at least one year.
    D. attested.

67. Which of the following terms could be found in a lease or a mortgage?
    A. Escalation clause
    B. Alienation clause
    C. Subjugation clause
    D. Redemption clause

68. A property manager signed a two-year property management agreement with the owner. Has an agency relationship been created, and if so, what type of agent is the property manager?
    A. Yes, authority has been given for the property manager to act on the owner's behalf, and the property manager is a general agent.
    B. Yes, authority has been given for the property manager to act on the owner's behalf, and the property manager is a special agent.
    C. No, because to create agency, the term of the agreement must be at least three years.
    D. No, because property management agreements do not create agency relationships.

69. To compute the return on investment, a property manager would need all of the following figures EXCEPT
   A. potential gross income.
   B. expenses.
   C. cap rate.
   D. debt service.

70. A property manager signed a lease agreement with a new tenant and collected a $500 security deposit check. The manager deposited the security deposit in the business bank account and did not disclose to the tenant the location of the money. Were these actions legal?
   A. Yes, if those were the instructions from the tenant.
   B. Yes, as long as the check was deposited within three business days.
   C. No, because the check should be deposited into a separate bank account for that purpose.
   D. No, because the manager did not inform the friend of the court of the location of the money.

MATCHING QUIZ

The column on the right contains a brief definition of important terms in this section. Write the letter of the matching term on the appropriate line.

A. ROI

B. Rent Control

C. Lease

D. Graduated Lease

E. Commingle

F. Covenant of Quiet Enjoyment

G. Fidelity Bond

H. Corrective Maintenance

I. Risk Management

J. Leasing Agent

K. Management Agreement

L. Operating Budget

M. Tenancy For Years

N. Periodic Tenancy

O. Estate at Will

P. Estate at Sufferance

Q. Holdover

R. Constructive Eviction

S. Routine Maintenance

T. Warranty of Habitability

1. _____ This lease may be used to entice tenants to rent spaces that are difficult to rent.

2. _____ The landlord's duty to honor the tenant's right of possession.

3. _____ The government's right to set the rent that landlords can charge.

4. _____ Repairing equipment and amenities to keep the building functional for the tenant.

5. _____ The property manager's report of anticipated revenues and expenses.

6. _____ Lease with definite beginning and ending dates.

7. _____ The landlord's duty to keep the property in good repair.

8. _____ The tenant has the right to possess the property with the consent of the landlord, but the lease can be terminated at any time by either party.

9. _____ When a tenant remains in possession after the lease expires, the tenant is given this title.

10. _____ The landlord breaches the lease and the tenant must leave the premises.

11. _____ This estate is created when the tenant remains in possession after the lease has expired.

12. _____ This document is a bilateral contract that gives exclusive possession to the tenant.

13. _____ The owner may require the property manager to purchase this to protect the owner should the manager mishandle monies.

14. _____ Housekeeping and maintenance of the common areas and grounds.

15. _____ Used to compute the profitability of the investment.

16. _____ A lease that will automatically renew unless proper notice is given.

17. _____ To place funds in the wrong bank account, such as placing the security deposit in a business account.

18. _____ Identifying risk and deciding to avoid, control, retain, or transfer the risk.

19. _____ If a brokerage is hired to rent property, this agreement is negotiated between the brokerage firm and the owner.

20. _____ Responsible for securing a qualified tenant for the owner.

CHAPTER 6 TEST ANSWERS

1. **(A)** The property manager is expected to be in an on-going business relationship and is a general agent of the owner.

2. **(B)** When negotiating contracts that are binding to the owner, the property manager should be aware of his/her duty of care and skill.

3. **(A)** The leasing agent is only responsible for finding a qualified tenant.

4. **(D)** The property management agreement is classified as a personal service contract that is also bilateral because both the owner and the manager have duties to perform.

5. **(D)** The nondisturbance clause would benefit the tenant. If the owner defaults on the mortgage and the tenant agrees to pay the lender, the tenant will not be evicted.

6. **(C)** The owner is responsible for the lease agreement, not the property manager.

7. **(B)** The lease agreement must give exclusive possession of the property to the tenant.

8. **(C)** When a tenant remains in possession after the expiration of the lease, the tenant is called a holdover.

9. **(D)** When an apartment building is sold, the new owner would be required to honor the existing leases.

10. **(B)** The landlord does not make the rent payments.

11. **(A)** If there is a low vacancy rate, the property manager should probably raise the rent.

12. **(B)** Unless the lease agreement stipulated otherwise, it would be the responsibility of the owner/lessor to maintain the property.

13. **(A)** In an assignment, the original tenant is the assignor, and the new tenant receiving the assignment would be the assignee.

14. **(C)** The landlord can evict the school, and it is called actual eviction.

15. **(D)** There would be two landlord tenant relationships in a sublease.

16. **(D)** Security deposits belong to the tenant and should be placed in a trust account for that person. If the security deposit is placed in a business account, it is called commingling, and this is illegal.

17. **(A)** Filling in a swimming pool is an example of avoiding the risk.

18. **(A)** Rent is paid in advance, meaning the tenant pays on the first of the month and is allowed to live there for the month. If the tenant does not pay on the agreed-upon date, the owner may start eviction procedures.

19. **(A)** An escalation clause would be found in an index lease, which would allow the rent payment to adjust based on an index outside of the control of the landlord or tenant.

20. **(B)** The rate of return is calculated to measure the profitability of the property.

21. **(B)** For properties built prior to 1978, tenants must be given copies of prior inspections and reports regarding lead-based paint.

22. **(A)** The word commingle means to mix together. Security deposit checks must be placed in a separate escrow or trust account for that purpose.

23. **(A)** If the tenant breaches the lease, the lessor may file a suit for possession. (Actual eviction)

24. **(B)** Making sure the building's equipment is in working order is corrective maintenance.

25. **(D)** Rent control is established by state or local governments to restrict the rent that can be charged.

26. **(A)** The authorization of the payment of expenses would be a part of the agreement.

27. **(D)** The property manager is not responsible for the repair of a tenant's fixture.

28. **(A)** The income and expenses are used to develop all other reports the manager must provide to the owner, including the profit and loss statement.

29. **(C)** In a net lease, the tenant agrees to pay ownership expenses.

30. **(C)** The property manager may not accept a rebate from a service provider unless the owner has given permission for him to do so.

31. **(D)** All the answers provide methods that a property manager can use to attract tenants. Referrals from satisfied tenants are the best.

32. **(C)** Property managers are usually paid a percentage of the gross income.

33. **(A)** When qualifying a potential tenant, a property manager must consider many factors. The space requirements, financial history and projected moving date are the most important criteria.

34. **(C)** When the owner sells the property, the buyer must honor the existing lease.

35. **(C)** The property manager should discuss and give a copy of the rules and regulations to a tenant to minimize any problems.

36. **(A)** The primary goals of a property manager are to generate the highest net operating income while maintain the owner's investment.

37. **(B)** Workers' compensation would protect the owner from liability should an employee be injured.

38. **(D)** Potential gross income
    – Vacancy and rent losses
    + Additional income
    Total anticipated revenue
    – Expenses
    Net operating income before debt service

39. **(C)** The return on investment formula: after-tax cash flow ÷ equity × 100%.

40. **(B)** A graduated lease is used to attract tenants to properties that are difficult to lease.

41. **(A)** The purpose of a profit and loss statement is to analyze how the property was managed, what changes should be made, and projections for the new year.

42. **(D)** The property manager's compensation is not entered on a profit and loss statement.

43. **(A)** Asbestos, radon, and urea formaldehyde are all environmental hazards of which a property manager must be aware.

44. **(A)** Constructive eviction occurs when the landlord breaches the lease. If the tenant doesn't pay the rent, the tenant has breached the lease, which is actual eviction.

45. **(C)** The property manager can act only within the scope and authority of the employment contract negotiated with the owner.

46. **(D)** The landlord cannot refuse to rent to the blind tenant and may not charge a pet deposit fee. The landlord may charge for damages when the tenant leaves.

47. **(B)** When the property is sold, the current leases remain binding and effective.

48. **(D)** The marketing plan does not consider the hiring of maintenance employees.

49. **(D)** Management agreements do not authorize managers to receive kickbacks from service providers.

50. **(C)** PCBs can be found in electrical equipment.

51. **(D)** The owner's profit is not a term negotiated with a tenant.

52. **(A)** The property manager does not invest the owner's profit.

53. **(B)** The race of a potential tenant is not a consideration of the property manager when negotiating a lease.

54. **(A)** The death of the lessor does not affect the lease in any way.

55. **(B)** The debt service is not an operating expense.

56. **(A)** Smoking describes a behavior, not a person. Smokers are not a protected class under federal fair housing laws.

57. **(A)** A property management agreement is a personal service contract that would create a general agency relationship.

58. **(B)** The owner may require the manager to purchase a fidelity bond.

59. **(B)** A periodic tenancy would have an automatic renewal clause.

60. **(D)** In a gross lease, the tenant pays a fixed rent, and the owner pays all ownership expenses.

61. **(C)** Property management contracts are personal service contracts and terminate upon the death of either party. The executor may hire the same property manager, but the question does not provide that information and it should not be assumed.

62. **(A)** By definition of rent control.

63. **(B)** The Americans with Disabilities Act (ADA) requires that places of public accommodations be accessible by people with disabilities.

64. **(C)** In an assignment, a tenant transfers all the leasehold interest. In a sublease, a tenant transfers less than the leasehold interest in the property.

65. **(A)** The implied warranty of habitability requires that the landlord keep the property in good condition.

66. **(B)** Property management agreements must be in writing.

67. **(A)** An escalation clause is found in an index lease that will allow the lease payment to adjust. It is also found in an adjustable-rate mortgage to allow the interest rate to adjust.

68. **(A)** A property management agreement would create an agency relationship, and the property manager would be a general agent, given a broad range of powers on behalf of the owner.

69. **(C)** An appraiser uses the cap rate to compute the value, but it is not used to determine the return on investment.

70. **(C)** Most states require that security deposit checks be placed in a separate escrow or trust account.

A N S W E R S — M A T C H I N G   Q U I Z

1. **D**   6. **M**   11. **P**   16. **N**

2. **F**   7. **T**   12. **C**   17. **E**

3. **B**   8. **O**   13. **G**   18. **I**

4. **H**   9. **Q**   14. **S**   19. **K**

5. **L**   10. **R**   15. **A**   20. **J**

CHAPTER 7

Real Estate Calculations

AMP Outline

A. COMPENSATION, COMMISSION, AND FEES

This chapter will show you how to use the T method for solving math questions. It is a simple formula that can be used to solve most of the math questions that you will encounter on the exam. The formulas for brokerage, financing, appraising, area, and settlement math will also be reviewed.

 Answers to math questions may vary, depending on how many decimal places are carried out. For these questions, carry out the decimal to four places and round in the final step.

The T Method

Here is a math question that you can mentally compute. If an agent sold a property for $100,000 and the broker was paid a 7 percent commission, what was that commission? The answer is $7,000. Let's use this question to learn how the T method works.

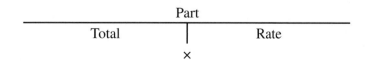

215

In the T, the total is placed on the bottom left, the *rate* on the bottom right, and the *part* at the top. Using the T for this question, it gives us this:

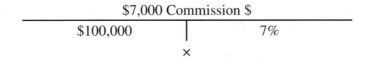

	$7,000 Commission $
$100,000	7%
×	

Rule 1   When given the two numbers in the bottom of the T, the total and the rate, the mathematical function is **multiplication**. $100,000 × 7 percent = $7,000.

Rule 2   When given the part, at the top of the T, and the rate, at the bottom, the mathematical function is **division**. It helps to remember TGIF: **T**op **G**oes **I**nto the calculator **F**irst.

> Example: If a broker received a $7,000 commission check and the selling price was $100,000, what was the commission rate?

The $7,000 is the part and goes at the top of the T. $100,000 is the sale price, or total, and goes in the lower left. Thus, $7,000 ÷ $100,000 = 7 percent.

	÷ $7,000 Commission $
$100,000	0.07 or 7%
Sale Price	Commission Rate

Rule 3   When given the part, at the top of the T, and the total, at the bottom, the mathematical function again is **division**. Remember TGIF, the **T**op number **G**oes **I**nto your calculator **F**irst.

> Example: The seller received $100,000 and the commission paid was 7 percent. What was the sale price of the property?

Notice how this question is different. Is the $100,000 a part or a total? It's a part, so it goes at the top of the T. It is equal to 93 percent of the selling price, so 93 percent goes in the lower right of the T. $100,000 ÷ 93% = $107,526.88.

	$100,000 Seller's Net ÷
$107,526.88	0.93 or 93%
Sale Price	Seller's %

Rule 4   When solving for the total, take the part and divide by the percent to which that part is equal.

> For example: Commission $ ÷ Commission Rate = Sale Price and Seller's $ ÷ Seller's % = Sale Price.

Brokerage math questions include computing commissions and determining the sale price when given the seller's dollars and the commission rate.

÷ Commission $ ÷	
Sale Price	Commission Rate

Sale Price × Commission Rate = Commission $

Commission $ ÷ Commission Rate = Sale Price

Commission $ ÷ Sale Price = Commission Rate

÷ Seller's Dollars $ ÷	
Sale Price	Seller's %

Sale Price × Seller's % = Seller's Dollars $

Seller's $ ÷ Seller's % = Sale Price

Seller's $ ÷ Sale Price = Seller %

COMPENSATION, COMMISSION, AND FEES QUESTIONS

Beginner Level

1. Ms. Seller is interviewing agents to list her property. She has the following quotes from two different companies: XYZ Realty, 7 percent commission; and Redford Realty, 5.5 percent commission. If her house sells for $225,000, how much will she save if she lists her property with Redford Realty?
   A. $3,357
   B. $3,375
   C. $4,500
   D. $5,400

2. At closing, the seller paid the broker $21,000, which was equivalent to 7 percent of the selling price. What was the selling price of the property?
   A. $147,000
   B. $210,000
   C. $300,000
   D. $400,000

3. A sales associate for XYZ Realty listed and sold a $175,000 home. The seller paid a 6 percent commission of which the agent received 2 percent for listing the property, and 1.5 percent for selling the property. How much was the broker's share of the commission?
   A. $10,500
   B. $5,250
   C. $6,125
   D. $4,375

4. A property sold for $235,000, and the selling broker's half of the commission was $8,225. What was the commission rate?
   A. 4 percent
   B. 5 percent
   C. 6 percent
   D. 7 percent

5. A broker and sales associate split commissions on a 60/40 basis. How much commission will the sales associate earn if he sells a property for $125,000, and a 6 percent commission is paid?
   A. $7,500
   B. $3,000
   C. $4,500
   D. $3,500

6. When, the seller listed a property, he agreed to pay a 7 percent commission. The property sold for $190,000. If the listing agent was paid 2 percent, and the selling agent was paid 1.5 percent, how much was the broker paid after paying his agents?
   A. $2,850
   B. $3,800
   C. $6,650
   D. $13,300

Intermediate Level

7. Ann listed her property with a XYZ Realty that charges a flat fee of $2,995 to list the property. If an agent within XYZ sells the property, the total commission paid is $2,995. However, if an agent from another company brings the buyer that purchases the property, the owner agreed to pay that company a 3 percent commission. An agent from JFK presented an offer of $425,000. If the offer is accepted, the total commission that the owner will pay is
   A. $15,745
   B. $12,750
   C. $11,250
   D. $10,500

8. A broker sold a property for $250,000. She was paid 6 percent on the first $100,000, 5 percent on the next $100,000, and 4 percent on the balance. How much was the broker paid?
   A. $6,000
   B. $5,000
   C. $13,000
   D. $24,000

9. An agent was paid $2,500, which was half of the 7 percent that the broker collected. What was the sale price of the property?
   A. $71,248
   B. $35,714
   C. $35,417
   D. $71,428

10. A broker and a sales associate split commissions on a 60/40 basis. If the broker's share of the commission was $3,500, and the sale price was $83,333, what was the commission rate?
    A. 6 percent
    B. 10.5 percent
    C. 7.5 percent
    D. 7 percent

11. When the owners sold their property, they paid a 6 percent commission. Their check after the commission was paid was $470,000. What was the selling price of the property?
    A. $500,000
    B. $783,333
    C. $800,000
    D. $900,000

Advanced Level

12. An owner sold her condo and paid 6 percent commission to the selling broker. If her net was $200,000, what was the sale price?
    A. $205,698.49
    B. $212,765.95
    C. $225,349.59
    D. $229,879.39

13. After closing expenses of $550 and a 6 percent commission was paid, the seller received a check for $149,850. What was the sale price of the property?
    A. $150,400
    B. $155,424
    C. $159,424
    D. $160,000

14. Mr. Seller wants to net a profit of $20,000 and agrees to pay a 7 percent commission. He also has selling expenses of $400 and a mortgage of $35,250. What is the minimum offer he could accept for the property?
    A. $59,839
    B. $59,545
    C. $58,565
    D. $59,656

15. Mr. and Mrs. Seller want to net a 12 percent profit after paying the brokerage firm a 6.5 percent commission. If the original purchase price was $104,500, what is the minimum offer they can accept?
    A. $125,716
    B. $117,040
    C. $125,176
    D. $124,647

B. VALUATION/MARKET SALE PRICE AND YIELDS

The appraisal formulas reviewed in this section are the income, the cost, and the gross rent multiplier approaches to appraising. This section also includes a review of capital gains, appreciation, and depreciation of property.

The income approach to appraising is used to convert the annual net operating income of investment property into a value by dividing it by the capitalization rate, which is also known as the rate of return.

Note that the appraiser will use the **market rent**, which is also known as the *economic rent*, to determine the potential gross income. The market rent is the rental income that real estate could command in the market at any given time versus **contract rent**, which is the income generated under the current lease contract. An appraiser has two options for computing the value of the property using the income approach to appraising. In the first example, the formula is

$$\text{Potential Gross Income} + \text{Additional Income} - \text{Vacancy Rate} =$$
$$\text{Effective Gross Income}$$

Example: Three apartments rent for $450 per month, three for $500 per month, and two for $550 per month. There is a 5 percent vacancy rate, $300 in monthly expenses, and $125 per month additional income. If the owner wants a 10 percent return on her investment, how much can she pay for the property?

$$3 \times \$450 \times 12 = \$16,200$$
$$3 \times \$500 \times 12 = \$18,000$$
$$2 \times \$550 \times 12 = \underline{\$13,200}$$
$$\$47,400 \text{ Potential Gross Income}$$
$$\$125 \times 12 = \underline{+\ 1,500 \text{ Additional Income}}$$
$$\$48,900$$
$$\underline{-\qquad 5\% \text{ Vacancy Rate}}$$
$$\$46,455 \text{ Effective Gross Income}$$
$$\$300 \times 12 = \underline{-\ 3,600 \text{ Expenses}}$$
$$\$42,855 \text{ Annual Net Operating Income}$$

$42,855 Annual Net Operating Income ÷	
$428,550	10%
Value	Cap Rate

The second option is to use the following formula:

Potential Gross Income – Vacancy Rate + Additional Income =
Effective Gross Income

$3 \times \$450 \times 12 =$ $16,200
$3 \times \$500 \times 12 =$ $18,000
$2 \times \$550 \times 12 =$ $13,200
$47,400 Potential Gross Income
– _____ 5% Vacancy Rate_____
$45,030
$125 \times 12 =$ + 1,500 Additional Income____
$46,530 Effective Gross Income
$300 \times 12 =$ – 3,600 Expenses_____
$42,930 Annual Net Operating Income

$42,930 Annual Net Operating Income ÷	
$429,300	10%
Value	Cap Rate

In this chapter, we will use the first formula to compute the value under the income approach to appraising. Check with your instructor to determine which method is used in your state.

The cost approach to appraising is used to determine the value of special-purpose properties, but it can also be used to appraise new buildings.

Example: The replacement cost of a building is $125,000. It has an annual depreciation of 10 percent, and a site value of $35,000. What is the value of the property?

$125,000 Replacement Cost
– _____10% Depreciation Rate___
$112,500
+ 35,000 Site Value_____
$147,500 Property Value

Replacement Cost
– Depreciation Rate
+ Site Value_____
Property Value

The **gross rent multiplier (GRM)** formula is used to appraise small income-producing properties, such as a single-family home or duplex that is investment property (use monthly rent). If this method is used to determine the value of a small shopping center, it is called the **gross income multiplier (GIM)**, and the annual rent is used.

Example: An appraiser has determined that the gross rent multiplier of a house that rents for $650 is 110. What is the value of the property?

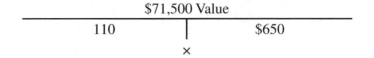

Gross Rent Multiplier × Rent

Gross Rent Multiplier × Monthly Rent = Value
Value ÷ Gross Rent Multiplier = Monthly Rent
Value ÷ Monthly Rent = Gross Rent Multiplier

Gross Income Multiplier × Annual Rent = Value
Value ÷ Gross Income Multiplier = Annual Rent
Value ÷ Annual Rent = Gross Income Multiplier

A capital gain is the profit that an owner makes when selling an asset, such as real estate.

Example: A buyer purchased a property for $90,000. He made $22,500 worth of improvements. Three years later, he sold the property for $130,000 and paid a 6 percent commission. What were his capital gains on the sale?

Step 1 $ 90,000   Original Investment
             + 22,500   Improvements
             $112,500   Adjusted Basis

Step 2 $7,800 Commission $
           _____
           $130,000 | 6%
           Sales Price × Commission %

Step 3 $130,000 – 7,800 = $122,200 Adjusted (Net)
           Sale Price (The sale price minus selling
           expenses equals the adjusted sale price)

Step 4 $122,200   Adjusted Sale Price
             –112,500   Adjusted Basis
             $ 9,700   Capital Gains

                  Original Investment
                + Improvements
                  Adjusted Basis

Selling Price
+ Selling Expenses
Adjusted Sale Price

Adjusted Sale Price
+ Adjusted Basis
Capital Gains

The previous formula is for computing the capital gains on an owner's principal place of residence. Under the new tax laws, which became effective May 7, 1997, first-time homebuyers may make a penalty-free withdrawal of up to $10,000 from their tax-deferred individual retirement fund or IRA for a down payment. Homeowners whose gain exceeds the maximum for exclusion must pay tax on the amount over the exclusion ($500,000 for married homeowners who file jointly, and $250,000 for single filers). The exclusion can be taken more than once. However, the home must have been used as a principal place of residence for two of the preceding five years.

Appraisal math may deal with the appreciation or depreciation of property value.

Example: The owners paid $80,000 for their property. This year, their property appreciated in value 10 percent. What is the value of the property today?

$88,000 Appreciated Value	
Original	100%
Investment	+ 10% Appreciation Rate
$80,000	× 110% Appreciated %

Appreciated Value	
Original	100%
Investment	+ Appreciation Rate
$80,000 ×	Appreciated %

Example: The owners paid $80,000 for their property. This year, their property depreciated in value 10 percent. What is the value of their property?

$72,000 Depreciated Value	
Original	100%
Investment	– 10% Appreciation Rate
$80,000	× 90% Depreciated %

Depreciated Value	
Original	100%
Investment	– Depreciation Rate
$80,000 ×	Depreciated %

VALUATION/MARKET SALE PRICE AND YIELDS QUESTIONS

Beginner Level

16. An apartment building with a $90,000 net operating income and an 8 percent cap rate has a value of
    A. $1,000,000.
    B. $1,125,000.
    C. $1,500,000.
    D. $1,720,000.

17. An apartment building has a semiannual net income of $48,000 and has been appraised for $1,250,000. What is the cap rate?
    A. 3.84 percent
    B. 4.38 percent
    C. 7.68 percent
    D. 7.86 percent

18. Last year, an apartment building had an effective gross income of $55,575 and expenses of $5,500. If the cap rate is 10 percent, what is the value?
    A. $555,555
    B. $555,750
    C. $500,000
    D. $500,750

19. If the gross rent multiplier of a property is 112 and the rent is $600 monthly, what is the value of the property?
    A. $76,200
    B. $62,700
    C. $27,600
    D. $67,200

20. Three years ago, a buyer paid $150,000 for a three-bedroom home. The property has appreciated at 5 percent each year. What is the value of the property today?
    A. $172,500
    B. $173,644
    C. $175,464
    D. $179,300

21. Two years ago, a buyer paid $175,000 for a house. Since that time, the property has depreciated 3 percent each year. What is the value of the property today?
    A. $164,500
    B. $164,658
    C. $185,500
    D. $185,657

Intermediate Level

22. The replacement cost of a building is $250,000. It has an annual depreciation of 8 percent, a site value of $50,000, and annual taxes of $3,950. What is the value of the property?
    A. $230,000
    B. $276,050
    C. 280,000
    D. $283,950

23. A building has a semiannual effective gross income of $250,000. If the annual expenses are 20 percent of the effective gross income, what is the net operating income?
    A. $500,000
    B. $200,000
    C. $100,000
    D. $400,000

24. Three years ago, the owner paid $165,000 for her property. During her period of ownership, she added a family room valued at $16,500 and $10,000 worth of other improvements. If she sells the property for $240,000 and pays a 7 percent commission, what capital gains may she exclude?
    A. $25,300
    B. $31,700
    C. $37,100
    D. $48,500

25. A property was purchased for $250,000. The owner added a tennis court at a cost of $10,000. Two years later, the property sold for $325,000 and the seller paid a 7 percent commission plus $250 in attorney fees. If he purchases another property for $350,000, how much capital gains will he exclude?
    A. $22,750
    B. $42,000
    C. $42,250
    D. $42,520

Advanced Level

26. The rent collected in a 12-unit building is as follows: three apartments, $550; three apartments, $600; and three apartments, $650. There is a vacancy rate of 4 percent, additional annual income of $2,400, and annual expenses of $5,000. With a cap rate of 9 percent, how much should the buyer pay for this property?
    A. $661,244
    B. $698,534
    C. $717,866
    D. $773,422

27. Five apartments rent for $550 per month, and five others for $600 per month. There is an 8 percent vacancy rate and monthly expenses of $250. If a buyer wants to yield an 8 percent return, what should he pay for the property?
    A. $790,375
    B. $765,000
    C. $756,000
    D. $790,735

28. A property is now worth $117,978. If it has appreciated 6 percent each year for the past two years, what was the original investment?
    A. $111,300
    B. $105,000
    C. $104,245
    D. $110,899

29. A property is now worth $98,250. If it has depreciated in value 5 percent each year for the past two years, what was the original investment?
    A. $103,421
    B. $103,241
    C. $108,864
    D. $108,320

C. TAX AND OTHER PRORATIONS

The calculation of real estate property taxes involves two math formulas. Taxes are computed on the assessed value, which is a percentage of the market value. The assessed value is then multiplied by the tax rate to give the annual property tax.

> Example: The market value of a property is $70,000, and it is assessed at 40 percent of the market value. If the tax rate is $5.50 per $100, what is the annual property tax?

The word *per* in a math question means divide. Thus, $5.50 ÷ $100 = 0.055 tax rate.

$$\frac{\$28,000 \text{ Assessed Value}}{\$70,000 \quad | \quad 40\%}$$
Market Value × Assessment Rate

$$\frac{\$1,540 \text{ Annual Property Taxes}}{\$28,000 \quad | \quad 0.055}$$
Assessed Value × Tax Rate

Market Value × Assessment Rate = Assessed Value
Assessed Value ÷ Market Value = Assessment Rate
Assessed Value ÷ Assessment Rate = Market Value

Assessed Value × Tax Rate = Annual Property Taxes
Annual Property Taxes ÷ Assessed Value = Tax Rate
Annual Property Taxes ÷ Tax Rate = Assessed Value

The previous formulas also can use the appraised value instead of the market value of the property.

The tax rate also can be expressed as mills, which means 1/1,000 of a dollar. Thus, whenever you see the tax rate expressed as mills, divide that number by 1,000.

> Example: If the tax rate is 55 mills, that means 55 ÷ 1,000 = 0.055 for the tax rate. If the tax rate is 555 mills, that means 555 ÷ 1,000 = 0.555 for the tax rate.

TAX QUESTIONS

Beginner Level

30. A property appraised for $125,000. If the assessment rate is 100 percent and the tax rate is $1 per $100, what are the annual property taxes?
    A. $1,250
    B. $1,520
    C. $1,350
    D. $1,550

Intermediate Level

31. If the market value of a property is $169,000, it is assessed at 35 percent, and the tax rate is $4.25 per $100, what are the monthly property taxes?
    A. $2,513.88
    B. $2,531.88
    C. $409.49
    D. $209.49

32. The appraised value of a property is $52,350. It is assessed at 38 percent of the appraised value, and the tax rate is 95 mills. What are the quarterly property taxes?
    A. $472.45
    B. $1,889.83
    C. $1,998.83
    D. $1,589.83

Advanced Level

33. The market value of a property is $65,000 and is assessed for 45 percent of its value. If the owner's semiannual tax bill was $511.88, what was the tax rate per $100?
    A. $3.50
    B. 350 mills
    C. $1.75
    D. 175 mills

34. The owners received a semiannual tax bill of $984.38. Property in the jurisdiction is assessed at one-fourth the market value. If the tax rate is $4.50 per $100, what is the estimated market value of the property?
    A. $43,750
    B. $175,000
    C. $195,000
    D. $53,750

Insurance Proration

To prorate an expense means to divide or distribute it proportionately. Sometimes, the buyer assumes the seller's insurance policy. Insurance is always paid in advance; thus, this entry is a debit to the buyer and a credit to the seller. The following shows one way to compute the number of days to prorate when more than one calendar year is involved.

■ The beginning date is the date the policy was written.

■ The prorate date is the closing date.

■ The ending date will be for the term of the policy and will end at midnight, which is one day prior to the date the policy was written.

Example: A one-year policy was written on June 15, 2010, and the premium for the policy was $425. The property was sold and closed on November 23, 2010. What is the approximate credit for the seller on the settlement sheet? (Use a 360-day calendar year.)

If a one-year policy was written on June 15, 2010, it would end at 11:59 PM one year later.

Beginning date:	June 15, 2010
Prorate date:	November 23, 2010
Ending date:	June 14, 2011

November 23–30:	7 days
December–May:	180 days
June 1–14:	14 days
Total:	201 days

$425 ÷ 360 = $ 1.1805 × 201 = $237.28 CS, DB

INSURANCE QUESTIONS

Beginner Level

35. A person purchased a new home, and her one-year insurance policy began on September 14, 2005, with a premium cost of $504. Her company transferred her, and when she sold her house, the buyer assumed her policy at the closing on January 25, 2006. How much will be credited to the seller on the closing statement (use a 360-day year)?
    A. $183.40
    B. $138.40
    C. $320.60
    D. $319.20

Advanced Level

36. The lender required the buyer to insure 100 percent of the value of improvements. The appraiser determined her property value, including the site, to be $335,000. The site was 20 percent of the value. The buyer purchased a two-year insurance premium that began on the closing date of November 15, 2005. The premium was $879. Her company transferred her on July 11, 2006, and a new buyer assumed her policy at the closing on the same day. Which of the following will be entered on the HUD-1 statement (use a 360-day year)?
    A. $288.13 CS, DB
    B. $288.13 DB, CS
    C. $589.26 CS, DB
    D. $590.87 DB, CS

D. NET TO SELLER, COST TO BUYER (CREDITS AND DEBITS)

The settlement sheet is a history of the buyer's and seller's debits and credits in a sales transaction. (See Figure 7.1.) If the entry is a debit, the party owes it at the closing table. If the entry is a credit, the party receives it at the closing table. The following worksheet shows the normal entries on a settlement sheet. Discount points can be paid by buyer or seller, so read the question carefully.

FIGURE 7.1

Settlement Sheet

Settlement Date: February 18, 2011	Buyer's Statement		Seller's Statement	
	Debit	Credit	Debit	Credit
Sales Price	DB			CS
Earnest Money Deposit		CB		
New Loan		CB		
Interest—New Loan	DB			
Loan Balance			DS	
Assumed Loan		CB	DS	
Interest—Assumed Loan		CB	DS	
Purchase-Money Mortgage		CB	DS	
Interest—Purchase-Money Mortgage	DB			CS
Commission			DS	
Property Taxes—Paid in Advance	DB			CS
Property Taxes—Paid in Arrears		CB	DS	
Assumed Insurance Policy	DB			CS
Credit Report	DB			
Origination Fees	DB			
Survey	DB			
Title Expenses	DB			
Appraisal Fee	DB			
Recording Fee	DB			
Transfer Fee			DS	

Discount points (these could be a DS or DB, so read the question to determine how it is to be entered.)

A 360-day or 365-day year may be used to compute interest, taxes, insurance, and so forth. Check to determine how they are computed in your state.

To compute proration problems, use a 360-day year, with each month having 30 days, unless the question states otherwise. Each proration question has a beginning date, prorate date, and ending date.

- The beginning date is always January 1, unless the question states otherwise.

- The prorate date is normally the closing date, but can be the date of the sale.

- The ending date is December 30, unless the question states otherwise.

- If paid in arrears, count from the beginning date to the prorate date, then debit the seller and credit the buyer.

■ If paid in advance, count from the prorate date to the ending date, then credit the seller and debit the buyer.

■ When the borrower is assuming the loan, the seller will owe from the first of the month through the closing date. The buyer will owe until the end of the month.

Example:
Closing date – August 14 (365-day year)
The seller will owe interest from August 1 through 14, or 14 days. The buyer will owe 17 days' interest. (31 – 14 = 17 days)

■ When the borrower is securing a *new loan*, the borrower will owe interest from the closing date through the end of that month.

Example:
Closing date – September 23 (365-day year)
The buyer will owe seven days' interest at the closing table.
(30 – 23 = 7 days)

Principal and interest payments are made in arrears. If the buyer's loan closed on September 23, the first PI payment would not be due until November 1. The interest for the month of October would be paid in the November 1 payment.

Figure 7.2 can be used if a 365-day year is needed to solve the question.

FIGURE 7.2	Month	Number of Days	Month	Number of Days
Settlement Sheet (365-day year)	January	31	July	31
	February	28*	August	31
	March	31	September	30
	April	30	October	31
	May	31	November	30
	June	30	December	31

*Remember, if the question states that it is a leap year, February will have 29 days.

Example: The property taxes of $1,250 have been paid for the year. If the property closes on June 23, how much is credited to the seller on the settlement sheet?

Step 1   January 1   The taxes have been paid, so count from the prorate
         June 23   date to the ending date and credit the seller, debit
                        the buyer.

         December 30   June 23 to June 30   =   7 days
                        July through December   = 180 days
                        Total   = 187 days CS, DB

Step 2 $1,250 ÷ 360 = $ 3.47 daily tax rate

Step 3   ×   187 days
         $648.89 CS, DB

PRORATION QUESTIONS

Beginner Level

37. On January 1, the seller paid the $2,345 in taxes for the current year. If he sold the property on June 23 of that same year, how much would he be credited at closing? (Use a 360-day year.)
    A. $1,158.78
    B. $1,218.10
    C. $1,293.53
    D. $1,772.50

38. The owners live in a county were taxes are paid in arrears and 360 days are used to compute the property tax bill. The house closed on April 13. If the annual tax bill is $3,355, how much will be credited the buyer on the settlement statement for taxes for this year?
    A. $946.57
    B. $959.96
    C. $2,407.78
    D. $2,441.84

Intermediate Level

39. Semiannual property taxes of $450 were paid only for the first half of the year. The property sold on July 11 and closed on September 19. If the taxes were prorated between the buyer and seller as of the date of sale, which of the following is TRUE?
    A. $252.50 CS, DB
    B. $252.50 DS, CB
    C. $27.50 DS, CB
    D. $497.50 CS, DB

40. A buyer negotiated a $75,000 loan at 8 percent interest for 30 years, with the first payment due in arrears on April 1. If the closing takes place on February 26, how much interest must the buyer pay on the day of closing (use a 360-day year)?
    A. $566.78
    B. $656.78
    C. $56.68
    D. $66.68

Advanced Level

41. A buyer offer of $295,000 was accepted, and a loan was negotiated for 80 percent at 7 percent for 25 years. The closing took place on January 5, and the buyer's first PITI payment is due March 1. Using a 365-day year, how much interest would the buyer be debited on the closing statement?
    A. $226.30
    B. $1,222.02
    C. $1,276.67
    D. $1,652.00

42. The buyer assumed a loan of $50,000 at 8.25 percent interest. Payments are due on the first of the month, in arrears. The last payment was made on April 1, and the closing took place on April 20. Which of the following is TRUE?
    A. $119.60 CS, DB
    B. $119.60 DB, CS
    C. $229.20 CS, DB
    D. $229.20 DS, CB

43. The buyer had a 20 percent down payment on a property she purchased for $89,500. She also must pay a 1 percent origination fee, $350 for title insurance, and one discount point. How much money will the buyer owe at the closing?
    A. $18,966
    B. $19,682
    C. $17,423
    D. $20,350

44. After the borrower made his payment on September 1, his loan balance was $12,259. His monthly payment is $124.34 per month paid in arrears on the first of the month. The interest rate on the loan is 9 percent. On October 1, he paid the lender for the October 1 payment, then paid off the entire mortgage balance. If the prepayment penalty was 2 percent, his prepayment penalty charge was approximately
    A. $244.53.
    B. $245.18.
    C. $232.40.
    D. $247.93.

E. AMORTIZATION

Financing math questions include computing the loan amount, annual interest dollars, discount points, loan origination fees, prepayment penalties, and amortization of a loan. Remember, the lender negotiates the loan on the sale price or appraised value, whichever is less.

> Example: A seller agreed to pay $85,000 for a property, but it appraised for $83,500. The lender agreed to negotiate a 90 percent loan. What was the loan amount?

$75,150 Loan

$83,500	90%

Appraised Value × Loan-to-Value Ratio
Sale Price or Appraised Value × Loan-to-Value Ratio = Loan
Loan ÷ Sale Price or Appraised Value = Loan-to-Value Ratio
Loan ÷ Loan-to-Value Ratio = Sale Price or Appraised Value

A question may ask for the annual, semiannual, quarterly, monthly, or daily interest that is due on a loan.

> Example: Sterling negotiated a $125,000 loan at 8.75 percent annual interest. How much interest will she pay the first year?

$10,937.50 Annual Interest $

$125,000	8.75%

Loan × Interest Rate
Loan × Interest Rate = Annual Interest $
Annual Interest $ ÷ Loan = Interest Rate
Annual Interest $ ÷ Interest Rate = Loan

F. POINTS

Discount points are computed as a percentage of the loan amount: 1 point = 1 percent of the loan, and 2 points = 2 percent of the loan.

> Example: Fred secured an $89,000 loan and was required to pay three discount points. How much did he pay in points?

$2,670 Discount Points $

$89,000	3%

Loan × Discount Points %
Loan × Discount Points % = Discount Points $
Discount Points $ ÷ Loan = Discount Points %
Discount Points $ ÷ Discount Points % = Loan

G. PREPAYMENT PENALTIES

The prepayment penalty is computed just like the discount points; it is calculated as a percentage of the loan amount.

> Example: The principal balance is $149,352.79. When the property transfers, the lender will charge a prepayment penalty of 3 percent. How much will the debited the seller for the prepayment penalty.

$4,480.58 Prepayment Penalty $

$149,352.79	3%
Loan	Prepayment Penalty %

×

Loan × Prepayment Penalty % = Prepayment Penalty $
Prepayment Penalty $ ÷ Loan = Prepayment Penalty %
Prepayment Penalty $ ÷ Prepayment Penalty % = Loan

A lender's cash outflow is the loan minus the discount points percent.

> Example: Ms. Buyer secured an $89,000 loan and had to pay one point. What was the cash outflow of the lender?

$89,000	Loan
− 1%	Discount Points %
$88,110	Cash Outflow

H. LOAN-TO-VALUE RATIOS

To determine the effective yield to the lender, remember this rule of thumb: For each discount point that the lender charges, the lender's yield is increased by 1/8 percent on a 30-year loan.

> Example: Warren negotiated an $80,000 loan for 30 years at an 8.25 percent rate of interest and had to pay two points. What was the effective yield to the lender?

Step 1   1 ÷ 8 = 0.125

Step 2   0.125 × 2 = 0.25 increase

Step 3   8.25% interest + 0.25% increase = 8.5% effective yield
0.125 × Discount Points = Increase
Interest Rate + Increase = Effective Yield

The loan origination fee also is computed as a percentage of the loan amount.

Example: The buyer secured a $50,000 loan and had to pay a 1.5 percent origination fee. How much did the buyer have to pay for the origination fee?

$$\frac{\text{\$750 Origination Fee \$}}{\text{\$50,000} \quad | \quad 1.5\%}$$

Loan × Origination Fee $
Loan × Origination Fee % = Origination Fees $
Origination Fee $ ÷ Loan = Origination Fee %
Origination Fee $ ÷ Origination Fee % = Loan

The word *amortize* means to reduce the debt by making payments that include both principal and interest. The principal and interest payment is normally given in the question about loan amortization.

Example: Sandy negotiated a $100,000 loan at 10 percent interest for 30 years. Her monthly payments are $877.58 per month. What is her loan balance after the first payment?

Step 1
$$\frac{\text{\$10,000 Annual Interest \$}}{\text{\$100,000} \quad | \quad 10\%}$$
Loan × Interest Rate

Step 2 $10,000 Annual Interest $ ÷ 12 months = $833.33 Monthly Interest

Step 3 $877.58 P&I – $833.33 Monthly Interest = $44.25 Principal

Step 4 $100,000 – 44.25 = $99,955.75 Loan Balance after First Payment

AMORTIZATION, POINTS, PREPAYMENT, AND LOAN-TO-VALUE QUESTIONS

Beginner Level

45. A property was purchased for $175,000. If the loan was $131,250, what was the loan-to-value ratio?
    A. 90 percent
    B. 80 percent
    C. 75 percent
    D. 70 percent

46. A lender negotiated an $82,250 loan, which was 80 percent of the appraised value. The appraised value of the property is
    A. $65,800.50
    B. $68,500.50
    C. $82,250.50
    D. $102,812.50

47. The buyers applied for a VA loan to purchase a property for $79,500. The property appraised at $79,000. They agreed to pay a 1 percent loan origination fee. How much did they pay in origination fees?
    A. $790
    B. $970
    C. $975
    D. $795

Intermediate Level

48. A lender agreed to a 90 percent loan-to-value ratio with an interest rate of 7 percent. If the annual interest is $17,640, what was the loan amount?
    A. $176,400
    B. $252,000
    C. $280,000
    D. $290,000

49. The semiannual interest paid on a loan was $4,387.50. If the interest rate is 6.5 percent, what was the loan amount?
    A. $67,500
    B. $135,000
    C. $270,000
    D. $540,000

50. A loan officer is paid 45 percent of the origination fee that her company charges. The loan officer negotiated a reverse mortgage, and her company was paid 2 percent of the appraised value of $190,000. How much was the loan officer paid?
    A. $1,710
    B. $3,800
    C. $5,200
    D. $6,400

51. What is the rate of interest if the mortgagor makes quarterly interest payments of $1,340.63 on a $65,000 loan?
    A. 2.06 percent
    B. 8.25 percent
    C. 7.75 percent
    D. 9.25 percent

52. To secure a $100,000 loan, the buyer paid $3,000 in discount points, and the seller paid $2,000 in discount points. How many points were charged?
    A. 3
    B. 2
    C. 5
    D. 4

53. A savings and loan agreed to make a $65,000 mortgage at 8 percent interest for 30 years and charged three points to negotiate the loan. What was the effective yield to the lender?
    A. 8.375 percent
    B. 8.735 percent
    C. 8.25 percent
    D. 8.35 percent

54. The lender negotiated a $55,000 loan and charged three discount points. What was the cash outflow of the lender?
    A. $56,560
    B. $56,650
    C. $53,530
    D. $53,350

Advanced Level

55. One lender charges 6.5 percent interest and the second lender charges 7 percent. How much money will the borrower save the first year on a $150,000 loan if he goes with the first lender?
    A. $500
    B. $650
    C. $750
    D. $850

56. The buyers secured an $82,000 loan at 9.25 percent interest for 30 years. Their monthly payment is $674.59. How much of their first payment will be applied to the principal balance?
    A. $42.51
    B. $64.51
    C. $632.08
    D. $785.55

57. The listing price of a property was $135,000. The buyer made an offer of 90 percent of the listing price, which was accepted by the sellers. The property appraised for $135,000, and the buyers secured an 85 percent loan at 9 percent interest for 30 years. How much interest will be paid in the first payment?
    A. $774.56
    B. $747.56
    C. $860.62
    D. $839.24

58. This month's interest payment is $585.70. If the buyer secured a 90 percent loan at an 8.75 percent annual rate of interest, what was the sale price?
    A. $80,325
    B. $80,235
    C. $89,250
    D. $89,500

59. A borrower secured an $80,000 loan at 8.25 percent interest, and the lender's cash outflow was $77,600. What was the effective yield to the lender?
    A. 8.50 percent
    B. 8.625 percent
    C. 8.375 percent
    D. 8.85 percent

I. MEASUREMENT (E.G., SQUARE FOOTAGE, ACREAGE, VOLUME)

The following are the formulas and rules that you must know to compute area math questions.

- The area of a rectangle or square is found by multiplying length × width.

- The area of a triangle is found by multiplying ½ base × height.

- The area of a circle is found by multiplying π (3.1416) × radius squared.

- The area of a trapezoid is found by adding the parallel lines, dividing by 2, and then multiplying by the height.

- To compute square feet, multiply length × width.

- To compute cubic feet, multiply length × width × height.

- There are 9 square feet in 1 square yard.

- To convert square feet to square yards, divide by 9.

- There are 27 cubic feet in 1 cubic yard.

- To convert cubic feet to cubic yards, divide by 27.

- To convert square feet to acres, divide by 43,560.

- To convert acres to square feet, multiply by 43,560.

- There are 5,280 feet in 1 mile.

- The front footage is the first dimension in a lot size.

    Example: A lot measures 200' × 250' and sells for $55,000. Another lot in that same area measuring 150' × 175' would likely sell for what price?

    Step 1   A = 200' × 250'
               A = 50,000 square feet

    Step 2 $55,000 ÷ 50,000 = $1.10 per sq. ft.

    Step 3   A = 150' × 175'
               A = 26,250 square feet

    Step 4   26,250 × $1.10 = $28,875

Example: How many square feet are in a triangular-shaped area that has a base of 60' and a height of 130'?

$$A = ½(b) \times h$$

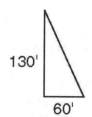

Step 1 $A = ½(60') \times 130'$

$A = 30' \times 130'$

$A = 3,900$ square feet

Example: A circle has a diameter of 90'. How many square feet does it contain? (The radius is one-half of the diameter.)

$$A = \pi r2$$

Step 1 $A = 3.1416 \times 45' \times 45'$

$A = 6,361.74$ square feet

How many square yards does it contain?

$6,361.74 \div 9 = 706.86$ square yards

Example: The two parallel sides of a trapezoid are 60' and 90'. The height is 50'. How many square feet does it contain?

$$A = [(\text{parallel lines}) \div 2] \times h$$

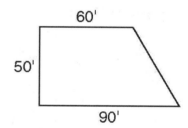

Step 1 $A = [(60' + 90') \div 2] \times 50'$

$A = 75' \times 50'$

$A = 3,750$ square feet

How many acres does it contain?

$3,750 \div 43,560 = 0.0861$ acres

Example: A storage room that measures 20' × 30' × 10' contains how many cubic feet?

$$V = L \times W \times H$$

Step 1 $V = 20' \times 30' \times 10'$

$V = 6,000$ cubic feet

How many cubic yards does it contain?

$6,000 \div 27 = 222.22$ cubic yards

MEASUREMENT QUESTIONS

Beginner Level

60. If a circular property has a diameter of 50' and costs $120 per square foot, what is the cost of the property?
    A. $235,620
    B. $942,480
    C. $1,235,620
    D. $2,356,200

61. The N½ of the SW¼ of the NE¼ sold for $2,500 per acre. What was the selling price?
    A. $10,000
    B. $20,000
    C. $40,000
    D. $50,000

62. A lot contains 9/10 of an acre. What is the depth of the lot if the front measures 150'?
    A. 216.36'
    B. 261.36'
    C. 322.67'
    D. 323.67'

Intermediate Level

63. A two-story house measures 25' × 50'. A one-story family room was added that measures 20' × 20'. At a cost of $9.95 per square yard for carpet and $2.50 per square yard for installation, how much will it cost to carpet the house and family room?
    A. $2,282.50
    B. $36,105.00
    C. $20,542.50
    D. $4,011.67

64. The rooms in Sandy's house measure as follows: living room, 20' × 25'; dining room, 18' × 20'; bedroom, 14' × 26'; bedroom, 15' × 15'; bedroom, 12' × 14'. The carpet she has selected costs $9.95 per square yard. How much will it cost to carpet the entire house?
    A. $732.39
    B. $836.91
    C. $950.77
    D. $1,787.68

65. A rectangular lot measures 200' × 300'. Property in the area is selling for $150,000 per acre. If the broker charges 8 percent, how much is she paid?
    A. $16,529
    B. $15,290
    C. $16,730
    D. $19,243

66. A building measures 30' × 80' × 15'. A buyer made an offer of $35 per square foot on the property. The owner made a counteroffer of $2.75 per cubic foot. How much more will it cost the buyer if he accepts the counteroffer?
    A. $18,000
    B. $15,000
    C. $17,000
    D. $16,000

Advanced Level

67. A buyer purchased a property that is one mile square and another that measures 511.23' × 511.23'. At a cost of $2,000 an acre, how much did she pay for the property?
    A. $1,291,999
    B. $1,921,999
    C. $1,733,435
    D. $1,373,435

68. How many cubic yards of concrete must a builder buy to pour a sidewalk that measures 45' × 3.25' and is five inches thick?
    A. 60.9375
    B. 2.2571
    C. 0.4167
    D. 6.7708

69. Using the dimensions in the following diagram, what is the approximate cost to purchase at $4,000 per acre?
   A. $3,214
   B. $6,428
   C. $9,213
   D. $12,856

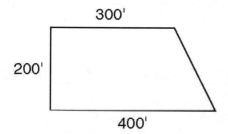

300'

200'

400'

70. How many square feet of living area are in the following house?
   A. 2,087.5
   B. 2,150.0
   C. 2,775.0
   D. 2,990.5

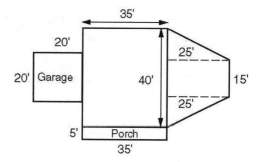

35'

20'

20' Garage

25'

40'

15'

25'

5'   Porch

35'

J. PROPERTY MANAGEMENT/INVESTMENT (E.G., RATE OF RETURN)

An agent acting as a property manager may be paid a percentage of the gross or net income as commission. Normally, the manager is paid a percentage of the gross income, but read the question carefully.

> Example: The annual gross rent collected on a building is $124,000. If the property manager is paid a 6 percent commission on the rents collected, how much is he paid annually?

$$\begin{array}{c|c} \multicolumn{2}{c}{\text{\$7,440 Commission \$}} \\ \hline \text{\$124,000} & \text{6\%} \end{array}$$

Gross Rent × Commission Rate = Commission $

Gross or Net Rent × Commission Rate = Commission $
Commission $ ÷ Commission Rate = Gross or Net Rent
Commission $ ÷ Gross or Net Rent = Commission Rate

Read the question carefully to determine if you are solving for the annual, semiannual, quarterly, or monthly commission.

The commission also may be computed as so many dollars per square foot of the space leased.

> Example: A tenant leased a 60 ft. × 100 ft. space for $8 per square foot annually. If the property manager is paid 8 percent of the rent collected, how much is she paid annually?

Step 1   60' × 100' = 6,000 square feet

Step 2   6,000 square feet × $8 = $48,000 annual rent

Step 3
$$\begin{array}{c|c} \multicolumn{2}{c}{\text{\$3,840 Commission \$}} \\ \hline \text{\$48,000} & \text{8\%} \end{array}$$

Gross Rent × Commission Rate

Though there are several types of percentage leases, this is usually how they are negotiated: the tenant pays a fixed monthly rent or base rent, plus a percentage of all income over a certain amount. The rent also could be paid on all income.

Example: A shop owner entered into a percentage lease with the lessor in which she agreed to pay a fixed rental of $650 per month; and when gross sales reached $175,000, she pays 5 percent of sales over that amount. This year, her gross sales were $225,000. What was the total rent paid at the end of the year?

Step 1 $650 \times 12 = \$7,800$ fixed rent

Step 2 $\$225,000 - 175,000 = \$50,000$ gross sales over $175,000

Step 3

$2,500 Commission $	
$50,000	5%

Gross Sales × Commission Rate

Step 4 $\$7,800 + 2,500 = \$10,300$ Total Commission Paid

In a graduated lease, the rents increase, or *step up* on a gradual basis over the life of the lease.

Example: A tenant entered into a 12-year graduated lease with the owner of a building. He agreed to pay $400 per month for the first four years, $450 per month for the next four years, and $500 per month for the remaining term. If the property manager is paid 6 percent of the total rent collected, how much will he be paid at the end of the leasing term?

Step 1 $\$400 \times 12 \times 4 = \$19,200$
         $\$450 \times 12 \times 4 = \$21,600$
         $+ \$500 \times 12 \times 4 = \$24,000$
         $\qquad\qquad\qquad \$64,800$

Step 2 $\$7,800 + 2,500 = \$10,300$ Total Commission Paid

Step 3

$3,888 Commission $	
$64,800	6%

×

Gross Rent × Commission Rate

RATE OF RETURN QUESTIONS

Beginner Level

71. A tenant pays rental of $15.50 per square foot annually for her office, which measures 25' × 50'. If the leasing agent is paid 7 percent of her rent collected, how much is she paid?
    A. $19,375
    B. $14,233
    C. $3,345
    D. $1,356

72. A space was leased for $1,200 per month. The owner pays a property manager 8 percent of the gross income as commission. How much does the owner pay annually?
    A. $1,512
    B. $1,152
    C. $1,215
    D. $96

73. A property manager negotiated a 15-year graduated lease with the following terms: The lessee will pay $550 per month for the first five years, with a $50 a month increase every five years thereafter. If the property manager is paid a 6.75 percent commission, what will be the total commission paid at the end of the term?
    A. $7,290
    B. $7,087
    C. $7,429
    D. $7,920

Intermediate Level

74. The lease agreement for Julia's Fine Arts store was as follows: $1,200 fixed monthly rent plus 4 percent commission on all sales over $850,000. This year, her gross sales were $1,500,000. How much was paid in rent?
    A. $14,400
    B. $26,000
    C. $40,400
    D. $35,000

75. A tenant entered into a 20-year graduated lease. She will pay $500 per month for the first 5 years, and $575 per month for the next 15 years. The property manager is paid 6 percent of the total rent collected, and he has another five buildings with the same agreement. How much will he be paid over the life of the leases?
    A. $40,050
    B. $48,060
    C. $50,260
    D. $55,350

76. The XYZ store leased a space in the mall with the following agreement: $575 fixed monthly rent, plus a 5.25 percent commission on all sales over $225,000. The gross sales were $389,250 for the year. What was the total rent paid by XYZ?
    A. $15,523
    B. $8,623
    C. $9,600
    D. $15,253

Advanced Level

77. The KLM store leased a space in the mall with a percentage lease and agreed to pay $425 monthly fixed rent and 6 percent on all sales over $175,000. This year, the total rent paid was $9,321. What were the gross sales?
    A. $184,849
    B. $213,350
    C. $213,530
    D. $245,350

78. VonTrapp Heirlooms' percentage lease reads as follows: The tenant agrees to pay $800 per month fixed rent plus 4 percent on all sales over one million dollars. If the total rent paid was $49,600, the gross sales were
    A. $1,000,000.
    B. $1,500,000.
    C. $2,000,000.
    D. $2,500,000.

EXTRA MATH QUESTIONS

Beginner Level

79. A home is valued at $250,000 and is insured for 80 percent of its value. The one-year insurance policy was purchased on January 12, 2008, at a cost of $550. The property was sold, and the buyer assumed the owner's policy on December 23, 2009. How much will the owner be credited at the closing?
    A. $522.50
    B. $432.70
    C. $27.50
    D. $29.03

80. The seller's net after paying a 6 percent commission was $355,000. The approximate sale price of the property was
    A. $377,660.
    B. $379,850.
    C. $376,300.
    D. $381,720.

81. An agent who works for XYZ Realty in Illinois and referred a buyer to an agent, who works for ABC Realty in Georgia. The referring agent is to receive 25 percent of buyer agent's commission when the transaction closes. The buyer purchased a $350,000 home, and the 7 percent commission was split as follows: listing broker, 2 percent; listing agent, 2 percent; selling broker, 1.5 percent; selling agent, 1.5 percent. How much was the referring agent paid?
    A. $24,500.00
    B. $7,000.00
    C. $5,250.50
    D. $1,312.50

82. An agent works for JKJ Realty in North Dakota, and she referred a buyer to an agent who works for ASD Realty in South Dakota. The referring agent's check was for $2,062.50, or 25 percent of the buyer agent's portion. The 7 percent commission was split as follows: listing broker, 2 percent; listing agent, 2 percent; selling broker, 1.5 percent; selling agent, 1.5 percent. What was the sale price of the property?
    A. $500,000
    B. $550,000
    C. $600,000
    D. $650,000

83. A property was listed for $450,000. A buyer's offer of 95 percent of the list price was accepted. He had a 20 percent down payment and secured a 30-year fixed rate loan at 6.75% interest. How much interest will he pay the first month of the loan?
    A. $1,923.75
    B. $3,847.50
    C. $7,695.00
    D. $23,085.00

84. An investment property had a net operating income of $75,230, expenses of $4,900, additional income of $2,500, and a cap rate of 8 percent. What is the effective gross income?
    A. $77,730
    B. $79,500
    C. $80,130
    D. $82,630

85. A rectangular lot is 275 feet deep, and it contains ⅔ of an acre. What is the length of the lot?
    A. 158.4'
    B. 106.5'
    C. 290.04'
    D. 105.6'

Intermediate Level

86. Four years ago, a buyer purchased a property for $148,000. For three years, it appreciated 4 percent each year, but the fourth year it depreciated 4 percent. What was the approximate value of the property at the end of the fourth year?
    A. $159,020
    B. $159,130
    C. $159,820
    D. $159,900

87. A first-time buyer paid $135,500 for her property. Taxes in her community are assessed at 80 percent of the market value. If the tax rate is 700 mills per $100, how much will be escrowed for taxes for her monthly PITI payment?
    A. $63.00
    B. $63.23
    C. $75.60
    D. $75.88

88. The owners pay $137.81 in monthly property taxes. If the tax rate is $3.50 per $100 and the assessment rate is 35 percent, what is the value of the property?
    A. $153,998.69
    B. $143,997.45
    C. $166,532.72
    D. $134,997.54

89. An agent is managing a 15-unit apartment building and is paid 9 percent of the gross income. She leases five apartments for $500, five for $550, and five for $600. There is a 3 percent vacancy rate and additional income of $450 per month. The monthly operating expenses are $1,749, and the owner is generating an 8 percent return on the investment. What is the effective gross income on the building?
    A. $99,000
    B. $96,030
    C. $80,442
    D. $101,430

90. Four units are renting for $450 each per month. There is a 5 percent vacancy factor, and annual expenses are $3,547. The owner wants an 8 percent return on her investment, and the property has additional monthly income of $464. What is the effective gross income of the property?
    A. $21,796
    B. $21,976
    C. $20,984
    D. $26,088

91. The buyers secured a loan with a 75 percent loan-to-value ratio. The interest rate was 7.125 percent, and the term was for 30 years. The first month's interest payment was $477.82. What was the appraised value of the property?
    A. $107,300
    B. $80,475
    C. $103,700
    D. $79,239

92. An owner wants to receive a net of $82,000 after selling her home. She has an existing mortgage of $32,500 and will have selling expenses of $444. If the broker is to receive a 7 percent commission, what is the LOWEST offer that she can accept for the property?
    A. $122,990.08
    B. $122,515.08
    C. $123,595.70
    D. $123,959.70

93. A homeowner has a property valued at $125,000 that is assessed at 35 percent of its value. If the local tax rate is 6,400 mills per $100 of the assessed value, what are the monthly taxes?
    A. $280.00
    B. $140.33
    C. $480.00
    D. $233.33

Advanced Level

94. An offer was made for 90 percent of the $120,900 list price of a property. The offer was accepted, and the lender agreed to negotiate an 80 percent loan at 8 percent interest for 30 years. The buyer had a $5,000 earnest money deposit, paid $350 for title expenses, $250 for attorney fees, and had other expenses of $749. How much money does the buyer need to close on the property?
    A. $18,111
    B. $23,111
    C. $10,159
    D. $15,159

95. A homeowner sold his property for $99,500. He paid a real estate commission of 6 percent, paid an attorney $250, paid a transfer tax of $99.50, paid his existing mortgage of $50,140, and agreed to a purchase-money mortgage of $10,000. What were his net proceeds at the closing?
    A. $43,050.40
    B. $33,040.50
    C. $53,040.50
    D. $33,050.40

96. An owner of a fourplex has one unit that rents for $450 a month, one unit that rents for $475 per month, and two units that rent for $500 per month. The vacancy rate is 4 percent, and the monthly expenses average $350. If the rate of return on the property is 10 percent, what is the value?
    A. $218,260
    B. $118,260
    C. $189,760
    D. $179,760

97. A house is now worth $105,000. The lot is now worth $50,000. If the house depreciated 4 percent each year for the past two years, and the lot appreciated 6 percent each year for the past two years, what was the approximate combined original value of the house and lot?
    A. $156,544
    B. $113,932
    C. $109,375
    D. $170,112

98. A borrower negotiated a loan of $150,000 at 4.75% interest for 30 years. His monthly P&I payment was $782.47. After making his payment on December 1, his principal balance was $144,212.71. The note contained a prepayment penalty of 2 percent. After making his payment on January 1, the borrower paid off the remaining mortgage balance. How much was he charged for the prepayment penalty?
    A. $2,875.77
    B. $2,880.02
    C. $2,884.25
    D. $2,925.34

99. A buyer assumed the seller's insurance policy on June 24, 2009. The owner paid $649.50 for a three-year policy on April 30, 2008. Which of the following is TRUE? (Use a 360-day year.)
    A. $249.90 DS, CB
    B. $249.90 CB, DS
    C. $399.00 CS, DB
    D. $399.00 DB, CS

100. On September 20, 2008, a buyer closed on her new $160,000 home, and she insured 80 percent of its value. Her premium on the two-year policy was $3.75 per $1,000. On November 11, 2009, she sold the property, and the buyer assumed the policy. Using a 360-day year, how much will the buyer be debited at the closing?
    A. $480.00
    B. $273.99
    C. $205.34
    D. $274.01

MATH ANSWERS

1. **(B)**

$$\frac{\$15,750}{\$225,000 \mid 7\%}$$
$$\times$$

$$\frac{\$12,375}{\$225,000 \mid 5.5\%}$$
$$\times$$

$$\begin{array}{r} \$15,750 \\ -\ 12,375 \\ \hline \$3,375 \end{array}$$

2. **(C)**

$$\frac{\$21,000 \div}{\$300,000 \mid 7\%}$$

3. **(D)**

2% + 1.5% = 3.5% Agent's share
6% – 3.5% = 2.5% Broker's share

$$\frac{\$4,375}{\$175,000 \mid 2.5\%}$$
$$\times$$

4. **(D)**

$8,225 \times 2 = \$16,450$ total commission paid

$$\frac{\div \$16,450}{\$235,000 \mid 0.07 \text{ or } 7\%}$$

5. **(B)**

$$\frac{\$7,500}{\$125,000 \mid 6\%}$$
$$\times$$

$$\frac{\$3,000}{\$7,500 \mid 40\%}$$
$$\times$$

6. **(C)**

7% – 2% – 1.5% = 3.5% to the broker

$$\frac{\$6,650}{\$190,000 \mid 3.5\%}$$
$$\times$$

7. **(A)**

$$\frac{\$12,750}{\$425,000 \mid 3\%}$$
$$\times$$

$12,750 + 2,995 = \$15,745$

8. **(C)**

$$\frac{\$6,000}{\$100,000 \mid 6\%}$$
$$\times$$

$$\frac{\$5,000}{\$100,000 \mid 5\%}$$
$$\times$$

$$\frac{\$2,000}{\$50,000 \mid 4\%}$$
$$\times$$

$$\begin{array}{r} \$\ 6,000 \\ 5,000 \\ +\ 2,000 \\ \hline \$13,000 \end{array}$$

9. **(D)**

$2,500 × 2 = $5,000

$$\frac{\$5,000 \div}{\$71,428.57 \mid 7\%}$$

10. **(D)**

$$\frac{\$3,500 \div}{\$5,933.33 \mid 60\%}$$

$$\frac{\div \$5,833.33}{\$83,333 \mid 0.07 \text{ or } 7\%}$$

11. **(A)**

100% – 6% = 94% Seller's percent

$$\frac{\$470,000 \div}{\$500,000 \mid 94\%}$$

12. **(B)**

100% – 6% = 94% Seller's percent

$$\frac{\$200,000 \div}{\$212,765.95 \mid 94\%}$$

13. **(D)**

$$
\begin{array}{rr}
100\% & \$149,850 \\
-\ 6\% & +\quad 550 \\
\hline
94\% & \$150,400
\end{array}
$$

$$\frac{\$150,400 \div}{\$160,000 \mid 94\%}$$

14. **(A)**

$$
\begin{array}{rr}
100\% & \$20,000 \\
-\ 7\% & 35,250 \\
\hline
93\% & +\quad 400 \\
& \$55,650
\end{array}
$$

$$\frac{\$55,650 \div}{\$59,838.71 \mid 93\%}$$

15. **(C)**

$$
\begin{array}{rr}
100\% & \$104,500 \\
-\ 6.5\% & +\quad 12\% \\
\hline
93.5\% & \$117,040
\end{array}
$$

$$\frac{\$117,040 \div}{\$125,176.47 \mid 93.5\%}$$

16. **(B)**

$$\frac{\$90,000 \div}{\$1,125,000 \mid 0.08\ (8\%)}$$
$$\times$$

17. **(C)**

$48,000 × 2 = $96,000

$$\frac{\div \$96,000}{\$1,250,000 \mid 0.0768 \text{ or } 7.68\%}$$

18. **(D)**

$$
\begin{array}{r}
\$55,575 \\
-\ 5,500 \\
\hline
\$50,075
\end{array}
$$

$$\frac{\$50,075 \div}{\$500,750 \mid 10\%}$$

19. **(D)**

$$\frac{\$67,200}{112 \mid \$600}$$
$$\times$$

20. **(B)** $150,000 + 5\% + 5\% + 5\% = \$173,643.75$ or $173,644

21. **(B)** $175,000 – 3\% – 3\% = \$164,657.50$ or $164,658

22. **(C)**

$250,000		$230,000
– 8%		+ 50,000
$230,000		$280,000

23. **(D)**

$250,000		$500,000
× 2		– 20%
$500,000		$400,000

24. **(C)**

$165,000		$240,000		$223,200
+ 16,500		– 7%		– 191,500
+ 10,000		$223,200		$ 31,700
+191,500				

25. **(B)**

$250,000		$325,000		$302,000
+ 10,000		– 7%		– 260,000
$260,000		$302,250		$ 42,000
		– 250		
		$302,000		

26. **(A)**

$550 × 12 × 3 = $19,800	$64,800	$67,200	$64,512	$59,512 ÷
$600 × 12 × 3 = $21,600	+ 2,400	– 4%	– 5,000	$661,244 | 0.09%
$650 × 12 × 3 = $23,400	$67,200	$64,512	$59,512	
$64,800				

27. **(C)**

5 × $550 × 12 =	$33,000	
5 × $600 × 12 =	$36,000	
	$69,000	
	– 8%	
	$63,480	$60,480 ÷
$250 × 12 =	– 3,000	$756,000 | 8%
	$60,480	

28. **(B)**

$117,978 ÷			$111,300 ÷	
$111,300	100%		$105,000	100%
	+ 6%			+ 6%
	106%			106%

29. **(C)**

$98,250 ÷			$103,421 ÷	
$103,421	100%		$108,864	100%
	− 5%			− 5%
	95%			95%

30. **(A)**

$1 ÷ 100 = 0.01 Tax rate

$1,250	
$125,000	0.01
×	

31. **(D)**

$4.25 ÷ 100 = 0.0425

$59,150	
$169,000	35%
×	

$2,513.875 ÷ 12 = $209.49

$59,150	
	0.0425
×	

32. **(A)**

95 ÷ 1,000 = 0.095

$19,893	
$52,350	38%
×	

$1,889.83 ÷ 4 = $472.45

$19,893	
	0.095
×	

33. **(A)**

$29,250	
$65,000	45%
×	

$511.88	
×	2
$1,023.75	

÷ $1,023.76

$29,250	0.035

	0.035
	× 100
	$3.50

34. **(B)**

$4.50 ÷ 100 = 0.045
$984.38 × 2 = $1,968.76

$1,968.76 ÷	
$43,750	0.045

$43,750 ÷	
$175,000	25%

35. **(D)**

Beginning Date: September 14, 2005
Prorate Date: January 25, 2006
Ending Date: September 13, 2006
January 25–30 = 5 days
February–August = 210 days
September = 13 days
Total = 228 days
$504 ÷ 360 = $1.40 × 228 = **$319.20**

36. **(C)**

Beginning Date:	November 15, 2005
Prorate Date:	July 11, 2006
Ending Date:	November 14, 2007

July 2006: 11–30 = 19 days

August 2006 – October 2007 = 15 months
× 30 days = 450 days

November = 14 days

Total = 483 days

360 days per year × 2 = 720

$879 ÷ 720 = $1.22 × 483 = **$589.26**

37. **(B)**

January 1   The taxes were paid in advance, so count from June 23 through December 30.

June 23   June 30 – 23 = 7 days

December 30   July through December = 30 × 6 = 180 days

180 + 7 = 187 days

$2,345 ÷ 360 = $6.5139 daily tax

187 × $6.5139 = **$1,218.10** credit to seller at closing

38. **(B)**

January through March	90 days
April 13	+13 days
Total	103 days

$3,355 ÷ 360 = $9.32 per day

103 × $9.32 = **$959.96**

39. **(C)** July 1 – 11 = 11 days

$450 ÷ 180 = $2.50

$ 2.50
× 11
$27.50 DS, CB

40. **(D)**

February 26   February 30 – 26 = 4 days

February 30

$6,000 ÷ 360

$75,000 | 8%

×

$16.67
× 4
$66.68

41. **(B)**

$236,000

$295,000 | 80%
×

$16,520

$236,000 | 7%
×

$16,520 ÷ 365 = $45.26 (January 5–31 = 27 days)

× 27
$1,222.02

42. **(D)**

April 1   April 1 – 20 = 20 days

April 20

$$\frac{\$4,125 \div 360}{\$50,000 \mid 8.25\%} = \$11.46$$
$$\times$$

$$\begin{array}{r} \$11.46 \\ \times \quad 20 \\ \hline \mathbf{\$229.20} \end{array}$$

43. **(B)**

$$\frac{\$71,600}{\$89,500 \mid 80\%}$$
$$\times$$

$$\begin{array}{r} \$89,500 \\ -71,600 \\ \hline \$17,900 \end{array}$$

$$\frac{\$716}{\$71,600 \mid 1\%}$$
$$\times$$

$$\begin{array}{rl} \$ & 716 \quad \text{discount points} \\ & 716 \quad \text{original fee} \\ & 350 \quad \text{insurance} \\ +17,&900 \quad \text{down payment} \\ \hline \mathbf{\$19,}&\mathbf{682} \end{array}$$

44. **(A)**

$$\frac{\$1,103.31 \div 12 = \$91.94}{\$12,259 \mid 9\%}$$
$$\times$$

$$\begin{array}{r} \$124.34 \\ -\ 91.94 \\ \hline \$\ 32.40 \end{array}$$

$$\begin{array}{r} \$12,259.00 \\ -\quad 32.40 \\ \hline \$12,226.60 \end{array}$$

$$\begin{array}{c} \mathbf{\$244.53} \\ \hline \$12,226.60 \mid 2\% \\ \times \end{array}$$

45. **(C)**

$$\frac{\div \$131,250}{\$175,000 \mid 0.75 \text{ or } 75\%}$$

46. **(D)**

$$\frac{\$82,250 \div}{\$102,812.50 \mid 80\%}$$

47. **(A)**

$$\frac{\$790}{\$79,000 \mid 1\%}$$
$$\times$$

48. **(B)**

$$\frac{\$17,640 \div}{\$252,000 \mid 7\%}$$

49. **(B)**

$4,387.50 \times 2 = \$8,775$ annual interest

$$\frac{\$8,775 \div}{\$135,000 \mid 6.5\%}$$

50. **(A)**

$$\frac{\$3,800}{\$190,000 \mid 2\%}$$
$$\times$$

$$\frac{\$1,710}{\$3,800 \mid 45\%}$$
$$\times$$

51. **(B)**

$$\begin{array}{r} \$1,340.63 \\ \times\qquad 4 \\ \hline \$5,362.52 \end{array}$$

$$\begin{array}{c} \div 5,362.52 \\ \hline \$65,000 \quad\big|\quad 8.25\% \\ \times \end{array}$$

52. **(C)**

$$\begin{array}{r} \$3,000 \\ +2,000 \\ \hline \$5,000 \end{array}$$

$$\begin{array}{c} \div \$5,000 \\ \hline \$100,000 \quad\big|\quad 0.05 \text{ or 5 points} \end{array}$$

53. **(A)** $0.125 \times 3 = 0.375$
            $8\% + 0.375 = 8.375\%$

54. **(D)**

$$\begin{array}{r} \$55,000 \\ -\qquad 3\% \\ \hline \$53,350 \end{array}$$

or

$$\begin{array}{c} \$1,650 \\ \hline \$55,000 \quad\big|\quad 3\% \\ \times \end{array}$$

$$\begin{array}{r} \$55,000 \\ -\quad 1,650 \\ \hline \$53,350 \end{array}$$

55. **(C)**

$$\begin{array}{c} \$9,750 \\ \hline \$150,000 \quad\big|\quad 6.5\% \\ \times \end{array}$$

$$\begin{array}{c} \$10,500 \\ \hline \$150,000 \quad\big|\quad 7\% \\ \times \end{array}$$

$$\begin{array}{r} \$10,500 \\ -\quad 9,750 \\ \hline \$\quad 750 \end{array}$$

56. **(A)**

$$\begin{array}{c} \$7,585 \\ \hline \$82,000 \quad\big|\quad 9.25\% \\ \times \end{array}$$

$$\$7,585 \div 12 = \$632.08$$

$$\begin{array}{r} \$674.59 \\ -\ 632.08 \\ \hline \$\ 42.51 \end{array}$$

57. **(A)**

$$\begin{array}{c} \$121,500 \\ \hline \$135,000 \quad\big|\quad 90\% \\ \times \end{array}$$

$$\begin{array}{c} \$103,275 \\ \hline \$121,500 \quad\big|\quad 85\% \\ \times \end{array}$$

$$\$9,294.75 \div 12 = \$774.56$$
$$\begin{array}{c} \hline \$103,275 \quad\big|\quad 9\% \\ \times \end{array}$$

58. **(C)**

$$\begin{array}{r} \$\ 585.75 \\ \times\qquad 12 \\ \hline \$7,028.40 \end{array}$$

$$\begin{array}{c} \$7,028.40 \div \\ \hline \$80,324.57 \quad\big|\quad 8.75\% \\ \times \end{array}$$

$$\begin{array}{c} \$80,324.57 \div \\ \hline \$89,249.52 \quad\big|\quad 90\% \\ \times \end{array}$$

59. **(B)**

$$\begin{array}{r} \$80,000 \\ -\ 77,600 \\ \hline \$\ 2,400 \end{array}$$

$$\begin{array}{c} \div 2,400 \\ \hline \$80,000 \quad\big|\quad 3 \text{ pts.} \\ \times \end{array}$$

$0.125 \times 3 = 0.375$
$8.25\% + 0.375 = 8.625\%$

60. **(A)** $A = 3.1416 \times 25' \times 25'$
            $A = 1,963.5 \text{ sq. ft.} \times \$120 = \$235,620$

61. **(D)** 640 ÷ 4 ÷ 4 ÷ 2 = 20 acres (See page 121 for explanation)
    20 × $2,500 = $50,000

62. **(B)** 9 ÷ 10 = 90%
    43,560 × 90% = 39,204
    39,204 ÷ 150 = 261.36

63. **(D)**

A = 25' × 50'	A = 20' × 20'	2,500	2,900 ÷ 9 =	322.222
A = 1,250 sq. ft.	A = 400 sq. ft.	+ 400	$9.95 + 2.50 =	× 12.45
× 2		2,900		$4,011.67
2,500				

64. **(D)**

20' × 25' = 500 sq. ft.   1,617 ÷ 9 = 179.6667 square yards
18' × 20' = 360 sq. ft.   179.667 × $9.95 = $1,787.68 for entire house
14' × 26' = 364 sq. ft.
15' × 15' = 225 sq. ft.
12' × 14' = 168 sq. ft.
Total   1,617 sq. ft.

65. **(A)** 200' × 300' = 60,000 sq. ft. ÷ 43,560 = 1.3774 acres
    1.3774 × $150,000 = $206,610
    $206,610 × 8% = $16,528.80 or $16,529

66. **(B)**

A = 30' × 80'   V = 30' × 80' × 15' $99,000
A = 2,400 sq. ft.   V = 36,000 cubic ft.   −84,000
× $35   × $2.75 $15,000
$84,000 $99,000

67. **(A)** 5,280 × 5,280 = 27,878,400
    27,878,400 ÷ 43,560 = 640
    511.23 × 511.23 = 261,356.1129
    261,356.1129 ÷ 43,560 = 5.9999
    640 + 5.9999 = 645.9999
    645.9999 × $2,000 = $1,291,999

68. **(B)**

5" ÷ 12" = 0.4167'   60.9423 ÷ 27 = 2.2571 cubic yds.
V = 45' × 3.25' × 0.4167'
V = 60.9423 cubic ft.

69. **(B)**

A = [(300' + 400') ÷ 2)] × 200'   70,000 ÷ 43,560 = 1.6070 acres
A = (700' ÷ 2) × 200'   1.6070 × $4,000 = $6,427.91 or $6,428
A = 350' × 200'
A = 70,000 sq. ft.

70. **(A)** A = 35' × 40'

   A = 1,400 sq. ft.

   A = [(15' + 40') ÷ 2 × 25']

   A = 687.5 sq. ft.

   $$\begin{array}{r} 1,400 \\ +\ 687.5 \\ \hline 2,087.5 \end{array}$$

71. **(D)**

   25' × 50' = 1,250 sq. ft.

   1,250 × $15.50 = $19,375 Annual rent

   $$\dfrac{\$1,356.25}{\$19,375\ \big|\ 7\%}$$
   ×

72. **(B)**

   $$\begin{array}{r} \$1,200 \\ \times\quad 12 \\ \hline \$14,400 \end{array}$$

   $$\dfrac{\$1,152}{\$14,400\ \big|\ 8\%}$$
   ×

73. **(A)**

   $550 × 12 × 5 = $ 33,000

   $600 × 12 × 5 = $ 36,000

   $650 × 12 × 5 = $ 39,000

   $108,000

   $$\dfrac{\$7,290}{\$108,000\ \big|\ 6.75\%}$$
   ×

74. **(C)**

   $$\begin{array}{r} \$1,500,000 \\ -\ \ 850,000 \\ \hline \$\ \ 650,000 \end{array}$$

   $$\dfrac{\$26,000}{\$650,000\ \big|\ 4\%}$$
   ×

   $1,200 × 12 = $14,400

   $$\begin{array}{r} \$26,000 \\ +\ 14,400 \\ \hline \$40,400 \end{array}$$

75. **(B)**

   $500 × 12 × 5 = $ 30,000

   $575 × 12 × 15 = $103,500

   $133,500

   $$\dfrac{\$48,060}{\$801,000\ \big|\ 6\%}$$
   ×

   $133,500 × 6 = $801,000

76. **(A)**

   $$\begin{array}{r} \$575 \\ \times\ 12 \\ \hline \$6,900 \end{array}$$

   $$\begin{array}{r} \$389,250 \\ -225,000 \\ \hline \$164,250 \end{array}$$

   $$\dfrac{\$8,623}{\$164,250\ \big|\ 5.25\%}$$
   ×

   $$\begin{array}{r} \$8,623 \\ +\ 6,900 \\ \hline \$15,523 \end{array}$$

77. **(D)**

   $$\begin{array}{r} \$\ 425 \\ \times\ 12 \\ \hline \$5,100 \end{array}$$

   $$\begin{array}{r} \$9,321 \\ -5,100 \\ \hline \$4,221 \end{array}$$

   $$\dfrac{\$4,221 \div}{\$70,350\ \big|\ 6\%}$$

   $$\begin{array}{r} \$175,000 \\ +\ 70,350 \\ \hline \$245,350 \end{array}$$

78. **(C)**

$$\$800 \times 12 = \$9,600 \qquad \begin{array}{r} \$49,600 \\ -\ 9,600 \\ \hline \$40,000 \end{array} \qquad \frac{\$40,000 \div}{\$1,000,000 \mid \ 4\%} \qquad \begin{array}{r} \$1,000,000 \\ +\ 1,000,000 \\ \hline \$2,000,000 \end{array}$$

79. **(C)**

Beginning Date:	January 12, 2008
Prorate Date:	December 23, 2009
Ending Date:	January 11, 2009

December 30–23 = 7 days

January 1–11 = 11 days

Total = 18 days

$\$550 \div 360 = 1.5277 \times 18 = \$27.50$

80. **(A)**

$$100\% - 6\% = 94\% \qquad \frac{\$355,000 \div}{\$377,659.57 \mid \ 94\%}$$

81. **(D)**

$$\frac{\$5,250}{\$350,000 \mid \ 1.5\%} \qquad \frac{\$1,312.50}{\$5,250 \mid \ 25\%}$$
$$\times \qquad\qquad\qquad \times$$

82. **(B)**

$$\frac{\$2,062.50 \div}{\$8,250 \mid \ 25\%} \qquad \frac{\$8,250 \div}{\$550,000 \mid \ 1.5\%}$$

83. **(A)**

$$\frac{\$427,500}{\$450,000 \mid \ 95\%} \quad \begin{array}{c} 100\% - 20\% = \\ 80\% \text{ Loan} \end{array} \quad \frac{\$342,000}{\$427,500 \mid \ 80\%} \quad \frac{\$23,085}{\$427,500 \mid \ 6.75\%}$$
$$\times \qquad\qquad\qquad\qquad\qquad \times \qquad\qquad\qquad \times$$
$$\$23,085 \div 12 = \$1,923.75$$

84. **(C)** $\begin{array}{r} \$75,230 \text{ net operating income} \\ +\ 4,900 \text{ expenses} \\ \hline \$80,130 \text{ effective gross income} \end{array}$

85. **(D)** $43,560 \div 3 = 14,520 \times 2 = 29,040$ sq. ft.

  $29,040 \div 275' = 105.60$ ft.

  OR $2 \div 3 = 0.6667$

  $43,560 \times 0.6667 = 29,041.45$ sq. ft.

  $29,041.45 \div 275' = 105.6052$ ft.

86. **(C)**

$$\frac{\$153,920}{\$148,000 \mid 104\%} \qquad \frac{\$160,076.80}{\$153,920 \mid 104\%} \qquad \frac{\$166,479.87}{\$160,076.80 \mid 104\%} \qquad \frac{\$159,820.68}{\$164,479.87 \mid 96\%}$$
$$\times \qquad\qquad\qquad \times \qquad\qquad\qquad \times \qquad\qquad\qquad \times$$

87. **(B)**

700 mills ÷ 1,000 = 0.7 ÷ 100 = 0.007 tax rate

$$\frac{\$108,400}{\$135,500 \mid 80\%} \qquad\qquad \frac{\$758.80}{\$108,400 \mid 0.007}$$
$$\times \qquad\qquad\qquad\qquad\qquad \times$$

$758.80 ÷ 12 = $63.23

88. **(D)**

$137.81 × 12 = $1,653.72

$3.50 ÷ 100 = 0.035

$$\frac{\$1,653.72 \div}{\$47,249.14 \mid 0.035} \qquad\qquad \frac{\$47,249.14 \div}{\$134,997.54 \mid 35\%}$$

89. **(D)** 5 × $500 × 12 = $30,000
5 × $550 × 12 = $33,000
5 × $600 × 12 = $36,000
Total PGI = $99,000

$99,000 $450 × 12 = $5,400 $ 96,030

–   3%   +   5,400

$96,030 $101,430

90. **(D)**

4 × $450 × 12 = $21,600   PGI

–   5% VR

$20,520

$464 × 12 =   +   5,568   AI

$ 26,088   EGI

91. **(A)**

$477.82 × 12 = $5,733.84 Annual Interest $

$$\frac{\$5,733.84 \div}{\$80,475 \mid 7.125\%} \qquad\qquad \frac{\$80,475 \div}{\$107,300 \mid 75\%}$$

92. **(C)**

100% $82,000 $114,944 ÷

– 7%   32,500 $123,595.70 | 93%

93%   +   444

$114,944

93. **(D)**

6,400 mills ÷ 1,000 = 6.40 ÷ 100 = 0.064

$$\frac{\$43,750}{\$125,000 \mid 35\%} \qquad\qquad \frac{\$2,800}{\$43,750 \mid 0.064}$$
$$\times \qquad\qquad\qquad\qquad\qquad \times$$

$2,800 ÷ 12 = $233.33

94. **(A)**

$108,810				$87,048			Debits	Credits

$$\frac{\$108,810}{\$120,900 \;\big|\; 90\%}$$
$$\times$$

$$\frac{\$87,048}{\$108,810 \;\big|\; 80\%}$$
$$\times$$

Debits	Credits
$108,810	$87,048
350	5,000
250	
749	
$110,159	$92,048

$110,159 – 92,048 = $18,111

95. **(B)**

Debits	Credits
$ 5,970.00	$99,500
250.00	
99.50	
50,140.00	
10,000.00	
$66,459.50	$99,500

$$\frac{\$5,970}{\$99,500 \;\big|\; 6\%}$$
$$\times$$

$99,500 – 66,459.50 = $33,040.50

96. **(D)**

$$
\begin{aligned}
1 \times \$450 \times 12 &= \$ 5,400 \\
1 \times \$475 \times 12 &= \$ 5,700 \\
2 \times \$500 \times 12 &= \underline{\$12,000}
\end{aligned}
$$

	$23,100	PGI
	− 4%	VR
	$22,176	EGI
$350 × 12 =	− 4,200	EXP
	$17,975	ANOI

$$\frac{\$17,976 \div}{\$179,760 \;\big|\; 10\%}$$

97. **(D)**

$$\frac{\$105,000 \div}{\$109,375 \;\big|\; 100\%}$$
$$- 4\%$$
$$96\%$$

$$\frac{\$109,375 \div}{\$113,932.29 \;\big|\; 100\%}$$
$$- 4\%$$
$$96\%$$

$$\frac{\$53,000}{\$50,000 \;\big|\; 100\%}$$
$$+ 6\%$$
$$\times 106\%$$

$$\frac{\$56,180}{\$53,000 \;\big|\; 100\%}$$
$$+ 6\%$$
$$\times 106\%$$

113,932.29 + 56,180 = $170,112.29

98. **(B)**

$$\frac{\$6{,}850.11}{\$144{,}212.71 \mid 4.75\%}$$
$$\times$$

$6,850.11 \div 12 = \$570.84$ Monthly Interest

$782.47 P&I	$144,212.71 Principal Balance		$2880.02 Prepayment Penalty
− 570.84 I	− 211.63 Principal Payment		$144,001.08 \mid 2%
$211.63 P	$144,001.08 New Principal Balance		

99. **(C)**

$649.50 \div 1{,}080 = 0.60$

Beginning Date:	April 30, 2008
Prorate Date:	June 24, 2009
Ending Date:	April 29, 2011

June 24–June 30 = 6 days
July 2009–April 29, 2011 = 659 days
Total = 665 days
$665 \times 0.60 = \$399$ CS, DB

100. **(C)**

$$\frac{\$128{,}000}{\$160{,}000 \mid 80\%} \qquad \$3.75 \div 1.000 = 0.00375$$
$$\times$$

$$\frac{\$480}{\$128{,}000 \mid 0.00375}$$
$$\times$$

$480 \div 720 = 0.6667$

Beginning Date:	September 20, 2008
Prorate Date:	November 11, 2009
Ending Date:	September 19, 2010

November 11–November 30 = 19 days
December 2009–August 2010 = 270 days
September 2010 = 19 days
Total = 308 days

$308 \times 0.6667 = \$205.34$

SALES EXAM I

1. A buyer working with an agent makes an offer on a property offered for sale by owner. The offer is contingent on the buyer's securing an FHA loan. Does this loan have to follow RESPA guidelines?
   A. No, because FHA and VA loans do have to meet HUD guidelines, but not RESPA guidelines.
   B. No, because the offer was made by a buyer working with a broker.
   C. Yes, because an FHA loan is guaranteed by the government.
   D. Yes, because it is a single-family residential property.

2. Which of the following is a typical characteristic of an FHA or VA loan?
   A. They are backed by the government and are not assumable.
   B. The down payment on these loans can normally be financed.
   C. Prepayment penalties cannot be charged on these loans.
   D. Typically, these loans must be repaid within 15 years.

3. A parent wants to transfer her property to her daughter who will take over the payments on the loan. The loan balance is $75,000. The property can be transferred if the loan does NOT contain a(n)
   A. alienation clause.
   B. acceleration clause.
   C. defeasance clause.
   D. nondisturbance clause.

4. Mr. Buyer purchased two parcels of land. One was one mile square and the other contained ten acres. If the land cost $2,500 an acre, what was the cost of the land?
   A. $1,265,000
   B. $1,625,000
   C. $1,526,000
   D. $1,600,000

5. An offer has been accepted on a property. After the title search, who gives an opinion of title?
   A. An attorney
   B. The seller
   C. The buyer
   D. The broker

6. The buyers just purchased their first house, which sits on five acres. They intend to keep goats on the property. Which of the following would allow or disallow them to keep goats?
   A. Federal ordinances
   B. State restrictions
   C. Zoning ordinances
   D. Neighbor restrictions

7. A buyer made an offer of $250,000 on a property with no contingencies, and the offer was accepted. The buyer planned to build a shopping center but never mentioned it to the agent. Just before the closing, the buyer discovered that he could not build the shopping center. What is the status of the sales contract?
   A. Valid
   B. Void
   C. Voidable
   D. Unenforceable

8. A disabled person moved into an apartment. At his own expense, he lowered the light switches, lowered the kitchen cabinets, installed handrails, and widened the doorways. At the expiration of the lease, which of the following would the tenant LEAST LIKELY have to return to its original condition?
   A. Light switches
   B. Kitchen cabinets
   C. Handrails
   D. Doorways

9. Which of the following BEST defines physical depreciation?
   A. Functional obsolescence caused by a poor design
   B. External obsolescence caused by any outside factor
   C. Deterioration caused by the age of the building
   D. Deterioration caused by normal wear and tear of the property

10. Which of the following must be disclosed when an agent is showing a house?
    A. Mortgage balance
    B. The asking price of other homes in the neighborhood
    C. That the property is in a flood plain zone
    D. Original cost of the property

11. What type of interest is normally computed on a residential loan?
    A. Simple
    B. Compound
    C. Annual
    D. Monthly

12. Which of the following is an example of an emblement?
    A. A stand of walnut trees
    B. A field of corn
    C. An apple orchard
    D. A vineyard

13. A buyer's agent is usually considered to be in what relationship to the seller?
    A. Client
    B. Customer
    C. Agency
    D. Subagency

14. A mortgage document and mortgage note are
    A. nonnegotiable instruments.
    B. used by mortgagees to release debt from property.
    C. used by mortgagors to secure liens on a property.
    D. standard security instruments.

15. Who is the optionee in an option contract?
    A. Vendor
    B. Vendee
    C. Grantor
    D. Grantee

16. J sells a property to H. Then H leases it back to J. At the conclusion of this transaction, what is the status of J's interest in the property?
    A. Fee simple absolute
    B. Fee simple defeasible
    C. A freehold interest
    D. A nonfreehold interest

17. Which of the following is a physical characteristic of real estate?
    A. Mobility
    B. Scarcity
    C. Uniqueness
    D. Transferability

18. Which of the following entities normally purchase mortgages in the secondary mortgage market?
    A. Mortgage banking companies
    B. Freddie Mac (FHLMC)
    C. Federal Housing Administration
    D. Department of Veterans Affairs

19. A broker listed a property, but the owner secured the buyer. The broker collected the commission. The type of listing agreement the seller signed is a(n)
    A. exclusive-right-to-sell listing.
    B. exclusive agency listing.
    C. open listing.
    D. net listing.

20. The federal Truth-in-Lending Act
    A. requires a lender to estimate a borrower's loan closing charges on all mortgages.
    B. regulates advertising that contains information regarding mortgage terms.
    C. prevents brokers from using phrases like "FHA-VA financing available" in classified ads.
    D. dictates that all mortgage loan applications be made on specially prepared government forms.

21. Recording a deed provides the greatest benefit for the
    A. grantor.
    B. public.
    C. attorney.
    D. grantee.

22. Which of the following documents is only signed by the seller(s) in the transaction?
    A. Purchase agreement
    B. Listing agreement
    C. Option
    D. Deed

23. The ability to pay for a home is the foremost consideration in choosing a home. What is the second consideration?
    A. Specification
    B. Age
    C. Improvements
    D. Location

24. The MOST important test in determining whether something is a fixture is
    A. its weight and/or size.
    B. its amount of utilization.
    C. the price paid for the item.
    D. the intention of the party who attached it.

25. A section of real estate
    A. contains 460 acres.
    B. is 1 mile square.
    C. contains 43,560 acres.
    D. is numbered to indicate either north or south.

26. A married couple decided to sell their home. The husband owned the property in severalty. Thirty minutes before the agent was scheduled to arrive, the wife had to leave for an emergency. The husband stayed for the appointment. Who must sign the listing agreement?
    A. Only the husband needs to sign the listing.
    B. Only the wife needs to sign the listing.
    C. The husband should sign the listing on behalf of both himself and his wife.
    D. As a married couple, both the husband and wife should sign the listing agreement.

27. Which of the following is NOT necessary in a listing contract?
    A. The signature of all parties on the deed.
    B. The beginning and ending dates of the agreement.
    C. The signature of the broker and/or agent.
    D. The signature of the buyer.

28. A couple owns their property as tenants by the entirety. The agent secured the signature of one spouse on the listing contract. Which of the following is TRUE?
    A. Both signatures are required on the listing contract.
    B. One spouse can sign because they each have an equal interest in the property.
    C. Only one spouse is required to sign because they are married.
    D. If it's an open listing, the agent has the proper signature.

29. A real estate tax lien takes priority over which of the following?
    A. Encroachment
    B. Encumbrance
    C. Mortgage lien
    D. Deed restrictions

30. The principles of appraising include which of the following?
    A. Reserves for replacement
    B. Operating expense ratio
    C. Highest and best use
    D. Holding period

31. Agents of Happy Valley Realty recently sold a home for $143,500. The brokerage charged the sellers a 6.5 percent commission. The broker paid the agent who secured the buyer 25 percent of the commission and the listing agent 30 percent of the commission collected. How much was the listing salesperson paid?
    A. $3,731
    B. $2,332
    C. $2,798
    D. $6,529

32. The interest portion of a borrower's last monthly payment was $291.42. If the borrower is paying interest at the rate of 8.25 percent, what was the outstanding balance of their loan before that last payment was made?
   A. $43,713.00
   B. $42,388.36
   C. $36,427.50
   D. $34,284.70

33. A home is valued at $65,000. Property in their area is assessed at 60 percent of its value, and the local tax rate is $2.85 per hundred. How much are the owner's monthly taxes?
   A. $1,111.50
   B. $926.30
   C. $111.15
   D. $92.63

34. An investor leases 12 apartments for a total monthly rental of $3,000. If this figure represents an 8 percent annual return on the investment, what was the original cost of the property?
   A. $450,000
   B. $360,000
   C. $45,000
   D. $36,000

35. A broker receives a check for earnest money from a buyer and deposits the money in an escrow or trust account. He does this to protect himself from the charge of which of the following?
   A. Commingling
   B. Novation
   C. Puffing
   D. Fraud

36. By paying the debt after a foreclosure sale, the mortgagor has the right to regain the property. What is this right called?
   A. Acceleration
   B. Redemption
   C. Reversion
   D. Recovery

37. A grandmother grants a life estate to her grandson and stipulates that, upon his death, the title will pass to her son-in-law. What is the son-in-law's estate called?
   A. Estate in reversion
   B. Estate in remainder
   C. Estate for years
   D. Estate in recapture

38. Under joint tenancy
   A. there is a right of survivorship.
   B. there is never more than two owners.
   C. the fractional undivided interest may be different.
   D. the estate is inheritable.

39. In some states, a lender holds title to the mortgaged property. These states are known as
   A. title-theory states.
   B. lien-theory states.
   C. statutory share states.
   D. dower rights states.

40. The borrower's offer of $190,000 was accepted. She has a 10 percent down payment and would like to avoid paying for private mortgage insurance. Is there a loan that would allow her to accomplish her goal?
   A. Yes, she can borrow $19,000 from a private source, tell the lender she has a 20 percent down payment instead of a 10 percent down payment, and avoid private mortgage insurance.
   B. Yes, if the seller will negotiate a purchase-money mortgage for $19,000 and agree to be in a second lien position on the property, she can avoid private mortgage insurance.
   C. No, because all borrowers must pay private mortgage insurance when negotiating any type of loan.
   D. No, because private mortgage insurance is always paid when a borrower has less than a 20 percent down payment.

41. Which of the following is NOT an example of a common subdivision rule and regulation?
    A. The agreement that the property cannot be sold and used as a waste disposal site
    B. The agreement that a tree house cannot be built on the property
    C. The agreement that walls and fences cannot exceed four feet in height
    D. The agreement that no structure of a temporary character can be constructed on any lot

42. Which of the following is NOT an example of an appurtenance that would transfer when the property is sold?
    A. Easement
    B. Lease
    C. Deed restriction
    D. License

43. A couple wants to list a home they have lived in for 38 years because they have decided to move to Florida. They want a quick sale. The listing agent is aware that zoning may change in the area, which would greatly increase the value of their property. The agent should
    A. say nothing in case the zoning does not change.
    B. inform the sellers of all the facts she has regarding the zoning change.
    C. tell the seller that if they list at a reduced price, he has buyers that might make an offer.
    D. say nothing because if the zoning does change, the listing contract will be void anyway.

44. Which of the following is NOT a depreciation factor when assessing the value of a property?
    A. A house with four bedrooms on the second floor and the bath located on the first floor
    B. A hog farm located one-half mile down the road from a $250,000 home
    C. A house located next to a city park
    D. A house, which cost $50,000 to build 40 years ago, with major cracks in the foundation

45. What is a tenancy at will?
    A. A tenancy created by the consent of the landlord
    B. A tenancy that expires on a specific date
    C. A tenancy created by the death of the owner
    D. A tenancy created by the testator

46. The value of a parcel of land
    A. is the present worth of future benefits.
    B. includes the money invested in past expenditures.
    C. is what a buyer pays for the property.
    D. is the same as the market price.

47. A seller wants to net $65,000 on his house after paying the broker's fee of 6 percent. The house must sell for at LEAST
    A. $69,149.
    B. $68,900.
    C. $67,035.
    D. $66,091.

48. A buyer is purchasing a condominium in a new subdivision and obtaining financing from a local savings and loan association. Which of the following BEST describes the borrower?
    A. Vendor
    B. Mortgagee
    C. Grantor
    D. Mortgagor

49. All of the following terminate an offer EXCEPT
    A. revocation of the offer before acceptance.
    B. death of the offeror before acceptance.
    C. a counteroffer by the offeree.
    D. an offer from a third party.

50. A buyer is purchasing a house under a contract for deed. Until the contract is paid, the buyer has
    A. legal title to the premises.
    B. no interest in the property.
    C. a legal life estate in the premises.
    D. equitable title in the premises.

51. A broker receives an earnest money deposit with a written offer that gives the seller ten days to accept. On the fifth day, and prior to acceptance by the seller, the buyer notifies the broker he is withdrawing his offer and demands that his deposit be returned. In this situation, the
    A. buyer cannot withdraw the offer; it must be held open for the full ten days.
    B. buyer has the right to revoke his offer and secure the return of the deposit at any time before the seller accepts the offer.
    C. broker can notify the seller that the buyer is withdrawing the offer and that each of them can retain one-half of the deposit.
    D. broker can declare the deposit forfeited and retain it for his services and commission.

52. Two people are joint tenants. One person sells his interest to another friend. What is the relationship of the friend of the other joint tenant?
    A. They are automatically joint tenants.
    B. They are tenants in common.
    C. There is no relationship between the parties.
    D. Each owns a divided one-half interest.

53. A homeowner who always maintains his house just discovered that he has termite infestation. This is an example of
    A. incurable physical obsolescence.
    B. possible curable physical obsolescence.
    C. possible curable economic obsolescence.
    D. incurable internal obsolescence.

54. When appraising property, the appraiser considers which of the following?
    A. The original price paid for the property, if purchased within three years.
    B. The reconciliation of the values determined by the different methods of appraising.
    C. The average cost of the comparable properties, after adjustments are made.
    D. The cost for updating the subject property, other than the cost of replacing the carpet.

55. When appraising a property, the appraiser determines the most probable price that a buyer would be willing to pay for a property. This is known as a(n)
    A. objective value/fair market value.
    B. subjective value/fair market value.
    C. plottage value.
    D. use value.

56. On Monday, an agent receives an offer from a buyer for $120,000 on a vacant lot he has for sale. On Tuesday, the seller rejects the offer and counteroffers at $130,000. The counteroffer gives the buyer three days to accept. On Friday, the buyer rejects the counteroffer, and upon being informed of the rejection, the seller says he will accept the buyer's original offer. Under these conditions, there is
    A. a valid agreement between the buyer and seller because $120,000 is the market value of the property.
    B. a valid agreement because the buyer's original can be accepted by the seller within three days.
    C. not a valid agreement because the buyer's original offer was rejected.
    D. not a valid agreement because the buyer's offer was not accepted by Thursday.

57. Due to the economic growth in an area, a house designed by a famous architect is now located in a flight pattern from the nearby airport. This is an example of
    A. incurable external obsolescence.
    B. curable external obsolescence.
    C. incurable functional obsolescence.
    D. curable functional obsolescence.

58. In an appurtenant easement, the property burdened by the easement is known as a
    A. prescriptive estate.
    B. dominant estate.
    C. condemned estate.
    D. servient estate.

59. Which of the following is NOT found in the appraisal report?
    A. Date of the inspection
    B. Condition of the subject property
    C. Adjustments of the subject property
    D. Signature of the appraiser

60. Unless stated otherwise in the sales contract, at the closing, the buyer will MOST LIKELY be transferred
    A. air rights, surface rights, and subsurface rights.
    B. air rights and surface rights.
    C. air rights and subsurface rights.
    D. air rights and mineral rights.

61. A house sold for $84,500 and the commission rate was 7 percent. The commission is split 60/40 between the selling broker and the listing broker. Each broker splits his share of the commission evenly with his salesperson. How much will the listing salesperson earn from the sale of the house?
    A. $1,774
    B. $1,183
    C. $1,020
    D. $2,366

62. The purchase price of a property is $84,500. The buyers wrote an earnest money check for $2,000 and obtained a new mortgage of $67,600. The closing is scheduled for March 15. The buyers and sellers will pro-rate the taxes of $1,880.96, which have been prepaid. The sellers' closing costs are $1,250, and the buyer's closing costs are $850. How much cash must the buyers bring to the closing? (Use a 360-day year.)
    A. $17,239.09
    B. $17,639.09
    C. $16,541.87
    D. $19,639.09

63. A loan is originated for 80 percent of the appraised value. The mortgage interest rate is 8 percent, and the first month interest is $460. What is the appraised value of the house?
    A. $86,250
    B. $71,875
    C. $69,000
    D. $92,875

64. A building is 100 feet by 150 feet and sits on a lot valued at $25,000. The replacement cost of the property is $25 per square foot, and it has depreciated 5 percent. What is the value of the property?
    A. $375,000
    B. $381,250
    C. $481,250
    D. $318,250

65. After a broker listed a property, he discovered that the client had previously been declared incompetent by a court of law. The listing is
    A. binding, as the broker was acting in good faith as the seller's agent.
    B. void because the owner had been declared incompetent.
    C. valid because the owner signed the agreement.
    D. voidable by the seller if he changes his mind within the first week.

66. An owner defaulted on his home loan payments, and the lender obtained a court order to foreclose on the property. At the foreclosure sale, the owner's house sold for $29,000, and the unpaid balance at the time of foreclosure was $40,000. What must the lender do to recover the $11,000 the defaulted borrower still owes?
    A. Sue for damages
    B. Sue for specific performance
    C. Seek a judgment by default
    D. Seek a deficiency judgment

67. All of the following are exemptions from the federal Fair Housing Act of 1968 EXCEPT
    A. the sale of a single-family home where the listing broker does not advertise the property.
    B. the rental of a unit in an owner-occupied, three-family dwelling where no advertisement is placed in the paper.
    C. the restriction of noncommercial lodgings by a private club to members of that club.
    D. the property is a state or local housing program designed specifically for the elderly.

68. A vacant lot that measures 100' by 125' is listed at $250 per front foot. The commission that the broker will collect is 8 percent. If the property sells for its full asking price, what will be the broker's fee?
   A. $2,500
   B. $2,000
   C. $1,500
   D. $1,250

69. A house was listed for $47,900. An Hispanic couple saw the house and was interested in purchasing it. When they asked the price of the house, the listing agent said it was $53,000. Under the federal Fair Housing Act of 1968, such a statement is
   A. legal because all that is important is that everyone be given the right to buy the house.
   B. legal because the statement was made by the agent and not the owner.
   C. illegal because the difference in the listed price and the quoted price was greater than $5,000.
   D. illegal because the terms of the sale were changed for the Hispanic couple.

70. The market rent for a duplex is $650 per month per unit. If the GRM is 125, what is the value of the property?
   A. $81,250
   B. $162,500
   C. $126,500
   D. $216,500

71. House keys are considered to be
   A. personal property because they are movable.
   B. personal property because they are not attached.
   C. real property because sale contracts stipulate that they will be transferred.
   D. real property because of the adaptation to the real estate.

72. In the lease agreement, a tenant has agreed to build out a commercial space to meet her needs at her own expense. The chattel fixtures that she adds to the property are the
   A. property of the landlord upon the expiration of the lease because they are now attached to the property.
   B. tenants' as long as they are removed from the property on or before the expiration of the lease and she leaves the property in good repair.
   C. tenants' as long as they are removed from the property on or before the expiration of the lease because she paid for them.
   D. property of the landlord automatically upon their addition, and the property must be left in good repair.

73. A, B, and C are co-owners of property. When C dies testate, A and B are the devisees to her one-third interest in the property. How do they own the property?
   A. Joint tenancy
   B. Tenancy in common
   C. Severalty
   D. Partnership tenancy

74. Which of the following is an example of a freehold inheritable estate?
   A. Life estate
   B. Dower estate
   C. Estate at will
   D. Fee simple defeasible estate

75. A buyer moved into a condominium that boasted of many common facilities, including a swimming pool, tennis courts, and a putting green. Under a typical condominium arrangement, these common elements are owned by
   A. an association of homeowners organized as a limited liability company.
   B. a corporation in which the owners of all the units own stock.
   C. the owners of all the units in the form of an undivided percentage interest.
   D. the owners of all the units in the form of divided interests.

76. In a graduated-payment loan
    A. mortgage payments decrease.
    B. mortgage payments balloon in five years.
    C. mortgage payments increase for a period of time and then level out.
    D. the interest rate on the loan adjusts annually.

77. A buyer feels that he has been the victim of an unfair discriminatory practice by a local broker. His complaint must be filed with HUD within
    A. 3 months of the alleged discrimination.
    B. 6 months of the alleged discrimination.
    C. 9 months of the alleged discrimination.
    D. 12 months of the alleged discrimination.

78. A mortgage using both real and personal property as security is a
    A. blanket mortgage.
    B. package mortgage.
    C. dual mortgage.
    D. wraparound mortgage.

79. If a buyer obtains a mortgage for $50,000 and pays four points, how much will she be charged by the lender at closing for the points?
    A. $6,000
    B. $200
    C. $2,000
    D. $600

80. A borrower obtained a second mortgage loan for $7,000. The payments are $50 per month, at 6 percent interest over a period of five years. The final installment is a balloon payment for the outstanding principal. What type of loan is this?
    A. Fully amortized loan
    B. Straight loan
    C. Partially amortized loan
    D. Accelerated loan

81. A buyer bought property in a secluded area adjacent to the Atlantic Ocean. Shortly thereafter, he noticed that people from town often walked along the shore in front of his property. He later learned that the locals had been walking along this beach for years. The owner went to court to try to stop people from walking along the water's edge in front of his property. He is likely to be
    A. unsuccessful because the local citizens were walking there before he bought the property, and thus had an easement.
    B. unsuccessful because under the doctrine of littoral rights, he owns the property only to the high-water mark, and the public can use the land beyond that mark.
    C. successful because of the doctrine of riparian rights.
    D. successful because he has the right to control access to his own property.

82. All of the following are true about the concept of adverse possession EXCEPT
    A. the person taking possession of the property must do so without the consent of the owner.
    B. occupancy of the property by the person taking possession must be continuous over a specified period.
    C. the person taking possession of the property must compensate the owner at the end of the adverse possession period.
    D. the person taking possession of the property may end up owning the property.

83. Reconciliation is an appraisal term used to describe the
    A. appraiser's determination of a property's highest value.
    B. average values for properties similar to the one being appraised.
    C. appraiser's analysis and comparison of the results of each appraisal approach.
    D. method used to determine a property's most appropriate capitalization rate.

84. In consideration of $15,000, an owner gives a potential buyer the option to purchase a property for $200,000 within 60 days. In this contract, the buyer is a(n)
    A. optionor.
    B. escrowee.
    C. optionee.
    D. grantor.

85. When a mortgage loan has been paid in full, which of the following is the MOST important thing for the borrower to confirm has been finalized?
    A. Put the paid note and all canceled papers in a safe-deposit box
    B. Arrange to receive and pay future real estate tax bills
    C. Be sure the mortgagor signs a satisfaction of mortgage
    D. Record the satisfaction of mortgage

86. Normally, the priority of general liens is determined by the
    A. order in which they are filed or recorded.
    B. order in which the cause of action arose.
    C. size of the claim.
    D. clerk of the court.

87. When property is held in tenancy by the entirety
    A. the owners must be husband and wife.
    B. either owner may half the property by signing a quitclaim deed.
    C. there is no right of survivorship.
    D. the property must be commercial.

88. The practice of directing potential buyers into or out of neighborhoods based on a protected class is known as
    A. canvassing.
    B. blockbusting.
    C. redlining.
    D. steering.

89. A broker was paid a commission when the sellers found the buyer. The brokerage firm MOST LIKELY had a(n)
    A. exclusive-agency listing contract with the sellers.
    B. net listing contract with the sellers.
    C. exclusive-right-to-sell listing contract with the sellers.
    D. open listing contract with the sellers.

90. A broker listed a property under a valid written listing agreement. After the sale was completed, the owner was not obligated to pay the broker's fee. The broker had MOST LIKELY entered into a(n)
    A. pocket listing.
    B. exclusive-right-to-sell listing.
    C. in-house listing.
    D. open listing.

91. All of the following are tests for determining a fixture EXCEPT
    A. intent of the parties.
    B. size of the item.
    C. method of attachment of the item.
    D. adaptation of the item to the particular real estate.

92. When real estate is sold under an installment land contract, the vendee's interest in the property is
    A. a legal title interest.
    B. an equitable title interest.
    C. kept by the mortgagor until the full purchase price is paid.
    D. held by the mortgagee until the full purchase price is paid.

93. To start a condominium, a developer usually files which of the following?
    A. Judgment
    B. Lien
    C. Certificate
    D. Declaration

94. A buyer agrees to purchase a property for $153,000, and the broker deposits a $5,300 earnest money check into the trust account. The seller is unable to provide a good and marketable title, so the buyer demands the return of his earnest money as provided in the contract. What should the broker do?
    A. Deduct his commission and return the balance to the buyer
    B. Deduct his commission and pay the balance to the seller
    C. Return the entire amount of the earnest money to the buyer
    D. Pay the entire amount to the seller to spend to get the title updated

95. The annual rate of interest on a mortgage loan is 8.5 percent, and the monthly interest payment is $201.46. What is the loan amount?
    A. $2,417.52
    B. $28,441.41
    C. $2,844.14
    D. $14,270.00

96. All of the following are contracts between the brokerage and a principal EXCEPT
    A. open listing.
    B. net listing.
    C. multiple listing.
    D. exclusive listing.

97. An owner and a builder enter into a contract to build a structure on the owner's vacant land. There were no contingency clauses in the contract. The builder discovers that because of the nature of the soil, the supports for the structure must be dug much deeper than he had anticipated. The additional work will cause the builder to lose money on the project. Under these circumstances, the builder
    A. does not have to continue with the contract, under the doctrine of impossibility.
    B. does not have to continue with the contract because the owner does not have the right to force the builder to lose money.
    C. can force the owner to renegotiate the contract.
    D. is liable for breach of contract if he fails to perform.

98. A seller represents to the listing agent that a new freeway will be built near his undeveloped land. The listing agent shares that information with a potential buyer, and neither the agent nor the buyer check with zoning to confirm the plans for the freeway. The buyer purchases the land without representation from any real estate agent. Several months after the closing, the buyer discovers that the freeway is not going to be built. Did the listing agent breach a fiduciary duty to the buyer?
    A. Yes. The agent breached the duty of reasonable care and skill by not checking with zoning as to the status of the freeway before sharing the information with a potential buyer.
    B. Yes. The agent breached the fiduciary duty of disclosure by sharing information without verification.
    C. No. The listing agent did not breach the fiduciary duty to the seller.
    D. No. The listing agent did not breach the fiduciary duty to the buyer.

99. The market value of a house is $84,500, the assessment ratio is 35 percent, and the tax rate is 30 mills. What are the monthly taxes?
    A. $887.25
    B. $942.50
    C. $73.94
    D. $87.72

100. An owner seeks relief from zoning regulations on the grounds of nonconforming use. Effective arguments to the zoning authorities would include all of the following EXCEPT
    A. that the nonconforming use existed prior to the passing of the zoning ordinance.
    B. that he would earn more by using the property for purposes that do not conform with the zoning ordinance.
    C. that the nonconforming use didn't harm the public health, safety, and welfare.
    D. that conforming to the zoning ordinance would create an undue hardship.

101. To create a bird sanctuary, an owner would like to purchase part of his neighbor's property. If the owner has the properties surveyed, all of the following terms would most likely be found in the survey EXCEPT
    A. datum.
    B. monument.
    C. point of beginning.
    D. linear distance.

102. An option contract
    A. sets a time limit to keep an offer open.
    B. is an open-end agreement.
    C. does not set the sale price for the property.
    D. transfers title when it is signed by the seller.

103. What is the legal procedure or action that may be brought by either the buyer or the seller to enforce the terms of a contract?
    A. Injunction
    B. Suit for specific performance
    C. Lis pendens
    D. Attachment

104. In an option to purchase real estate, the optionee
    A. must purchase the property, but may do so at any time within the option period.
    B. has no obligation to purchase the property.
    C. as a matter of law can receive a refund of the option consideration if the option is exercised.
    D. is the prospective seller of the property.

105. Which of the following contracts would become void upon the death of one of the principals?
    A. Listing contracts
    B. Sales contracts
    C. Mortgage
    D. Note

106. Lot A measured 200' × 300' and sold for $30,000 per acre. Lot B, which is located down the street, measures 150' × 200'. If it sells for the same price per acre as Lot A, what is the price of Lot B?
    A. $21,780
    B. $20,661
    C. $41,322
    D. $51,229

107. A borrower negotiated a $25,000 term mortgage for one year. His semiannual interest was $875. What was the interest rate?
    A. 3.5 percent
    B. 4.0 percent
    C. 5.0 percent
    D. 7.0 percent

108. The seller left the closing table with a check for $145,250. She paid a 6 percent commission to the brokerage. What was the sale price of the property?
    A. $153,965
    B. $154,521
    C. $155,418
    D. $155,525

109. A seller netted $275,500 after paying a 6.5 percent commission and $5,000 in other closing costs. What was the sale price?
    A. $280,500
    B. $285,500
    C. $295,000
    D. $300,000

110. An investment property has annual expenses of $15,000, and the annual net operating income is $50,000. If the value is $500,000, what is the cap rate?
    A. 1 percent
    B. 10 percent
    C. 15 percent
    D. 20 percent

SALES EXAM I ANSWERS

1. **(D)** RESPA covers one-to-four-family residential loans financed by a federally related mortgage loan.

2. **(C)** Prepayment penalties cannot be charged on FHA or VA mortgages.

3. **(A)** The alienation clause in a mortgage document allows the lender to call the note due and payable on the conveyance of the property.

4. **(B)** 640 + 10 = 650 acres × $2,500 = $1,625,000 (1 mile square = 640 acres).

5. **(A)** An attorney gives an opinion of title and issues a title certificate.

6. **(C)** The local zoning laws regulate the type of animals that can be kept on a property.

7. **(A)** A contract with no contingencies is a valid, enforceable contract.

8. **(D)** The tenant would least likely be responsible for returning the doorways to their original width.

9. **(D)** Deterioration caused by normal wear and tear of the property best describes depreciation.

10. **(C)** Any material fact or property defect must be disclosed to potential buyers of a property.

11. **(A)** The lender normally computes simple interest on residential loans.

12. **(B)** Emblements are crops that require annual planting. The crop that has been harvested is an emblement.

13. **(B)** The seller is normally considered to be the customer to a buyer's agent.

14. **(D)** By definition of mortgage document and mortgage note.

15. **(B)** In an option contract, the optionee is the vendee or buyer.

16. **(D)** In this sale-leaseback transaction, J is the lessee and has a nonfreehold (leasehold) interest in the property.

17. **(C)** Heterogeneity, immobility, and durability are the physical characteristics of real estate. Heterogeneity, or nonhomogeneity, means that every parcel of land is unique.

18. **(B)** Fannie Mae, Ginnie Mae, and Freddie Mac buy and sell mortgages on the secondary market.

19. **(A)** In an exclusive-right-to-sell listing, the broker collects a commission even if the seller sells the property.

20. **(B)** Truth-in-lending laws require the disclosure of the cost of financing the loan expressed as an APR and regulates the advertising of mortgage loans.

21. **(D)** It is to the benefit of the buyer to give constructive notice to the world that she or he is the owner of the property.

22. **(D)** A deed is a transfer of title, and the party currently holding title is required to sign.

23. **(D)** The location of the property affects its price today and in the future. People purchase homes because of their preference for certain locations.

24. **(D)** Courts have held that the intention of the parties is the most important factor in determining when an item is a fixture.

25. **(B)** A section of land is one mile square.

26. **(D)** Even though the husband owns the house in severalty, both the husband and wife should sign the listing to release any marital rights the wife has in the property.

27. **(D)** The buyer is not a party to the listing contract.

28. **(A)** Both spouses' signatures are required on the listing because it is owned as tenancy by the entirety.

29. **(C)** Real estate taxes and special assessments take priority over all other liens.

30. **(C)** The highest and best use of the property is its most profitable use.

31. **(C)** $143,500 × 6.5% = $9,327.50
    $9,327.50 × 0.30 = $2,798.25

32. **(B)** $291.42 × 12 = $3,497.04
    $3,497.04 ÷ 8.25% = $42,388.36

33. **(D)** $2.85 ÷ 100 = 0.0285
    $65,000 × 60% = $39,000
    $39,000 × 0.0285 = $1,111.50
    $1,111.50 ÷ 12 = $92.625

34. **(A)** $3,000 × 12 = $36,000
    $36,000 ÷ 8% = $450,000

35. **(A)** All money received in a fiduciary relationship must be placed in an escrow account to prevent commingling.

36. **(B)** The equitable right of redemption is the owner's right to regain property before foreclosure. The statutory right of redemption is the owner's right to regain the property after foreclosure.

37. **(B)** The son-in-law is a remainderman, and his interest is an estate in remainder.

38. **(A)** Joint tenancy is characterized by right of survivorship.

39. **(A)** By definition of title-theory state.

40. **(B)** If the seller would lend her $19,000 as a purchase-money mortgage, she could avoid private mortgage insurance.

41. **(A)** This is an example of a deed condition placed on the property by a grantor that is binding on all future owners.

42. **(D)** A license is the revocable permission for a temporary land use granted to another, but it does not transfer with the property.

43. **(B)** The agent must inform the sellers of all facts that she has regarding the possible zoning change and the consequences of their decision should they accept any offers on the property before the decision about the zoning is finalized.

44. **(C)** Depreciation does not occur because a house is located next to a city park.

45. **(A)** A tenancy at will is a lease that is created at the consent of the landlord.

46. **(A)** By definition of value.

47. **(A)** 100% – 6% = 94%
    $65,000 ÷ 94% = $69,148.94

48. **(D)** The borrower or the mortgagor.

49. **(D)** An offer from a third party does not terminate an offer.

50. **(D)** When the legal title in the property is held by another party, the buyer's interest is an equitable interest.

51. **(B)** An offer can be withdrawn at any time prior to acceptance.

52. **(B)** When a joint tenant sells an interest in a property, the new owner becomes a tenant in common with the other joint tenants.

53. **(B)** Unless termite infestation has been present on a property for an extended period of time, it is curable. Because the question states that the homeowner always maintained his house and the termite infestation was just discovered, then the physical obsolescence is probably curable.

54. **(B)** Appraisers reconcile the values as determined by the different methods of appraising, but they do not consider any of the factors in the other answers.

55. **(A)** The appraiser determines the most probable price that a buyer will pay for the property. This is known as the fair market value and should be an objective value.

56. **(C)** Once an offer has been rejected, it cannot be accepted later.

57. **(A)** A change outside the property has affected the property's value. This is external obsolescence.

58. **(D)** In an appurtenant easement, the servient estate is burdened by the easement and the dominant estate benefits from it.

59. **(C)** Adjustments are never made in the subject property, only in the comparable properties.

60. **(A)** Any rights that are not being transferred should be in the listing contract and sales contract.

61. **(B)** $84,500 × 7% = $5,915
$5,915 × 40% = $2,366
$2,366 ÷ 2 = $1,183

62. **(A)**

Debit	Credit
$84,500.00	$ 2,000
$ 1,489.09	$67,600
$ 850.00	$69,600
$86,839.09	

Jan. 1
March 15—Count from March 15 through Dec. 30 = 285 days
Dec. 30

$1,880.96 ÷ 360 = $5.22489 per day
$5.22489 × 285 days = $1,489.09

$86,839.09 − $69,600 = $17,639.09

63. **(A)** $460 × 12 = $5,520
$5,520 ÷ 80% = $69,000
$69,000 ÷ 8% = $86,250

64. **(B)** A = 100' × 150' = 15,000 sq. ft.
15,000 square feet × $25 = $375,000
− 5%
$356,250
+ 25,000
$381,250

65. **(B)** The listing is void because a legally incompetent party does not have the ability to contract. The listing agent should enter into the listing agreement with the guardian of the incompetent party.

66. **(D)** By definition of deficiency judgment.

67. **(A)** There are circumstances in which the Fair Housing Act does not apply to single-family homeowners, but none of these apply when an owner uses the services of a broker.

68. **(B)** 100' × $250 = $25,000
$25,000 × 8% = $2,000

69. **(D)** It is discriminatory to change the terms of the listing agreement.

70. **(B)** $650 × 2 = $1,300
125 × $1,300 = $162,500

71. **(D)** House keys are adapted to the use of a specific property and are considered real property.

72. **(B)** Trade fixtures must be removed from the property on or before the lease expires. The tenant is responsible for any damage caused by the removal of the fixtures. Those that are not removed become the property of the landlord.

73. **(B)** Tenancy in common is an inheritable estate. When C wrote her will, she made the other co-owners her devisees.

74. **(D)** Fee simple absolute and fee simple defeasible estates are freehold inheritable estates.

75. **(C)** Common areas are owned by the condo owners in an undivided percentage interest.

76. **(C)** By definition of graduated-payment mortgage.

77. **(D)** Complaints must be filed with HUD within one year.

78. **(B)** By definition of package mortgage.

79. **(C)** $50,000 × 4% = $2,000

80. **(C)** By definition of partially amortized loan.

81. **(B)** By definition of littoral rights.

82. **(C)** The adverse possessor does not compensate the owner at the end of the adverse possession period.

83. **(C)** By definition of reconciliation.

84. **(C)** The potential buyer is the optionee.

85. **(D)** The satisfaction of mortgage or mortgage release needs to be recorded to release the lender's (mortgagee's) interest in the property.

86. **(A)** The priority of liens is usually determined by the order in which they are filed or recorded.

87. **(A)** Tenancy by the entirety involves a husband and wife who own property.

88. **(D)** By definition of channeling and steering.

89. **(C)** By definition of exclusive-right-to-sell listing.

90. **(D)** In an exclusive agency listing or an open listing, the seller has the right to sell the property and not pay a commission to a brokerage firm.

91. **(B)** The size of an item is not one of the tests to determine if it is a fixture.

92. **(B)** The buyer's interest in the property in a land contract is an equitable title interest, but the seller retains legal title. A land contract is not a mortgage.

93. **(D)** To develop a condominium community, the developer must file a declaration.

94. **(C)** The earnest money check should be returned to the buyer. The broker must pursue the seller for the commission.

95. **(B)** $201.46 × 12 = $2,417.52
$2,417.52 ÷ 8.5% = $28,441.41

96. **(C)** The multiple-listing service is an agreement between brokers, not between an agent and a principal.

97. **(D)** Because there were no contingencies in the contract, the builder must fulfill the contract.

98. **(D)** The buyer did not have an agent representing him in the transaction, so the listing agent did not breach a fiduciary duty to the buyer.

99. **(C)** 30 ÷ 1,000 = 0.03
$84,500 × 35% = $29,575
$29,575 × 0.03 = $887.25
$887.25 ÷ 12 = $73.94 (202)

100. **(B)** The fact that the owner could earn more money is not a valid reason to grant relief from zoning regulations.

101. **(A)** A datum is a point, line, or surface from which elevations are measured to determine the heights of structures or grades of streets and would not be found in a survey between two neighbors' properties.

102. **(A)** By definition, option contract.

103. **(B)** By definition, suit for specific performance.

104. **(B)** The optionee (buyer) has no obligation to purchase the property. The buyer has purchased an option on the property and is not entitled to a refund of the option money if the buyer does not purchase it.

105. **(A)** Listing contracts would terminate on the death of either party.

106. **(B)** 150' × 200' = 30,000 square feet
30,000 ÷ 43,560 = 0.6887 acres
$30,000 × 0.6887 = $20,661

107. **(D)** $875 × 2 = $1,750 annual interest
$1,750 ÷ $25,000 = 0.07 = 7%

108. **(B)** 100% − 6% = 94%
$145,250 ÷ 94% = $154,521

109. **(D)** $275,500 + $5,000 = $280,500
100% − 6.5% = 93.5%
$280,500 ÷ 93.5% = $300,000

110. **(B)** $50,000 ÷ $500,000 = 0.1 = 10%

SALES EXAM II

1. A house sold for $137,500, and the buyers secured an FHA mortgage. The required down payment was 3 percent for the first $50,000, and 5 percent for any amount over $50,000. What was the amount of the mortgage?
   A. $1,500
   B. $4,375
   C. $133,125
   D. $131,625

2. After a neighborhood had been hit by vandals on a number of occasions, an owner offered to pay $100 to anyone providing information leading to the arrest and conviction of the guilty party. Shortly thereafter, a person supplied the needed information and received the reward. This is an example of a(n)
   A. gift.
   B. option.
   C. unilateral contract.
   D. voidable contract.

3. A broker pays her salespeople 20 percent of the commission for listing property and 40 percent of the commission for selling it. The commission rate is 5 percent. What was the selling price of a house if the salesperson who both listed and sold it received $3,600?
   A. $120,000
   B. $200,000
   C. $72,000
   D. $100,000

4. Which of the following is a loan in which only interest is payable during the term of the loan and all principal is payable at the end of the loan period?
   A. Amortized loan
   B. Flexible loan
   C. Fixed installment loan
   D. Term loan

5. A property owned solely by one spouse
   A. is owned in trust.
   B. is owned in severalty.
   C. is immune from seizure by creditors.
   D. cannot be homesteaded.

6. When a property fails to sell at a court foreclosure for an amount sufficient to satisfy the mortgage debt, the mortgagee may seek which of the following against the defaulted borrower?
   A. Attachment by default
   B. Deficiency judgment
   C. Satisfaction of mortgage
   D. Damages adjudication

7. A property is registered as Torrens property. In connection with the purchase, the
   A. buyer should have an attorney review the abstract and render an opinion about prior transfers.
   B. Torrens certificate is proof of ownership.
   C. buyer should check for adverse prescription.
   D. execution of the deed automatically transfers title.

8. A buyer purchased a property and accepted a quitclaim deed. The buyer can be certain that
   A. the seller had a good title to the property.
   B. whatever the seller's interest may be, it is being transferred.
   C. the seller will convey after-acquired title.
   D. there are no liens against the property that adversely affect marketable title.

9. The broker and seller entered into an open listing agreement. Under such an agreement, the seller
   A. does not have to pay the broker a commission if the broker finds a buyer.
   B. does not have to pay the broker a commission if the seller finds a buyer.
   C. must pay a commission if either the seller or brokerage finds a buyer.
   D. must pay a commission if anyone other than the seller finds a buyer.

10. When a buyer signs a purchase agreement and the seller accepts, the buyer acquires an interest in the real estate. The buyer's interest is known as
    A. equitable title.
    B. equitable justice.
    C. statutory rights.
    D. servient tenement.

11. A property has been sold. All of the following documents could be used to convey title EXCEPT
    A. warranty deed.
    B. quitclaim deed.
    C. trustee's deed.
    D. deed in lieu of foreclosure.

12. The ABC Real Estate Company listed a property at $4.50 per square foot. The land dimensions were 50 feet by 137 feet. If the commission rate was set at 7.25 percent, how much did the seller pay the ABC Real Estate Company?
    A. $1,005.50
    B. $2,234.81
    C. $22,348.12
    D. $10,055.00

13. To purchase a home, a buyer obtained a $142,500 mortgage at 7.75 percent interest for 25 years. The mortgage was closed on June 15, with the first P&I payment due in arrears on August 1. At the closing, which of the following occurred?
    A. The buyer paid a $490.83 interest adjustment.
    B. The seller paid a $490.83 interest adjustment.
    C. The seller paid a $920.31 interest adjustment.
    D. The buyer paid a $920.31 interest adjustment.

14. To be valid, a deed must be signed by which of the following?
    A. Grantors
    B. Attorney at law
    C. Grantees
    D. Broker

15. To have a valid conveyance, all of the following are necessary EXCEPT
    A. legal capacity to execute.
    B. recital of consideration.
    C. designation of any limitations.
    D. proof of heirship.

16. Which of the following scenarios are exempt from the federal Fair Housing Act?
    A. Rental of rooms in an owner-occupied, one-to-four-family dwelling
    B. Alteration of the terms or conditions of mortgage
    C. Property for sale above $250,000
    D. Property sold on an installment sales contract

17. A brokerage manages a number of income-producing properties for a large landholder in the city. The management agreement stipulates that the property manager shall be responsible for finding new tenants and maintaining the properties. The property management fee the brokerage may charge for its services is MOST LIKELY a percentage of the
    A. net income earned from the properties.
    B. gross income earned from the properties.
    C. total expenses incurred in maintaining the properties.
    D. ROI.

18. On a settlement statement, the commission owed to the listing broker is a
    A. debit to the sellers.
    B. debit to the buyers.
    C. credit to the sellers and a debit to the buyers.
    D. credit to the buyers.

19. The closing for a rental property is to take place September 15. On September 1, the owners collected the rent for the month of September from the tenant. Under the terms of the purchase agreement, the buyers are entitled to any rent received covering the period subsequent to the closing. At the closing, the prepaid rent will appear as a
   A. credit to the sellers and a debit to the buyers.
   B. debit to the sellers and a credit to the buyers.
   C. credit to the buyers.
   D. debit to the sellers.

20. Under the provisions of the Real Estate Settlement Procedures Act, certain disclosures are required from the
   A. seller in a residential real estate transaction.
   B. buyer in a residential real estate transaction.
   C. lender in a residential real estate transaction.
   D. agent in a residential real estate transaction.

21. Which of the following real estate documents will LEAST LIKELY be recorded at the county recorder's office?
   A. Contract for deed
   B. Long-term lease
   C. Option agreement
   D. Purchase agreement

22. Under most state laws, an advertisement for listed property should include the
   A. broker or brokerage name.
   B. seller's name.
   C. agent's name.
   D. sale price.

23. A buyer's offer was accepted. MOST state laws would require that the buyers
   A. will make a loan application.
   B. have a copy of the sales contract.
   C. have a down payment.
   D. have inspected the home.

24. The sellers have executed three open listings with three brokers around town. All three brokers would like to place "For Sale" signs on the seller's property. Under these circumstances
   A. a broker does not have to obtain the seller's permission before placing a sign on the property.
   B. only one For Sale sign may be placed on the property at one time.
   C. upon obtaining the seller's written consent, all can place signs on the property.
   D. the first listing broker must consent to all signs.

25. For a parcel of real estate to have value, it must have
   A. utility.
   B. scarcity.
   C. transferability.
   D. all of these.

26. Under the income approach to estimating the value of real estate, the capitalization rate is the
   A. rate at which the property increases in value.
   B. rate of return the property earns on an investment.
   C. rate of capital required to keep a property operating by its most effective method.
   D. maximum rate of return allowed by law on an investment.

27. An appraiser makes adjustments to the selling prices of comparable properties. The adjustments will reflect differences in
   A. location and amenities of the properties.
   B. gross rent multiplier of other properties.
   C. expired properties.
   D. current listed properties.

28. The final step in the appraisal process is to
   A. make copies for the lender.
   B. create an invoice.
   C. adjust the subject property.
   D. reconcile the differences.

29. If a landlord breaches the lease, and because the unit is uninhabitable, what action can the tenant take?
    A. Pursue a suit for possession
    B. Consider the action a constructive eviction
    C. Resort to tenancy at sufferance
    D. Pursue a covenant for quiet possession

30. How can tenancy at sufferance be created?
    A. By failure to surrender possession
    B. By payment of rent
    C. By bringing an unlawful detainer action
    D. By giving 30 days' written notice

31. If the title will pass to a third party upon the death of the life tenant, what was the third party's interest in the property?
    A. Remainder interest
    B. Reversionary interest
    C. Conditional interest
    D. Redemption interest

32. What is the interest of the grantee when real estate is conveyed only for as long as specified conditions are met?
    A. Defeasible fee
    B. Indefeasible fee
    C. Restrictive fee
    D. Base fee

33. FHA insurance regulations state that the
    A. FHA must set the interest rate.
    B. buyer and/or seller may pay the points.
    C. mortgage insurance premium be paid by the seller.
    D. closing costs be paid by the buyer.

34. The United States uses both lien theory and title theory in mortgage law. In title theory states, the
    A. mortgagor has title to the property.
    B. mortgagee has title to the property.
    C. mortgagor and mortgagee jointly hold title.
    D. buyer holds title in trust.

35. Brokers who conspire to set commission rates or enter into an agreement to allocate a specific market are subject to which of the following?
    A. Sherman Antitrust Act
    B. Law of agency
    C. Blue-sky laws
    D. Securities Act of 1933

36. Which of the following affects the control and regulation of land use?
    A. Public and private land-use controls
    B. Zoning ordinances
    C. Deed restrictions
    D. All of these

37. Under a percentage lease, the lessee pays $400 per month plus 2.75 percent of gross sales. Last month's gross sales were $198,210. How much is the rent?
    A. $5,450.78
    B. $5,850.78
    C. $5,540.78
    D. $5,580.78

38. What type of lease requires the lessee to pay taxes, insurance, and repairs?
    A. Net lease
    B. Percentage lease
    C. Variable lease
    D. Gross lease

39. After signing a lease, the lessor obtains which of the following interests in real estate?
    A. Freehold estate
    B. Leased fee interest
    C. Leasehold interest
    D. Remainderman interest

40. The market value of a property is $72,000, and it is assessed at 67 percent of value. What are the monthly taxes if the tax rate for the area is $6.50 per $100 of the assessed value?
    A. $3,157.38
    B. $4,857.50
    C. $261.30
    D. $485.75

41. A $50,000 mortgage on a property represents an 80 percent loan-to-value ratio. The real estate was assessed at 82 percent, the taxes were based on $4 per $100 of assessed value, and the owners paid $2,050 annual property taxes. What was the sale price of the home?
    A. $62,500
    B. $51,250
    C. $41,000
    D. $50,000

42. Which of the following is a method of fore-closure that does not require civil action?
    A. Judicial foreclosure
    B. Strict foreclosure
    C. Sheriff's foreclosure
    D. Nonjudicial foreclosure

43. A home sells for $65,900. The mortgage requires a 40 percent down payment, a 1 percent origination fee, and $450 in clos-ing costs. How much does the buyer need to close?
    A. $26,623.60
    B. $27,205.40
    C. $27,173.59
    D. $26,360.00

44. A building is 200 feet wide, 300 feet long, and five stories high (each story 12 feet in height). How much does the building cost at $0.79 per cubic foot?
    A. $237,000
    B. $275,982
    C. $568,880
    D. $2,844,000

45. Prorated items that represent prepaid expenses of the seller should be shown on the settlement statement as a
    A. credit to the seller and debit to the buyer.
    B. debit to the seller and credit to the buyer.
    C. credit to the buyer.
    D. debit to the seller.

46. A mortgagor can get direct financing from all of the following EXCEPT
    A. mortgage banking companies.
    B. savings and loan associations.
    C. commercial banks.
    D. Ginnie Mae.

47. After the statute of limitations has run out, a contract that has been breached is which of the following?
    A. Unenforceable
    B. Rescinded
    C. Terminated
    D. Discharged

48. In the event the parties to a contract wish to delete a provision in the printed agreement form, they should
    A. execute a supplement to the purchase agreement.
    B. cross out the provisions to be deleted.
    C. have their signatures notarized.
    D. arrive at an oral agreement to make the changes.

49. A licensed real estate broker
    A. becomes an agent of the vendee upon obtaining a valid listing.
    B. can disclose any truthful information received from the principal.
    C. becomes an agent of the vendor when a buyer is found.
    D. must disclose all material facts to the principal.

50. How many acres are in the S½ of the NW¼ of the SE¼ of a section?
    A. 10
    B. 20
    C. 40
    D. 120

51. An owner listed his home with the XYZ Brokerage Company under an open listing agreement. After the sale of the property, a dispute arose between XYZ Brokerage and Sunday Brokerage. Each brokerage firm claimed to be entitled to a commission. In this situation, the commission should be paid to the broker who
    A. listed the property.
    B. advertised the property.
    C. obtained the first offer.
    D. was the procuring cause of the sale.

52. A broker has an exclusive-right-to-sell listing. When the seller is out of town on business, a buyer makes an offer contingent upon the seller taking a purchase money mortgage of $10,000. The buyer must have a commitment from the seller prior to the seller's scheduled return to the city. Under these circumstances, the
    A. broker may enter into a binding agreement on behalf of the seller.
    B. broker may collect a commission because he found a ready, willing, and able buyer.
    C. buyer is deemed to have an option until the seller returns.
    D. broker must obtain the signature of both parties in order to earn a commission.

53. Two people are co-owners of a parcel of real estate. Each owns an undivided interest. One person owns two-thirds and the other owns one-third. This form of ownership is
    A. tenancy in common.
    B. joint tenancy.
    C. tenancy by the entirety.
    D. community property ownership.

54. A buyer made an offer on a property with a contingency clause entitling the buyer to a refund of his earnest money deposit if the seller's accepted and signed contract was not delivered to him within two days of the contract date. The owner signed the contract the next day. On the third day, the broker attempted to deliver the signed copy to the buyer but learned that he had been killed in an accident. In these circumstances
    A. the estate of the deceased buyer is liable for completion of the contract.
    B. the contract, by its terms, is void.
    C. death cancels all real estate contracts.
    D. the broker can collect a commission from the seller.

55. An investor leases a property to a tenant under an oral one-year lease. If the tenant defaults, the investor may
    A. not bring court action because of parol evidence rule.
    B. not bring court action because of the statute of frauds.
    C. bring a court action because one-year leases need not be in writing to be enforced.
    D. bring a court action because the statute of limitations does not apply to oral leases.

56. An acceleration clause will be found in which of the following documents?
    A. Listings
    B. Sales contracts
    C. Mortgages
    D. Leases

57. The federal Fair Housing Act of 1968 makes it illegal to discriminate because of
    A. age.
    B. marital status.
    C. public assistance.
    D. religion.

58. A person owns a large parcel of undeveloped property, in severalty, near a large urban area. A developer, who believes the property could be developed for commercial purposes, buys the property. At the closing, the developer insists that the spouse sign the deed. The purpose of obtaining the signature of the spouse is to
    A. terminate any rights the spouse may have in the property.
    B. attest that the deed is accurate and correct.
    C. provide the developer with a sale-lease-back agreement.
    D. subordinate the spouse's interest to the developer.

59. A broker enters into a listing agreement where the seller will receive $120,000 from the sale of a vacant lot. The broker is to receive any sale proceeds over and above that amount. The broker and seller entered into a(an)
    A. gross listing.
    B. exclusive right-to-sell listing.
    C. exclusive agency listing.
    D. net listing.

60. The annual net income from a commercial property is $22,000, and the capitalization rate is 8 percent. What is the value of the property using the income approach?
    A. $275,000
    B. $176,000
    C. $200,000
    D. $183,000

61. A storage tank that measures 12' × 9' × 8' was designed to store natural gas. The cost of natural gas is $1.82 per cubic foot. What will it cost to fill the tank to one-half its capacity?
    A. $864.00
    B. $1,572.48
    C. $786.24
    D. $684.58

62. A real estate sales contract becomes valid when it has been signed by which of the following?
    A. Buyer
    B. Buyer and seller
    C. Seller
    D. Broker and seller

63. ABC Investment Company enters into a five year lease agreement with XYZ Retail store. Two years later, XYZ Retail wants to sell his business to JFK Incorporated. ABC Investment Company releases XYZ Retail of liability and signs a new contract with JFK Inc. The term that BEST describes this scenario is
    A. assignment.
    B. novation.
    C. secondary agreement.
    D. sublease.

64. All of the following situations are in violation of the federal Fair Housing Act of 1968 EXCEPT
    A. the refusal of the property manager to rent an apartment to a Catholic couple who are otherwise qualified.
    B. the policy of a loan company not to grant home improvement loans to individuals in *changing* neighborhoods.
    C. the intentional neglect of a broker to show a black family any properties in all-white neighborhoods.
    D. the insistence of an owner of a single family home to rent her spare bedroom only to females.

65. A house sold for $140,000, and the buyer obtained an FHA mortgage in the amount of $136,500. How much money would the buyer pay if he was charged four points?
    A. $5,420
    B. $5,460
    C. $5,600
    D. $5,640

66. What is a tenancy at will?
    A. Tenancy with the consent of the landlord
    B. Tenancy that expires on a specific date
    C. Tenancy created by the death of the owner
    D. Tenancy created by the testator

67. Which of the following BEST describes a datum?
    A. Undersized or fractional section
    B. Imaginary line from which heights are measured
    C. Primary township
    D. Imaginary line that measures longitude

68. A licensed salesperson is authorized by law to
    A. sign a closing statement.
    B. collect a commission directly from a principal for performing assigned duties.
    C. advertise listed property under the salesperson's own name.
    D. act under the supervision of a real estate broker.

69. Which of the following BEST describes steering?
    A. Leading prospective homeowners to or away from certain areas
    B. Refusing to make loans to persons in certain areas
    C. A requirement to join MLS
    D. Practice of setting commissions

70. Other than property taxes and special assessments, lien priority is established by
    A. county laws.
    B. the recording date at the court house.
    C. the date on which the debt was incurred.
    D. the date the broker listed the property.

71. An agreement between an owner and the property management agreement would MOST LIKELY have a(an)
    A. statement of owner's purpose.
    B. estoppel certificate.
    C. joint and several liability.
    D. waiver of subrogation.

72. Three days before the closing, a buyer notified his agent that he would not buy. What legal action can the seller take to enforce the terms of the contract?
    A. File an adverse possession claim
    B. File a lis pendens notice
    C. Serve a notice of redemption
    D. Sue for specific performance

73. The annual tax bill of $743.25 is due on December 31 of each year and is paid in arrears. The property was sold and closed on August 12. Which of the following is TRUE? (Use a 360-day year.)
    A. $284.91 DS, CB
    B. $458.32 DS, CB
    C. $284.91 CB, DS
    D. $458.32 CS, DB

74. The Federal Reserve regulates the supply of money in the market by setting the
    A. reserve requirements and discount rates.
    B. interest rate that local lenders can charge.
    C. number of loans that FHA can approve each year.
    D. discount points that sellers pay on VA guaranteed loans.

75. In estimating the value of commercial property, what is the appraiser's MOST important consideration?
    A. Reproduction cost
    B. Net income
    C. Gross rent multiplier
    D. Gross income

76. All of the following are examples of a specific lien EXCEPT
    A. real estate taxes.
    B. an IRS lien.
    C. a mortgage.
    D. a mechanic's lien.

77. Which of the following types of ownership are characterized by the right of survivorship?
    A. Joint tenancy and tenancy by the entireties
    B. Joint tenancy and severalty
    C. Joint tenancy and tenancy in common
    D. Joint tenancy and condominium tenancy

78. The type of ownership that blends severalty and tenancy in common ownership is a
    A. periodic tenancy.
    B. condominium.
    C. cooperative.
    D. life estate.

79. K grants a life estate to L based on the life of M. L dies before M. What is the status of the life estate?
    A. It belongs to K in fee simple absolute ownership.
    B. It belongs to K's remainderman.
    C. It belongs to M and the heirs of M.
    D. It belongs to L's heirs until the death of M.

80. A subdivision has a deed restriction that does not allow the building of tree houses. An architect moves into the subdivision and builds a tree house in the back yard. How many neighbors will it take to enforce the deed restriction, and what action should be taken?
    A. Seventy-five percent of the neighbors must sign a petition that will be given to the local zoning board for enforcement.
    B. Only one neighbor needs to take action through the local zoning board.
    C. Only one neighbor needs to take action through the court system.
    D. Seventy-five percent of the neighbors must take action through private court action.

81. A developer discovers that a proposed swimming pool in a condominium community meets all local zoning requirements except for the side yard line on one side of the clubhouse. The developer should
    A. take no action because it is only on one side of the clubhouse.
    B. file for a variance with the local zoning board.
    C. file for a nonconforming use with the local zoning board.
    D. continue with the construction and later file for an adverse possession claim to the property.

82. A lot is valued at $75,000. The two-story house measures 30' × 50' and is valued at $100 a square foot. If the owner is willing to pay a 6 percent commission, the agent should list the property for at LEAST what amount?
    A. $375,000
    B. $389,350
    C. $397,500
    D. $398,936

83. Which of the following situations would terminate a listing agreement without legal liability?
    A. Death of the salesperson
    B. Destruction of the broker's office
    C. Death of the seller
    D. Bankruptcy of the agent

84. An exclusive-right-to-sell listing is usually an
    A. executory bilateral contract.
    B. exculpatory bilateral contract.
    C. executed unilateral contract.
    D. executed implied contract.

85. An agent listed a property for $89,000 and five days later received an offer of $89,000. There were no contingencies. Which of the following is TRUE?
    A. The seller must accept the offer because it is for the listed price.
    B. The buyer cannot withdraw the offer because it is for the listed price.
    C. The seller does not have to sell and he does not have to pay the broker's commission.
    D. The buyer may withdraw the offer prior to its acceptance.

86. A contract gives the buyer the right to purchase a property within a specified timeframe. The purchase price and other specific terms have been agreed upon by both parties. The buyer gave the seller a $10,000 check with the contract, which will not be returned if the buyer does not purchase. The seller gave the buyer a(n)
    A. sales contract.
    B. lease.
    C. offer.
    D. option.

87. Which of the following statements is NOT true?
    A. A land contract is also known as an installment contract.
    B. If time is of the essence is in a contract, the duties are expected to be performed within a reasonable time.
    C. An equitable title is transferred when the deed is signed by the grantor at the closing table.
    D. Liquidated damages are agreed to in advance by the parties.

88. Which of the following is NOT false?
    A. An earnest money deposit is necessary to create a legally binding contract.
    B. The death of the salesperson will affect the status of listing contracts.
    C. If time is of the essence is found in a contract, then the contract must be performed within the time limit specified.
    D. A contract entered into under duress, undue influence, or misrepresentation is void.

89. Because the cost of clean-up and removal of hazardous waste can be greater than the value of the property, an agent is expected to have
    A. technical expertise in possible hazardous substances found within buildings.
    B. technical expertise in the area of asbestos, which is present in so many buildings.
    C. taken a class on how to identify asbestos, because it is present in so many buildings.
    D. a basic knowledge of hazardous substances and be aware of environmental issues in a real estate transaction.

90. The primary objectives of a property manager are to
    A. generate the highest net operating income of the property while maintaining and preserving the owner's investment.
    B. secure tenants by offering the lowest possible rents that the budget allows.
    C. negotiate contracts with service providers that give the manager the most advantageous kickbacks.
    D. cut expenses in any way necessary to generate a profit for the owner.

91. A lease with a definite beginning, a definite ending, and where no notice is required to terminate the lease is a(n)
    A. estate for years.
    B. periodic tenancy.
    C. estate at will.
    D. estate at sufferance.

92. A tenant entered into a three-year lease that was an estate for years agreement. On termination of the lease agreement, the tenant remained in possession of the property. Which of the following is TRUE?
    A. If the landlord accepted payment for another month, the original lease would automatically renew for another two years.
    B. The landlord could evict the tenant or treat the holdover tenant as a periodic tenancy.
    C. The tenant had the right to remain in the property because the landlord did not give proper notice.
    D. The tenant had the right to remain in the property because the landlord does not have it rented to anyone anyway.

93. Which of the following is NOT a requirement for a valid lease?
    A. Offer and acceptance
    B. Description of the leased premises
    C. Capacity to contract
    D. An option agreement

94. A tenant pays $700 per month in fixed rent, plus 4 percent of all gross sales of more than $350,000. How much were the gross sales if the total rent paid for the year was $14,975?
    A. $414,375
    B. $164,375
    C. $356,375
    D. $514,375

95. A homeowner purchased a first principal place of residence for $69,000. In the next five years, she made $10,000 worth of improvements. The property sold for $109,000, and a 6 percent commission was paid. Which of the following is TRUE regarding the capital gains?
    A. The adjusted basis is $102,460.
    B. The capital gain is $23,460.
    C. The capital gain is $33,460.
    D. The adjusted basis is $89,000.

96. Which of the following would not be associated with mortgage fraud?
    A. Rescue scams
    B. Straw buyers
    C. Silent second
    D. Home equity loan

97. What is the priority of the following liens?
    A. IRS liens, then property taxes
    B. IRS liens, then special assessments
    C. First mortgage, then property taxes
    D. Property taxes, then first mortgage

98. A borrower purchased mortgagee's title insurance on a property. After the final payment was made on the mortgage, a title defect was found. The borrower may have recourse through the
    A. previous owner if a general warranty deed was transferred at the closing.
    B. previous owner if a quitclaim deed was transferred at the closing.
    C. title insurance company because a title policy was secured when the property was purchased.
    D. title insurance company because a mortgagee's title insurance was secured when the property was purchased.

99. What is the major difference between constructive notice and actual notice?
    A. Constructive notice is direct knowledge, while actual notice is legal notice.
    B. Constructive notice is given annually, while actual notice is given monthly.
    C. Constructive notice is recorded by an attorney, while actual notice can be recorded by anyone.
    D. Constructive notice is notice that the law presumes we have, while actual notice is what a party actually knows.

100. Which of the following is NOT true regarding RESPA?
    A. RESPA requirements apply when a residential purchase is financed by a federally related mortgage loan.
    B. RESPA was enacted to eliminate kickbacks and other referral fees that increase the cost of settlement.
    C. RESPA requires that a good-faith estimate of settlement costs be provided to the buyer within two days of loan application.
    D. The settlement statement must be made available for inspection by the borrower at or before settlement.

101. The owners of a cooperative will
    A. become stockholders in a corporation that owns the building where they will reside.
    B. receive a deed and title to the building where they will reside.
    C. take out a mortgage to purchase the building where they will reside.
    D. receive a 20-year lease for the unit in which they will reside.

102. Which of the following is NOT an example of a legal description?
    A. Geodetic survey
    B. Lot and block
    C. Metes and bounds
    D. Torrens system

103. A buyer is purchasing a single-family home. The appraiser will MOST LIKELY use which method to appraise the property?
    A. Income
    B. GIM
    C. Cost
    D. Market data

104. In appraising a residential property, the appraiser would make a
   A. positive adjustment to the subject property if the subject property had an amenity the comparable did not.
   B. negative adjustment to the subject property if the subject property had an amenity the comparable did not.
   C. positive adjustment to the comparable property if the subject property had an amenity the comparable did not.
   D. negative adjustment to the comparable property if the comparable property did not have an amenity the subject property had.

105. Which of the following terms is associated with real estate property taxes?
   A. Caveat emptor
   B. Caveat venditor
   C. Annuit coeptis
   D. Ad valorem

106. The closing date was scheduled for October 31, and the seller made her mortgage payment on October 1. The loan balance after the October 1 payment was $125,000, and the interest rate was 8 percent. If there were no prepayment penalties, the loan payoff would be
   A. $135,000.00.
   B. $8,333.33.
   C. $125,833.33.
   D. $124,166.67.

107. The sellers accepted an offer of $510,000 for their property. On the closing statement, their mortgage balance was $200,000, the commission paid was 6 percent, and they had $5,000 in other closing costs. The net to the sellers is
   A. $30,600.
   B. $274,400.
   C. $310,000.
   D. $479,400.

108. On April 1, a borrower made her monthly payment principal and interest payment of $212.47, and her loan balance was $6,945.23. On May 1, she made another principal and interest payment and paid off the loan. If the interest rate was 10 percent, what was her payoff?
   A. $6,790.64
   B. $6,887.35
   C. $6,250.71
   D. $6,125.99

109. A lender charged $4,000 in discount points on a $100,000 loan. How many discount points were charged?
   A. 1
   B. 10
   C. 4
   D. 40

110. A borrower negotiated a 90 percent loan and the lender is charging two points. If his offer of $190,000 is accepted, what is the minimum cash he will need to close?
   A. $22,420
   B. $19,000
   C. $25,239
   D. $22,240

SALES EXAM II ANSWERS

1. **(D)** $137,500 – 50,000 = $87,500
   $50,000 × 3% = $1,500
   $87,500 × 5% = $4,375
   $4,375 + 1,500 = $5,875
   $137,500 – 5,875 = $131,625

2. **(C)** Only party bound to the contract; therefore, it is a unilateral contract. (56)

3. **(A)** 20% + 40% = 60%
   $3,600 ÷ 60% = $6,000
   $6,000 ÷ 5% = $120,000

4. **(D)** By definition of term loan.

5. **(B)** Ownership in severalty is ownership by one party.

6. **(B)** A deficiency judgment allows a mortgagee to sue for the balance owned when the security for a loan is insufficient to satisfy the debt.

7. **(B)** The Torrens system is a method of registering land, and the Torrens certificate is proof of ownership.

8. **(B)** A title transferred by a quitclaim deed provides no warranties. It transfers whatever interest the grantor has in the property.

9. **(B)** In an open listing, the seller retains the right to sell the property and not pay a commission to the broker.

10. **(A)** The buyer's interest in the property when legal title is held by another party is known as equitable title.

11. **(D)** A deed in lieu of foreclosure conveys title to the lender, but it does not indicate the sale of property.

12. **(B)** A = 50' × 137'
    A = 6,850 sq. ft.
    6,850 × $4.50 = $30,825
    $30,825 × 7.25% = $2,234.81

13. **(A)** The buyer owes interest from June 15 through June 30, or 16 days.
    $142,500 × 7.75% = $11,043.75
    $11,043.75 ÷ 360 = $30.6770
    $30.6770 × 16 = $490.83

14. **(A)** To transfer a title, a deed is signed by the grantors.

15. **(D)** Proof of heirship is not one of the requirements for a valid deed.

16. **(A)** The rental of rooms in an owner-occupied one- to four-family dwelling is exempt from the federal Fair Housing Act. No broker can be used and the owner cannot discriminate in advertising.

17. **(B)** Property managers are usually paid a percentage of the gross income.

18. **(A)** The commission is a debit to the seller on a settlement sheet.

19. **(B)** The sellers owe the remaining balance of the month's rent to the buyer.

20. **(C)** RESPA requires that the lender make the proper disclosures.

21. **(D)** A purchase agreement would least likely be recorded at the county recorder's office.

22. **(A)** Most state laws require that all listed property be advertised in the name of the broker or brokerage.

23. **(B)** State laws require that parties receive a copy of all contracts they sign.

24. **(C)** If consent is secured from the seller, all the brokers in the open listing can place signs on the property. (Some states require written consent.)

25. **(D)** DUST is the acronym to remember the characteristics of value. Demand, utility, scarcity, and transferability make real estate valuable.

26. **(B)** By definition of capitalization rate.

27. **(A)** Adjustments are made in the amenities of the comparable properties.

28. **(D)** The final step in the appraisal process is to reconcile the difference to arrive at the value.

29. **(B)** If the property is uninhabitable, the tenant may leave the property. This is known as constructive eviction.

30. **(A)** Tenancy at sufferance is created when the tenant refuses to surrender possession of the property upon the expiration of the lease.

31. **(A)** By definition of remainder interest.

32. **(A)** A fee simple defeasible title, or defeasible fee, is transferred when the real estate is conveyed with specified conditions.

33. **(B)** The buyer and/or seller may pay the points in FHA-insured loans.

34. **(B)** In title-theory states, the lender has title to the property.

35. **(A)** The Sherman Antitrust Act and state laws prohibit price fixing.

36. **(D)** All are examples of public and private land-use controls.

37. **(B)** $198,210 \times 2.75\% = \$5,450.78$
$\$5,450.78 + 400 = \$5,850.78 \ (195)$

38. **(A)** By definition of net lease.

39. **(B)** The landlord's interest is a leased fee interest, while the tenant's interest is a leasehold interest.

40. **(C)** $\$6.50 \div 100 = 0.065$
$\$72,000 \times 67\% = \$48,240$
$\$48,240 \times 0.065 = \$3,135.60$
$\$3,135.60 \div 12 = \$261.30$

41. **(A)** $\$50,000 \div 80\% = \$62,500$

42. **(D)** Nonjudicial foreclosure does not involve civil action. The lender is allowed to foreclose by advertisement.

43. **(B)**

Debit	Credit
$65,900.00	$39,540.00
395.40	
450.00	
$66,745.40	$39,540.00

$\$65,900 \times 40\% = \$26,360$
$\$65,900 - 26,360 = \$39,540$
$\$39,540 \times 1\% = \$395.40$
$\$66,745.40$ Debits $- \$39,540.00$ Credits $= \$27,205.40$

44. **(D)** $V = 200' \times 300' \times 12' = 720,000$ cu. ft.
$720,000 \times 0.79 = \$568,880 \times 5 = \$2,844,000$

45. **(A)** Prepaid expenses are a credit to the seller and a debit to the buyer.

46. **(D)** Ginnie Mae does not negotiate loans.

47. **(A)** A contract not performed within the statutory time period is unenforceable.

48. **(A)** To delete a provision in an agreement, the parties should execute a supplement to the purchase agreement.

49. **(D)** A broker is required by the law of agency to disclose all material facts to the principal.

50. **(B)** $640 \div 4 \div 4 \div 2 = 20$ acres

51. **(D)** The party who is the procuring cause of the sale should be paid the commission.

52. **(D)** The broker must obtain the signature of both parties in order to get earn a commission.

53. **(A)** Tenancy in common ownership allows unequal shares of the real estate.

54. **(B)** The signed contract was not received by the buyer within two days, and upon the death of the buyer, became void.

55. **(C)** According to the statute of frauds, leases for less than one year need not be in writing and are enforceable.

56. **(C)** An acceleration clause in the mortgage allows the lender to call the entire mortgage balance due and payable.

57. **(D)** Religion is a protected class under the federal Fair Housing Act.

58. **(A)** The buyer wants to terminate any rights the spouse may have or may acquire in the property, such as homestead or dower rights.

59. **(D)** By definition of net listing.

60. **(A)** $22,000 ÷ 8\% = \$275,000$

61. **(C)** $V = 12' \times 9' \times 8' = 864$ cu. ft.
    $864 \times \$1.82 = \$1,572.48 ÷ 2 = \$786.24$

62. **(B)** The sales contract becomes valid when signed by the buyer and seller.

63. **(B)** By definition of novation.

64. **(D)** A homeowner can rent a spare bedroom and discriminate because of gender.

65. **(B)** $\$136,500 \times 4\% = \$5,460$

66. **(A)** A tenancy at will is a lease for an uncertain duration that is created with the consent of the landlord.

67. **(B)** By definition of datum.

68. **(D)** An agent can work only under the authority of a broker.

69. **(A)** By definition of steering.

70. **(B)** Unless there are unusual circumstances, the date on which the lien was recorded determines priority.

71. **(A)** A management agreement must contain a statement of the owner's purpose.

72. **(D)** By definition of specific performance. Real estate is unique; therefore, a suit for specific performance is an option upon default.

73. **(B)** Count from January 1 through August 12 for 222 days.
    $\$743.25 ÷ 360 = \$2.0645$
    $\$2.0645 \times 222 = \$458.32$ DS, CB

74. **(A)** The purpose of the Federal Reserve is to regulate the flow of money by regulating reserve requirements and discount rates.

75. **(B)** The annual net operating income is used to compute the value of the property.

76. **(B)** An IRS lien is a general lien against real and personal property.

77. **(A)** By definition of joint tenancy and tenancy by the entireties.

78. **(B)** When an owner purchases a condominium, the air space is owned in severalty; whereas the land and the improvements on the land are owned by all members in the condominium community as tenancy in common.

79. **(D)** L has been granted a life estate pur autre vie based on the life of M. Should L predecease M, L's heirs inherit the life estate and have rights as long as M is alive.

80. **(C)** Only one neighbor is necessary to enforce the deed restrictions through court action.

81. **(B)** A variance may be granted to relieve the harshness of a zoning ordinance.

82. **(D)** 100% – 6% = 94%
A = 30' × 50' = 1,500 × 2 = 3,000 sq. ft.
3,000 × $100 = $300,000
$300,000 + 75,000 = $375,000
$375,000 ÷ 94% = $398,936.17 or
$398,936

83. **(C)** Upon the death of either the principal broker or the seller, the listing is void.

84. **(A)** A listing contract is an executory contract in that something remains to be performed by one or more parties. It is a bilateral contract because all parties are bound to the contract.

85. **(D)** An offer can be rescinded at any time prior to its acceptance. The seller does not have to accept a full price offer, but a commission is due the broker.

86. **(D)** By definition of option contract.

87. **(C)** The legal title is transferred to the buyer at the closing, not equitable title.

88. **(C)** When time is of the essence is stated in a contract, it means that the contract must be performed within the specified time limit. Any party that does not perform within the proper time period is liable for breach of contract.

89. **(D)** Agents are not expected to be experts in the area of hazardous substances, but they should have a basic knowledge so all parties in the transaction can make informed decisions.

90. **(A)** The objectives of a property manager are to generate the highest net operating income from a property while maintaining, modernizing, and preserving the owner's interest.

91. **(A)** By the definition of estate for years.

92. **(B)** If the tenant remains in possession of the property after the expiration of the lease, the landlord may evict the tenant or accept payment from the tenant and create a periodic tenancy.

93. **(D)** A lease does not have to contain an option agreement to be valid.

94. **(D)** $700 × 12 = $8,400
$14,975 – $8,400 = $6,575
$6,575 ÷ 4% = $164,375
$164,375 + $350,000 = $514,375

95. **(B)** $69,000 + $10,000 = $79,000 adjusted basis
$109,000 – 6% = $102,460 net to seller
$102,460 – $79,000 = $23,460 capital gains

96. **(D)** Home equity loans are not a type of mortgage scam.

97. **(D)** Property taxes and special assessments are paid before all other liens.

98. **(A)** If a general warranty deed was given, there may be recourse through the previous owner.

99. **(D)** By definitions of constructive and actual notice.

100. **(C)** The good-faith estimate must be given to the buyer within three business days of loan application.

101. **(A)** When purchasing a cooperative, the owner receives stock in the company (cooperative) and a proprietary lease for the apartment.

102. **(D)** The Torrens system is a system of land registration, not a legal description.

103. **(D)** The appraiser would use the market data approach to determine value.

104. **(C)** If the subject property has an amenity that the comparable does not, then the appraiser makes a positive adjustment (adds) to the comparable property.

105. **(D)** Property taxes are also called ad valorem taxes.

106. **(C)** $125,000 × 8% = $10,000
$10,000 ÷ 12 = $833.33
$125,000 + $833.33 = $125,833.33

107. **(B)** $510,000 × 6% = $30,600
$510,000 − $200,000 − $30,600 − 5,000
= $274,400

108. **(A)** $6,945.23 × 10% = $694.52 ÷ 12 =
$57.88
$212.47 − $57.88 = $154.59
$6,945.23 − $154.59 = $6,790.64

109. **(C)** $4,000 ÷ $100,000 = 0.04 = 4 percent or
4 points

110. **(A)** $190,000 × 90% = $171,000
$171,000 × 2% = $3,420
$190,000 − $171,000 = $19,000
$19,000 + $3,420 = $22,420

State-Specific Questions to Know

Before you take your exam, be sure you can answer these questions about your state.

1. Is an agency disclosure form used in your state? ____ yes ____ no

2. If yes, when must it be given to the buyer, seller, landlord, tenant?
   _____

3. Is a dual agency legal in your state? ____ yes ____ no

4. If yes, when and how is it required to be disclosed?
   _____

5. Is designated agency offered in your state? ____ yes ____ no

6. Is a property disclosure statement used in your state? ____ yes ____ no

7. If yes, when is it given to the buyer? _____

8. How long are transaction files required to be kept in your state?
   _____

9. Does your company have a buyer agency agreement? ____ yes ____ no

    If yes, please read to determine how the buyer agent will be compensated.

10. Does your state have a law regarding stigmatized properties? _____ yes _____ no

    If yes, please review the legal duties when dealing with a stigmatized property.

11. Does your broker's listing agreement contain a broker protection clause? ____ yes ____ no

12. If yes, what is the standard time frame for the clause?
    _____

13. Does your state require property management agreements to be in writing? ___ yes ___ no

14. Does your state have a Landlord-Tenant Act? _____ yes _____ no

15. If yes, can the security deposits be placed in an interest-bearing account? _____ yes _____ no

16. In your community, who pays for the survey? _____ seller _____ buyer

17. In your community, who pays for the lender's title policy? _____ seller _____ buyer

18. Is your state a lien-theory, a title-theory, or an intermediate-theory state? _____

19. Under your state law, when must the earnest money check be deposited into the escrow account? _____

20.   In your state, under what conditions may the earnest money check be withdrawn from the escrow account? _____

21.   If the broker's license is suspended or revoked, what is the status of the sales associate's license? _____

Forms

FIGURE B.1

IRS Form 8300

IRS Form **8300** (Rev. June 2011) OMB No. 1545-0892 Department of the Treasury Internal Revenue Service	**Report of Cash Payments Over $10,000 Received in a Trade or Business** ▶ See instructions for definition of cash. ▶ Use this form for transactions occurring after June 30, 2011. Do not use prior versions after this date. For Privacy Act and Paperwork Reduction Act Notice, see the last page.	FinCEN Form **8300** (Rev. June 2011) OMB No. 1506-0018 Department of the Treasury Financial Crimes Enforcement Network

1 Check appropriate box(es) if: **a** ☐ Amends prior report;   **b** ☐ Suspicious transaction.

Part I   Identity of Individual From Whom the Cash Was Received

2 If more than one individual is involved, check here and see instructions . . . . ▶ ☐

3 Last name	**4** First name	**5** M.I.	**6** Taxpayer identification number

7 Address (number, street, and apt. or suite no.)	**8** Date of birth . . ▶ M M D D Y Y Y Y (see instructions)

9 City	**10** State	**11** ZIP code	**12** Country (if not U.S.)	**13** Occupation, profession, or business

14 Identifying document (ID)	**a Describe ID** ▶ ------------- **c Number** ▶	**b Issued by** ▶ -------------

Part II   Person on Whose Behalf This Transaction Was Conducted

15 If this transaction was conducted on behalf of more than one person, check here and see instructions . . . . ▶ ☐

16 Individual's last name or organization's name	**17** First name	**18** M.I.	**19** Taxpayer identification number

20 Doing business as (DBA) name (see instructions)	Employer identification number

21 Address (number, street, and apt. or suite no.)	**22** Occupation, profession, or business

23 City	**24** State	**25** ZIP code	**26** Country (if not U.S.)

27 Alien identification (ID)	**a Describe ID** ▶ ------------- **c Number** ▶	**b Issued by** ▶ -------------

Part III   Description of Transaction and Method of Payment

28 Date cash received M M D D Y Y Y Y	**29** Total cash received $ .00	**30** If cash was received in more than one payment, check here . . . ▶ ☐	**31** Total price if different from item 29 $ .00

32 Amount of cash received (in U.S. dollar equivalent) (must equal item 29) (see instructions):

a U.S. currency	$ .00	(Amount in $100 bills or higher $ _____ .00)
b Foreign currency	$ .00	(Country ▶ _____)
c Cashier's check(s)	$ .00	Issuer's name(s) and serial number(s) of the monetary instrument(s) ▶
d Money order(s)	$ .00	-------------
e Bank draft(s)	$ .00	-------------
f Traveler's check(s)	$ .00	

33 Type of transaction

- **a** ☐ Personal property purchased
- **b** ☐ Real property purchased
- **c** ☐ Personal services provided
- **d** ☐ Business services provided
- **e** ☐ Intangible property purchased
- **f** ☐ Debt obligations paid
- **g** ☐ Exchange of cash
- **h** ☐ Escrow or trust funds
- **i** ☐ Bail received by court clerks
- **j** ☐ Other (specify in item 34) ▶

34 Specific description of property or service shown in 33. Give serial or registration number, address, docket number, etc. ▶ ------------- -------------

Part IV   Business That Received Cash

35 Name of business that received cash	**36** Employer identification number

37 Address (number, street, and apt. or suite no.)	Social security number

38 City	**39** State	**40** ZIP code	**41** Nature of your business

42 Under penalties of perjury, I declare that to the best of my knowledge the information I have furnished above is true, correct, and complete.

Signature ▶ _____   Title ▶ _____
         Authorized official

43 Date of signature M M D D Y Y Y Y	**44** Type or print name of contact person	**45** Contact telephone number

IRS Form **8300** (Rev. 6-2011)   Cat. No. 62133S   FinCEN Form **8300** (Rev. 6-2011)

FIGURE B.1

IRS Form 8300 (continued)

IRS Form **8300** (Rev. 6-2011)   Page **2**   FinCEN Form **8300** (Rev. 6-2011)

Multiple Parties
(Complete applicable parts below if box 2 or 15 on page 1 is checked)

Part I   Continued—Complete if box 2 on page 1 is checked

3 Last name	4 First name	5 M.I.	6 Taxpayer identification number

7 Address (number, street, and apt. or suite no.)	8 Date of birth . . . ▶ (see instructions)	M M D D Y Y Y Y

9 City	10 State	11 ZIP code	12 Country (if not U.S.)	13 Occupation, profession, or business

14 Identifying document (ID)	a Describe ID ▶	b Issued by ▶
	c Number ▶	

3 Last name	4 First name	5 M.I.	6 Taxpayer identification number

7 Address (number, street, and apt. or suite no.)	8 Date of birth . . . ▶ (see instructions)	M M D D Y Y Y Y

9 City	10 State	11 ZIP code	12 Country (if not U.S.)	13 Occupation, profession, or business

14 Identifying document (ID)	a Describe ID ▶	b Issued by ▶
	c Number ▶	

Part II   Continued—Complete if box 15 on page 1 is checked

16 Individual's last name or organization's name	17 First name	18 M.I.	19 Taxpayer identification number

20 Doing business as (DBA) name (see instructions)	Employer identification number

21 Address (number, street, and apt. or suite no.)	22 Occupation, profession, or business

23 City	24 State	25 ZIP code	26 Country (if not U.S.)

27 Alien identification (ID)	a Describe ID ▶	b Issued by ▶
	c Number ▶	

16 Individual's last name or organization's name	17 First name	18 M.I.	19 Taxpayer identification number

20 Doing business as (DBA) name (see instructions)	Employer identification number

21 Address (number, street, and apt. or suite no.)	22 Occupation, profession, or business

23 City	24 State	25 ZIP code	26 Country (if not U.S.)

27 Alien identification (ID)	a Describe ID ▶	b Issued by ▶
	c Number ▶	

Comments – Please use the lines provided below to comment on or clarify any information you entered on any line in Parts I, II, III, and IV

IRS Form **8300** (Rev. 6-2011)   FinCEN Form **8300** (Rev. 6-2011)

IRS Form 8300 (continued)

IRS Form 8300 (Rev. 6-2011)   Page **3**   **FinCEN Form 8300** (Rev. 6-2011)

Section references are to the Internal Revenue Code unless otherwise noted.

Important Reminders

• Section 6050I (26 United States Code (U.S.C.) 6050I) and 31 U.S.C. 5331 require that certain information be reported to the IRS and the Financial Crimes Enforcement Network (FinCEN). This information must be reported on IRS/FinCEN Form 8300.

• Item 33, box i, is to be checked only by clerks of the court; box d is to be checked by bail bondsmen. See *Item 33* under *Part III,* later.

• The meaning of the word "currency" for purposes of 31 U.S.C. 5331 is the same as for the word "cash" (See *Cash* under *Definitions,* later).

General Instructions

Who must file. Each person engaged in a trade or business who, in the course of that trade or business, receives more than $10,000 in cash in one transaction or in two or more related transactions, must file Form 8300. Any transactions conducted between a payer (or its agent) and the recipient in a 24-hour period are related transactions. Transactions are considered related even if they occur over a period of more than 24 hours if the recipient knows, or has reason to know, that each transaction is one of a series of connected transactions.

Keep a copy of each Form 8300 for 5 years from the date you file it.

Clerks of federal or state courts must file Form 8300 if more than $10,000 in cash is received as bail for an individual(s) charged with certain criminal offenses. For these purposes, a clerk includes the clerk's office or any other office, department, division, branch, or unit of the court that is authorized to receive bail. If a person receives bail on behalf of a clerk, the clerk is treated as receiving the bail. See *Item 33* under *Part III,* later.

If multiple payments are made in cash to satisfy bail and the initial payment does not exceed $10,000, the initial payment and subsequent payments must be aggregated and the information return must be filed by the 15th day after receipt of the payment that causes the aggregate amount to exceed $10,000 in cash. In such cases, the reporting requirement can be satisfied either by sending a single written statement with an aggregate amount listed or by furnishing a copy of each Form 8300 relating to that payer. Payments made to satisfy separate bail requirements are not required to be aggregated. See Treasury Regulations section 1.6050I-2.

Casinos must file Form 8300 for nongaming activities (restaurants, shops, etc.).

Voluntary use of Form 8300. Form 8300 may be filed voluntarily for any suspicious transaction (see *Definitions,* later) for use by FinCEN and the IRS, even if the total amount does not exceed $10,000.

Exceptions. Cash is not required to be reported if it is received:

• By a financial institution required to file Form 104, Currency Transaction Report;

• By a casino required to file (or exempt from filing) Form 103, Currency Transaction Report by Casinos, if the cash is received as part of its gaming business;

• By an agent who receives the cash from a principal, if the agent uses all of the cash within 15 days in a second transaction that is reportable on Form 8300 or on Form 104, and discloses all the information necessary to complete Part II of Form 8300 or Form 104 to the recipient of the cash in the second transaction;

• In a transaction occurring entirely outside the United States. See Publication 1544, Reporting Cash Payments of Over $10,000 (Received in a Trade or Business), regarding transactions occurring in Puerto Rico and territories and possessions of the United States; or

• In a transaction that is not in the course of a person's trade or business.

When to file. File Form 8300 by the 15th day after the date the cash was received. If that date falls on a Saturday, Sunday, or legal holiday, file the form on the next business day.

Where to file. File the form with the Internal Revenue Service, Detroit Computing Center, P.O. Box 32621, Detroit, MI 48232.

Statement to be provided. You must give a written or electronic statement to each person named on a required Form 8300 on or before January 31 of the year following the calendar year in which the cash is received. The statement must show the name, telephone number, and address of the information contact for the business, the aggregate amount of reportable cash received, and that the information was furnished to the IRS. Keep a copy of the statement for your records.

Multiple payments. If you receive more than one cash payment for a single transaction or for related transactions, you must report the multiple payments any time you receive a total amount that exceeds $10,000 within any 12-month period. Submit the report within 15 days of the date you receive the payment that

causes the total amount to exceed $10,000. If more than one report is required within 15 days, you may file a combined report. File the combined report no later than the date the earliest report, if filed separately, would have to be filed.

Taxpayer identification number (TIN). You must furnish the correct TIN of the person or persons from whom you receive the cash and, if applicable, the person or persons on whose behalf the transaction is being conducted. You may be subject to penalties for an incorrect or missing TIN.

The TIN for an individual (including a sole proprietorship) is the individual's social security number (SSN). For certain resident aliens who are not eligible to get an SSN and nonresident aliens who are required to file tax returns, it is an IRS Individual Taxpayer Identification Number (ITIN). For other persons, including corporations, partnerships, and estates, it is the employer identification number (EIN).

If you have requested but are not able to get a TIN for one or more of the parties to a transaction within 15 days following the transaction, file the report and attach a statement explaining why the TIN is not included.

Exception: *You are not required to provide the TIN of a person who is a nonresident alien individual or a foreign organization if that person or foreign organization:*

• *Does not have income effectively connected with the conduct of a U.S. trade or business;*

• *Does not have an office or place of business, or a fiscal or paying agent in the United States;*

• *Does not furnish a withholding certificate described in §1.1441-1(e)(2) or (3) or §1.1441-5(c)(2)(iv) or (3)(iii) to the extent required under §1.1441-1(e)(4)(vii); or*

• *Does not have to furnish a TIN on any return, statement, or other document as required by the income tax regulations under section 897 or 1445.*

Penalties. You may be subject to penalties if you fail to file a correct and complete Form 8300 on time and you cannot show that the failure was due to reasonable cause. You may also be subject to penalties if you fail to furnish timely a correct and complete statement to each person named in a required report. A minimum penalty of $25,000 may be imposed if the failure is due to an intentional or willful disregard of the cash reporting requirements.

Penalties may also be imposed for causing, or attempting to cause, a trade or business to fail to file a required

FIGURE B.1

IRS Form 8300 (continued)

report; for causing, or attempting to cause, a trade or business to file a required report containing a material omission or misstatement of fact; or for structuring, or attempting to structure, transactions to avoid the reporting requirements. These violations may also be subject to criminal prosecution which, upon conviction, may result in imprisonment of up to 5 years or fines of up to $250,000 for individuals and $500,000 for corporations or both.

Definitions

Cash. The term "cash" means the following.

• U.S. and foreign coin and currency received in any transaction; or

• A cashier's check, money order, bank draft, or traveler's check having a face amount of $10,000 or less that is received in a designated reporting transaction (defined below), or that is received in any transaction in which the recipient knows that the instrument is being used in an attempt to avoid the reporting of the transaction under either section 6050I or 31 U.S.C. 5331.

Note. Cash does not include a check drawn on the payer's own account, such as a personal check, regardless of the amount.

Designated reporting transaction. A retail sale (or the receipt of funds by a broker or other intermediary in connection with a retail sale) of a consumer durable, a collectible, or a travel or entertainment activity.

Retail sale. Any sale (whether or not the sale is for resale or for any other purpose) made in the course of a trade or business if that trade or business principally consists of making sales to ultimate consumers.

Consumer durable. An item of tangible personal property of a type that, under ordinary usage, can reasonably be expected to remain useful for at least 1 year, and that has a sales price of more than $10,000.

Collectible. Any work of art, rug, antique, metal, gem, stamp, coin, etc.

Travel or entertainment activity. An item of travel or entertainment that pertains to a single trip or event if the combined sales price of the item and all other items relating to the same trip or event that are sold in the same transaction (or related transactions) exceeds $10,000.

Exceptions. A cashier's check, money order, bank draft, or traveler's check is not considered received in a designated reporting transaction if it constitutes the proceeds of a bank loan or if it is received as a payment on certain promissory notes, installment sales contracts, or down payment plans. See Publication 1544 for more information.

Person. An individual, corporation, partnership, trust, estate, association, or company.

Recipient. The person receiving the cash. Each branch or other unit of a person's trade or business is considered a separate recipient unless the branch receiving the cash (or a central office linking the branches), knows or has reason to know the identity of payers making cash payments to other branches.

Transaction. Includes the purchase of property or services, the payment of debt, the exchange of cash for a negotiable instrument, and the receipt of cash to be held in escrow or trust. A single transaction may not be broken into multiple transactions to avoid reporting.

Suspicious transaction. A suspicious transaction is a transaction in which it appears that a person is attempting to cause Form 8300 not to be filed, or to file a false or incomplete form.

Specific Instructions

You must complete all parts. However, you may skip Part II if the individual named in Part I is conducting the transaction on his or her behalf only. For voluntary reporting of suspicious transactions, see *Item 1* next.

Item 1. If you are amending a prior report, check box 1a. Complete the appropriate items with the correct or amended information only. Complete all of Part IV. Staple a copy of the original report to the amended report.

To voluntarily report a suspicious transaction (see *Suspicious transaction* above), check box 1b. You may also telephone your local IRS Criminal Investigation Division or call the FinCEN Financial Institution Hotline at 1-866-556-3974.

Part I

Item 2. If two or more individuals conducted the transaction you are reporting, check the box and complete Part I for any one of the individuals. Provide the same information for the other individual(s) on the back of the form. If more than three individuals are involved, provide the same information on additional sheets of paper and attach them to this form.

Item 6. Enter the taxpayer identification number (TIN) of the individual named. See *Taxpayer identification number (TIN),* earlier, for more information.

Item 8. Enter eight numerals for the date of birth of the individual named. For example, if the individual's birth date is July 6, 1960, enter 07 06 1960.

Item 13. Fully describe the nature of the occupation, profession, or business (for example, "plumber," "attorney," or "automobile dealer"). Do not use general or nondescriptive terms such as "businessman" or "self-employed."

Item 14. You must verify the name and address of the named individual(s). Verification must be made by examination of a document normally accepted as a means of identification when cashing checks (for example, a driver's license, passport, alien registration card, or other official document). In item 14a, enter the type of document examined. In item 14b, identify the issuer of the document. In item 14c, enter the document's number. For example, if the individual has a Utah driver's license, enter "driver's license" in item 14a, "Utah" in item 14b, and the number appearing on the license in item 14c.

Note. You must complete all three items (a, b, and c) in this line to make sure that Form 8300 will be processed correctly.

Part II

Item 15. If the transaction is being conducted on behalf of more than one person (including husband and wife or parent and child), check the box and complete Part II for any one of the persons. Provide the same information for the other person(s) on the back of the form. If more than three persons are involved, provide the same information on additional sheets of paper and attach them to this form.

Items 16 through 19. If the person on whose behalf the transaction is being conducted is an individual, complete items 16, 17, and 18. Enter his or her TIN in item 19. If the individual is a sole proprietor and has an employer identification number (EIN), you must enter both the SSN and EIN in item 19. If the person is an organization, put its name as shown on required tax filings in item 16 and its EIN in item 19.

Item 20. If a sole proprietor or organization named in items 16 through 18 is doing business under a name other than that entered in item 16 (for example, a "trade" or "doing business as (DBA)" name), enter it here.

Item 27. If the person is not required to furnish a TIN, complete this item. See *Taxpayer identification number (TIN),* earlier. Enter a description of the type of official document issued to that person in item 27a (for example, a "passport"), the country that issued the document in item 27b, and the document's number in item 27c.

FIGURE B.1

IRS Form 8300 (continued)

Note. You must complete all three items (a, b, and c) in this line to make sure that Form 8300 will be processed correctly.

Part III

Item 28. Enter the date you received the cash. If you received the cash in more than one payment, enter the date you received the payment that caused the combined amount to exceed $10,000. See *Multiple payments,* earlier, for more information.

Item 30. Check this box if the amount shown in item 29 was received in more than one payment (for example, as installment payments or payments on related transactions).

Item 31. Enter the total price of the property, services, amount of cash exchanged, etc. (for example, the total cost of a vehicle purchased, cost of catering service, exchange of currency) if different from the amount shown in item 29.

Item 32. Enter the dollar amount of each form of cash received. Show foreign currency amounts in U.S. dollar equivalent at a fair market rate of exchange available to the public. The sum of the amounts must equal item 29. For cashier's check, money order, bank draft, or traveler's check, provide the name of the issuer and the serial number of each instrument. Names of all issuers and all serial numbers involved must be provided. If necessary, provide this information on additional sheets of paper and attach them to this form.

Item 33. Check the appropriate box(es) that describe the transaction. If the transaction is not specified in boxes a–i, check box j and briefly describe the transaction (for example, "car lease," "boat lease," "house lease," or "aircraft rental"). If the transaction relates to the receipt of bail by a court clerk, check box i, "Bail received by court clerks." This box is only for use by court clerks. If the transaction relates to cash received by a bail bondsman, check box d, "Business services provided."

Part IV

Item 36. If you are a sole proprietorship, you must enter your SSN. If your business also has an EIN, you must provide the EIN as well. All other business entities must enter an EIN.

Item 41. Fully describe the nature of your business, for example, "attorney" or "jewelry dealer." Do not use general or nondescriptive terms such as "business" or "store."

Item 42. This form must be signed by an individual who has been authorized to do so for the business that received the cash.

Comments

Use this section to comment on or clarify anything you may have entered on any line in Parts I, II, III, and IV. For example, if you checked box b (Suspicious transaction) in line 1 above Part I, you may want to explain why you think that the cash transaction you are reporting on Form 8300 may be suspicious.

Privacy Act and Paperwork Reduction Act Notice. Except as otherwise noted, the information solicited on this form is required by the IRS and FinCEN in order to carry out the laws and regulations of the United States Department of the Treasury. Trades or businesses, except for clerks of criminal courts, are required to provide the information to the IRS and FinCEN under both section 6050I and 31 U.S.C. 5331. Clerks of criminal courts are required to provide the information to the IRS under section 6050I. Section 6109 and 31 U.S.C. 5331 require that you provide your social security number in order to adequately identify you and process your return and other papers. The principal purpose for collecting the information on this form is to maintain reports or records which have a high degree of usefulness in criminal, tax, or regulatory investigations or proceedings, or in the conduct of intelligence or counterintelligence activities, by directing the federal government's attention to unusual or questionable transactions.

You are not required to provide information as to whether the reported transaction is deemed suspicious. Failure to provide all other requested information, or providing fraudulent information, may result in criminal prosecution and other penalties under 26 U.S.C. and 31 U.S.C.

Generally, tax returns and return information are confidential, as stated in section 6103. However, section 6103 allows or requires the IRS to disclose or give the information requested on this form to others as described in the Internal Revenue Code. For example, we may disclose your tax information to the Department of Justice, to enforce the tax laws, both civil and criminal, and to cities, states, the District of Columbia, and U.S. commonwealths and possessions, to carry out their tax laws. We may disclose this information to other persons as necessary to obtain information which we cannot get in any other way. We may disclose this information to federal, state, and local child support agencies; and to other federal agencies for the purposes of determining entitlement for benefits or the eligibility for and the repayment of loans. We may also provide the records to appropriate state, local, and foreign criminal law enforcement and regulatory personnel in the performance of their official duties. We may also disclose this information to other countries under a tax treaty, or to federal and state agencies to enforce federal nontax criminal laws and to combat terrorism. In addition, FinCEN may provide the information to those officials if they are conducting intelligence or counter-intelligence activities to protect against international terrorism.

You are not required to provide the information requested on a form that is subject to the Paperwork Reduction Act unless the form displays a valid OMB control number. Books or records relating to a form or its instructions must be retained as long as their contents may become material in the administration of any law under 26 U.S.C. or 31 U.S.C.

The time needed to complete this form will vary depending on individual circumstances. The estimated average time is 21 minutes. If you have comments concerning the accuracy of this time estimate or suggestions for making this form simpler, you can write to the Internal Revenue Service, Tax Products Coordinating Committee, SE:W:CAR:MP:T:T:SP, 1111 Constitution Ave. NW, IR-6526, Washington, DC 20224. Do not send Form 8300 to this address. Instead, see *Where to file,* earlier.

FIGURE B.2

Lead-Based Paint Lessor Disclosure

Disclosure of Information on Lead-Based Paint and/or Lead-Based Paint Hazards

Lead Warning Statement
Housing built before 1978 may contain lead-based paint. Lead from paint, paint chips, and dust can pose health hazards if not managed properly. Lead exposure is especially harmful to young children and pregnant women. Before renting pre-1978 housing, lessors must disclose the presence of known lead-based paint and/or lead-based paint hazards in the dwelling. Lessees must also receive a federally approved pamphlet on lead poisoning prevention.

Lessor's Disclosure

(a) Presence of lead-based paint and/or lead-based paint hazards (check (i) or (ii) below):

    (i) _____ Known lead-based paint and/or lead-based paint hazards are present in the housing (explain).

    _____

    _____

    (ii) _____ Lessor has no knowledge of lead-based paint and/or lead-based paint hazards in the housing.

(b) Records and reports available to the lessor (check (i) or (ii) below):

    (i) _____ Lessor has provided the lessee with all available records and reports pertaining to lead-based paint and/or lead-based paint hazards in the housing (list documents below).

    _____

    _____

    (ii) _____ Lessor has no reports or records pertaining to lead-based paint and/or lead-based paint hazards in the housing.

Lessee's Acknowledgment (initial)

(c) _____ Lessee has received copies of all information listed above.

(d) _____ Lessee has received the pamphlet *Protect Your Family from Lead in Your Home.*

Agent's Acknowledgment (initial)

(e) _____ Agent has informed the lessor of the lessor's obligations under 42 U.S.C. 4852d and is aware of his/her responsibility to ensure compliance.

Certification of Accuracy
The following parties have reviewed the information above and certify, to the best of their knowledge, that the information they have provided is true and accurate.

Lessor	Date	Lessor	Date
Lessee	Date	Lessee	Date
Agent	Date	Agent	Date

Lead-Based Paint Seller Disclosure

Disclosure of Information on Lead-Based Paint and/or Lead-Based Paint Hazards

Lead Warning Statement

Every purchaser of any interest in residential real property on which a residential dwelling was built prior to 1978 is notified that such property may present exposure to lead from lead-based paint that may place young children at risk of developing lead poisoning. Lead poisoning in young children may produce permanent neurological damage, including learning disabilities, reduced intelligence quotient, behavioral problems, and impaired memory. Lead poisoning also poses a particular risk to pregnant women. The seller of any interest in residential real property is required to provide the buyer with any information on lead-based paint hazards from risk assessments or inspections in the seller's possession and notify the buyer of any known lead-based paint hazards. A risk assessment or inspection for possible lead-based paint hazards is recommended prior to purchase.

Seller's Disclosure

(a) Presence of lead-based paint and/or lead-based paint hazards (check (i) or (ii) below):

   (i) _____ Known lead-based paint and/or lead-based paint hazards are present in the housing (explain).

_____

   (ii) _____ Seller has no knowledge of lead-based paint and/or lead-based paint hazards in the housing.

(b) Records and reports available to the seller (check (i) or (ii) below):

   (i) _____ Seller has provided the purchaser with all available records and reports pertaining to lead-based paint and/or lead-based paint hazards in the housing (list documents below).

_____

   (ii) _____ Seller has no reports or records pertaining to lead-based paint and/or lead-based paint hazards in the housing.

Purchaser's Acknowledgment (initial)

(c) _____ Purchaser has received copies of all information listed above.

(d) _____ Purchaser has received the pamphlet *Protect Your Family from Lead in Your Home.*

(e) Purchaser has (check (i) or (ii) below):

   (i) _____ received a 10-day opportunity (or mutually agreed upon period) to conduct a risk assessment or inspection for the presence of lead-based paint and/or lead-based paint hazards; or

   (ii) _____ waived the opportunity to conduct a risk assessment or inspection for the presence of lead-based paint and/or lead-based paint hazards.

Agent's Acknowledgment (initial)

(f) _____ Agent has informed the seller of the seller's obligations under 42 U.S.C. 4852d and is aware of his/her responsibility to ensure compliance.

Certification of Accuracy

The following parties have reviewed the information above and certify, to the best of their knowledge, that the information they have provided is true and accurate.

Seller	Date	Seller	Date
Purchaser	Date	Purchaser	Date
Agent	Date	Agent	Date

GLOSSARY

abandonment   The voluntary and permanent cessation of use or enjoyment with no intention to resume or reclaim one's possession or interest. May pertain to an easement or a property.

abrogation   Tenants cannot sign away their rights in advance of signing the lease.

abstract of title   A condensed version of the history of title to a particular parcel of real estate as recorded in the county clerk's records; consists of a summary of the original grant and all subsequent conveyances and encumbrances affecting the property.

abutting   The joining, reaching, or touching of adjoining land. Abutting parcels of land have a common boundary.

accelerated depreciation   A method of calculating for tax purposes the depreciation of income property at a faster rate than would be achieved using the straight-line method. Note that any depreciation taken in excess of that which would be claimed using the straight-line rate is subject to recapture as ordinary income to the extent of gain resulting from the sale. *See also* straight-line method

acceleration clause   A provision in a written mortgage, note, bond, or conditional sales contract that, in the event of default, the whole amount of principal and interest may be declared to be due and payable at once.

accretion   An increase or addition to land by the deposit of sand or soil washed up naturally from a river, lake, or sea.

accrued depreciation   The actual depreciation that has occurred to a property at any given date; the difference between the cost of replacement new (as of the date of appraisal) and the present appraised value.

acknowledgment   A declaration made by a person to a notary public, or other public official authorized to take acknowledgments, that an instrument was executed by that person as a free and voluntary act

actual eviction   The result of legal action originated by a lessor, whereby a defaulted tenant is physically ousted from the rented property pursuant to a court order. *See also* eviction.

actual notice   Express information or fact; that which is known; actual knowledge.

adjustable-rate mortgage   A mortgage in which the interest rate changes at predetermined intervals. The mortgage has caps, or a ceiling, that limits the amount it can change at the predetermined intervals.

administrator   The party appointed by the county court to settle the estate of a deceased person who died without leaving a will.

ad valorem tax   A tax levied according to value; generally used to refer to real estate tax. Also called the general tax.

adverse possession   The right of an occupant of land to acquire title against the real owner, where possession has been actual, continuous, hostile, visible, and distinct for the statutory period.

affidavit   A written statement signed and sworn to before a person authorized to administer an oath.

agent   One who represents or has the power to act for another person (called the principal). The authorization may be express or implied. A fiduciary relationship is created under the law of agency when a property owner, as the principal, executes a listing agreement or management contract authorizing a licensed real estate broker to be the owner's agent.

agreement of sale   A written agreement whereby the purchaser agrees to buy certain real estate and the seller agrees to sell, upon terms and conditions set forth in the agreement.

air lot   A designated airspace over a piece of land. Air lots, like surface property, may be transferred.

air rights   The right to use the open space above a property, generally allowing the surface to be used for another purpose.

alienation   The act of transferring property to another. Alienation may be voluntary, such as by gift or sale; or involuntary, such as through eminent domain or adverse possession.

alienation clause   The clause in a mortgage or deed of trust that states that the balance of the secured debt becomes immediately due and payable at the mortgagee's option if the property is sold by the mortgagor. In effect, this clause prevents the mortgagor from assigning the debt without the mortgagee's approval.

alluvion   New deposits of soil as the result of accretion.

amenities   The tangible and intangible features that increase the value or desirability of real estate.

Americans with Disabilities Act   The ADA is a federal law that became effective in 1992. It is designed to eliminate discrimination against individuals with disabilities by mandating equal access to jobs, public accommodations, public transportation, telecommunications, and government services.

amortization   The liquidation of a financial burden by installment payments.

amortized loan   A loan in which the principal, as well as the interest, is payable in monthly or other periodic installments over the term of the loan.

antitrust laws   The laws designed to preserve the free enterprise of the open marketplace by making illegal certain private conspiracies and combinations formed to minimize competition. Violations of antitrust laws in the real estate business generally involve either price fixing (brokers conspiring to set fixed compensation rates) or allocation of customers or markets (brokers agreeing to limit their areas of trade or dealing to certain areas or properties).

appraisal   An estimate of the quantity, quality, or value of something. The process through which conclusions of property value are obtained; also refers to the report setting forth the process of estimation and conclusion of value.

appraised value   An estimate of a property's present worth.

appreciation   An increase in the worth or value of a property due to economic or related causes that may prove to be either temporary or permanent; opposite of depreciation.

appurtenant   Belonging to; incident to; annexed to. For example, a garage is appurtenant to a house, and the common interest in the common elements of a condominium is appurtenant to each apartment. Appurtenances pass with the land when the property is transferred.

arbitration   A means of settling a controversy between two parties through the medium of an impartial third party whose decision on the controversy (it is agreed) will be final and binding.

assemblage   The process of merging two or more parcels of real estate to create one parcel.

assessment   The imposition of a tax, charge, or levy, usually according to established rates.

assignment   The transfer in writing of rights or interest in a bond, mortgage, lease, or other instrument.

assumption of mortgage   The transfer of title to property to a grantee wherein he assumes liability for payment of an existing note secured by a mortgage against the property. Should the mortgage be foreclosed and the property sold for a lesser amount than that due, the grantee-purchaser who has assumed and agreed to pay the debt secured by the mortgage is personally liable for the deficiency. Before a seller may be relieved of liability under the existing mortgage, the lender must accept the transfer of liability for payment of the note.

attachment   The method by which a debtor's property is placed in the custody of the law and held as security pending outcome of a creditor's suit.

attorney-in-fact   The holder of a power of attorney.

attorney's opinion of title   An instrument written and signed by the attorney who examines the title, stating the attorney's opinion as to whether a seller may convey good title.

automatic extension   A clause in a listing agreement that states that the agreement will continue automatically for a certain period of time after its expiration date. In many states, use of this clause is discouraged or prohibited.

avulsion   The sudden removal of land by natural forces, such as an earthquake.

balloon payment   The final payment of a mortgage loan that is considerably larger than the required periodic payments because the loan amount was not fully amortized.

bargain and sale deed   A deed that carries with it no warranties against liens or other encumbrances, but that does imply that the grantor has the right to convey title. Note that the grantor may add warranties to the deed at his or her discretion.

base line   One of a set of imaginary lines running east and west and crossing a principal meridian at a definite point, used by surveyors for reference in locating and describing land under the rectangular survey system (or government survey method) of property description.

bench mark   A permanent reference mark or point established for use by surveyors in measuring differences in elevation.

beneficiary   The person for whom a trust operates, or in whose behalf the income from a trust estate is drawn. Also refers to a lender who lends money on real estate and takes back a note and deed of trust from the borrower.

bequest   A provision in a will providing for the distribution of personal property.

bilateral contract   A contract in which each party promises to perform an act in exchange for the other party's promise to perform.

bill of sale   A written instrument given to pass title to personal property.

binder   An agreement that may accompany an earnest money deposit for the purchase of real property as evidence of the purchaser's good faith and intent to complete the transaction.

blanket mortgage   A mortgage covering more than one parcel of real estate, providing for each parcel's partial release from the mortgage lien upon repayment of a definite portion of the debt.

blockbusting   The illegal practice of inducing homeowners to sell their properties by making representations regarding the entry, or prospective entry, of minority persons into the neighborhood.

blue-sky laws   The common name for those state laws that regulate the registration and sale of investment securities.

branch office   A secondary place of business apart from the principal or main office from which real estate business is conducted. A branch office generally must be run by a licensed real estate broker working on behalf of the broker operating the principal office.

breach of contract   The failure, without legal excuse, of one of the parties to a contract to perform according to the contract.

broker   One who buys and sells for another for a commission. *See also* real estate broker.

brokerage   The business of buying and selling for another for a commission.

budget loan or budget mortgage   A loan in which the monthly payments made by the borrower cover not only interest and a payment on the principal, but also one-twelfth of such expenses as taxes, insurance, assessments, and similar charges. The monthly payment is called a *PITI payment.*

buffer zone   A zone or space between two different use districts. An example of a buffer zone would be a park between a residential district and a commercial district.

building code   An ordinance specifying minimum standards of construction of buildings for the protection of public safety and health.

building line   A line fixed at a certain distance from the front and/or sides of a lot beyond which no structure can project; a setback line used to ensure a degree of uniformity in the appearance of buildings and unobstructed light, air, and view.

building restrictions   The limitations on the size or type of property improvements established by zoning acts or by deed or lease restrictions.

bulk zoning   Bulk zoning controls the density of the development on land to avoid overcrowding.

bundle of legal rights   The theory that land ownership involves ownership of all legal rights to the land, such as possession, control within the law, and enjoyment, rather than ownership of the land itself.

buydown mortgage   A mortgage in which the interest rate is reduced by paying interest in advance. A temporary buydown is for the initial years of the loan. A permanent buydown is for the life of the loan.

capacity of parties   The legal ability of persons to enter into a valid contract. Most persons have full capacity to contract, and are said to be competent parties.

capital gains   A tax on the profits realized from the sale of a capital asset.

capital improvement   Any improvement that is made to extend the useful life of a property or add to its value.

capital investment   The initial capital and the long-term expenditures made to establish and maintain a business or investment property.

capitalization   The process of converting into present value (or obtaining the present worth of) a series of anticipated future periodic installments of net income. In real estate appraising, it usually takes the form of discounting. The formula is expressed as follows: Income ÷ Rate = Value

capitalization rate   The rate of return a property will produce on the owner's investment.

cash flow   The net spendable income from an investment, determined by deducting all operating and fixed expenses from the gross income. If expenses exceed income, a negative cash flow is the result.

casualty insurance   A type of insurance policy that protects a property owner or other person from loss or injury sustained as a result of theft, vandalism, or similar occurrences.

caveat emptor   A Latin phrase meaning "Let the buyer beware."

caveat venditor   A Latin phrase meaning "Let the seller beware."

certificate of eligibility   A certificate given by the federal government to qualified veterans to show their remaining eligibility for a VA-guaranteed loan.

certificate of occupancy   A certificate of occupancy is issued after the building is inspected to make sure it complies with building codes.

certificate of reasonable value   A certificate issued by the Veterans Administration certifying the value, as determined by an approved VA appraiser, of property secured by a VA mortgage.

certificate of reduction   A document issued by the lender to verify the loan balance.

certificate of sale   The document generally given to a purchaser at a tax foreclosure sale. A certificate of sale does not convey title; generally, it is an instrument certifying that the holder received title to the property after the redemption period had passed and that the holder paid the property taxes for that interim period.

certificate of title   A statement of opinion on the status of the title to a parcel of real property based on an examination of specified public records.

cession deed   The type of deed used when land is donated to the government.

chain of title   The succession of conveyances from some accepted starting point whereby the present holder of real property derives a title.

chattel   Personal property.

City Planning Commission   A local governmental organization designed to direct and control the development of land within a municipality.

cloud on title   A claim or encumbrance that may affect title to land.

codicil   An addition to a will that alters, explains, adds to, or confirms the will, but does not revoke it.

coinsurance clause   A clause in insurance policies covering real property that requires the policyholder to maintain fire insurance; coverage is generally equal to at least 80 percent of the property's actual replacement cost.

collateral   Something of value given or pledged to a lender as security for a debt or obligation.

commercial property   A classification of real estate that includes income-producing property, such as office buildings, restaurants, shopping centers, hotels, and stores.

commingled property   That property of a married couple that is so mixed or commingled that it is difficult to determine whether it is separate or community property. Commingled property becomes community property.

commingling   The illegal act of a real estate broker who mixes the money of other people with that of his or her own; by law, brokers are required to maintain a separate trust account for the funds of other parties held temporarily by the broker.

commission   The payment made to a broker for services rendered, such as in the sale or purchase of real property; usually a percentage of the selling price of the property.

common elements   Those parts of a property that are necessary or convenient to the existence, maintenance, and safety of a condominium, or are normally used in common by all of the condominium residents. All condominium owners have an undivided ownership interest in the common elements.

common law   The body of law based on custom, usage, and court decisions.

community property   A system of property ownership based on the theory that each spouse has an equal interest in the property acquired by the efforts of either spouse during marriage.

Community Reinvestment Act   A part of the Housing and Community Development Act passed in 1977. The purpose of the act is to prevent the practice of redlining and disinvestment by lenders in certain areas of a city.

comparables   The properties listed in an appraisal report that are substantially equivalent to the subject property.

competent parties   Those persons who are recognized by law as being able to contract with others; usually those of legal age and sound mind.

condemnation   A judicial or administrative proceeding to exercise the power of eminent domain, by which a government agency takes private property for public use and compensates the owner.

conditional-use permit   A permit granted that allows the holder to build a special-purpose property that is inconsistent with zoning in the area. A conditional permit is generally issued to allow buildings for the good of the public, such as hospitals and houses of worship in a residential area.

condominium   The absolute ownership of an apartment or a unit, generally in a multiunit building, based on a legal description of the airspace that the unit actually occupies, plus an undivided interest in the ownership of the common elements that are owned jointly with the other condominium unit owners. The entire tract of real estate included in a condominium development is called a *parcel*, or *development parcel*. One apartment or space in a condominium building, or a part of a property intended for independent use and having lawful access to a public way is called a *unit*. Ownership of one unit also includes a definite undivided interest in the common elements.

conformity   The maximum value is achieved when the property is in harmony with its surroundings.

consideration   Something of value that induces one to enter into a contract. Consideration may be valuable (money or commodity), or good (love and affection).

constructive eviction   Acts done by the landlord that so materially disturb or impair the tenant's enjoyment of the leased premises that the tenant is effectively forced to move out and terminate the lease without liability for any further rent. Also refers to a purchaser's inability to obtain clear title.

constructive notice   Notice given to the world by recorded documents. All persons are charged with knowledge of such documents and their contents, whether or not they have actually examined them. Possession of property is also considered constructive notice that the person in possession has an interest in the property.

contingency   A provision in a contract that requires completion or that a certain event must occur before the contract becomes binding.

contract   An agreement entered into by two or more legally competent parties by the terms of which one or more of the parties, for a consideration, undertakes to do or to refrain from doing some legal act or acts. A contract may be either unilateral, where only one party is bound to act, or bilateral, where all parties to the instrument are legally bound to act as prescribed.

contract for deed   A contract for the sale of real estate wherein the sales price is paid in periodic installments by the purchaser, who is in possession, although title is retained by the seller until final payment. Also called an *installment contract* or a *land contract*.

contract for exchange of real estate   A contract of sale of real estate in which the consideration is paid wholly or partly in property.

contract rent   Rental income received under the current lease agreement. *See also* market rent.

contribution   The value of any part of the property is measured by its effect on the value of the whole.

conventional insured mortgage   A mortgage (loan) wherein the borrower has less than a 20 percent down payment. The lender may require that the borrower purchase private mortgage insurance to reduce the lender's risk.

conventional life estate   A life estate created by the grantor rather than by law.

conventional mortgage   A mortgage (loan) where real property is used as security for the payment of the debt and the loan is not insured through FHA or guaranteed by VA.

conventional uninsured mortgage   A mortgage (loan) wherein the borrower has a 20 percent or greater down payment, and the lender accepts the creditworthiness of the borrower and the property as security for the loan.

conversion   The process of changing from one form of ownership to another, such as apartment use to condo use.

conveyance   A written instrument that evidences transfer of some interest in real property from one person to another.

cooperative   A residential multiunit building whose title is held by a trust or corporation, which is owned by and operated for the benefit of persons living within the building, who are the beneficial owners of the trust or stockholders of the corporation, each having a proprietary lease.

corporation   An entity or organization created by operation of law whose rights of doing business are essentially the same as those of an individual. The entity has continuous existence until dissolved according to legal procedures.

correction lines   Used in the government survey to compensate for the curvature of the earth.

cost approach   The process of estimating the value of a special purchase property. The formula is as follows: Reproduction or replacement cost – Depreciation + Land = Value

counseling   The business of providing people with expert advice on a subject, based on the counselor's extensive, expert knowledge of the subject.

counteroffer   A new offer made as a reply to an offer received, having the effect of voiding the original offer, which cannot be accepted thereafter unless revived by the offeror's repeating it.

covenant   A promise to do or to refrain from doing an act. The covenants found in a general warranty deed are seisin, encumbrances, further assurance, quiet enjoyment, and warranty forever.

covenant of quiet enjoyment   In a deed, this covenant ensures that the grantee and the grantee's heirs have the right to the property free from interference from the acts or claims of third parties. In a lease, this covenant ensures the tenants' right of possession without interference from the landlord or third parties.

cul-de-sac   A dead-end street that widens sufficiently at the end to permit an automobile to make a U-turn.

curable depreciation   When the cost of fixing the property does not exceed the value of the property.

curtesy   A life estate, usually a fractional interest, given by some states to the surviving husband in real estate owned by his deceased wife. Many states have abolished curtesy.

cycle   A recurring sequence of events that regularly follow one another, generally within a fixed interval of time. The cycle of real estate is growth, stability, decline, and restoration.

datum   A horizontal plane from which heights and depths are measured.

dba   Doing business as.

debenture   A note or bond given as evidence of debt and issued without security.

debt   Something owed to another; an obligation to pay or to return something.

debt service   A borrower's periodic payment, comprising principal and interest, on the unpaid balance of a mortgage.

decreasing returns   When adding improvements to the land does not produce a proportional increase in the property value.

deed   A written instrument that, when executed and delivered, conveys title to, or an interest in, real estate.

deed in trust   A three-party instrument in which the trustor conveys legal title to the trustee for the benefit of the beneficiary. That trustee has full power to sell, mortgage, and subdivide a parcel of real estate. The beneficiary controls the trustee's use of these powers under the provisions of the trust agreement.

deed of reconveyance   The instrument used to reconvey title to a trustor under a deed of trust once the debt has been satisfied.

deed of trust   An instrument used to create a mortgage lien by which the mortgagor conveys title to a trustee, who holds it as security for the benefit of the note holder (the lender); also called a *trust deed*.

deed restrictions   The clauses in a deed limiting the future uses of the property. Deed restrictions may impose a vast variety of limitations and conditions, such as limiting the density of buildings, dictating the types of structures that can be erected, and preventing buildings from being used for specific purposes or from being used at all.

default   The nonperformance of a duty, whether arising under a contract or otherwise; failure to meet an obligation when due.

defeasance   A provision or condition in a deed or in a separate instrument that, being performed, renders the instrument void.

defeasible fee estate   An estate in land in which the holder has fee simple title subject to being divested on the happening of a specified condition. Two categories: (1) fee simple determinable or special limitation, and (2) fee simple subject to a condition subsequent.

deficiency judgment   A personal judgment levied against the mortgagor when a foreclosure sale does not produce sufficient funds to pay the mortgage debt in full.

delinquent taxes   Those unpaid taxes that are past due.

delivery   The legal act of transferring ownership. Documents, such as deeds and mortgages, must be delivered and accepted to be valid.

delivery in escrow   Delivery of a deed to a third person until the performance of some act or condition by one of the parties.

demand   The willingness of a number of people to accept available goods at a given price; often coupled with supply.

density zoning   The zoning ordinances that restrict the average maximum number of houses per acre that may be built within a particular area, generally a subdivision.

depreciation   In appraisal, a loss of value in property due to all causes, including physical deterioration, functional depreciation, and economic obsolescence. In real estate investment, an expense deduction for tax purposes taken over the period of ownership of income property.

descent   The hereditary succession of an heir to the property of a relative who dies intestate.

designated agent   An agent who has been appointed by a broker to act for a specific principal or client.

determinable fee estate   A defeasible fee estate in which the property automatically reverts to the grantor upon the occurrence of a specified event or condition. Also known as *special limitation*.

devise   A transfer of real estate by will or last testament. The donor is the devisor and the recipient is the devisee.

diminishing returns   The principle of diminishing returns applies when a given parcel of land reaches its maximum percentage return on investment, and further expenditures for improving the property yield a decreasing return.

discount points   An added loan fee charged by a lender to make the yield on a lower-than-market-value FHA or VA loan competitive with higher-interest conventional loans.

discount rate   The rate of interest a commercial bank must pay when it borrows from its Federal Reserve bank. Consequently, the discount rate is the rate of interest the banking system carries within its own framework. Member banks may take certain promissory notes that they have received from customers and sell them to their district Federal Reserve bank for less than face value. With the funds received, the banks can make further loans. Changes in the discount rate may cause banks and other lenders to reexamine credit policies and conditions.

dispossess   To oust from land by legal process.

dominant tenement   A property that includes in its ownership the appurtenant right to use an easement over another's property for a specific purpose.

dower   The legal right or interest recognized in some states that a wife acquires in the property her husband held or acquired during their marriage. During the lifetime of the husband, the right is only a possibility of an interest; on his death, it can become an interest in land. Many states have abolished dower.

dual agency   This occurs when an agent represents both parties in the same transaction. Both parties are clients.

due diligence   Reasonable care and protection agents owe any party that is their client (buyer, seller, principal broker, owner of the property in a property management agreement); the obligation of a person to use good-faith efforts to perform the terms of a contract, such as the buyer's responsibility to make efforts to obtain financing if that was a term of the sales contract.

due-on-sale clause   A clause in a mortgage allowing the lender the right to implement the acceleration clause in the mortgage if the borrower transfers title to the property.

duress   The use of unlawful constraint that forces action or inaction against a person's will.

earnest money deposit   An amount of money deposited by a buyer under the terms of a contract.

easement   A right to use the land of another for a specific purpose, such as for a right-of-way or for utilities; an incorporeal interest in land. An easement appurtenant passes with the land when conveyed.

easement by necessity   An easement allowed by law as necessary for the full enjoyment of a parcel of real estate; for example, a right of ingress and egress over a grantor's land.

easement by prescription   An easement acquired by continuous, open, uninterrupted, exclusive, and adverse use of the property for the period of time prescribed by state law.

easement in gross   An easement that is not created for the benefit of any land owned by the owner of the easement but that attaches personally to the easement owner. For example, a right to an easement granted by Eleanor Franks to Joe Fish to use a portion of her property for the rest of his life would be an easement in gross.

economic life   The period of time over which an improved property will earn an income adequate to justify its continued existence.

economic obsolescence   The impairment of desirability or useful life arising from factors external to the property, such as economic forces or environmental changes that affect supply and demand relationships in the market. Loss in the use and value of a property arising from the factors of economic obsolescence is to be distinguished from loss in value from physical deterioration and functional obsolescence, both of which are inherent in the property. Also referred to as *locational obsolescence* or *environmental obsolescence*.

emblements   Those growing crops produced annually through the tenant's own care and labor, and that can be taken away after the tenancy is ended. Emblements are regarded as personal property even prior to harvest, so if the landlord terminates the lease, the tenant may still reenter the land and remove such crops. If the tenant terminates the tenancy voluntarily, however, the tenant is not generally entitled to the emblements.

eminent domain   The right of a government or municipal quasi-public body to acquire property for public use through a court action called *condemnation*, in which the court determines that the use is a public use and determines the price or compensation to be paid to the owner.

employee status   One who works as a direct employee of an employer. The employer is obligated to withhold income taxes and Social Security taxes from the compensation of employees. *See also* independent contractor.

employment contract   A document evidencing formal employment between employer and employee or between principal and agent. In the real estate business, this generally takes the form of a listing agreement or management agreement.

encroachment   A fixture, or structure, such as a wall or fence that invades a portion of a property belonging to another.

encumbrance   Any lien, such as a mortgage, tax, or judgment lien, an easement, a restriction on the use of the land, or an outstanding dower right that may diminish the value of the property.

Equal Credit Opportunity Act   The ECOA is a federal act that prohibits discrimination by lenders on the basis of race, color, religion, sex, national origin, age, or marital status in any aspect of a credit transaction.

equalization   The raising or lowering of assessed values for tax purposes in a particular county or taxing district to make them equal to assessments in other counties or districts.

equitable lien   A lien that arises out of common law, wherein the parties have agreed in writing that a certain property will be held as security for a debt.

equitable right of redemption   The right of a defaulted borrower to redeem property before foreclosure upon full payment of the outstanding debt, as well as accrued interest and related costs prior to the foreclosure.

equitable title   The interest held by a vendee under a contract for deed or a sales contract; the equitable right to obtain absolute ownership to property when legal title is held in another's name; an insurable interest.

equity   The interest or value that an owner has in a property over and above any mortgage indebtedness.

erosion   The gradual wearing away of land by water, wind, and general weather conditions; the diminishing of property caused by the elements.

errors and omissions insurance   An insurance that protects brokers from loss due to errors, mistakes, and negligence.

escalation clause   A clause found in a mortgage or lease that allows the payment to adjust over the life of the mortgage or lease.

escheat   The reversion of property to the state in the event the owner thereof dies without leaving a will and has no heirs to whom the property may pass by lawful descent.

escrow   The closing of a transaction through a third party, called an *escrow agent* or *escrowee*, who receives certain funds and documents to be delivered on the performance of certain conditions in the escrow agreement.

estate for years   An interest for a certain, exact period of time in property leased for a specified consideration.

estate in land   The degree, quantity, nature, and extent of interest that a person has in real property.

estate in severalty   An estate owned by one person.

estoppel certificate   A legal instrument executed by a mortgagor showing the amount of the unpaid balance due on a mortgage and stating that the mortgagor has no defenses or offsets against the mortgagee at the time of execution of the certificate. Also called a *certificate of no defense*.

ethical   Conforming to professional standards of conduct.

eviction   A legal process to oust a person from possession of real estate.

evidence of title   A proof of ownership of property, which is commonly a certificate of title, a title insurance policy, an abstract of title with lawyer's opinion, or a Torrens registration certificate.

exchange   A transaction in which all or part of the consideration for the purchase of real property is the transfer of like-kind property (that is, real estate for real estate).

exclusive-agency buyer agency agreement   A buyer brokerage agreement wherein the broker is entitled to a payment only if the broker locates the property the buyer purchases. The buyer can find property without the services of the agent.

exclusive-agency listing   A listing contract under which the owner appoints a real estate broker as an exclusive agent for a designated period of time to sell the property on the owner's stated terms for a commission. However, the owner reserves the right to sell without paying anyone a commission by selling to a prospect who has not been introduced or claimed by the broker.

exclusive buyer agency agreement   An exclusive-agency agreement wherein the buyer is legally bound to compensate the agent whenever the buyer purchases a property of the type described in the contract. This is true even if the buyer finds the property.

exclusive-right-to-sell listing   A listing contract under which the owner appoints a real estate broker as the owner's exclusive agent for a designated period of time to sell the property on the owner's stated terms and agrees to pay the broker a commission when the property is sold, whether by the broker, the owner, or another broker.

exculpatory clause   A hold harmless clause that may be found in contracts excusing a party for injuries to another.

executed contract   A contract in which all parties have fulfilled their promises and thus performed the contract.

execution   The signing and delivery of an instrument. Also, a legal order directing an official to enforce a judgment against the property of a debtor.

executor   The male designated in a will to handle the estate of the deceased.

executory contract   A contract under which something remains to be done by one or more of the parties.

executrix   The female designated in a will to handle the estate of the deceased. The probate court must approve any sale of property by the executrix.

expenses   The short-term costs that are deducted from an investment property's income, such as minor repairs, regular maintenance, and renting costs.

expressed contract   An oral or written contract in which the parties state their terms and express their intentions in words.

familial status   A protected class under federal fair housing law. A landlord cannot refuse to rent to a head of the household with minor children or to a pregnant woman.

federal Fair Housing Act   The term for Title VIII of the Civil Rights Act enacted in 1968 that prohibits discrimination based on race, color, sex, religion, or national origin in the sale and rental of residential property.

Federal Home Loan Bank System   A system created by the Federal Home Loan Bank Act of 1932 to provide for a central reserve credit system for savings institutions engaged in home mortgage finance (predominantly savings and loans). The system is divided into 12 federal home loan bank districts with an FHLB in each district. The FHLBs maintain a permanent pool of credit to maintain liquidity of members or to provide means for mortgage lending when local funds are insufficient. Three sources of funds are available for the operation of the FHLB: (1) capital stock, (2) deposits of member institutions, and (3) consolidated obligations sold on the market. When member associations need funds, they obtain money by borrowing from FHLB. The FHLB Board supervises the system. The board is composed of three members appointed by the president of the United States with the advice and consent of the Senate.

Federal Home Loan Mortgage Corporation   A member of the secondary mortgage market that primarily buys conventional loans.

Federal Housing Administration (FHA)
A federal administrative body created by the National Housing Act in 1934 to encourage improvement in housing standards and conditions, to provide an adequate home financing system through the insurance of housing mortgages and credit, and to exert a stabilizing influence on the mortgage market.

federal income tax An annual tax based on income, including monies derived from the lease, use, or operation of real estate.

Federal National Mortgage Association (FNMA) Fannie Mae is the popular name for this federal agency that creates a secondary market for existing mortgages. FNMA does not loan money directly, but rather buys VA, FHA, and conventional loans.

Federal Reserve banks The government controls banks located in each of the 12 Federal Reserve districts, established by the Federal Reserve Act of 1913. The Board of Governors, working closely with the president and the U.S. Treasury, controls the Federal Reserve. The Federal Reserve system (through the 12 central banks) supervises and examines members' commercial banks; clears and collects checks drawn on commercial banks; and may influence the cost, supply, and availability of money.

fee simple absolute The highest form of ownership recognized by law. Also known as *fee simple* or *ownership in fee.*

fee simple defeasible with a special limitation Also known as a *fee simple determinable estate.* An estate created with a special limitation. Title would automatically revert back to the grantor or the grantor's heirs if the estate ceased to be used for the special limitation.

fee simple estate The maximum possible estate or right of ownership of real property continuing forever. Sometimes called a *fee* or *fee simple absolute.*

fee simple subject to a condition subsequent A defeasible fee estate in which the grantor reserves right of reentry to the property when the condition of ownership is violated.

FHA appraisal A Federal Housing Administration (FHA) evaluation of a property as security for a loan. Includes study of the physical characteristics of the property and surroundings; the location of the property; the prospective borrower's ability and willingness to repay a loan; and the mortgage amount and monthly payments.

FHA loan A loan insured by the FHA and made by an approved lender in accordance with the FHA's regulations.

fiduciary relationship A relationship of trust and confidence, as between trustee and beneficiary, attorney and client, and principal and agent.

financing statement *See* Uniform Commercial Code.

first mortgage A mortgage that creates a superior voluntary lien on the property mortgaged relative to other charges or encumbrances against same.

fixture An article that was once personal property, but has been so affixed to real estate that it has become real property.

floor area ratio (FAR) The FAR indicates the relationship between a building area and land, or the relationship between the square footage of the building and the square footage of the land.

forcible entry and detainer A summary proceeding for restoring to possession of land one who is wrongfully kept out or has been wrongfully deprived of the possession.

foreclosure A legal procedure whereby property used as security for a debt is sold to satisfy the debt in the event of default in payment of the mortgage note or default of other terms in the mortgage document. The foreclosure procedure brings the rights of all parties to a conclusion and passes the title in the mortgaged property to either the holder of the mortgage or a third party who may purchase the realty at the foreclosure sale, free of all encumbrances affecting the property subsequent to the mortgage.

formal will A will written by an attorney, with two subscribing witnesses and with necessary language. Such a will may appoint the executor of the estate as independent agent and avoid the necessity of a bond.

fractional sections   An oversized or undersized section that is not exactly one mile by one mile is a fractional section; used only in the government or rectangular survey.

fraud   A misstatement of a material fact made with intent to deceive or made with reckless disregard of the truth and that actually does deceive.

freehold estate   An estate in land in which ownership is for an indeterminate length of time, in contrast to a leasehold estate.

front feet   A unit of linear measurement of the side of a property that faces the street.

functional obsolescence   The impairment of functional capacity or efficiency. Functional obsolescence reflects the loss in value brought about by factors that affect the property, such as overcapacity, inadequacy, or changes in the design. The inability of a structure to perform adequately the function for which it is currently employed.

future interest   A person's present right to an interest in real property that will not result in possession or enjoyment until some time in the future, such as a reversion or right of reentry.

gap   A defect in the chain of title of a particular parcel of real estate; a missing document or conveyance that raises doubt as to the present ownership of the land.

general agent   A party authorized to perform all acts of the principal's affairs within the continued operation of a particular job or business.

general contractor   A construction specialist who enters into a formal construction contract with a landowner or master lessee to construct a real estate building or project. The general contractor often contracts with several subcontractors specializing in various aspects of the building process to perform individual jobs.

general lien   A lien on all real and personal property owned by a debtor.

general partnership   See partnership.

general tax   See ad valorem tax.

general warranty deed   A deed that states that the title conveyed therein is good from the sovereignty of the soil to the grantee therein; no one else can claim the property.

GI-guaranteed mortgage   See VA loan.

government lot   Those fractional sections in the rectangular (government) survey system that are less than one full quarter-section in area.

Government National Mortgage Association (GNMA)   Ginnie Mae, a federal agency and division of HUD that operates special assistance aspects of federally aided housing programs and participates in the secondary market through its mortgage-backed securities pools.

graduated lease   A lease that provides for periodic step increases in the rental payments.

graduated payment mortgage   A loan in which smaller payments are made in the early years and larger payments at some predetermined time. This may create negative amortization.

grant   The act of conveying or transferring title to real property.

grant deed   A type of deed that includes three basic warranties: (1) the owner warrants the right to convey the property, (2) the owner warrants that the property is not encumbered other than with those encumbrances listed in the deed, and (3) the owner promises to convey any after-acquired title to the property. Grant deeds are popular in states that rely heavily on title insurance.

grantee   A person to whom real estate is conveyed; the buyer.

granting clause   That portion of the deed that states the grantor's intention to transfer title and type of ownership interest conveyed.

grantor   A person who conveys real estate by deed; the seller.

gross lease   A lease of property under which a landlord pays all property charges regularly incurred through ownership, such as repairs, taxes, insurance, and operating expenses. Most residential leases are gross leases.

gross rent multiplier (GRM)   A figure used as a multiplier of the gross rental income of a property to produce an estimate of the property's value.

ground lease   A lease of land only, on which the tenant usually owns a building or is required to build his or her own building as specified in the lease. Such leases are usually long-term net leases; a tenant's rights and obligations continue until the lease expires or is terminated through default.

growing-equity mortgage   A loan in which the monthly payments increase, with the increased amount being applied directly to the outstanding principal balance, thus decreasing the loan term.

guaranteed sale plan   An agreement between broker and seller that if the seller's real property is not sold before a certain date, the broker will purchase it for a specified price.

guardian   One who guards or cares for another person's rights and property. A guardian has legal custody of the affairs of a minor or a person incapable of taking care of his own interests, called a *ward*.

habendum clause   The deed clause beginning *to have and to hold* that defines or limits the extent of ownership in the estate granted by the deed.

heir   One who might inherit or succeed to an interest in land under the state law of descent when the owner dies without leaving a valid will.

highest and best use   That possible use of land that will produce the greatest net income and thereby develop the highest land value.

holdover tenancy   A tenancy whereby a lessee retains possession of leased property after the lessee's lease has expired and the landlord, by continuing to accept rent from the tenant, agrees to the tenant's continued occupancy as defined by state law.

holographic will   A will that is written, dated, and signed in the handwriting of the maker, and that does not need to be notarized or witnessed to be valid.

homeowners' insurance policy   A standardized package insurance policy that covers a residential real estate owner against financial loss from fire, theft, public liability, and other common risks.

homeowners warranty program   An insurance program offered to buyers by some brokerages, warranting the property against certain defects for a specified period of time.

homestead   The land, and the improvements thereon, designated by the owner as the owner's homestead and, therefore, protected by state law from forced sale by certain creditors of the owner.

HUD   The Department of Housing and Urban Development, which regulates FHA and GNMA.

hypothecation   A pledge of property to the lender without giving up possession rights.

implied contract   A contract under which the agreement of the parties is demonstrated by their acts and conduct.

implied grant   A method of creating an easement. One party may be using another's property for the benefit of both parties; for example, a sewer on a property.

improvement   (1) Improvements on land—any structure, usually privately owned, erected on a site to enhance the value of the property; for example, buildings, fences, and driveways. (2) Improvements to land—usually a publicly owned structure, such as a curb, sidewalk, or sewer.

income approach   The process of estimating the value of an income-producing property by capitalization of the annual net income expected to be produced by the property during its remaining useful life.

increasing returns   When increased expenditures for improvements to a given parcel of land yield an increasing percentage return on investment, the principle of increasing returns applies.

incurable depreciation   The cost of fixing the property will be more than the increase in value or the corrections are not physically possible.

indefeasible fee   A title that cannot be defeated. Example: fee simple absolute.

indemnification   An agreement to compensate someone for a loss.

independent contractor   One who is retained to perform a certain act, but who is subject to the control and direction of another only as to the end result and not as to how he or she performs the act. Unlike an employee, an independent contractor pays for all his or her expenses, income and Social Security taxes, and receives no employee benefits. Many real estate salespeople are independent contractors.

index lease   A lease in which the rental payment is tied to some agreed-on index, such as the Consumer Price Index or the Wholesale Price Index.

industrial property   All land and buildings used or suited for use in the production, storage, or distribution of tangible goods.

installment contract   *See* contract for deed.

installment sale   A method of reporting income received from the sale of real estate when the sales price is paid in two or more installments over two or more years. If the sale meets certain requirements, a taxpayer can postpone reporting such income to future years when the taxpayer's other income may be lower.

insurable title   A title to land that a title company will insure.

insurance   The indemnification against loss from a specific hazard or peril through a contract (called a *policy*) and for a consideration (called a *premium*).

intangible property   Personal property that cannot be physically touched, such as stock or a lease.

interest   A charge made or paid by a lender for the use of money.

interim financing   A short-term loan usually made during the construction phase of a building project, often referred to as a *construction loan*.

inter vivos trust   A living trust created by an owner during the owner's lifetime.

intestate   The condition of a property owner who dies without leaving a will. Title to such property will pass to the owner's heirs as provided in the state law of descent.

invalid   In regard to contracts, it means having no legal force or effect.

invalidate   To render null and void.

investment   Money directed toward the purchase, improvement, and development of an asset in expectation of income or profits. A good financial investment has the following characteristics: safety, regularity of yield, marketability, acceptable denominations, valuable collateral, acceptable duration, required attention, and potential appreciation.

involuntary alienation   The transfer of property against an owner's will. Example: foreclosure.

involuntary lien   A lien that is placed on the property without the consent of the owner.

IRS tax lien   A general, statutory, involuntary lien on all real and personal property owned by a debtor.

joint tenancy   The ownership of real estate between two or more parties who have been named in one conveyance as joint tenants. Upon the death of a joint tenant, that tenant's interest passes to the surviving joint tenant or tenants by the right of survivorship.

joint venture   The joining of two or more people to conduct a specific business enterprise. On the one hand, a joint venture is similar to a partnership in that it must be created by agreement between the parties to share in the losses and profits of the venture. On the other hand, it is unlike a partnership in that the venture is for one specific project only, rather than for a continuing business relationship.

judgment   The official decision of a court on the respective rights and claims of the parties to an action or suit. When a judgment is entered and recorded with the county recorder, it usually becomes a general lien on the property.

judgment clause   A provision that may be included in notes, leases, and contracts by which the debtor, lessee, or obligor authorizes any attorney to go into court to confess a judgment against the debtor for a default in payment. Also called a *cognovit*.

judicial sale   A type of foreclosure in which the lender enforces the acceleration clause in the mortgage and files a suit to foreclose on the property.

laches   An equitable doctrine used by courts to bar a legal claim or to prevent the assertion of a right because of undue delay, negligence, or failure to assert the claim or right.

land The earth's surface extending downward to the center of the earth and upward infinitely into space.

land contract The seller finances the property instead of a traditional lender. The seller holds title until final payment is made.

landlocked Property that does not have access to a public road to enter (ingress) or leave (egress) the land. This situation may create an easement by necessity.

latent defect A hidden defect in the property.

law of agency *See* agent.

lawyer's opinion of title *See* attorney's opinion of title.

lease A contract between a landlord (the lessor) and a tenant (the lessee) transferring the right to exclusive possession and use of the landlord's real property to the lessee for a specified period of time and for a stated consideration (rent). By state law, leases for longer than a certain period of time (generally one year) must be in writing to be enforceable.

leased fee interest The landlord's retained interest in the leased property is the leased fee interest.

leasehold estate A tenant's right to occupy real estate during the term of a lease, generally considered to be a personal property interest.

leasehold interest The tenant's interest in the leased property is the leasehold interest.

lease option This lease gives the tenant the option right to purchase the property within or at the end of the lease.

lease purchase The tenant leases property for a period of time with the intention of purchasing it.

legal description A description of a specific parcel of real estate sufficient for an independent surveyor to locate and identify it. The most common forms of legal description are rectangular survey; metes and bounds; lot, block (plat), and subdivision.

legality of object An element that must be present in a valid contract. All contracts that have for their object an act that violates the laws of the United States, or the laws of a state to which the parties are subject, are illegal, invalid, and not recognized by the courts.

legal life estate A life estate created by law; dower, curtesy, and homestead.

legatee A person who receives personal or real property under a will.

lessee The tenant who leases a property.

lessor One who leases property to a tenant.

leverage The use of borrowed money to finance the bulk of an investment.

levy To assess; to seize or collect. To levy a tax is to assess a property and set the rate of taxation. To levy an execution is to seize officially the property of a person to satisfy an obligation.

license (1) A privilege or right granted to a person by a state to operate as a real estate broker or salesperson. (2) The revocable permission for a temporary use of land—a personal right that cannot be sold.

lien A right given by law to certain creditors to have their debt paid out of the property of a defaulting debtor, usually by means of a court sale.

lienee The party whose property is subject to a lien.

lienor The party holding the lien right.

lien-theory state A state in which the mortgage gives the mortgagee the right to place a lien on the property and the mortgagor retains title to the property.

life estate An interest in real or personal property that is limited in duration to the lifetime of its owner or some other designated person.

life tenant A person in possession of a life estate.

liquidated damages An amount predetermined by the parties to a contract as the total compensation the aggrieved party will receive should the other party breach the contract.

liquidity The ability to sell an asset and convert it into cash at a price close to its true value.

lis pendens Latin for action pending, which is recorded to give constructive notice that an action affecting the property (lawsuit) has been filed, but a judgment has not been decreed. A lis pendens notice renders the property unmarketable.

listing agreement   A contract between a land-owner (as principal) and a licensed real estate broker (as agent) by which the broker is employed as agent to sell real estate on the owner's terms within a given time, for which service the landowner agrees to pay a commission.

listing broker   The broker in a multiple-listing situation from whose office a listing agreement is initiated, as opposed to the selling broker, from whose office negotiations leading up to a sale are initiated. The listing broker and the selling broker may, of course, be the same person. *See also* multiple listing.

littoral rights   (1) A landowner's claim to use water in large lakes and oceans adjacent to the landlord's property. (2) The ownership's rights to land bordering these bodies of water up to the high-water mark.

loan-to-value   The relationship between the amount of a loan and the appraised value of a property. It is expressed as a percentage of the appraised value.

lock-in clause   (1) The lender's agreement to lock in an interest rate for a specified time period. (2) A condition in a promissory note that prohibits prepayment of the note.

lot-and-block description   A description of real property that identifies a parcel of land by reference to lot and block numbers within a subdivision, as identified on a subdivided plat duly recorded in the county recorder's office.

management agreement   A contract between the owner of income property and a management firm or individual property manager outlining the scope of the manager's authority.

marketable title   A good or clear salable title reasonably free from risk of litigation over possible defects; also called a *merchantable title*.

market-date approach   That approach in analysis that is based on the proposition that an informed purchaser would pay no more for a property than the cost to him of acquiring an existing property with the same utility. This approach is applicable when an active market provides sufficient quantities of reliable data that can be verified from authoritative sources. The approach is relatively unreliable in an inactive market or in estimating the value of properties for which no real comparable sales data are available. It is also questionable when sales data cannot be verified with principals to the transaction. Also referred to as the *market comparison* or *direct sales comparison approach*.

market price   The actual selling price of a property.

market rent   Also known as *economic rent*; the rental income that real estate could command in the market at any given time, versus *contract rent*, which is the income generated under the current lease contract.

market value   The highest price that a property will bring in a competitive and open market under all conditions requisite to a fair sale. The price at which a buyer would buy and a seller would sell, each acting prudently and knowledgeably, and assuming the price is not affected by undue stimulus.

master deed   A document that legally establishes the condominium regime. It is referred to as a *condominium declaration* and fully describes each unit and common elements, as well as specific essential elements of ownership that govern its operation.

master plan   A master plan provides the guidelines for the future development of a community.

mechanic's lien   A statutory lien created in favor of contractors, laborers, and materialmen who have performed work or furnished materials in erecting or repairing a building.

metes-and-bounds description   A legal description of a parcel of land that begins at a well-marked point and follows the boundaries, using direction and distances around the tract back to the place of beginning.

mill One-tenth of 1¢ (0.001). Some states use a mill rate to compute real estate taxes; for example, a rate of 52 mills would be 0.052 tax for each dollar of assessed valuation of a property.

millage rate A property tax rate obtained by dividing the total assessed value of all the property in the tax district into the total amount of revenue needed by the taxing district. This millage rate is then applied to the assessed value of each property in the district to determine individual taxes.

ministerial acts Acts performed by a licensee for a consumer that are informative in nature, but do not rise to the level of active representation, such as responding to inquiries about a property's price range or providing other facts.

misrepresentation To represent falsely; to give an untrue idea of a property. May be accomplished by omission or concealment of a material fact.

money judgment A court judgment ordering payment of money rather than specific performance of a certain action. *See also* judgment.

money market Those institutions—such as banks, savings and loan associations, and life insurance companies—whose function it is to supply money and credit to borrowers.

month-to-month tenancy A periodic tenancy; the tenant rents for one period at a time. In the absence of a rental agreement (oral or written), a tenancy is generally considered to be month to month.

monument A fixed natural or artificial object used to establish real estate boundaries for a metes-and-bounds description.

mortgage A conditional transfer or pledge of real estate as security for a loan. Also, the document creating a mortgage lien.

mortgage bankers A firm or individual who originates loans for sale to other investors.

mortgage broker A mortgage broker is a firm or person who brings borrowers and lenders together, and the finders' fee is normally paid by the lender, but it could be paid by the borrower.

mortgage fraud The lender is provided with false or misleading information on a loan application, or with falsified documents in the loan process.

mortgagee The lender who receives a pledge from a borrower to repay a loan.

mortgage lien A lien or charge on a mortgagor's property that secures the underlying debt obligations.

mortgagor One who, having all or part of title to property, pledges that property as security for a debt; the borrower.

multiple listing An exclusive listing (generally, an exclusive-right-to-sell) with the additional authority and obligation on the part of the listing broker to distribute the listing to other brokers in the multiple-listing organization.

municipal ordinances The laws, regulations, and codes enacted by the governing body of a municipality.

mutual rescission The act of putting an end to a contract by mutual agreement of the parties.

negative amortization A loan in which the loan balance increases with each payment rather than decreasing because the payment amount is not sufficient to cover the interest.

negligence Carelessness and inattentiveness resulting in violation of trust. Failure to do what is required.

net income The gross income of a property minus operating expenses (not including debt service).

net lease A lease requiring the tenant to pay not only rent, but also all costs incurred in maintaining the property, including taxes, insurance, utilities, and repairs.

net listing A listing establishing a price, which must be expressly agreed on, below which the owner will not sell the property and at which price the broker will not receive a commission; the broker receives the excess over and above the net listing price as commission.

nonconforming loan A loan that does not meet secondary market standards.

nonconforming use   A use of property that is permitted to continue after a zoning ordinance prohibiting it has been established for the area. Also, a use of property that is not conforming to current zoning because of a change in zoning, such as property being used for residential purposes, but currently zoned commercial.

nondisturbance clause   A clause found in a lease that protects the tenant. If the landlord defaults on payments to the lender, the lender has the right to collect rent from the tenant. If the tenant pays the lender, the tenant cannot be evicted.

nonhomogeneity   A lack of uniformity; dissimilarity. As no two parcels of land are exactly alike, real estate is said to be unique or nonhomogeneous.

nonjudicial foreclosure   Also known as *foreclosure by advertisement* because it is a foreclosure procedure where the lender does not have to involve the courts.

nonrecourse loan   A loan in which the property being pledged as collateral is the sole security for the loan. The borrower cannot be held personally liable for the note.

notarize   To certify or attest to a document, as by a notary.

notary public   A public official authorized to certify and attest to documents, take affidavits, take acknowledgments, administer oaths, and perform other such acts.

note   An instrument of credit given to attest a debt.

notice of abandonment   An instrument filed to release a recorded declaration of homestead.

novation   Substituting a new contract for an old one and the release of liability.

obligee/promisee   The lender in the note.

obligor/promissor   The borrower in a note.

obsolescence   To be obsolete; as used in appraising the loss of value because it is outdated or less useful.

offer and acceptance   The two components of a valid contract; a *meeting of the minds*.

officer's deed   A deed by sheriffs, trustees, guardians, and the like.

one hundred-percent-commission plan   A salesperson compensation plan whereby the salesperson pays the salesperson's broker a monthly service charge to cover the costs of office expenses and receives 100 percent of the commissions from the negotiated sales.

open buyer agency agreement   A nonexclusive agency contract between a broker and a buyer wherein the buyer may enter into similar agreements with an unlimited number of brokers; the broker is paid who locates the property the buyer purchases.

open-end mortgage   A mortgage loan that is expandable by increments up to a maximum dollar amount, all of which is secured by the same original mortgage.

open listing   A listing contract under which the broker's commission is contingent on the broker's producing a ready, willing, and able buyer before the property is sold by the seller or another broker; the principal (owner) reserves the right to list the property with other brokers.

open mortgage   An open mortgage is a mortgage without a prepayment clause. FHA-insured and VA-guaranteed mortgages are open mortgages.

option   The right to purchase property within a definite time at a specified price. No obligation to purchase exists, but the seller is obligated to sell if the option holder exercises right to purchase.

optionee   The party that receives and holds an option.

optionor   The party that grants or gives an option.

ownership   The exclusive right to hold, possess, or control and dispose of a tangible or intangible thing. Ownership may be held by a person, corporation, or political entity.

package mortgage   A method of financing in which the loan that finances the purchase of a home also finances the purchase of certain items of personal property, such as a washer, dryer, refrigerator, stove, and other specified appliances.

participation financing   A mortgage in which the lender participates in the income of the mortgaged venture beyond a fixed return, or receives a yield on the loan in addition to the straight interest rate.

partnership   An association of two or more individuals who carry on a continuing business for profit as co-owners. Under the law, a partnership is regarded as a group of individuals, rather than as a single entity. A general partnership is a typical form of joint venture, in which each general partner shares in the administration, profits, and losses of the operation. A limited partnership is a business arrangement whereby the operation is administered by one or more general partners and funded by limited or silent partners who are by law responsible for losses only to the extent of their investment.

party wall   A wall that is located on or at a boundary line between two adjoining parcels for the use of the owners of both properties.

patent defect   A defect that can be found by normal inspection of the property.

payee   The party that receives payment.

payor   The party that makes payment to another.

percentage lease   A lease commonly used for retail property in which the rental is based on the tenant's gross sales at the premises; often stipulates a base monthly rental plus a percentage of any gross sales above a certain amount.

periodic estate   An interest in leased property that continues from period to period—week to week, month to month, or year to year.

personal property   Those items, called chattels, that are not classified as real property; tangible and movable objects.

physical deterioration   A reduction in utility resulting from an impairment of physical condition. For purposes of appraisal analysis, it is most common and convenient to divide physical deterioration into curable and incurable components.

plat   A map of a town, section, or subdivision indicating the location and boundaries of individual properties.

plat book   A record of recorded subdivisions of land.

plottage   The value that is created when two or more tracts of land are merged into a single, larger one.

point   A unit of measurement used for various loan charges. One point equals 1 percent of the amount of the loan. *See also* discount points.

point of beginning   The starting point of the survey situated in one corner of the parcel in a metes-and-bounds legal description. All metes-and-bounds descriptions must follow the boundaries of the parcel back to the point of beginning.

police power   The government's right to impose laws, statutes, and ordinances to protect the public health, safety, and welfare, including zoning ordinances and building codes.

power of attorney   A written instrument authorizing a person (the attorney-in-fact) to act on behalf of the maker to the extent indicated in the instrument.

premises   The specific section of a deed that states the names of the parties, recital of consideration, operative words of conveyance, legal property description, and appurtenance provisions.

prepayment penalty   A charge imposed on a borrower by a lender for early payment of the loan principal to compensate the lender for interest and other charges that would otherwise be lost.

prepayment privilege clause   The statement of the terms upon which the mortgagor may pay the entire or stated amount of the mortgage principal at some time prior to the due date.

prescription   The right or easement to land that is acquired by adverse possession or *squatter's rights*. It must be acquired under certain conditions as required by law.

prescriptive title   A title that is acquired by an adverse possession claim.

price fixing   *See* antitrust laws.

primary mortgage market   The market where a person or business goes to negotiate a loan.

principal   (1) A sum lent or employed as a fund or investment, as distinguished from its income or profits. (2) The original amount (as in a loan) of the total due and payable at a certain date. (3) A main party to a transaction—the person for whom the agent works.

principal meridian   One of 37 north and south survey lines established and defined as part of the rectangular (government) survey system.

principle of conformity   The appraisal theory stating that buildings that are similar in design, construction, and age to other buildings in the area have a higher value than they would in a neighborhood of dissimilar buildings.

principle of substitution   The appraisal theory that states that no one will pay more for a property than the cost of buying or building a similar property; or, in the case of investments, the price of a substitute investment.

priority   The order of position or time. The priority of liens is generally determined by the chronological order in which the lien documents are recorded; tax liens, however, have priority even over previously recorded liens.

private mortgage insurance (PMI)   Insurance written by a private company (not government) that protects a lender against loss if a borrower defaults.

probate   The formal judicial proceeding to prove or confirm the validity of a will.

procuring cause   The effort that brings about the desired result. Under an open listing, the broker who is the procuring cause of the sale receives the commission.

progression   When a small structure is placed in an area of larger more expensive structures, the value of the smaller structure will increase.

property management   The operation of the property of another for compensation. Includes marketing of space; advertising and rental activities; collection, recording, and remitting of rents; maintenance of the property; tenant relations; hiring of employees; keeping proper accounts; and rendering periodic reports to the owner.

property tax   Those taxes levied by the government against either real or personal property. The right to tax real property in the United States rests exclusively with the states, not with the federal government.

proprietary lease   A lease given by the corporation that owns a cooperative apartment building to the shareholder, giving the shareholder (tenant) the right to occupy one of the units.

proration   The proportionate division or distribution of expenses of property ownership between two or more parties. Closing statement prorations generally include taxes, rents, insurance, interest charges, and assessments.

prospectus   A printed advertisement, usually in pamphlet form, presenting a new development, subdivision, business venture, or stock issue.

public utility easement   A right granted by a property owner to a public utility company to erect and maintain poles, wires, and conduits on, across, or under the owner's land for telephone, electric power, gas, water, or sewer installation.

puffing   An exaggerated opinion, many times in regards to a property's amenity.

pur autre vie   A term meaning for the life of another. A life estate pur autre vie is a life estate that is measured by the life of a person other than the grantee.

purchase-money mortgage   A note secured by a mortgage or deed of trust given by a buyer, as mortgagor, to a seller, as mortgagee, as part of the purchase price of the real estate.

pyramiding   Obtaining additional investment property by borrowing against the equity of existing investments.

qualification   The act of determining the prospect's needs, abilities, and urgency to buy and then matching these with available properties.

quiet enjoyment   A covenant in a deed that the title being given is good against third parties.

quiet title lawsuit   A suit to clear up any defects or clouds on a title.

quitclaim deed   A conveyance by which the grantor transfers whatever interest the grantor has in the real estate without warranties or obligations.

range   A strip of land six miles wide, extending north and south and numbered east and west according to its distance from the principal meridians in the rectangular survey system (government survey method) of land description.

ready, willing, and able buyer   One who is prepared to buy property on the seller's terms and is ready to take positive steps to consummate the transaction.

real estate   Land; a portion of the earth's surface extending downward to the center of the earth and upward infinitely into space, including all things permanently attached thereto, whether by nature or by man; any and every interest in land.

real estate broker Any person, partnership, association, or corporation that sells (or offers to sell), buys (or offers to buy), or negotiates the purchase, sale, or exchange of real estate, or that leases (or offers to lease) or rents (or offers to rent) any real estate or the improvements thereon for others and for compensation or valuable consideration. A real estate broker may not conduct business without a real estate broker's license.

real estate investment trust (REIT) Trust ownership of real estate wherein a group of individuals purchases certificates of ownership in the trust, which purchases property and distributes the profits back to the investors free of corporate income tax.

Real Estate Settlement Procedures Act (RESPA) The federal law ensuring that the buyer and seller in a real estate transaction have knowledge of all settlement costs when the purchase of a one- to four-family residential dwelling is financed by a federally related mortgage loan. Federally related loans include those made by savings and loans, insured by the FHA or VA, administered by HUD, or intended to be sold by the lender to an agency.

reality of consent An element of all valid contracts. Offer and acceptance in a contract are usually taken to mean that reality of consent is also present. This is not the case if any of the following are present, however: mistake, misrepresentation, fraud, undue influence, or duress.

real property Real property, or real estate as it is often called, consists of land, anything affixed to it so as to be regarded as a permanent part of the land, that which is appurtenant to the land, and that which is immovable by law.

REALTOR® A registered trademark term reserved for the sole use of active members of local REALTOR® boards affiliated with the National Association of REALTORS®.

receiver The court-appointed custodian of property involved in litigation, pending final disposition of the matter before the court.

reconciliation The final step in the appraisal process, in which the appraiser reconciles the estimates of value received from the market-data, cost, and income approaches to arrive at a final estimate of market value for the subject property.

recording The act of entering or recording documents affecting or conveying interests in real estate in the recorder's office established in each county. Until recorded, a deed or mortgage generally is not effective against subsequent purchases or mortgage liens.

recovery fund A fund established in some states from real estate license funds to cover claims of aggrieved parties who have suffered monetary damage through the actions of a real estate licensee.

rectangular survey system A system established in 1785 by the U.S. government, providing for surveying and describing land by reference to principal meridians and base lines.

redemption period A period of time established by state law during which a property owner has the right to redeem his or her real estate from a foreclosure or tax sale by paying the sales price, interest, and costs. Many states do not have mortgage redemption laws.

redlining The illegal practice of some institutions of denying loans or restricting their number for certain areas of a community.

regression When a large structure is placed in an area of smaller, less expensive structures, the value of the larger structure will decrease.

release To relinquish an interest in or claim to a parcel of property.

reliction When water recedes, new land is acquired by reliction.

relocation service An organization that aids a person in selling a property in one area and buying another property in another area.

remainder The remnant of an estate that has been conveyed to take effect and be enjoyed after the termination of a prior estate, such as when an owner conveys a life estate to one party and the remainder to another.

remainder interest A third party who has a future ownership interest in the property upon the death of the life tenant. *See also* life estates.

rent   A fixed, periodic payment made by a tenant of a property to the owner for possession and use, usually by prior agreement of the parties.

rent control   The regulation by the state or local government agencies restricting the amount of rent landlords can charge their tenants.

rent schedule   A statement of proposed rental rates, determined by the owner or the property manager or both, based on a building's estimated expenses, market supply, and demand and the owner's long-range goals for the property.

replacement cost   The cost of construction at current prices of a building having utility equivalent to the building being appraised but built with modern materials and according to current standards, design, and layout. The use of the replacement cost concept presumably eliminates all functional obsolescence, and the only depreciations to be measured are physical deterioration and economic obsolescence.

reproduction cost   The cost of construction at current prices of an exact duplicate or replica using the same materials, construction standards, design, layout, and quality of workmanship and embodying all the deficiencies, superadequacies, and obsolescences of the subject building.

rescission   The termination of a contract by mutual agreement of the parties.

reservation in a deed   The creation by a deed to property of a new right in favor of the grantor. Usually involves an easement, life estate, or a mineral interest.

restriction   A limitation on the use of real property, generally originated by the owner or subdivider in a deed.

reverse mortgage   A mortgage that allows senior homeowners 62 years of age or older to release a percent of the equity in their property without making monthly payments. The loan is repaid when the borrower no longer resides in the property.

reversion   The remnant of an estate that the grantor holds after the grantor has granted a life estate to another person; the estate will return or revert to the grantor; also called a *reverser*.

reversionary right   An owner's right to regain possession of leased property upon termination of the lease agreement.

rezoning   The process involved in changing the existing zoning of a property or area.

right of first refusal   A potential buyer's right to meet the terms of the sales contract.

right of survivorship   *See* joint tenancy.

riparian rights   An owner's rights in land that borders on or includes a stream, river, lake, or sea. These rights include access to and use of the water.

sale and leaseback   A transaction in which an owner sells his or her improved property and, as part of the same transaction, signs a long-term lease to remain in possession of the premises.

sales comparison approach   Also known as the *market approach to appraising*. It is used to appraise residential property or vacant land that will be used for residential purposes. It is based on the principle of substitution.

sales contract   A contract containing the complete terms of the agreement between buyer and seller for the sale of a particular parcel or parcels of real estate.

salesperson   A person who performs real estate activities while employed by, or associated with, a licensed real estate broker.

sandwich lease   The lessee's interest in a sublease is the sandwich lease.

satisfaction   A document acknowledging the payment of a debt.

secondary mortgage market   A market for the purchase and sale of existing mortgages, designed to provide greater liquidity for mortgages; also called the *secondary money market*.

section   A portion of a township under the rectangular survey system (government survey method). A township is divided into 36 sections numbered 1 to 36. A section is a square with mile-long sides and an area of 1 square mile or 640 acres.

security deposit   A payment made by the tenant that the landlord holds during the lease term and that may be kept wholly or in part on default or destruction of the premises by the tenant.

selling broker   *See* listing broker.

separate property   The real property owned by a husband or wife prior to their marriage.

servient tenement   The land on which an easement exists in favor of an adjacent property (called a *dominant estate*); also called a *servient estate*.

setback   The amount of space local zoning regulations require between a lot line and a building line.

severalty   The ownership of real property by one person only, also called *sole ownership*.

severance   The process of changing real property to personal property.

shared participation mortgage   A type of participation mortgage in which the lender shares in the appreciation of the mortgage property when the property is sold.
short sale. A lender process where the bank and seller agree to take less than the amount owed on the property.

situs   The personal preference of people for one area over another, not necessarily based on objective facts and knowledge.

sole ownership   *See* severalty.

special agent   A party authorized to perform with limited authority given by the principal.

special assessment   A tax or levy customarily imposed against only those specific parcels of real estate that will benefit from a proposed public improvement, such as a street or sewer.

special warranty deed   A deed in which the grantor warrants or guarantees the title only against defects arising during the period of the grantor's tenure and ownership of the property and not against defects existing before that time, generally using the language, *by, through, or under the grantor but not otherwise.*

specific lien   A lien affecting or attaching only to a certain, specific parcel of land or piece of property.

specific performance suit   A legal action brought in a court of equity in special cases to compel a party to carry out the terms of a contract. The basis for an equity court's jurisdiction in breach of a real estate contract is the fact that land is unique and mere legal damages would not adequately compensate the buyer for the seller's breach.

sponsoring broker   A duly licensed real estate broker who employs a salesperson. Under law, the broker is responsible for the acts of the broker's salespeople.

squatter's rights   Those rights acquired through adverse possession. By *squatting* on land for a certain statutory period under prescribed conditions, one may acquire title by limitations. If an easement only is acquired, instead of title to the land itself, one has title by prescription.

statute of frauds   The part of a state law that requires that certain instruments, such as deeds, real estate sales contracts, and certain leases, be in writing in order to be legally enforceable.

statute of limitation   That law pertaining to the period of time within which certain actions must be brought to court.

statutory lien   A lien imposed on property by statute, such as a tax lien, in contrast to a voluntary lien that an owner places on the owner's own real estate, such as a mortgage lien.

statutory right of redemption   In some states, defaulted borrowers have the statutory right of redemption, which allows them to buy back their property after the foreclosure sale by paying the sales price, interest, and costs.

steering   The illegal practice of channeling home seekers to particular areas, either to maintain the homogeneity of an area or to change its character in order to create a speculative situation.

stigmatized property   A property is considered stigmatized or undesirable because of events that have occurred on the property.

straight-line method   A method of calculating depreciation for tax purposes, computed by dividing the adjusted basis of a property less its estimated salvage value by the estimated number of years of remaining useful life.

strict foreclosure   A foreclosure procedure in which the lender secures title and all equity to the property.

subagent   An agent of an agent. The broker is the agent of the principal. The salesperson is a subagent of the principal.

subcontractor   *See* general contractor.

subdivision   A tract of land divided by the owner, known as the *subdivider*, into blocks, building lots, and streets according to a recorded subdivision plat, which must comply with local ordinances and regulations.

subletting   The leasing of premises by a lessee to a third party for part of the lessee's remaining term. *See also* assignment.

subordination   A relegation to a lesser position, usually in respect to a right or security.

subrogation   The substitution of one creditor for another, with the substituted person succeeding to the legal rights and claims of the original claimant. Subrogation is used by title insurers to acquire rights to sue from the injured party to recover any claims they have paid.

substitution   An appraisal principle that states that the maximum value of a property tends to be set by the cost of purchasing an equally desirable and valuable substitute property, assuming that no costly delay is encountered in making the substitution.

suit for partition   A legal action to divide the ownership interests in a property.

suit for possession   A court suit initiated by a landlord to evict a tenant from leased premises after the tenant has breached one of the terms of the lease or has held possession of the property after the lease's expiration.

suit for specific performance   A legal action brought by either a buyer or a seller to enforce performance of the terms of a contract.

suit to quiet title   A legal action intended to establish or settle the title to a particular property, especially when there is a cloud on the title.

summation appraisal   An approach under which value equals estimated land value plus reproduction costs of any improvements, after depreciation has been subtracted.

supply   The amount of goods available in the market to be sold at a given price. The term is often coupled with demand.

surety bond   An agreement by an insurance or bonding company to be responsible for certain possible defaults, debts, or obligations contracted for by an insured party; in essence, a policy insuring one's personal and/or financial integrity. In the real estate business, a surety bond is generally used to ensure that a particular project will be completed at a certain date or that a contract will be performed as stated.

survey   The process by which boundaries are measured and land areas are determined; the on-site measurement of lot lines, dimensions, and positions of buildings on a lot, including the determination of any existing encroachments or easements.

syndicate   A combination of two or more persons or firms to accomplish a joint venture of mutual interest. Syndicates dissolve when the specific purpose for which they were created has been accomplished.

tacking   Combining successive periods of property use; associated with adverse possession claims.

tangible property   Property that can be seen and touched.

taxation   The process by which a government or municipal quasi-public body raises monies to fund its operation.

tax deed   An instrument, similar to a certificate of sale, given to a purchaser at a tax sale. *See also* certificate of sale.

taxes   A compulsory contribution required by the government from persons, corporations, and other organizations, according to a law, for the general support of the government and for the maintenance of public services.

tax lien   A charge against property created by operation of law. Tax liens and assessments take priority over all other liens.

tax rate   The rate at which real property is taxed in a tax district or county. For example, in a certain county, real property may be taxed at a rate of 56¢ per dollar of assessed valuation.

tax sale   A court-ordered sale of real property to raise money to cover delinquent taxes.

tax shelters   Allow a taxpayer to reduce current tax liability by offsetting income from one source with losses from another source.

tenancy at sufferance   The tenancy of a lessee who lawfully comes into possession of a landlord's real estate, but who continues to occupy the premises improperly after the lessee's lease rights have expired.

tenancy at will   An estate that gives the lessee the right to possession until the estate is terminated by either party; the term of this estate is indefinite.

tenancy by the entirety   The joint ownership, recognized in some states, of property acquired by husband and wife during marriage. Upon the death of one spouse, the survivor becomes the owner of the property.

tenancy in common   A form of co-ownership by which each owner holds an undivided interest in real property as if that owner was the sole owner. Each individual owner has the right to partition. Unlike a joint tenancy, there is no right of survivorship between tenants in common.

tenant   One who holds or possesses lands or tenements by any kind of right or title.

tenement   Everything that may be occupied under a lease by a tenant.

termination (lease)   The cancellation of a lease by action of either party. A lease may be terminated by expiration of term, surrender and acceptance, constructive eviction by lessor, or option when provided in lease for breach of covenants.

termination (listing)   The cancellation of a broker-principal employment contract; a listing may be terminated by death or insanity of either party, expiration of listing period, mutual agreement, sufficient written notice, or the completion of performance under the agreement.

term mortgage   A nonamortized loan in which the borrower makes periodic interest payments to the lender and the principal balance is due on maturity. Also known as a *straight mortgage*.

testamentary trust   A trust created through a will after a property owner's death.

testate   Having made and left a valid will.

testator   A male willmaker.

testatrix   A female willmaker.

time is of the essence   A phrase in a contract that requires the performance of a certain act within a stated period of time.

time-share estate   A fee simple interest in an interval ownership of property for a specified time period. The owner's occupancy is limited to the time period purchased.

time-share use   The right to use and occupy the property for a certain number of years. A time-share use may be conveyed by a lease or license.

title   The legal evidence of ownership rights to real property.

title insurance   Insurance that is designed to indemnify the holder for loss sustained for reason of defects in a title, up to and including the policy limits.

title-theory states   A state in which a security instrument gives the mortgagee the title to the property.

Torrens system   A method of evidencing title by registration with the proper public authority, generally called the registrar. Named for its founder, Sir Robert Torrens.

township   The principal unit of the rectangular (government) survey system. A township is a square with 6-mile sides and an area of 36 square miles.

township lines   The lines running at six-mile intervals parallel to the base lines in the rectangular (government) survey system.

trade fixtures   The articles installed by a tenant under the terms of a lease and removable by the tenant before the lease expires. These remain personal property and are not true fixtures.

transaction broker   A person who represents neither party in a transaction. Both parties are treated as customers.

transfer taxes   Real estate transfer taxes or RETT are state, county, and/or municipal sales taxes most often used as general revenue.

trust   A fiduciary arrangement whereby property is conveyed to a person or institution, called a *trustee*, to be held and administered on behalf of another person, called a *beneficiary*.

trust deed   An instrument used to create a mortgage lien by which the mortgagor conveys title to a trustee, who holds it as security for the benefit of the note holder (the lender); also called a *deed of trust*.

trustee   One who as agent for others handles money or holds title to their land.

trustee's deed   A deed executed by a trustee conveying land held in a trust.

trustor   A borrower in a deed of trust; a grantor in a deed in trust.

Truth-in-Lending Act   Also known as Regulation Z, this act requires that the lender disclose the true cost of credit to individual borrowers for certain types of loans. It also regulates the advertisement of creditors.

unconventional mortgage   An unconventional mortgage (loan) is backed by the government to reduce the lender's risk. Examples: FHA-insured loans and VA-guaranteed loans.

unenforceable contract   A contract in which neither party can sue the other to force performance, such as a contract missing the signature of the person authorized to perform.

undivided interest   An interest in a property that cannot be physically divided. *See also* tenancy in common.

Uniform Commercial Code (UCC)   A codification of commercial law adopted in most states that attempts to make uniform all laws relating to commercial transactions, including chattel mortgages and bulk transfers. Security interests in chattels are created by an instrument known as a *security agreement*. Article 6 of the code regulates bulk transfers—the sale of a business as a whole, including all fixtures, chattels, and merchandise.

unilateral contract   A one-sided contract wherein one party makes a promise in order to induce a second party to do something. The second party is not legally bound to perform; however, if the second party does comply, the first party is obligated to keep the promise.

unity of ownership   The four unities that are traditionally needed to create a joint tenancy—unity of title, unity of time, unity of interest, and unity of possession.

universal agent   An agent that represents a principal in all activities, such as someone given full power of attorney.

useful life   In real estate investment, the number of years a property will be useful to the investors.

usury   The practice of charging more than the rate of interest allowed by law.

valid contract   A contract that complies with all the essentials of a contract and is binding and enforceable on all parties to it.

valid deed   An enforceable deed that has a competent grantor and grantee, consideration, conveyance, legal description of land, signature of grantor, acknowledgment, delivery, and acceptance.

valid lease   An enforceable lease that has the following essential parts: lessor and lessee with contractual capacity, offer and acceptance, legality of object, description of the premises, consideration, signatures, and delivery. Leases for more than one year must also be in writing.

VA loan   A mortgage loan on approved property made to a qualified veteran by an authorized lender and guaranteed by the Department of Veterans Affairs to limit possible loss by the lender.

variance   The permission obtained from zoning authorities to build a structure or conduct a use that is expressly prohibited by the current zoning laws; an exception from the zoning ordinances.

vendee   The buyer or purchaser.

vendor   The seller.

voidable contract   A contract that seems to be valid but that may be rejected or disaffirmed by one of the parties.

void contract   A contract that has no legal force or effect because it does not meet the essential elements of a contract.

voluntary lien   A lien that is created intentionally by the property owner, such as a mortgage.

voluntary transfer   *See* alienation.

waiver   The intentional or voluntary relinquishment of a known claim or right.

warranty deed   A deed in which the grantor fully warrants good clear title to the premises. Used in most real estate deed transfers, a warranty deed offers the greatest protection of any deed.

warranty of habitability   In a lease, this warranty requires that the landlord keep the property in good condition; that is to maintain the property, equipment, and to comply with state and local codes.

waste   An improper use or an abuse of a property by a possessor who holds less than fee ownership, such as a tenant, life tenant, mortgagor, or vendee. Such waste generally impairs the value of the land or the interest of the person holding the title or the reversionary rights.

will   A written document, properly witnessed, providing for the transfer of title to property owned by the deceased, called the *testator*.

wraparound mortgage   A method of refinancing in which the new mortgage is placed in a secondary, or subordinate, position. In essence, it is an additional mortgage in which another lender refinances a borrower by lending an amount over the existing first-mortgage amount without disturbing the existence of the first mortgage.

writ of attachment   Action taken by a creditor wherein the court retains custody of the property while a lawsuit is being decided, thus preventing the debtor from transferring unsecured real estate before a judgment is rendered. This ensures that the property will be available to satisfy the judgment.

writ of execution   A court order that authorizes and directs the proper officer of the court (usually the sheriff) to sell the property of a defendant as required by the judgment or decree of the court.

year-to-year tenancy   A periodic tenancy in which rent is collected from year to year.

zoning ordinance   An exercise of police power by a municipality to regulate and control the character and use of property.

INDEX

House stealing, 101
Housing-to-income ratio, 365
Hypothecation, 93, 360

I

Immobility, 128
Implied agency, 1, 343
Implied contract, 5, 345
Implied covenant of quiet enjoy-
    ment, 383
Impound account, 344
Improvements, 124, 128
Inactive license, 348
Incentive zoning, 65
Income approach, 131, 368
Increasing returns, 124, 369
Incurable depreciation, 125
Indemnification clause, 10, 347
Independent contractor, 23–24, 348
Index, 86
Index lease, 52, 351
Individual retirement account
    (IRA), 223
Ingress, 59
Installment contract, 346
Insurance companies, 81, 357
Insurance policy, 140, 228, 347,
    373
Intangible property/appurtenance,
    44, 367
Intention, 129
Interest
    in land, 45
    only, 85
    rate, 80, 93, 357
Interim loan, 86
Intermediate-theory state, 95, 357
Internal BPO, 126
Internal Revenue Code, 23
    Section 1031, 17, 374
Internal Revenue Service
    Form 1099-S, 139
    Form 8300, 27, 348
    tax lien, 58, 353
Interstate securities, 352
Interval ownership, 48
Inter vivos trust, 137, 372
Intestate, 138, 372
Intrastate
    securities, 352
Involuntary lien, 58, 353

J

Joint and several liability, 160
Joint tenancy, 45, 46, 349
Joint venture, 57, 352

Jones v. Mayer, 170, 378
Judgment, 58, 135, 353
Judicial foreclosure, 96
Judicial sale, 96
Junk Fax Prevention Act of 2005,
    167

L

Land, 127
Land contract, 8, 90, 346
Landlord
    disclosure, lead warning state-
        ment, 153
    responsibilities, 54
Land measurement, 123
Land use, 64, 355
Latent defect, 162, 376
Laws of descent and distribution,
    138, 372
Lead-based paint, 374
    contractor ruling, 156
    disclosure statement, 374
    warning statement, 153–154
Lead-Based Paint Hazard Reduc-
    tion Act, 199
Lead poisoning, 156
Lease, 49, 191–192, 349, 351
    default/non-performance rem-
        edies, 54
    option, 8, 51, 346, 351
    preexisting, 60
    provisions, 52–53
    purchase, 51, 351
    termination, 52, 193
    types, 192–193
Leased fee interest, 49
Leasehold estate/interest, 43, 49,
    350–351
Leasing agent, 196–197, 380
Legacy, 138, 372
Legal description, 136, 367
Lender's (mortgagee's) title policy,
    370
Lending process, 365
Liabilities, 105
Libel, 164, 377
License, 25, 60, 354
    suspension, revocation, 348
Licensee information, 348
Lien, 57–58, 353
Lienee, 58
Lienor, 58
Lien-theory state, 94–95, 357
Life cycle, 124, 369
Life estate(s), 44
    pur autre vie, 349

Life-of-the-loan, 86
Life safety program, 198–199,
    380–381
Life tenant, 349
Like-kind exchange/property, 17,
    126, 374
Limited common area, 350
Limited liability company, 56
Limited partnership, 55, 352
Liquidated damages clause, 10–11,
    346, 347
Lis pendens notice, 135, 353
Listing, 22, 126
Listing agent duties, 14–15
Listing agreement/contract, 3, 13,
    344
    provisions, 13–14
    remuneration, 19–20
    termination, 18–19
    types of, 20–21
Littoral rights, 127, 366
Livability space ratio, 123, 367
Livable area, 122–123
Loan
    application, 365
    commitment letter, 105, 365
    origination fee, 104, 365
    payment, 79
    term, 79
Loan-to-value ratio, 79, 88, 234,
    356
Location, 124, 368
Lock-in clause, 93, 104, 361
Lot-and-block, 122, 367
Loyalty, 3

M

Maintenance, 199
Maintenance fee, 47
Management agreement, 188–189
Management plan, 188, 380
Margin, 86, 359
MARIA, 129, 366
Marketable title, 132, 370
Market analysis, 196
Market data approach, 129–130,
    368
Market price, 123–124, 368
Market rent, 220
Market value, 123
Master deed, 47, 350
Material fact, 163, 376, 380
Measurements, 238–239
Mechanic's lien, 58, 353
Meeting of the minds, 5, 11–12
Megan's Law, 199

This review section was created to provide a review of key real estate concepts in the days or hours prior to your exam. The pages can be removed and carried with you from classroom to home to office. The review terms follow the outline of this book. For additional terms, please review your glossary before your exam.

CHAPTER 1—AGENCY RELATIONSHIPS AND CONTRACTS

Agency Relationships

1. When the owner of a property hires a broker to find a buyer, an *agency relationship* is created. The owner (principal) delegates to the broker (agent) the right to act on the owner's behalf, creating a *fiduciary relationship* of trust and confidence.

2. Representing only one party in a transaction creates a *single agency*. Representing both parties creates a *dual agency*. A dual agency must be disclosed in writing to all parties. In a dual agency, both parties would have client status.

3. A *facilitator* or *transaction broker* does not represent either party in the transaction. Both parties are treated as customers.

4. A *designated seller's agent* would be the agent representing only the seller. A *designated buyer's agent* would be the agent representing only the buyer. In designated agency, the principal broker or manager would be a dual agent.

5. *Ministerial acts* are those acts that a licensee may perform for a consumer that are informative in nature and do not rise to the level of active representation. *Puffing* is the exaggeration of a fact.

6. A *general agency* is created when the principal delegates a broad range of powers to the agent. A *special agency* is created when the principal delegates only a specific act or business transaction with detailed instructions.

7. In an *express agency,* the parties state the contract's terms and express their intention either orally or in writing. An *implied agency* occurs when the actions or conduct of the parties communicate that there is an agreement.

8. The acronym COALD represents the duties of the agent to the principal: care, obedience, accountability, loyalty, and disclosure.

9. A *listing agreement* is a personal service contract employing the brokerage firm to find a ready, willing, and able buyer. Most states require that the listing agreement be in writing to be enforceable.

10. In an *exclusive-right-to-sell listing,* one broker is hired to list and sell the property. If the seller gives the listing broker permission to work with cooperating brokers, then other brokers may sell the property. If the property sells during the listing term, the seller must pay the commission even if the seller finds the buyer.

11. In an *exclusive-agency listing*, the seller retains the right to sell the property and authorizes one broker to list the property. If the seller grants the listing broker authority to place the property in the MLS, then other brokers may sell the property. If the seller secures the buyer, no commission is due. If a broker secures the buyer, a commission must be paid.

12. In an *open listing,* the seller enters into listing agreements with any number of brokerage firms and also retains the right to sell the property. If the seller secures the buyer, no commission is due. If a broker secures the buyer, a commission must be paid.

13. A *net listing* stipulates that the seller will receive a specified amount of money and anything over that amount is the broker's commission. Net listings are illegal in most states.

14. A *listing contract* is considered an employment contract. If a seller does not accept a full list price offer, a commission is due the broker because the broker procured a ready, willing, and able buyer.

15. In the *exclusive buyer agency,* the broker is due a commission whenever a property is purchased.

16. In an *exclusive-agency buyer agency,* the broker is entitled to payment only if the broker locates the property purchased by the buyer.

17. In an *open buyer agency,* the buyer may have contracts with several agents, and pays only the broker who finds suitable property.

18. A party should immediately receive a copy of any document the party has just signed.

19. A broker should keep copies of all records pertaining to the property. State laws determine how long they are kept.

20. A *trust account,* also known as an *escrow* or *impound account,* is set up by a broker to hold the money of others. State laws regulate the establishment, maintenance, and auditing of the account(s) that a broker is required to have.

21. *Commingling* a client's money with a broker's personal or business account is not allowed in most states. Embezzlement or using someone else's money is illegal.

22. State laws determine the length of time that brokers must keep complete and accurate records of all business transactions.

Contracts

1. A valid and enforceable contract must contain the following essential elements: legally competent parties, offer and acceptance, proper legal form, legal purpose, consideration, reality of consent, and the signature(s) of the party or parties authorized to perform.

2. To *offer* means to put forward for acceptance, rejection, or consideration. An offer becomes a contract when accepted without changes.

3. The *offeror* makes the offer; the *offeree* receives it.

4. The terms of the offer must be clear and definite and have a time frame for acceptance. An offer can be revoked at any time before acceptance. The acceptance is not effective until the offeror receives notice of the acceptance. Offers may be terminated by notice of revocation, death or insanity of either party, or a counteroffer.

5. If any change is made in an offer, the original offer is void. If a *counteroffer* is made, the legal positions of the parties are reversed.

6. Only one party is obligated to perform in a *unilateral contract.* Open listings and options are unilateral contracts.

7. Both parties are obligated to perform in a *bilateral contract.* Exclusive listings, leases, and sales contracts are bilateral contracts.

8. In an *express contract,* the parties have specifically agreed, either orally or in writing, to enter into a contract.

9. In an *implied contract,* the parties by their actions or conduct enter into a contract.

10. One or both parties still have duties to perform in an *executory contract.*

11. In an executed contract, all parties have fulfilled their obligations.

12. A contract is *valid* when it meets all the essential elements and is enforceable.

13. A contract is *void* if it is missing an essential element and is unenforceable by either party.

14. A contract is *voidable* if it can be rescinded by one or both parties. Contracts entered into under duress, undue influence, misrepresentation, fraud, or with a minor or an incompetent person are voidable by the innocent party.

15. A contract is *unenforceable* if neither party can sue to force performance of the contract.

16. The statute of frauds requires that certain instruments, such as deeds, real estate sales contracts, and certain leases be in writing to be legally enforceable.

17. To change any of the provisions in the contract, or to insert additional terms, the parties should create an *addendum* or supplement to the contract. An addendum is a part of the original contract. After a contract has been created, if additional changes are made to the contract, the parties may *amend* the contract. Appropriate parties should sign or initial, and date the amendment.

Types of Contracts

1. Contract of sale, purchase and sale agreement, and offer to purchase are three of the different names that can be applied to the document that contains the seller's agreement to sell and the buyer's agreement to buy.

2. In an *option agreement,* the owner (optionor) agrees to keep open an offer to sell or lease real property for a specified time. The owner receives option money that may or may not apply toward the purchase price.

3. An *option contract* binds the optionor to sell should the optionee exercise the option.

4. An option contract is a *unilateral contract.* An option that has been exercised is a *bilateral contract.*

5. An option contract should contain the names and addresses of the parties, identification of the property, sales price, date of the expiration of the option, method of notice by which the option is to be exercised, and provisions for forfeiture of the option money if the option is not exercised. It may contain a clause forbidding assignment.

6. In a *lease option,* the lessee (tenant) has the right to purchase the property under specified conditions or to renew or extend the lease at its end. The rent or a portion of the rent may be applied to the purchase price.

7. In a *land contract,* the seller is the *vendor* and the buyer is the *vendee.* Typically, the seller retains legal title to the property until the final payment is made. A land contract is also known as a contract for deed, an installment contract, articles of agreement for warranty deed, bond for title, or an agreement of sale.

Contractual Terms

1. *Time is of the essence* means the contract must be performed within the time limit specified.

2. An *assignment* is a transfer of rights and/or duties from one contract to another or from one person to another person.

3. *Novation* means a new contract has been substituted for another; it releases liability from the original contract.

4. Any ambiguities in a contract will be construed against its writer. To add or delete a provision in a contract, an addendum should be signed by the parties.

5. *Contingencies* require the completion of a certain act or promise before the contract is binding.

6. In a sales contract, land contract, or trust deed, the buyer's interest in the property is an *equitable title.* Legal title is held by another party, and the buyer has an insurable interest in the property.

7. A *liquidated damages clause* requires that compensation be paid if one party breaches the contract.

8. A *forfeiture clause* means that under certain circumstances, one party must forfeit or give something to the other party. If found in the sales contract, the earnest money may be given to the seller if the buyer breaches the contract.

9. A *suit for specific performance* is legal action to enforce or compel the performance of the terms of a contract.

10. *Caveat emptor* means let the buyer beware. *Caveat venditor* means let the seller beware.

11. An *exculpatory clause* is a hold harmless clause that may be found in contracts relieving a party from liability for injuries to another.

12. If an *indemnification clause* is found in the contract, it means one party agrees to compensate another for a loss or damage that is sustained.

Performance and Damages

1. A contingency requires the completion of a certain act or promise before the contract is binding, or it may cancel contract obligations. Until the contingencies have been fulfilled, the contract is voidable or unenforceable.

2. *Liquidated damages* are those damages that have been pre-authorized by the contract.

3. *Actual damages* are those that compensate for the cost of that which has been lost.

4. *Punitive damages* are unrelated to the cost of the lost and merely awarded to punish the wrong-doer.

5. The process of *rescission* means the contract has been canceled, and the parties have returned to the legal positions they were in before they entered the contract.

Insurance

1. Most homeowners' insurance policies require that the owner maintain insurance equal to at least 80 percent of the replacement cost of the dwelling. The three general categories of risk that a homeowner's policy should include protection against are (1) destruction of the premises, (2) injury to others on the premises, and (3) theft of personal property of the homeowner or family members.

2. Buyers may hire their own property inspector. Lenders normally require a survey, pest inspection, flood certification, and environmental inspection before closing.

3. The *Comprehensive Loss Underwriting Exchange (CLUE)* is a database of consumer claims that insurance companies can access when they are underwriting or rating an insurance policy. The database contains property insurance claims for up to five years.

4. The *National Flood Insurance Reform Act of 1994* allows lenders to purchase flood insurance on behalf of borrowers/owners of properties in special flood-hazard areas and charge the cost back to the borrowers.

Licensee Information

1. For a salesperson to be operative in the real estate business, a broker must sponsor the salesperson's license. The salesperson is authorized to perform real estate activities on behalf of and in the name of the broker.

2. An *independent contractor* pays the income tax and Social Security and may not receive any employee benefits from the broker. The broker can regulate the working hours, office routine, and attendance at meetings of employees and may withhold income, Social Security, FICA, and state taxes.

3. Disputes within the office may be settled by company policies and procedures. Disputes between REALTORS® will be settled by arbitration. Disputes between non-REALTORS® may be settled through the court system.

4. In some states, if the broker's license is suspended or revoked, all of the licenses held by that broker are immediately suspended or rendered inactive until the licensees associate with another broker.

5. Federal and state antitrust laws do not allow groups of brokers to fix commission rates among or between them. Payments of commissions are negotiated between brokers and their clients.

6. Each broker should have a written agreement with the broker's licensees on how commissions will be divided. A salesperson may receive a commission only from the broker.

7. Most state laws require that an agent be licensed at the time of the transaction, have an employment contract (listing), and be the procuring cause of the sale to earn a commission. When the brokerage firm has secured a qualified buyer, the broker is due a commission.

8. If a *buyer agency* relationship has been created, agreement should state who is responsible for the payment of the commission.

9. Listed properties should be advertised through the broker.

10. Parties should receive a copy of all documents they sign.

11. Each person engaged in a trade or business who receives more than $10,000 in cash in one transaction, or in two or more related transactions, must file Form 8300 with the Internal Revenue Service. The form must be filed by the 15th day after the date the cash was received. If that date falls on a Saturday, Sunday, or legal holiday, the form must be filed by the next business day.

CHAPTER 2 REAL PROPERTY OWNERSHIP/ INTEREST

Freehold Estates

1. An *estate in land* refers to a party's legal interests or rights to a property. To be an estate, an interest must be possessory or may become possessory in the future. An easement is not an estate in land because it does not allow for the possession of the property.

2. The *bundle of rights* allows the owner to possess, enjoy, control, exclude, and dispose of the property.

3. *Freehold estates* include fee estates and life estates. A freehold estate exists for an uncertain duration. *Nonfreehold estates* include leasehold estates, which are based on calendar time.

4. *Fee simple absolute* is the highest ownership recognized by law. This possessory interest is freely transferable, of indefinite duration, and is an inheritable estate.

5. The two types of *fee simple defeasible estates* (title can be defeated) are *special limitation* and *condition subsequent*. When a title is transferred by special limitation with the possibility of reverter, the grantee has ownership interests so long as the property is used for that particular purpose.

6. When a title is transferred by condition subsequent with a right of reentry, the grantee ownership is on the condition that, which means there is an action or activity that the grantee must not perform. This deed condition is binding on the future owners of the property.

7. A *conventional life estate* is a freehold estate that is created by the grantor. It is not inheritable and is limited in duration to the life of the life tenant(s).

8. The *life tenant* has full enjoyment of the ownership as long as the life tenant is alive. On the death of the life tenant, the property reverts to the grantor or to a remainderman. The grantor's future interest is called a reversionary interest. The future interest of the remainderman is a *remainder interest*.

9. A life estate based on the life of a third party is called a life estate pur autre vie.

10. The life tenant has the right to sell, mortgage, or lease the property, but cannot allow the property to go to waste. A lease or deed signed by the life tenant becomes void on the death of the life tenant.

11. Dower, curtesy, and homestead are legal life estates that are created by law.

12. *Dower* is a wife's interest in real estate owned by her husband. *Curtesy* is a husband's interest in real estate owned by his wife. A *homestead* protects the owner from certain creditors.

13. *Severalty* means the title to real estate is owned by one party: an individual, a corporation, or a government body.

14. Characteristics of *tenancy in common* ownership are each tenant holds an undivided fractional interest; interests may be unequal; unity of possession; each co-owner can sell, convey, mortgage, or transfer his or her interest without the consent of the other owners; and it is an inheritable estate.

15. *Joint tenancy* is a concurrent form of ownership characterized by right of survivorship. There must be unities of time, interest, and possession for joint tenancy to be created. Each joint tenant has the right to sell, mortgage, or lease an interest without the consent of the other owners.

16. If one joint tenant sells his or her property, the new owner would be a tenant in common with the other joint tenants.

17. When cotenants cannot voluntarily agree to the termination of their co-ownership, a *suit for partition* can be filed in which the court dissolves the relationship.

18.   *Tenancy by the entirety* is recognized in some states and allows a husband and wife to each have an equal, undivided interest in the property that is characterized by survivorship.

19.   A *trust* is established to manage a property for the owner. The three parties in a trust agreement are the trustor, the trustee, and the beneficiary.

20.   Community property states regard any property acquired during marriage as obtained by mutual effort. When one spouse dies, the surviving spouse automatically owns one-half of the community property. Separate property, owned, inherited, or received as a gift by either spouse before or during marriage, can be sold or mortgaged without the signature of the nonowning spouse.

21.   To create a condominium community, the developer must record a declaration of condominium. The *master deed* allows the land to be converted to condominium use. The *bylaws* govern the operation of the homeowners' association.

22.   A party purchasing a residential condominium owns airspace in a unit and is a tenant in common with other community members in the land and improvements. A *limited common area* is owned by all but is limited to the use of the condo owners.

23.   Each condo owner is required to pay a homeowners' association fee to cover maintenance, insurance, and reserve funds. If the fee is not paid, the condo could be sold at foreclosure.

24.   In a *cooperative*, a corporation owns the property in severalty. Owners purchase stock in the company and receive a *proprietary lease*. Both are considered personal property. The maintenance fee includes each co-op owner's share of the corporations' expenses.

25.   Should a co-op owner default on a payment, the other shareholders are expected to pay. A co-op owner who defaults or breaches the lease may be evicted. If the co-op defaults on a payment to the lender, the lender can foreclose on the entire property.

26.   *Time-sharing* allows for an interval ownership or use by multiple purchasers of the property. When a *time-share estate* is conveyed, the owner holds a deed to the property. When a *time-share use* is conveyed, the buyer has the right to occupy the property for a stipulated time.

Leasehold Estates

1.   A *lease* gives the tenant the right to exclusive occupancy of the property and is considered personal property.

2.   An *estate for years* (tenancy for years) has a definite time period and no notice is needed to terminate. When the ending date arrives, the tenant is to vacate the premises.

3.   An *estate from period to period* (periodic tenancy) has an indefinite time period. This lease automatically renews until proper notice is given.

4. An *estate at will* (tenancy at will) gives the tenant the right to possess the property with the consent of the landlord. The lease can be terminated at any time by either party.

5. An *estate at sufferance* (tenancy at sufferance) is created when the tenant remains in possession of the property after the lease expires without the consent of the landlord. If the landlord gives permission to a tenant to remain on the property, a holdover tenancy is created.

6. A lease agreement can be oral or written. The owners' right to retake the property after the expiration of the lease is a *reversionary right.* Oral leases for 12 months and under are enforceable.

7. The lessor's interest is called a *leased fee interest*, and the lessee's interest is called a *leasehold interest.*

8. A tenant who transfers all the leasehold interests assigns the lease, creating a new landlord-tenant relationship between the lessor and the assignee. The lessor now expects payment from the assignee.

9. A *sublease* is created when a tenant transfers less than all the leasehold interests to a new tenant. In a sublease, there are two landlord-tenant relationships. One between the lessor and lessee in the original lease, and a second relationship between the lessee and the sublessee. The lessee can charge more rent and keep the profit. The lease between the sublessor and the sublessee is called a *sandwich lease.*

10. In a *lease option,* the tenant has the option to purchase a property at a specified price within a certain period.

11. In a *lease purchase,* the tenant agrees to purchase the property at a specified price within a certain period, usually the end of the lease.

12. In a *gross (straight) lease,* the tenant pays a fixed rental amount, and the owner pays all other ownership expenses for the property. The tenant normally pays for utilities.

13. The tenant who enters into a *net lease* agrees to pay ownership expenses, such as property taxes, insurance, and maintenance.

14. In a *percentage lease,* a commercial tenant agrees to pay a fixed base rental fee plus a percentage of the gross income in excess of a predetermined minimum amount of sales.

15. In a *sale-leaseback,* the grantor sells the property to the grantee and then leases it back.

16. A *graduated lease* allows for a periodic step-up of rent payments and may be used to attract tenants to a property that is difficult to rent.

17. In a net lease, the tenant agrees to pay ownership expenses, such as utilities, property taxes, and special assessments. The terms *net, double net,* and *triple net* can be used to describe the lease, depending on the ownership expenses the tenant agrees to pay.

18. In times of inflation, the property manager may negotiate an *index lease,* wherein the rent is tied to an index outside the control of either the landlord or the tenant. Index leases contain an *escalation clause* that allows the lease payment to change based on the index.

19. Leases may be terminated by the expiration of the term of the lease, proper notice as defined in the lease, surrender and acceptance, abandonment, merger, or destruction or condemnation of the property. The death of the lessor or lessee does not automatically terminate a lease.

20. Should the property be sold, the grantee takes the title subject to all existing leases and cannot make any changes until each lease expires.

21. Tenants should be aware that they cannot use their space in such a way as to infringe on the rights of others in the building or the community.

22. The Uniform Residential Landlord and Tenant Act does not allow abrogation where tenants sign away their rights in advance of signing the lease.

Forms of Business Ownership

1. A *sole proprietorship* is the simplest form of business ownership by a single person. Because there is no distinct legal difference between the person and the business, a person acting as a sole proprietor is accepting personal liability for the business.

2. A *partnership* is an association of two or more persons who establish a business for profit as co-owners. *General partners* are personally liable for business losses and obligations and are responsible for the operation of the business. *Limited partners* are liable for business losses only to the extent of their investment and do not participate in the operation of the business.

3. A *corporation* is a legal entity that is seen as an artificial person. A board of directors manages the business and a person is legally appointed to be responsible for the real estate activities. A licensee should ask for a copy of the corporate documents and minutes in order to identify the person that has the authority to enter into real estate contracts on behalf of the corporation.

4. The major advantage of the corporation is the corporate veil that limits the liability to the assets of the corporation. One of the major disadvantages is that profits are subject to double taxation. The corporation must pay taxes on the profits and shareholders must pay taxes on the dividends they receive.

5. A *security* is created when a party joins with others in the expectation of making a profit from the efforts of others. Securities sold *interstate* are regulated by the Securities and Exchange Commission. Securities sold *intrastate* (within state lines) are regulated by *blue-sky laws.*

6. A *syndicate* is formed when two or more people unite and pool their resources to own, develop, and/or operate an investment.

7. A *joint venture* is characterized by the intention of the parties to enter into a business relationship that is limited to a certain timeframe. The parties know that it will never be a permanent business relationship. Members of the joint venture share in capitol, revenues, expenses and assets.

8. The main advantage of a *real estate investment trust (REIT)* is that investors can avoid double taxation when certain requirements are met.

Restrictions on Real Property

1. A *lien* is a legal right that a creditor has in the borrower's property.

2. A *general lien* is a claim against all property of the lienee. A *specific lien* is a claim against one particular property.

3. A *voluntary lien* is established intentionally by the lienee. An *involuntary lien* is placed on the property without any action on the part of the owner.

4. A voluntary or involuntary lien may be statutory or equitable. A *statutory lien* is created by law, such as a judgment. An *equitable lien* is created by the court based on fairness.

5. Property taxes are specific, involuntary liens.

6. *Special assessments* are levied for the improvements made to property and are specific and statutory. They may be either voluntary or involuntary liens.

7. Property taxes *(ad valorem taxes)* and special assessments take priority over all other property liens.

8. A *mortgage lien* or *deed of trust* is a voluntary lien on real estate that secures the loan for the lender until the debt is paid in full.

9. A *mechanic's lien* is placed on the property by a party who performed labor or furnished material to improve the property. Generally, a mechanic's lien becomes effective on the day the work began or the materials were delivered.

10. A *judgment* is a decision by the court on the respective rights and claims of the parties in a suit. It is a general, involuntary, equitable lien on real and personal property in the county where the judgment is rendered.

11. A creditor may seek a *writ of attachment,* which allows the court to retain custody of the property while a suit is being decided. This prevents the debtor from transferring the real estate before a judgment is rendered.

12. A *lis pendens notice* gives constructive notice that an action affecting the property has been filed in court and that a future lien may be placed on the property. A lis pendens notice renders a property unmarketable.

13. An *IRS tax lien* is a general, statutory, involuntary lien on all real and personal property of the citizen who owes taxes. It does not supersede previously recorded liens.

14. The priority of liens is generally as follows: real estate taxes and special assessments, senior lien, and junior liens in the order of recording.

Easements and Deed Restrictions

1. An *easement* is the right to use the land of another; it does not include possession rights.

2. The parcel of land that benefits from an appurtenant easement is known as the *dominant estate.* The parcel of land burdened by the easement is known as the *servient estate.*

3. Personal gross easements terminate on the death of the easement owner and do not transfer when the property is sold. Commercial gross easements, such as a utility easement, transfer when the property is sold.

4. An *easement by necessity* is created for a landlocked property to provide the access rights of ingress (entry) and egress (exit).

5. An *easement by prescription* is created when a claimant uses another's property for a statutory period of time and follows the proper legal proceedings to secure the easement.

6. A license is a personal privilege to enter the land of another and use it for a specific purpose. It can be revoked at any time and terminates on the death of either party or the sale of the land.

7. A *profit a prendre* is the right to take crops, soil, or profit from the land of another. (Also known as profit.)

8. An *encumbrance* is any claim, lien, or liability that affects the value or the use of a property.

9. A *right-of-way* is exactly as the term implies: a right or privilege, to pass over the land of another. This right can be created by contract or the usage over a period of time. An easement is an example of a right-of-way.

10. An *encroachment* is an unauthorized intrusion onto the real property of another. A survey is the best way for a buyer to determine if there are any encroachments.

11. A party who has open, notorious, hostile, and continuous use of another's property for a statutory period may acquire title to the property by *adverse possession*. The rights of the party in possession are called *squatter's rights*.

12. Periods of ownership by different squatters can be combined, which is known as *tacking*.

13. To acquire a title through adverse possession, the claimant must file a suit to quiet title. The title received by the squatter is called a *title by prescription*.

14. *Deed restrictions* are provisions placed in deeds to control the future uses of the property. The restriction may be either a deed condition or a deed covenant.

15. A *deed condition* creates a conditional fee estate, which means that if the condition is breached, the title may revert to the grantor or the grantor's heirs.

16. Deed restrictions normally run with the land, meaning they transfer from one owner to the next. They may be found in the deed, in the subdivision rules and regulations created by the developer, or the homeowners' association of a condominium community, or in a separate document such as a Declaration of Restrictions.

17. *Private restrictions* may also be placed on the property by the owner, and these restrictions would be found in the deed. These restrictions may be enforced by any other property owner, the developer, the homeowners' association, or a lender. Any unusual deed restrictions should be included in the listing contract.

18. Deed restrictions can be enforced by an interested party, such as a neighbor, the homeowners' association or the developer.

19. Condominiums and other communities with a homeowner association, have documents to govern how the association is run. Some states require that if an association is involved in the management of the community, the seller must provide certain disclosures to the potential buyer.

20. The buyer must be given a certain timeframe to review the disclosures before the sales contract is valid. These disclosures generally include a copy of the declaration; a copy of the bylaws, rules and regulations; and a seller's certificate, which certifies certain information about the community.

Government Powers

1. The Americans with Disabilities Act (ADA) is intended to enable individuals with disabilities to become a part of the mainstream by mandating equal access to public accommodations, jobs, public transportation, telecommunications, and government services. Private clubs and religious organizations are exempt.

2. ADA stipulates that employers with 15 or more employees adopt nondiscriminatory employment procedures for the disabled, including making reasonable accommodations to allow a qualified person to perform job functions.

3. ADA requires that existing architectural and communication barriers be removed, if this can be accomplished in a readily achievable manner. Priority 1: Get the party to the door. Priority 2: Provide equal access to all areas where goods and services are available to the public. Priority 3: Make restroom facilities accessible. Priority 4: Provide free access to all remaining areas.

4. State enabling acts allow municipal governments to create zoning and planning boards to evaluate current needs and to project for future growth in a stable manner.

5. Public controls include the inherent right of the state to regulate land use for the health, safety, and welfare of the public. Such controls include land-use planning, zoning ordinances, subdivision regulations, building codes, and environmental protection legislation.

6. Private restrictions are placed on real estate by the developer to control and maintain the desirable quality and character of a subdivision or property. One neighbor can enforce a deed restriction through court action. Private restrictions are called covenants, conditions, and restrictions, or CC&Rs.

7. Municipalities and counties develop a master plan to guide long-term development. *Zoning ordinances* implement the master plan and regulate land use and structures. Zoning powers are given to the local government by *state enabling acts*.

8. *Land use* is regulated by dividing the land into residential, commercial, industrial, and agricultural use districts. A *buffer zone* separates two different use districts.

9. *Bulk zoning* controls density or the ratio of land area to structure area. Aesthetic zoning requires that new buildings conform to certain types of architectural styles. Incentive zoning requires that the street floors of office buildings be used for retail space.

10. When zoning changes, zoning boards must make decisions on *nonconforming properties*. An owner may be allowed to continue a nonconforming use of a property until the property is sold or destroyed.

11. A *variance* may be granted if the zoning creates an unnecessary hardship on the owner and the variance is not detrimental to zoning.

12. When a special-purpose property, such as a library, is to be built, a *conditional-use permit* must be secured.

13. *Spot zoning* is a change of zoning for a particular spot or lot and is generally not permitted.

14. Special study zones are used to control development in high-risk flood-prone or geological areas.

15. Performance standards regulate air, noise and water pollution in industrial properties and may also set standards for building codes.

16. *Police power* is the right of the government to regulate for the purpose of promoting the health, safety and welfare of the public.

17. The right of the government to take property for public use and pay just compensation to the owner is called *eminent domain*. The government exercises this right by the process of *condemnation*.

18. *Taxation* is the right of the government to charge the owner of real estate a fee to raise funds to meet public needs.

19. When a property owner dies intestate and the government can find no heirs, the property *escheats (reverts)* to the state or county.

CHAPTER 3 – FINANCE

Basic Concepts and Terminology

1. The difference between the current market value and any liens on the property is the owner's *equity*.

2. The lender will negotiate the loan on the sale price or the appraised value, whichever is less. The *loan-to-value ratio* is the relationship between the amount of a loan and the appraised value (sale price) of a property.

3. *Interest* is what a borrower pays when a loan is negotiated, and it is what is earned when the money is lent to other people, such as interest earned on a certificate of deposit or a savings account.

4. Interest on home loans is usually computed as *simple interest* and is paid in *arrears*, meaning the borrower has the benefit of the service and then pays the interest due. (As opposed to tenants who pay rent in advance, meaning they pay for the service before they have the benefit of living in the space.)

5. Some states have *usury laws* that limit the maximum interest rate that a lender can charge on certain types of loans. In times of emergencies, the federal government can set aside usury laws.

6. In a *lien-theory state,* the borrower receives the deed to the property, and the lender establishes a lien position by recording the note and mortgage.

7. In a *title-theory state*, the law construes the lender to have legal title to the property and the borrower to have an equitable title.

8. *Intermediate-theory states* are a combination of lien theory and title theory. The law interprets the lender as having a lien on the property unless the borrower defaults. On default, the title passes to the lender.

Primary Mortgage Market

9. The *primary mortgage market* includes savings and loan associations, mutual savings banks, commercial banks, insurance companies, mortgage bankers, mortgage brokers, credit unions, pension funds, and the Rural Economic and Community Development agency, formerly the Farmers Home Administration.

10. *Savings and loans* are an important source of funds for single-family home loans.

11. *Commercial banks* have specialized in short-term loans, but they are becoming more active in the negotiation of long-term residential loans.

12. *Insurance companies* specialize in large-scale, long-term loans that finance commercial and industrial properties. They may require an equity kicker or participation financing, meaning they become a partner with the borrower.

13. *Mortgage bankers* originate loans with money from insurance companies, pension funds, or individuals. They package and sell mortgages and continue to service a loan after it is sold. Mortgage brokers are financial middlemen between borrowers and lenders.

14. *Credit unions* are a source of funds for their members.

15. The Rural Economic and Community Development agency negotiates loans to people in rural areas for the purchase of property, to operate farms, and to purchase farm equipment. These loans can be originated through a private lender or directly from the agency.

16. In a *purchase-money mortgage,* the seller agrees to finance a portion or the entire purchase price. At the closing, the seller pays off the existing mortgage and takes back a mortgage on the property sold. Purchase-money mortgages usually create a junior lien on the property.

17. When a property is purchased subject to the mortgage, the original borrower or obligor remains liable for the debt. When a third party assumes the mortgage, the third party becomes primarily liable for the debt, and the original borrower is secondarily liable.

Secondary Mortgage Market

18. The *secondary mortgage markets* were created to stabilize the source of funds for lenders on the primary markets, especially when money is in short supply. Loans that are purchased by the secondary market are pooled (packaged) and sold to investors in the form of *mortgage-backed securities (MBS).* Investors purchase *pass-through participation certificates* that entitle the holders to pro-rata shares of all principal and interest payments made on the pool of loan assets.

19. The Federal National Mortgage Association, or Fannie Mae, is a government-sponsored enterprise (GSE) chartered by Congress. Fannie Mae buys mortgages on the secondary market, pools them, and sells them as mortgage-backed securities to investors on the open market. Fannie Mae was taken over by the federal government in September of 2008, and the Federal Housing Finance Agency (FHFA) was appointed conservator.

20. The Government National Mortgage Association, or Ginnie Mae, was created when Fannie Mae was reorganized in 1968. Ginnie Mae specializes in high-risk and special assistance programs and has the management and liquidating functions of the old Fannie Mae. The Ginnie Mae pass-through certificate provides for a monthly pass-through of principal and interest payments directly to the certificate holder.

21. The Federal Home Loan Mortgage Corporation, or Freddie Mac, was established to assist savings and loans as a secondary market for conventional mortgages, and is a publicly owned corporation. Freddie Mac purchases mortgages, pools them, and sells bonds in the open market as mortgage-backed securities. Freddie Mac was also taken over by the federal government in September of 2008, and the Federal Housing Finance Agency (FHFA) was appointed conservator.

22. The Federal Reserve stabilizes the economy by controlling the money supply and credit available in the country. It does this by (1) creating money, (2) regulating reserve requirements, and (3) setting the discount rate of interest it charges for loans to member banks.

Financing Terms

1. To *amortize* means to repay a loan in periodic payments that include principal and interest.

2. In a *fully amortized loan,* the principal balance is zero at the end of the loan term. In a *partially amortized loan,* the principal and interest payments do not pay off the entire loan. In a *nonamortized loan,* periodic interest payments are made to the lender, but no part of the payments is applied to the principal balance.

3. In a partially amortized loan, or *balloon mortgage,* the principal and interest payments do not pay off the entire loan. A balance remains when the final payment is made.

4. In a nonamortized loan, periodic interest payments are made to the lender, but nothing is applied to the principal balance. These loans are called *term mortgages* or *straight mortgages.*

5. A *construction loan* is an example of a nonamortized loan. With a construction loan, the borrower receives the money in stages, called draws, and makes periodic payments of interest. When the construction is complete, the borrower must have secured long-term financing and will pay off the entire principal balance.

6. An *adjustable-rate mortgage (ARM)* contains an escalation clause that allows the interest to adjust over the loan term. ARMs are tied to an index. The premium charged by the lender and added to the index to determine the interest charged is called the *margin*, which remains constant over the life of an ARM. A cap sets the maximum limit the interest rate can increase and the maximum limit of rate change at each adjustment interval.

7. An *unconventional mortgage* is backed by the government.

    Examples: FHA-insured and V.

8. In 1934, FHA was established to encourage improvements in housing standards, to encourage lenders to make loans, and to exert a stabilizing influence on the mortgage market. FHA does not negotiate loans.

9. With an FHA-insured loan, the borrower must purchase a mortgage insurance premium (MIP). A minimum cash down payment is required, which may be a gift. Interest rates are negotiable, and FHA does not set income limits for borrowers. No prepayment penalties are allowed on FHA-insured loans.

10. One of the purposes of the VA is to make loans available for qualified veterans and unremarried widows or widowers of veterans. The VA guarantees loans but normally does not make loans.

11. A qualified veteran can negotiate a loan with 100 percent loan-to-value ratio or with a minimum down payment. A qualified person can secure a VA-guaranteed loan on a one-to-four-family dwelling when the property will be owner-occupied.

12. Though the limit on the amount of loan that a veteran can obtain is determined by the lender, there is a limit that the VA will guarantee, based on a sliding scale of the value of the property. A veteran must apply for a certificate of eligibility, which establishes the maximum guarantee entitlement of the veteran. The VA also issues a *certificate of reasonable value (CRV)* for the property being purchased, which states the current market value based on a VA-approved appraisal and places a ceiling on the amount of a VA loan allowed. A veteran is not required to have a down payment unless the purchase price exceeds the amount cited in the CRV.

13. At the closing, the borrower or seller must pay a funding fee to the VA. This is a percentage of the loan amount and depends on the eligibility status and down payment of the veteran. The fee may be financed as a part of the loan. Discount points may be paid by the buyer or seller. No prepayment penalties are allowed on a VA loan.

14. A VA loan is *assumable* with VA approval. Another qualified veteran's certificate of eligibility may replace the existing certificate. The original borrower is granted *novation* by the lender, and full eligibility may be reinstated by the VA. If a nonveteran assumes the loan, the original borrower remains liable.

15.   A *conventional mortgage* is not backed by the government, and it can be insured or uninsured.

16.   In conventional financing, if a borrower has a 20 percent or greater down payment, the lender may accept the creditworthiness of the borrower and the security of the property to ensure the payment of debt. If a borrower has less than a 20 percent down payment, the lender may require that the borrower purchase *private mortgage insurance (PMI).* Should the borrower default, the lender may foreclose. At the foreclosure sale, if the property sells for less than the mortgage balance, the PMI pays the lender up to the amount covered in the policy.

17.   A *purchase-money mortgage (PMM)* is a creative financing technique that developed when interest rates were high. The seller agrees to finance a portion or the entire purchase price. The buyer will receive the deed and title at the closing and the seller will put a lien on the property. If the seller finances a portion of the purchase price, he records the note and be in a second lien position. If the seller finances the entire amount, he records the note and will be in a first lien position. A PMM is also known as a *take-back mortgage.*

Provisions of Financing Instruments

1.   A *security instrument* protects the lender's interest by providing collateral for the loan. Trust deeds and mortgages are standard security instruments. A land contract also is a security instrument.

2.   A *mortgage* is a pledge of property to the lender as security for the payment of the debt. The *mortgagor* is the borrower and the *mortgagee* is the lender. A *note* is evidence of the debt and states the terms of repayment. The borrower is the *obligor,* or *promissor,* because of the obligation to repay the debt. The lender is the *obligee/promisee.*

3.   *Hypothecation* means to pledge property to the lender as collateral, without giving up possession of it.

4.   In a *graduated-payment mortgage,* the borrower makes lower monthly payments for the first few years and then larger payments. If the lower monthly payments do not cover all the interest charges, the lender will add the unpaid interest to the principal balance. This creates *negative amortization,* which means the borrower owes more than the original loan amount.

5.   In a *growing-equity mortgage*, there are periodic increases in the monthly payment that are applied directly to the principal, thus reducing the term of the loan.

6.   In a *shared-appreciation mortgage,* the lender agrees to originate the loan at below-market interest rates in return for a guaranteed share of the appreciation the borrower will realize when the property is sold.

7.   A *reverse mortgage* allows homeowners 62 years of age or older to borrow against the equity in their homes and receive monthly payments, a lump sum, a line of credit, or a combination of any of these terms. The loan becomes due when the borrower no longer permanently resides in the property.

8. A *package mortgage* includes both real and personal property and is usually used in the sale of new homes in a subdivision or in resort condominium sales.

9. A *blanket mortgage* covers more than one tract of land and contains a partial release clause that allows the borrower to obtain a release of any one lot or parcel.

10. A *wraparound mortgage* is a junior loan that wraps around an existing senior loan when the original loan is assumable. It is also known as an *all-inclusive* or *overriding loan*. The lender wraps the junior loan around the existing first mortgage. The borrower makes only one monthly payment to the lender that is applied to both mortgages.

11. A *buydown mortgage* allows the borrower to buy down the interest rate, thus reducing the monthly payment for a number of years.

12. A *budget mortgage* includes principal, interest, taxes, and insurance payments. The tax and insurance portions of each payment are paid from an escrow account.

13. An *open-end mortgage* allows the mortgagor to borrow additional funds, up to a maximum dollar amount, all of which are secured by the same original mortgage.

    Example: Construction loan

14. The *prepayment privilege clause* found in an open mortgage allows a borrower to pay off the loan before the end of the term. Because of early repayment, some lenders charge a prepayment penalty, which is computed as a percentage of the remaining mortgage balance.

15. The *lock-in clause* in the note typically means that, upon loan application, the lender has agreed to lock the rate for a specified time period, or it could mean that the loan cannot be prepaid unless all interest is paid.

16. When the mortgage is paid, the lender must release its interest in the property. In lien-theory states, a *mortgage release* or *satisfaction piece* is recorded to release the lender's interest.

17. In title-theory states, a *defeasance clause* provides that the lender release its interest when the loan is paid in full.

18. If the mortgage document was a trust deed, the *reconveyance deed* must be recorded to release the lender's title interest.

19. A *due-on-sale clause* in a mortgage allows the lender to collect full payment from the mortgagor when the property is sold. Mortgages may also contain an *alienation clause,* stipulating that if the property is conveyed to any party, the lender can collect full payment.

20. In a *subordination agreement,* a lender with a first lien position agrees to take a second lien position on the property.

21. Notes, mortgages, and security instruments contain an *acceleration clause* that allows the lender to call the note payable in advance of the loan term. Default of the mortgage, destruction of the premises, or the sale of the property to another party may accelerate the payments.

22. Under a deed of trust, the borrower transfers legal title to the trustee, who holds the title for the benefit of the beneficiary (the lender). When the borrower has made the final payment to the lender, the lender's interest in the property has been defeated. The lender sends the proper documents to the trustee, who uses a deed of reconveyance to convey the title to the trustor.

23. Under a deed of trust, should the borrower default on the loan, the lender notifies the trustee. The borrower is given a time frame in which to make the payments current, pay a reinstatement fee, and reinstate the delinquent loan. If the borrower cannot, the trustee advertises and sells the property in a *foreclosure by advertisement*. This avoids the judicial foreclosure process found in lien-theory states.

Short Sales and Foreclosures

1. A *short sale* means that the lender and seller are willing to take less than the outstanding loan amount; however, the bank has the final approval of the selling price.

2. The *default clause* in a mortgage allows the lender to foreclose if there is a nonperformance of a duty or obligation on the part of the borrower.

3. *Foreclosure* is the legal process whereby a property is sold as security for the payment of a debt. State and local laws regulate foreclosure proceedings.

4. *Foreclosure by judicial sale* requires that the lender go to court and prove that the borrower has defaulted. The judge orders an appraisal of the property and sets a sale date. Creditors are notified, and the property is advertised. When the sale of the property is confirmed, the owner's rights to the property have been foreclosed.

5. An *equitable right of redemption* is the defaulted borrower's right to redeem the property before confirmation of the foreclosure. A *statutory right of redemption* is the defaulted borrower's right to redeem the property after confirmation of the foreclosure.

6. *Nonjudicial foreclosure* is used in states where the mortgage contains a *power-of-sale clause* that allows the lender to sell the property without going to court. The defaulted borrower has a specified time to pay delinquent payments and costs, after which the property is advertised and sold.

7. *Strict foreclosure* allows the lender to foreclose after appropriate notice has been given to the delinquent borrower and the proper papers have been filed. If full payment is not made, the property is sold, and the lender keeps all equity.

8. A *deficiency judgment,* which is a personal judgment, can be levied against the defaulted if the foreclosure sale price does not pay off the loan (principal plus costs of collection and foreclosure).

9. In a *nonrecourse loan*, the borrower is not held personally responsible for the note because the property is adequate collateral.

Government Oversight

Real Estate Settlement Procedures Act

1. The Real Estate Settlement Procedures Act (RESPA) requires the disclosure of settlement costs. Disclosures must be made on loans that are financed by federally related mortgages.

2. RESPA applies to first and second liens for the purchase or refinancing of one- to four-family dwellings. RESPA does not apply to a land contract; a purchase-money mortgage where the seller is financing the property; or a loan assumption where the lender charges less than $50 for the assumption.

3. RESPA requires that within three business days of loan application, the applicants must receive a copy of *Settlement Costs and You,* and a *good-faith estimate* of the settlement costs. The *Uniform Settlement Statement (HUD Form 1)* must be used to itemize all debits and credits. RESPA does not allow the lender to receive kickbacks from service providers.

4. Lenders cannot charge a fee for the preparation of the settlement statement. The settlement statement must be made available to the borrower for inspection one day prior to closing, with copies to the buyer and seller at the closing.

Truth in Lending

1. The Truth-in-Lending Act (Regulation Z) requires that lenders disclose the true cost of credit expressed as an APR, or *annual percentage rate.*

2. Finance fees that must be disclosed include loan fees, finders' fees, service charges, interest, and discount points. Fees that do not have to be disclosed include attorneys' fees, escrow fees, appraisals, surveys, inspections fees, title fees, and closing expenses. (RESPA does require the disclosure of these fees.)

3. Regulation Z covers all one- to four-family real estate financing for residential borrowers who are natural persons, but not loans that are used for business, commercial, or agricultural purposes; personal property credit transactions involving more than $25,000; and loans to the owner of a dwelling containing more than four housing units.

4. A borrower negotiating a home improvement loan or refinancing (but not a first mortgage or trust deed) has a three-day right of rescission in which to cancel the transaction.

5. Truth-in-Lending requires full disclosure by the lender if the following trigger items are used in an ad: monthly payment, number of payments, down payment, finance charges and the term of payment. If any of these items are used, the ad must include the purchase price; required down payment; number, amounts, and due dates of all payments; and the annual percentage rate.

6. Regulation Z defines a creditor as a person or an institution that extends consumer credit more than 25 times a year, or more than five times a year if the transaction involves a dwelling as security. The credit must be subject to a finance charge or payable in more than four installments by written agreement.

Sherman Antitrust Laws

1. The Sherman Antitrust laws prohibit price fixing, group boycotting, allocation of customers or markets, and tie-in agreements.

2. A brokerage firm can establish a brokerage policy regarding the commission rate that the brokerage will charge. *Commission rates* are negotiable between the parties. Brokers cannot conspire with other brokers to fix prices.

3. Brokers may not *group boycott* or conspire not to work with other brokers, or to withhold patronage to reduce competition.

4. Brokers may not allocate customers or markets by dividing the community into geographic areas and then agree not to compete with other brokers in that area. Brokers may not divide the market by price range or types of property they will sell.

5. Brokers cannot tie or agree to sell one product based on the purchase of another product. (This is sometimes seen as a tying agreement.)

Mortgage Fraud

1. *Mortgage fraud* means the lender was provided with false or misleading information on a loan application, or with falsified documents in the loan process. There are usually several players involved in mortgage fraud. These may include appraisers, title companies, lenders, real estate agents, and investors.

2. The types of mortgage fraud include, but is not limited to: equity skimming, house stealing, property flipping, straw buyers, silent second, stolen identity, and rescue scams, to name a few. There are many warning signs that a real estate agent can look for to prevent mortgage fraud. Agents can prevent fraud by ensuring the following:

    - The property address or legal description is clearly identified and legible on the sales contract and that all the blanks in the contract are filled in. Write the letters NA for not applicable, if the blank is not needed.

    - The sales contract accurately states the consideration to be paid by the buyer for the property. If after the contract is negotiated an agent is asked to change the consideration, the agent should not do it.

    - If the buyer wants the offer written contingent upon the use of a certain appraiser, the agent should not do it.

    - Any party that wants to place restrictions on how their participation is reported in the contract or HUD-1 should be reported.

    - The consideration stated in the sales contract and on the deed the buyer receives at closing are for the same amount.

    - Current comparables are used. Beware if the comparables that the appraiser used are a year old, but they are not the most recent sales in the neighborhood.

    - The sellers name/s should be the same on the sales contract and the deed given to the buyer at closing.

Other Federal Laws

1. The *Equal Credit Opportunity Act* prohibits discrimination based on race, color, religion, national origin, sex, marital status, age, or source of income in the granting of credit. Loan qualification is based on income, net worth, job stability, and credit rating.

2. Lenders have 30 days to inform a rejected applicant of the reasons why credit was denied.

3. The *Community Reinvestment Act* was passed to prevent redlining and disinvestment in central city areas. *Redlining* is the lender's refusal to negotiate loans in certain geographic areas, even to qualified borrowers.

Lending Process

1. Assessing the buyer's price range depends on three basic factors: (1) stable income, (2) net worth, and (3) credit history.

2. A *credit score* takes into account the applicant's payment and credit history.

3. A loan underwriter evaluates a loan application to determine the desirability of the loan.

4. The *mortgage-to-income ratio* (housing-to-income ratio) is the ratio of the monthly housing expense to gross monthly income. The mortgage expense can be no more than 28 percent of the gross monthly income. This can also be known as the housing-to-income ratio, or the *front-end ratio.*

5. The *debt service ratio* is the sum of the total monthly debt payments in relationship to the borrower's gross monthly income. This is also known as the debt-to-income ratio, or the *back-end ratio.*

6. In most conventional loans, the total debt-to-service ratio can be no more than 36 percent of the borrower's stable monthly income. FHA debt-to-service ratios are generally 29 percent, and debt-to-income ratio is 41 percent.

7. VA has no front-end ratio, and the back-end ratio is 41 percent of the gross monthly income.

8. The four basic steps for securing a loan for the purchase of real estate are applying for the loan, analysis of the borrower and the property, underwriting the loan, and closing the loan.

9. For a *loan application,* the lender requires a copy of the purchase and sale agreement; the residence, employment, and credit histories of the borrower; income information; a report of the borrower's assets and liabilities; and a copy of a gift letter, if applicable.

10. The *loan origination* fee covers the administrative costs of making the loan and is a percentage of the loan amount.

11. The *loan commitment letter* states that the loan has been approved pending a satisfactory title report, mortgagee's title insurance, homeowner's insurance policy, survey, verification of job status, affidavit of marital status, copy of the settlement sheet of the house sold, verification of bank accounts, payoff of a particular bill, inspection reports required by the lender, and repairs required by the appraiser.

CHAPTER 4 – REAL PROPERTY

Real Property and Personal Property

1. *Real estate* is the land and all attachments to the land. *Real property* is land, all attachments, plus the bundle of legal rights that are inherent in its ownership.

2. *Personal property* is also known as personalty, or chattels, and includes movable items not attached to the real estate. Real property can become personal property by *severance* from the land.

3. The acronym MARIA will help you remember the tests to determine if an item is real or personal property.

   Method of annexation—Was the item permanently attached? Can it be removed without causing damage?

   Adaptation to real estate—Is the item custom made? For example, house keys are movable but are considered to be real property because of their adapted use to the property.

   Relationship to the parties—Emblements are considered the personal property of the tenant, but in the purchase of a farm, emblements could belong to the seller or buyer, depending on what is negotiated.

   Intention—What was the intention of the owner when the item was installed? Did the owner intend for it to remain permanently or to take it when the property was sold? (Courts have ruled that this intention is the most important factor in determining if an item is real or personal property.)

   Agreement—What was the agreement in the sales contract?

4. *Fructus naturales,* or fruits of nature, do not require annual cultivation and are considered real property.

5. Crops that require annual planting are known as *emblements* and are considered personal property.

6. A *fixture* is personal property that has become affixed to the land or improvements so that it becomes real property. A *trade fixture* is personal property owned by a tenant, is attached to rented space, and is used in conducting a business. Trade fixtures generally become the property of the landlord if not been removed prior to the expiration of the lease.

7. *Riparian rights* are granted to owners of land along a river, stream, or lake. Land adjoining navigable rivers is usually owned to the water's edge; land adjoining nonnavigable streams and lakes is owned to the center of the stream or lake.

8. *Littoral rights* are granted to owners of land that borders on large, navigable lakes, seas, and oceans. Ownership is to the mean high-water mark.

9. An owner is entitled to all increases in land that result from accretion, which is the deposit of soil by water's action. These deposits are called *alluvion* or *alluvium*. When water recedes, the new land is acquired by *reliction*. Avulsion is the sudden loss of land, while *erosion* is the gradual wearing away of land.

10. The courts use four tests to determine if an item is real or personal property: (1) intention, (2) method of annexation, (3) adaptation to real estate, and (4) agreement.

Legal Descriptions and Square Footage

1. The *metes-and-bounds* legal description describes the land by metes (distance) and bounds (direction).

2. A *benchmark* is a permanent reference point placed by a government survey team to establish elevation or altitude above sea level.

3. The *lot-and-block* method of legal description is used to record subdivided land. *Contiguous* lots are adjacent to each other.

4. The *government, rectangular,* or *geodetic survey* is based on a system of imaginary lines. Principal meridian lines run north and south; base lines run east and west.

5. The largest area in the government survey is called a *check* and is 24 miles by 24 miles. Checks are divided into *townships*, which are 6 miles by 6 miles. Townships are divided into *sections*, which are 1 mile by 1 mile. Each section contains 640 acres. Oversized or undersized sections are called *fractional sections*. *Correction lines* are adjustments for the earth's curvature.

6. In computing the *gross living area (GLA)* of a building, use only the area above grade or ground level. Do not include the garage, porch, or patio.

7. The word *appurtenant* means attached. Tangible (touchable) appurtenances include personal property or fixtures that may or may not pass in the deed. *Intangible (cannot touch) appurtenances* include rights and privileges that belong to the land and pass in the deed.

8. A *finished area* is suitable for year-round use. The space must be connected to the house. This is sometimes referred to as the gross living area (GLA).

9. An *unfinished area* is not suitable for year-round use.

10. The area of the house that is entirely above grade or ground level is said to be *above grade.*

11. The area of a house that is wholly or partially below grade is said to be *below grade.*

12. The *floor area ratio* represents the floor area to the land area on which the building sits.

13. The *livability space ratio* requires a minimum square footage of nonvehicular outdoor area in a development for each square foot of total living area.

14. The front footage is the linear measurement of a property along the street line or water line is always given first when dimensions are stated (if a lot

measures 100' × 200', then the first dimension given [100'] refers to the front footage).

15. The *setback line* is the amount of space required between the lot line and the building line.

Appraisal

1. The purpose of an *appraisal* is to estimate the market value, or most probable price that a buyer will pay for the property in an arm's-length transaction.

2. The types of appraisal methods are: sales comparison (market data), income approach, and cost approach.

3. In the *market data approach* to appraising, the subject property's value is estimated by comparing recent sales of similar properties. The property with the fewest adjustments is used to determine the market value. Market data is used by the appraiser to determine value. General data would be appropriate for many properties. Specific data refers to information regarding the subject and comparable properties.

4. Adjustments are always made to the values of the comparable properties. Remember: SBA—Subject Better, Add; CBS—Comparable Better, Subtract

5. The *income or capitalization approach* is used to appraise investment property. The appraiser estimates the present worth of future rights to the income the property generates.

6. The *cost approach* is used to appraise unique properties, such as a house of worship, post office, library, or hospital.

7. *Replacement cost* is the dollar amount required to construct improvements of equal utility using current materials. *Reproduction cost* is the dollar amount required to construct an exact duplicate of the subject property.

8. *Situs (location)* is a major factor in determining the value of a property.

9. *Market price* is the actual selling price of the property. *Cost* is the actual dollars spent to produce an asset. Value, price, and cost could be the same, but they are usually different.

10. The *principle of anticipation* states that the value of the property will adjust with any anticipated change within the community, such as the change of zoning from residential to commercial, or the expansion of the airport that will increase the noise levels in nearby communities.

11. *Competition* is the interaction of supply and demand. Excess profits attract competition.

12. *Conformity* is the maximum value achieved when the property is in harmony with its surroundings.

13. *Contribution* is the value of any part of the property, measured by its effect on the value of the whole.

14. *Highest and best* use is the most reasonable, probable, and profitable use of the property.

15. *Increasing returns* is when money spent on an improvement increases the property value. (Remodeling the kitchen will usually increase the property's value.)

16. *Decreasing returns* is when adding improvements to the land does not produce a proportional increase in property values. (A swimming pool may not increase a property's value.)

17. *Plottage* is the value that is created when two or more tracts of land are merged into a single, larger one; *assemblage* is the process of merging the parcels of real estate.

18. *Progression* occurs when the value of a modest home increases if surrounded by larger, more expensive properties.

19. *Regression* occurs when a larger, more expensive home is adversely affected if surrounded by smaller, more modest homes.

20. *Substitution* is the foundation for all approaches to appraising; the maximum value of a property tends to be set by the cost of purchasing an equal substitute property.

21. *Supply* is the amount of goods available in the market, and demand is the need for the good.

22. *Depreciation* causes a property to lose value. Depreciation may be *curable* (reasonable and economically feasible to correct) or *incurable* (not economically feasible to correct).

23. *Physical depreciation* is caused by lack of maintenance and ordinary wear and tear.

24. *Functional obsolescence* occurs because of the absence or inadequacies of features in design or construction.

25. *External* or *environmental obsolescence* is incurable and occurs because of factors located outside the property.

26. The *life cycle* of a community includes growth, stability, decline, and gentrification or revitalization. An appraiser evaluates the community to determine which cycle the property is in and how that affects the value of the property.

27. The *economic base* is reviewed for activities that will attract business and income to the community. Other economic factors that will affect a property's value include interest rates, taxes, employment levels, and population.

28. DUST is the acronym to help you remember the four elements of value.

    D—Demand is the number of properties (goods) that people are willing and able to buy at a given price.

    U—Utility asks the question, "How has the land and improvement been utilized?" (A one-bedroom home versus a three-bedroom home.)

    S—Scarcity means that when the supply is limited, the price will increase.

    T—Transferability means that there must be a good and marketable title to the property.

29. A *comparative market analysis (CMA)* to help the seller determine the listed price, or to help buyers determine what they should offer.

30. Licensees may be hired by lenders to do a *Broker Price Opinion (BPO),* which can also be called a Broker Opinion of Value (BOV). Some lenders will use a BPO to determine the value of a property that is going into foreclosure, an estate sale, a short sale, or for a refinance or home equity loan.

Deeds and Title

1. A *deed* transfers the title from the grantor to the grantee. The *title* is found within the deed and is used to show ownership of land.

2. A *title search* is conducted to ensure that the buyer and the lender receive a marketable title or one that would not place either party in a position of legal liability.

3. An *abstract (of title)* is a condensed legal history of all transactions affecting the property; it includes conveyances, wills, records of judicial proceedings, recorded liens and encumbrances affecting the property, and their current status.

4. Easements, restrictions, violations of zoning ordinances, lis pendens notices, mortgages, liens, federal tax liens, property tax liens, and encroachments could render a title unmarketable. Slight encroachments usually do not render a title unmarketable.

5. A *marketable title* or *merchantable title* is one that is free from reasonable objections; that is, one that will not place the buyer in a position of legal liability or threaten the buyer's right to quiet enjoyment of the property.

6. *Title insurance* protects the policyholder against losses that arise from defects in the title. Prior defects and liens found in the title search, defects known to the buyer, and changes in zoning are not covered in a title policy. Standard coverage includes protection against forged documents, missing heirs, incompetent grantors, incorrect marital statements, improperly delivered deeds, and defects found in public records.

7. An *owner's (mortgagor's) title policy* is issued for the market value of the property and benefits the owner. A *lender's (mortgagee's) title policy* covers the loan balance and decreases as the balance is reduced.

8. A *cloud on title* is any claim that creates a defect of title or casts doubt on the title's validity.

9. When a title insurance company makes a payment to settle a claim, the company requires that a policyholder subrogate any rights to the claim. *Subrogation* is the substitution of one creditor for another. This gives the title insurance company the right to sue the guilty party to recover any monies it paid to settle a title claim.

10. A title search is carried out by a lawyer, abstractor, or title insurance company. It is a condensed legal history of all transactions affecting the property.

11. For there to be a valid transfer of real estate, the deed must be signed by the grantor and accepted by the grantee. (The deed must meet the requirements of state laws.) There is nothing that requires the grantee to record the deed.

However, to best protect the grantee's interest against the claims of other parties, it is recommended that the deed be recorded. When a deed is not recorded, it creates a gap in the title which can create a question regarding the ownership of the property.

12. *Constructive notice* is legal notice created by recording documents, such as deeds, mortgages, and long-term leases in the county where the property is located. Physical possession of the property also gives constructive notice of the rights of the parties that are in possession.

13. *Actual notice* is when a party has actual knowledge of the fact. When a party has actual notice of a third party's prior rights to a property and still accepts the deed to the property, the party accepts the deed subject to the third party's prior rights. For example, a person who accepts a deed with a judgment lien on the property becomes responsible for the judgment.

14. The *Torrens system* is a method of legal registration of land where title does not transfer and encumbrances are not effective against the property until the proper documents are registered at the Torrens office. In some states, this means that the title cannot be lost through adverse possession.

15. The essential elements of a valid deed are the name of the grantor, a grantee who is identified with reasonable certainty, consideration, a granting clause or *habendum clause* that defines the extent of ownership, limitations placed on the conveyance, an accurate legal description, the signature of the grantor, and delivery and acceptance by the grantee.

16. Most states require that a deed be acknowledged and attested before it can be recorded. *Acknowledgment* verifies that the person voluntarily signed the document and verifies the identity of the signer.

17. A *general warranty deed* is the best type of deed for the buyer to receive because it binds the seller to covenants back to the origins of the property.

18. The usual *covenants* found in a general warranty deed are the covenant of *seisin,* which promises that the grantor owns the property and has the right to convey title; the *covenant against encumbrances,* which promises that the property is free from liens and encumbrances except those stated in the deed; the *covenant of quiet enjoyment,* which promises that the grantor has a superior title to the property; the *covenant of further assurance,* which promises that the grantor will obtain and deliver any instrument needed to make the title good; and the *covenant of warranty forever,* which promises that the grantor will compensate the grantee for any loss sustained if the title fails in the future.

19. With a *special warranty deed,* the grantor's liabilities are limited to the grantor's period of ownership.

20. A *bargain and sale deed* makes no express promises or warranties against encumbrances. This deed implies that the owner holds title and has possession of the property.

21. A *quitclaim deed* provides the buyer with the least protection because it provides no promises or warranties. The grantee has no legal recourse against the grantor should a title defect be found in the future.

22. Quitclaim deeds are used to convey title, to release interests in real estate, or to correct errors found in a deed.

23. A *reconveyance deed* is used in a deed in trust or a deed of trust to reconvey the title to the trustor.

24. Administrator's, executor's, sheriff's, and guardian's deeds are examples of deeds executed pursuant to court order.

25. In a *deed in trust,* the trustor conveys title to a trustee, who manages the property for the beneficiary.

26. An *inter vivos trust* means to set up a trust during one's life.

27. A *testamentary trust* means that the trust is established by will.

28. Most states have imposed a *transfer tax,* which is normally paid by the seller.

Wills

1. When a person dies, that person's estate is distributed through a legal process called *probate*. All liabilities are paid from the assets, and the remaining property is distributed to the heirs.

2. A person can die *testate,* meaning with a will; or *intestate,* without a will.

3. A *valid will* has been written by someone of legal age, who is also of sound mind and that meets the state requirements for a valid will.

4. An *executor* (male) or *executrix* (female) is the party named in a will to settle the estate.

5. The *testator* is the writer of the will.

6. *Devise* is to leave real property to someone in a will.

7. *Devisee* is the title of the person receiving real property through a will.

8. *Bequest* is a gift left in a will.

9. *Legacy* is money that is left to someone in a will.

10. An *administrator* (male) or *adminstratrix* (female) is a person appointed by the court to settle the estate of someone who died intestate.

11. The *Laws of Descent and Distribution* are state laws that determine how the assets will be distributed when someone died intestate. If a person dies intestate and owns property in another state, the laws in the state where the property is located determine who receives the property.

12. *Descent* is the method of receiving real property when someone died intestate.

13. A *holographic will* is a handwritten will that is legal in many states.

14. A *nuncupative will* is an oral will in which someone distributes personal property on a deathbed. There must be at least two witnesses, and if a written will is found, the nuncupative will cannot contradict the written will.

Closing or Settlement

1. A *real estate settlement,* or *closing*, takes place to consummate or finalize a real estate transaction.

2. A *face-to-face closing* is a formal meeting of all parties involved, and a settlement agent presides over the closing. A *closing in escrow* means that a disinterested third party is authorized to act as an escrow agent for the buyer and the seller and to handle all closing activities.

3. A *settlement agent* could be a closing agent from the title company, an attorney, a lender, or a real estate agent.

4. An *affidavit of the seller* is a document in which the seller affirms that, from the time the sales contract was accepted until the date of closing, the seller has done nothing to burden the title that would not be revealed in the title search.

5. A *bill of sale* is used to show the transfer of personal property.

6. A *payoff statement* indicates the payoff of the seller's existing note(s).

7. An *insurance policy* is required by a buyer to show payment of homeowners' insurance.

8. *Real estate transfer taxes, or RETTs,* are state, county, and/or municipal sales taxes most often used as general revenue. Transfer taxes are normally paid by the seller or lessor when the property is conveyed by a deed, contract for deed, lease, sublease, or assignment. The transfer tax may be paid by the purchase of tax stamps and are sometimes called documentary stamp taxes.

9. Home ownership may provide the following tax deductions: mortgage interest payments on qualified residential first and second homes, real estate property taxes, certain loan discount points, certain loan origination fees, loan prepayment penalties, and casualty losses to real estate not covered by insurance.

10. *Tax shelters* reduce current tax liability by offsetting income from one source with losses from another source.

11. A *capital gain* is a taxable profit that is realized from the sale or exchange of a capital asset.

12. Married homeowners who file jointly may exclude up to $500,000 from capital gains tax for profits on the sale of a principal residence. Single filers may exclude up to $250,000 from capital gains tax for profits on the sale of a principal residence. If the capital gain exceeds the exclusion, capital gains tax must be paid on the excess amount. The exclusion can be taken more than once. The home must have been used as a principal place of residence for two of the preceding five years.

13. *Depreciation,* or cost recovery, is a form of tax deduction. It allows an investor to recover the cost of an income-producing property used in a trade or business.

14. The cost of the improvements may be depreciated or deducted over an arbitrary period of time. Land cannot be depreciated.

15. The Internal Revenue Code Section 1031 allows investors to trade *like-kind property.* If no boot, which is cash or its equivalent, is involved in the trade, it is a tax-free exchange. If boot is involved, tax must be paid on the boot.

16. A *capital improvement* is any improvement made to extend the useful life of a property or add to its value.

CHAPTER 5 – MARKETING REGULATIONS

Lead-Based Paint

1. A seller or landlord must provide a *lead-based paint disclosure statement* on residential properties built prior to 1978.

2. On acceptance of an offer, purchasers must be given ten days to inspect the property. This right may be waived. (Tenants do not have ten days to inspect the property before entering into a lease agreement.)

3. Buyers and tenants have the right to any prior inspection records and reports. Buyers and tenants must be given the booklet *Protect Your Family from Lead in Your Home.*

4. The law does not require any testing or removal of lead-based paint by sellers or landlords, and it does not invalidate leasing and sales contracts. Federal law requires that the disclosures be kept for three years.

5. Agents must ensure that

   ■ sellers and landlords are made aware of their obligations under this rule;

   ■ sellers and landlords disclose the proper information to lessors, buyers, and tenants; and

   ■ sellers give purchasers the opportunity to conduct an inspection. Lease and sales contracts contain the appropriate notification and disclosure language and proper signatures.

Radon

1. *Radon* is a cancer-causing radioactive gas that is produced by the natural decay of radium, which is produced by the natural decay of uranium. The two main sources of radon are air and water. The EPA Action Level is 4 pico-curies per liter of air (4 pCi/L).

2. Urea formaldehyde is used in building materials, especially insulation, and it emits gases that can cause respiratory problems and eye and skin irritations.

3. *Asbestos Containing Materials (ACMs)* include insulation, floor tiles, roof shingles, and siding, to name a few. Intact asbestos is generally not a hazard. Disturbed or exposed asbestos can release microscopic fibers, which is breathed into the lungs and can result in respiratory diseases.

4. *Friable ACM* is defined as any material containing more than 1 percent asbestos, and that, when dry, can be crumbled, pulverized, or reduced to powder by hand pressure.

5. *Non-friable ACM* is any material containing more than 1 percent asbestos that, when dry, cannot be crumbled, pulverized, or reduced to powder by hand pressure.

6. *Carbon monoxide* is an odorless and colorless gas that occurs as a byproduct of incomplete combustion when burning fuels, such as wood, oil, and natural gas. Proper ventilation is needed when burning these fuels. Carbon monoxide inhibits the blood's ability to transport oxygen, which can cause nausea and even death.

7. *Underground storage tanks (USTs)* are commonly found where gas stations, auto repair shops, printing and chemical plants, and dry cleaners used tanks for storage of chemicals. If USTs are used to store toxic wastes and the tanks are neglected, they may leak hazardous substances into the environment and thus contaminate the soil and groundwater. More than 90 percent of the world's total supply of drinking water is groundwater. Approximately half of the people in the United States use ground water for drinking water.

8. *Mold* is found almost everywhere, but excess moisture allows mold to grow rapidly and mold can destroy property. Some people are sensitive to mold, which can cause allergic reactions or more serious health problems.

9. *PCBs or Polychlorinated biphenyls* were formerly used in electrical transformers. Equipment leaking PCBs should be replaced because they are considered a health hazard.

10. Toxic Substances Control Act (TSCA) placed prohibitions on the manufacture, processing, and distribution of PCBs in commerce. The law requires *"Cradle to Grave"* management of PCBs from manufacturing to disposal.

11. Comprehensive Environmental Response, Compensation, and Liability Act (CERCLA) is a 1980 law that taxed the petroleum industry, created a national inventory of hazardous waste sites and identified *potentially responsible parties (PRPs)* for cleanup of the sites. The four classes of potentially liable parties are

    ■ current owners and operators of a facility;

    ■ past owners and operators of a facility at the time hazardous wastes were disposed;

    ■ generators and parties that arranged for the disposal or transport of the hazardous substances; and

    ■ transporters of hazardous waste that selected the site where the hazardous substances were brought.

    The law became known as the *Superfund* when Congress collected over $12 billion to cleanup sites when a PRP could not be identified.

12. Any real estate can involve an Environmental Site Assessment (ESA), and many commercial transactions involve a Phase I, Phase II, and/or Phase III assessment. The purpose of an ESA is to identify potential or existing environmental liabilities.

Property Condition

1. Many buyers write their offers contingent upon an inspection by an independent third party or property inspector. Buyers and lenders may require a pest control report showing that the property is free and clear of any live, visible infestation by wood-destroying organisms. Depending on the type of property, lenders may also require a flood certification and environmental assessment before negotiating a loan on the property.

2. Developers want to ensure that there is an adequate and safe water supply and that the disposal of sewage meets health and safety standards. To ensure the health, safety, and welfare of homeowners, there are local, state, or municipal building and construction standards that must be met. These standards include the regulation and control of design, construction, quality, use, occupancy, location, and maintenance of all buildings and structures.

3. *Building codes* are established to ensure the health, safety, and welfare of property owners. A certificate of occupancy is issued when a building meets code requirements.

4. A *building permit* is issued for construction of a new building or other improvement, substantial repair of an existing structure, or demolition of a building.

5. Property owners who use septic tanks are required to have a *percolation test* (perk test), which tests the soil's absorption or drainage capacity. Only if the soil has the ability to absorb and drain water can the land be developed.

6. A *latent defect* is a hidden defect; a patent defect is obvious.

7. An agent is liable for not disclosing known defects and may be liable for defects about which the agent should have known.

8. *Misrepresentation* means a party is making a decision based on information that is not true, and that may be intentional or negligent. The property is being misrepresented when defects are not disclosed to the buyer. The buyer may be able to rescind the sales contract or receive compensatory damages, which are actual damages for the repair of the defect. *Punitive damages* are damages assessed as punishment.

9. A *material fact* is defined as a fact that is significant or essential to the issue or matter at hand. It is information that, if known, could change the decision of the party. Agents must disclose material facts that would affect the value of a property, such as zoning, property taxes, land-use restrictions, and special assessments.

10. A property may become *stigmatized* because an undesirable event has occurred on the property or near the property. Brokers should seek legal counsel when dealing with such properties.

11. The illegal use of *methamphetamine* is a major drug threat in the United States. Meth labs can be set up almost anywhere and are often found in private residences, apartments, trailers, automobiles, campgrounds, and hotel and motel rooms. When a meth lab is found in a home, the site is deemed a toxic waste site. When these chemicals are dumped, contamination of soil and nearby water supplies is possible.

12. *A brownfield site* is real property, for which the expansion, redevelopment, or reuse is complicated by the presence, or potential presence, of a hazardous substance, pollutant, or contaminant. Brownfields include abandoned factories, former dry cleaners, vacant gas stations, illegal drug labs, old dumps, and mine-scarred lands.

Advertising

1. Whether advertising property, the brokerage firm, or self-promotion, state and federal advertising laws must be followed. Advertising should not be false, misleading or deceptive in any way.

2. Agents also need to be aware of the liability of postings on their Web sites and social media sites. *Defamation* is the act of harming the reputation of another by making a false statements to a third person. When the defamation assertion is expressed in a transitory form, especially speech**,** it is called *slander*. When a defamatory statement expressed in a fixed medium, especially writing but also a picture, sign, or electronic broadcast, it is called *libel*.

Do-Not-Call Laws

1. The two databases that a licensee should check before making a phone call to solicit business are the database maintained by the Federal Trade Commission (FTC) and brokerage firm database. Telemarketers are required to check the Do-Not-Call list every 31 days. The civil fine can be up to $11,000 per violation for calling someone on the Do-Not-Call list. Each call is a separate violation.

2. Telemarketers can call for any of the following reasons.

    ■   There has been a prior, or there is an existing business relationship with someone. This exception applies to existing clients and customers and extends for up to 18 months after the end of a transaction. Agents from other brokerage firms would need to check the Do-Not-Call list, and if the number is on the list, they cannot call.

    ■   If a consumer makes an inquiry, the telemarketer can call the person for up to three months after the inquiry.

    ■   There has been an express request from someone to call.

    ■   There is an existing debt or contract with the company.

    ■   They are soliciting only donations for charities.

    ■   They are promoting a political candidate.

    ■   They are calling a business.

3. A licensee may call a For Sale By Owner whose number in on the Do-Not-Call list if a buyer is interested in seeing the property.

4. A licensee may not call a For Sale By Owner whose number is on the Do-Not-Call list, to solicit the listing.

Do-Not-Email

1. Controlling the Assault of Non-Solicited Pornography and Marketing Act (CAN-SPAM Act) established the guidelines for sending unsolicited emails. If an email is commercial in nature, then it must follow these guidelines.

    ■ The header information cannot be false or misleading. The subject line cannot be deceptive.

    ■ The message must be identified as an advertisement.

    ■ Your message must include a valid physical postal address.

    ■ A method to opt-out from receiving future emails must be prominent.

    ■ Opt-out requests must be honored within 10 business days. (Opt-out mechanisms must be able to process the opt-out request for at least 30 days after the message is sent.)

    ■ If using a third party to send emails, you must monitor what others are doing on your behalf.

2. Email that is classified as transactional or contains relationship content, that facilitates an already agreed-upon transaction or updates a customer in an existing business relationship is not considered commercial email. It may not contain false or misleading routing information, but it is otherwise exempt from most of the provisions of the law.

3. There can be a fine of up to $16,000 for each separate unsolicited email.

Fair Housing

1. The Civil Rights Act of 1866 prohibits discrimination based on race in real estate and personal transactions. There are no exceptions to this law and no limits on punitive damages for racial discrimination.

2. A landlord must make *reasonable accommodations* in rules, policies, practices, and services to afford the disabled person equal opportunity to use and enjoy a dwelling. An owner cannot refuse to permit a disabled person to modify a dwelling, and the disabled person may be required to restore the unit to its original condition.

3. After March 12, 1991, multifamily dwellings must be designed to allow accessibility to the building and through units by persons in wheelchairs. New apartments built with elevators must be entirely accessible; the ground level of new apartment buildings without elevators must be accessible.

4. *Jones v. Mayer* is a 1968 Supreme Court case that upheld the Civil Rights Act of 1866.

5. Currently, *federal fair housing laws* prohibit discrimination based on race, color, religion, sex, national origin, familial status, and disability. Many state laws are stricter than federal regulations. Failure to comply with these laws is a criminal act and grounds for disciplinary action.

6. *Blockbusting* (panic peddling) occurs when an agent induces owners to sell because minority groups are moving into a neighborhood. *Steering*

(channeling) occurs when an agent directs buyers into or out of certain neighborhoods. These activities are illegal.

7. *Familial status* protects the head of a household responsible for a minor child or children, or a pregnant woman from discriminatory practices. Housing occupied or intended to be solely occupied by persons aged 62 or older is exempt from the law. If 80 percent of the units are occupied by someone 55 years of age or older, then the building also is exempt.

8. The sale or rental of a single-family home is exempt if the owner who is not occupying a home has only one sale in 24 months; no more than three homes are owned at any one time; the services of a broker or any other person engaged in the business of selling or leasing real estate are not used; and no discriminatory advertising is used.

9. A one- to four-family dwelling is exempt if the owner occupies one of the units, no discriminatory advertising is used, and a broker is not used. A nonprofit religious organization can discriminate on a religious basis, so long as membership in the organization is not discriminatory; a nonprofit private club may restrict rentals or occupancy of lodgings to members, so long as membership in the nonprofit private club is not discriminatory.

10. Complaints for violations of the federal Fair Housing Act may be filed with HUD or taken directly to a federal district court or to the Attorney general of the United States. An aggrieved party must file a complaint within one year of the discriminatory act.

11. Any person who fails to attend or provide testimony at a hearing or fails to answer lawful inquiries may be fined up to $100,000 and/or imprisoned for up to one year. An offender can be fined up to $16,000 for the first offense, $37,500 for the second offense within five years, and $65,000 for the third offense within seven years. Penalties for intimidation are up to $1,000 and/or up to one year in jail. Penalties for bodily injury are up to $10,000 and/or up to 10 years in jail; for death, the penalty can be any jail term up to life.

12. Refusing to make loans or issue insurance policies in specific areas for reasons other than the financial qualifications of the applicant is known as *redlining*. Redlining is illegal.

13. A disability is a physical or mental impairment or history of such impairment that substantially limits one or more of a person's major life activities. The law does not protect anyone using illegal drugs or controlled substances.

14. Real estate ads should state no discriminatory preference or limitation on account of race, color, national origin, sex, familial status, or handicap. Ads should describe property, not people.

CHAPTER 6 – PROPERTY MANAGEMENT

1. An owner can manager his own property without a license. In most states, an owner can hire an employee who does not have a real estate license, to manage the property of the owner. Review your state laws to determine under what circumstances a person would need a license to manage property for others. A property management agreement is *a personal service contract,* which means it is terminated upon the death of either party.

2. The owner may also enter into a contract with a brokerage firm to manage property. If the brokerage firm is hired to manage the property, an agent for the brokerage may be the property manager.

3. A *written management agreement* should stipulate the relationship between the property manager and the owner (employer-employee, principal-agent, or trustor-trustee), how compensation will be computed, and owners' and managers' rights and responsibilities.

4. The property manager has a fiduciary relationship with the owner. The objectives of a manager are to generate the highest net operating income while maintaining the property.

5. The property manager has a fiduciary relationship with the owner, which includes the duties of care, obedience, accounting, loyalty, and disclosure.

6. The *duty of care* means to use care and skill while managing the property and binding the owner to contracts, and to be responsible in every way to the owner.

7. The *duty of obedience* means to carry out, in good faith, the owner's instructions. The property manager should immediately terminate the relationship if asked to do something illegal or unethical.

8. The *duty of accounting* means to maintain and accurately report to the owner the status of all funds received on behalf of or from the property owner. The manager may not commingle funds.

9. The *duty of loyalty* means to put the property owner's interests first and act without self-interest in every transaction.

10. The *duty of disclosure* means to keep the owner informed of all material facts regarding the management of the property.

11. The property manager will be responsible for creating a *management plan* that meets the owner's objectives, a budget of projected revenues and expenses, and occupancy and absorption rates.

12. Most owners require that the property manager create a monthly report of income and expenses.

13. Only the interest portion of each mortgage payment should be deducted as an expense on the *profit and loss statement.*

14. The *return on investment (ROI)* is the ratio of the property's net income after taxes (ATCF) to the money invested (equity). The ROI also may be computed on a before-tax basis.

15. Material facts that a property manager should disclose to the tenant include location and return of security deposits, building rules, procedure for paying the rent, penalties for late payments, process for maintenance requests, and steps for renewal and termination of the lease.

16. A leasing agent is an independent contractor, and the agent's primary function is to show the property, follow up on prospective tenants, and lease the property.

17. The four goals of a life safety program are (1) preventing emergencies and security breaches by installing smoke detectors, sprinkler systems, paging

systems, closed-circuit television, video camera, and security alarms. (2) detecting a breach as early as possible, (3) containing or confining the damage or intrusion, and (4) counteracting the damage by prompt and proper action.

18. *Preventive maintenance* preserves the physical building and eliminates costly problems before major repairs become necessary.

19. *Corrective maintenance* includes keeping the building's equipment, utilities, and amenities functioning properly.

20. *Routine maintenance* includes maintenance of the common areas and grounds and the physical cleanliness of the building.

21. *New construction maintenance* occurs to meet the needs of the tenant, such as installing new carpeting or remodeling the property.

22. Property managers must be aware of state laws regulating security deposits and send the owner a monthly report of income and expenses.

23. Property managers must have a working knowledge of hazardous substances and the laws regulating owners. A *hazardous waste* is a byproduct of a manufactured item; a hazardous substance may include everyday items, such as household cleaning products.

Duties of the Parties

1. Owner's Duties

   ■ Provide specific goals and objectives to the property manager.

   ■ Provide the lease agreement to the property manager.

   ■ Keep the property safe and habitable. This includes snow and ice removal, adequate lighting in parking lots and hallways, working sprinkler systems, smoke detectors, etc.

   ■ Comply with health and building codes. Follow federal, state and local laws.

   ■ Give reasonable notice to inspect, make repairs for improvements, and enter the property.

   ■ If a residential tenant abandons the property before the lease expires, the owner must make reasonable efforts to rent the abandoned space.

   ■ Set up a trust or escrow account for security deposits. Note that some states prohibit security deposits from being commingled with earnest money deposits.

   ■ Set up a business account for other monies.

   ■ Maintain proper insurance on the property.

   ■ Provide lead-based paint disclosures and reports to tenants.

   ■ Follow eviction laws.

   ■ Unless paid by the tenant, the owner must pay property taxes, special assessments, and utilities.

- Provide the tenant with building rules and other laws that must be followed. (This will be a part of the lease agreement.)

- Notify the tenant of the location of the security deposit and the terms for its return. (This will be a part of the lease agreement.)

2. Property Manager's Duties

- Meeting the goals and objectives of the owner by generating the highest net operating income while maintaining the property.

- Development of a management plan, operating budget, profit and loss statement, cash flow reports, and budget comparison reports.

- Analyze rental rates, screen and select qualified tenants, collect the rent and evict tenants.

- Market and advertise the property. Comply with all advertising and fair housing laws.

- Maintain good relations with the tenant.

- Maintain the property by hiring qualified contractors to make repairs.

- Evaluate risk management and make recommendations to the owner.

- Comply with federal, state and local laws; such as providing the lead-based paint disclosures, and being in compliance with the Americans with Disabilities Act.

- Be aware of environmental issues and comply with laws.

- Be accountable for money, employees and service contracts.

- Hire, supervise and discharge employees and contractors.

- Enter into contracts with service providers on behalf of the owner. (Phone. electricity, water, trash removal, etc.)

3. Tenant Duties

- Read the lease agreement to make sure that the tenant understands and will comply with the terms.

- Use the property for legal purposes and keep the property in a habitable condition.

- Pay the full rent due in a timely manner.

- The tenant may not use the property in any way that interferes with the rights of neighbors or other tenants.

- The tenant may not alter the property unless it is allowed within the terms of the lease agreement.

- The tenant agrees to obey federal, state, and local laws in regards to the use of the property.

- Notify the owner or property manager of needed repairs.

- Give proper notice when moving. Proper notice is determined by state law or the terms of the lease. Generally, in a residential lease, proper notice is the timeframe when the rent is paid. If rent is paid every thirty days, then thirty days notice would be required. If rent is paid every two weeks, then two weeks' notice would be required.

4. By an *implied covenant of quiet enjoyment,* the lessor guarantees that the lessee will have exclusive possession, and the landlord will not interfere with the tenant's possession or use of the property.

5. A tenant is usually evicted because of nonpayment of rent, unlawful use of the premises, or noncompliance with health and safety codes. Filing a *suit for possession* is known as *actual eviction.*

6. The *warranty of habitability* requires that the landlord keep the property in good condition. If the landlord breaches the lease agreement and the tenant must leave the premises, the tenant may sue for constructive eviction.

7. *Rent control* is a regulation by the state or local government agencies restricting the amount of rent landlords can charge their tenants. The primary purpose of rent control was to remedy high rents caused by the imbalance between supply and demand in housing.

Notes

Notes

Notes